WAR IN THE TWENTIETH CENTURY

WAR
IN THE
TWENTIETH CENTURY

Sources in Theological Ethics

Richard B. Miller, Editor

Westminster/John Knox Press
Louisville, Kentucky

Book design by Ken Taylor

First edition

This book is printed on acid-free paper that meets the American National Standards Institute Z39.48 standard. ♾

Published by Westminster/John Knox Press
Louisville, Kentucky

PRINTED IN THE UNITED STATES OF AMERICA

9 8 7 6 5 4 3 2 1

Library of Congress Cataloging-in-Publication Data

War in the twentieth century : sources in theological ethics / Richard B. Miller, editor.
p. cm. — (Library of theological ethics)
Includes bibliographical references.
ISBN 0-664-25323-7 (pbk. : alk. paper)

1. War—Religious aspects—Christianity. 2. War—Moral and ethical aspects. 3. Just war doctrine. I. Miller, Richard Brian, 1953– . II. Series.
BT736.2.W3443 1992
241′.6242—dc20 92-2318

LIBRARY OF THEOLOGICAL ETHICS

General Editors' Introduction

The field of theological ethics possesses in its literature an abundant inheritance concerning religious convictions and the moral life, critical issues, methods, and moral problems. The Library of Theological Ethics is designed to present a selection of important texts that would otherwise be unavailable for scholarly purposes and classroom use. The series will engage the question of what it means to think theologically and ethically. It is offered in the conviction that sustained dialogue with our predecessors serves the interests of responsible contemporary reflection. Our more immediate aim in offering it, however, is to enable scholars and teachers to make more extensive use of classic texts as they train new generations of theologians, ethicists, and ministers.

The volumes included in the Library will comprise a variety of types. Some will make available English-language texts and translations that have fallen out of print; others will present new translations of texts previously unavailable in English. Still others will offer anthologies or collections of significant statements about problems and themes of special importance. We hope that each volume will encourage contemporary theological ethicists to remain in conversation with the rich and diverse heritage of their discipline.

Robin W. Lovin
Douglas F. Ottati
William Schweiker

CONTENTS

ACKNOWLEDGMENTS

Grateful acknowledgment is made for permission to reprint the following copyrighted material.

H. Richard Niebuhr, "The Grace of Doing Nothing." Copyright 1932 Christian Century Foundation. Reprinted by permission from the March 23, 1932, issue of *The Christian Century.*

Reinhold Niebuhr, "Must We Do Nothing?" Copyright 1932 Christian Century Foundation. Reprinted by permission from the March 30, 1932, issue of *The Christian Century.*

H. Richard Niebuhr, "A Communication: The Only Way Into the Kingdom of God." Copyright 1932 Christian Century Foundation. Reprinted by permission from the April 6, 1932, issue of *The Christian Century.*

Reinhold Niebuhr, "Why the Christian Church Is Not Pacifist." From *The Essential Reinhold Niebuhr,* ed. Robert McAfee Brown (New Haven, Conn.: Yale University Press, 1986). Copyright 1986 by Yale University.

H. Richard Niebuhr, "War as the Judgment of God." Copyright 1942 Christian Century Foundation. Reprinted by permission from the May 3, 1942, issue of *The Christian Century.*

Virgil Aldrich and H. Richard Niebuhr, "Is God in the War?" Copyright 1942 Christian Century Foundation. Reprinted by permission from the August 5, 1942, issue of *The Christian Century.*

H. Richard Niebuhr, "War as Crucifixion." Copyright 1943 Christian Century Foundation. Reprinted by permission from the April 28, 1943, issue of *The Christian Century.*

The Calhoun Commission, "The Relation of the Church to the War in the Light of the Christian Faith." *Social Action* 2 (1944), 5–79. Used by permission.

G. E. M. Anscombe, "The Justice of the Present War Examined." *Ethics, Religion, and Politics* (Oxford: Basil Blackwell, 1981). Used by permission of Basil Blackwell Publishers, Ltd.

John C. Ford, S. J. "The Morality of Obliteration Bombing." *Theological Studies* 5 (September 1944), 261–273, 308–309. Used by permission.

Paul Ramsey, "Is Vietnam a Just War?" From *The Just War: Force and Moral Responsibility* (New York: Charles Scribner's Sons, 1968). Used by permission of Marcia Ramsey Wood.

Ralph B. Potter, Jr., "The Moral Logic of War." *McCormick Quarterly* 23 (1970), 203–233. Used by permission.

LeRoy Walters, "A Historical Perspective on Selective Conscientious Objection." *Journal of the American Academy of Religion* 41 (June 1973), 201–211.

G. E. M. Anscombe, "Mr. Truman's Decree." *Ethics, Religion, and Politics* (Oxford: Basil Blackwell, 1981). Used by permission of Basil Blackwell Publishers, Ltd.

John Courtney Murray, S. J., "Remarks on the Moral Problem of War." *Theological Studies* 20 (1959), 40–61. Used by permission.

Karl Barth, "Freedom for Life." From *Church Dogmatics* III/4 (Edinburgh: T. & T. Clark, 1961). Used by permission.

Paul Ramsey, "A Political Ethics Context for Strategic Thinking." From *Speak Up for Just War or Pacifism* (University Park and London: Pennsylvania State University Press, 1988). Used by permission.

William V. O'Brien, "Just War Doctrine in a Nuclear Context." *Theological Studies* 44 (June 1983), 191–220. Used by permission of William V. O'Brien.

James F. Childress, "Just-War Criteria." From *Moral Responsibility in Conflicts: Essays on Nonviolence, War, and Conscience* (Baton Rouge: Louisiana State University Press, 1982). Copyright © 1982 by Louisiana State University Press. Used by permission.

U.S. Catholic Bishops. Excerpts from *The Challenge of Peace: God's Promise and Our Response,* copyright © 1983, United

States Catholic Conference, Washington, D.C., are used by permission. All rights reserved.

Jean Bethke Elshtain, "Reflections on War and Moral Discourse: Realism, Just War, and Feminism in a Nuclear Age." Copyright © 1985 by Sage Publications, Inc. *Political Theory* 13 (February 1985), 39–57. Reprinted by permission of Sage Publications, Inc.

The United Methodist Council of Bishops (U.S.A.). Excerpts from *In Defense of Creation: The Nuclear Crisis and a Just Peace* (Nashville: Graded Press), copyright © 1986 by Graded Press, are used by permission.

James Turner Johnson, "Just War Tradition and the War in the Gulf." Copyright 1991 The Christian Century Foundation. Reprinted by permission from the February 6–13, 1991, issue of *The Christian Century*.

John Langan, S. J., "An Imperfectly Just War." *Commonweal* (June 1, 1991), 361–365. Copyright © Commonweal Foundation. Used by permission.

Jim Wallis, "This War Cannot Be Justified." *Sojourners* (February 1, 1991). Reprinted with permission from *Sojourners*, Box 29272, Washington, DC 20017.

In producing this anthology I was greatly helped by my graduate assistant, Jennifer Girod, and by Jenny Mobley and Jill Rogers, secretaries in the Department of Religious Studies. I would also like to thank those students who discussed these materials with me in graduate courses, especially Cara Beth Lee, Jack Musselman, Lucinda Peach, and Todd Sullivan. William Meyer made helpful suggestions about how to improve the final draft, and Davis Perkins of Westminster/John Knox Press patiently shepherded this collection to its completion. Finally, I am grateful to Barbara Klinger and Matthew Miller for their good cheer, affection, and support.

RICHARD B. MILLER

Indiana University
March 1992

ACKNOWLEDGMENTS

States Catholic Conference, Washington, D.C., and used by permission. All rights reserved.

[illegible] Hollenbach, [illegible] and Moral [illegible] [illegible], Just War and Pacifism in a Nuclear Age. Copyright © [illegible] by [illegible]. [illegible] by permission of [illegible] Publications, Inc.

The United Methodist Council of Bishops, [illegible] excerpts from In Defense of Creation: The Nuclear Crisis and a Just Peace. [illegible] Copyright © [illegible]. Used by permission.

James Turner Johnson, [illegible] War Tradition and the Restraint of War [illegible]. Used by permission [illegible].

[illegible] used by permission.

[illegible] Washington, D.C. [illegible]

In addition [illegible] I was greatly helped by [illegible] John Kelsay [illegible] I am grateful [illegible].

Richard B. Miller

INTRODUCTION

This volume brings together nonpacifist materials in Protestant and Roman Catholic ethics, spanning the period from the Manchurian crisis in the early 1930s to the Allied war against Iraq in 1991. By *nonpacifist* I mean materials that do not provide an in-principled condemnation of the institution of war. Many of these materials draw from well-known representatives of the just-war tradition, and all of them have contributed significantly to our understanding of that tradition.

In producing this collection, I have chosen nonpacifist materials that, for the most part, attempt to engage in practical reasoning about war rather than to theorize about the possible justice of war, conceived in the abstract. The goal is to situate nonpacifist reasoning within the circumstances about which it found immediate relevance. Thus it might be possible to see how nonpacifist ideas, especially just-war tenets, have been interpreted and applied at various points over the last century in response to tangible problems in moral experience. If any principle of selection has organized this anthology, it is the Aristotelian idea that we shed light on the meaning of our moral principles as we try to apply them. Seen in this way, interpretation and social criticism are symbiotic.

DEFINING A JUST WAR

When viewed as a tradition rather than a static doctrine, the conditions that define a just war are forever protean, subject to development as international relations and technological discoveries provide new materials for ethical reflection. This tradition finds its origins in the writings of Augustine, and has been developed since then by canonists, theologians, codes of military practice, and political philosophers. Yet however diverse may be its sources, this tradition is nonetheless shaped by two fundamental, unchanging assumptions. First, it is premised on the notion that war may be an instrument of justice in relations between communities or nation-states, crude as that instrument may be. Second, it is premised on the idea that not all is fair in war, even for those whose cause in war is justified. Given these premises, this tradition has developed two sets of criteria for assessing the justice of war, the *jus ad bellum* and the *jus in bello.*

The *jus ad bellum* is designed to answer what might be called the "when" or "whether" question: When, if ever, is resort to war ethically acceptable? The components within the *jus ad bellum* consist of several moral criteria that seek to specify those circumstances in which resort to war may be justified.

The *jus in bello* is designed to answer what might be called the "how" or "methods" question: What methods are morally acceptable once recourse to war has been justified? Here the idea is that the justification of entering war does *not* extend to all possible methods of war itself: the ends do not justify the means.

In its broadest outlines, then, *ad bellum* criteria provide the basis for justifying war, whereas *in bello* criteria furnish the basis for morally limiting the methods of war. Various interpretations of these tenets and their relation have emerged since the time of Augustine, but we do a great disservice to the tradition if we ignore either set of just-war tenets.

Ad bellum criteria include the following:

1. *Just cause:* War is justifiable only in defense against threats to innocent life, conditions for the community's future, and basic human rights. War cannot be justified for purposes of revenge or domination.

2. *Competent authority:* This criterion precludes resort to war by private individuals, allowing only those who are responsible for the public order to declare war. This criterion obviously presumes that conditions of political legitimacy have been satisfied.

3. *Right intention:* Intention must be confined to self-defense. Intention here denotes the purpose or goal of war, not merely the psychological state of those who have entered war. Force may not be used to acquire control over the adversary, although this criterion does permit relevant parties to establish stronger conditions of peace than those that preceded war.

4. *Last resort:* This criterion holds that nonviolent means of settling disputes within reasonable reach of the relevant authorities must be tried before resort to war is justifiable. If successful defense of a just cause is reasonably possible using nonviolent methods, then there is a moral duty to use them.

5. *Relative justice:* Echoing Vitoria's idea of "ostensible simultaneous justice," this criterion holds that no state may act as if it possesses "absolute justice," that neither side may claim a monopoly on moral righteousness. Rather, the justice of war is relative, especially given the problems of measuring justice in the changing circumstances of war.

6. *Proportionality:* Within *ad bellum* criteria, proportionality requires one to ask, Will the prospective costs of war be balanced by the overall values that are being defended? Is the war, in moral terms, worth risking? What losses to ourselves and the world community can be morally sustained given the values in defense of which war might be fought?

7. *Reasonable hope for success:* A corollary of proportionality, this criterion excludes reckless fighting in defense of a cause. Although it may on occasion permit us to defend very noble values against huge odds, its general purpose is to prevent irrational uses of force.

In bello criteria, establishing the limits to the use of justifiable force, include the following:

1. *Discrimination:* This criterion prohibits the intentional attack of civilians, the shorthand for which is the phrase "noncombatant immunity." This criterion has two key distinctions.

The first distinction separates combatants from noncombatants. "Combatant" denotes those who are materially cooperating with the war effort, posing an objective threat to another community's political and social order. Combatants include soldiers and those working for war-related industries (e.g., bomb factories). Noncombatants would include, for example, children, the elderly, the sick, farmers, teachers, health-care professionals.

The second distinction draws a line between intentional (i.e., purposeful) and foreseen, but unintentional, effects of an act.

Putting these distinctions together produces the verdict that intentional attacks against noncombatants are tantamount to murder. Such attacks are directed against innocent people, where "innocent" is understood as a military or political, but not necessarily moral, category. The foreseen, unintentional loss of life *passes* the test of discrimination but is open to moral evaluation according to the second *in bello* criterion, proportionality.

2. *Proportionality:* The *in bello* principle of proportionality requires us to balance the foreseen, unintended losses against the values that are defended in a specific act of war. Here we must think about the morality of war's tactics: Is the good that is being pursued or defended commensurate with the unintended losses that may reasonably be expected? Even discriminate tactics can be immoral if the foreseen, unintended loss of life outweighs the defended values.

THE DEVELOPMENT OF NONPACIFIST ETHICS IN THIS CENTURY

In producing this anthology, I happened across some remarkable findings about how nonpacifist ethics has developed in this century.

First, and perhaps most notably, I was surprised to find that the systematic application of just-war criteria to assess the conduct of nations at war has occurred with greater rarity than one would expect, given the frequency of international conflict in this century. Among Christian nonpacifist ethicists and ecclesial authorities, there is a virtual silence about the Spanish-American War, the Boer War, the Great War, the Korean War, the Cuban Missile Crisis, and the Seven-Day War, to name a few. However much it may be true that most Christian authorities and writers eschewed a strict commitment to pacifism throughout most of this century, it remains the case that a disciplined use of just-war tenets in the twentieth century is no more than two generations old. And even in this more recent period, reference to just-war tenets has been, at best, sporadic, relying in large part on the efforts and influence of John Courtney Murray and Paul Ramsey.

Until Ramsey's work began to generate interest and commentary, just-war tenets were often associated with traditional Roman Catholic moral theology, drawing from the works of Augustine, Aquinas, Vitoria, and Suárez. Yet—and this was the second surprise—eccelesial sources in Roman

Catholicism did little to instruct laypeople about the ethics of war for a good part of this century. Popes Benedict XV, Pius XI, and Pius XII never systematically addressed the two world wars according to just-war tenets; most of their teachings addressed the need for global peace. Of these popes, Pius XII was most concerned about the horrors of modern technology and war, but it would take a John Courtney Murray to organize Pius XII's teachings, drawing largely on speeches from the postwar period.

Third, it will doubtless surprise many to note that just-war criteria have not been used exclusively or even primarily to baptize the institution of war or the practices within particular wars. It is more accurate to say, based on the sources collected here, that just-war tenets help to articulate the conditions necessary for a disciplined evaluation of specific wars or events in war. On this point it is instructive to note that the war that seems most likely to satisfy just-war tenets—the Second World War—was evaluated as a remarkably complex affair by commentators of the day. Virtually all who addressed this war eschewed self-congratulatory rhetoric or patriotic zealotry; one author, H. Richard Niebuhr, chose the metaphor of crucifixion to shed light on the effects of that war on the innocent. To insist that nonpacifist ethics have been forever co-opted by political interests would be to infer well beyond what the sources suggest. On this point it may also be instructive to observe that, over the past decade, several just-war theorists have sought to provide a theoretical framework to prevent interpretations and applications of the criteria from succumbing to the exigencies of realism or military efficiency.

Fourth, despite the growing interest in and knowledge about the just-war tradition, a consensus about the number, meaning, and relative weight of its criteria is still elusive. The principle of discrimination is interpreted as an absolute rule by some (e.g., Ramsey and the U.S. Catholic bishops), whereas others (e.g., William O'Brien) insist that it must be interpreted flexibly, given the duties or permissions implied by *ad bellum* criteria. Moreover, the kinds of efforts necessary to satisfy the condition of "last resort" have yet to be suggested. Nor is it clear how we are to evaluate motives and intentions when nations go to war. We often assume that motives and intentions are identical, overlooking questions about the morality of nations acting for a just cause with mixed motives. And, on questions of authority in allied causes or interventions, no one to date has specified the proper agency to authorize recourse to war in a collective action.

Finally, and related to the last point, the just-war tradition still lacks a systematic political philosophy to provide it with a theoretical framework. Generally, applications of just-war tenets hold two competing values in some balance: human rights and state sovereignty. The former allows for the recourse to force to protect or promote the conditions of human dignity. When viewed as the sole basis for justifying force, reference to rights can lead to a strong ethic of interventionism, even at the expense of state sovereignty. The latter allows for recourse to force when international boundaries have been trespassed. When viewed as the sole basis for justifying force, reference to sovereignty creates a strong presumption against intervention, even at the expense of human rights.

If we were to begin with a theory to make intelligible a nonpacifist ethic, then, a collection of twentieth-century theological sources would be impossible. No doubt for this reason, too, it is wise to eschew theories of the just war and turn instead to ways in which just-war criteria have been interpreted and applied as a vocabulary for social criticism. If this collection can stimulate further interest in teaching and research about the ethics of war, then its modest purpose will have been satisfied.

PART I

The Manchurian Crisis

INTRODUCTION:
NONINTERVENTION OR NONVIOLENT COERCION?

When the Kwantung Army of Japan set out to assume control of Manchuria on September 19, 1931, it was fulfilling nationalist and expansionist aspirations that had been brewing for at least four years in Tokyo. This is not to say that the Kwantung Army and its principal leader, Colonel Itagaki, acted under the approval of the imperial government. Quite the contrary: Itagaki and his forces incited the incident of Mukden and proceeded to take control of the region entirely on their own initiative. Established to protect Kwantung-leased territory at the southern tip of Manchuria along with the Southern Manchurian Railway, the army conspired to blow up the tracks in Mukden and within twenty-four hours eliminated virtually all local Chinese resistance. Three days later, they gained control of Kirin city, the seat of government of Kirin province. To compensate for the shortage of troops along the railway, the Kwantung Army enlisted the support of Japanese forces in Korea; those forces responded immediately, without imperial sanction. A month later, Itagaki's forces bombed the city of Chinchow, the headquarters of Chinese forces, and by November had control of the last of Manchuria's eastern provinces, Tsitsihar.

Both the Tokyo government and world leaders would soon have to reckon with the army's control of the region, positioned between Russian presence to the north and a decreasingly powerful Chinese government to the west, in Beijing. To that end, officials in Japan drafted the "Outline of Principles for the Solution to the China Problem" in January 1932, stating that Mongolia and Manchuria would be made an essential part of the existence of the empire, thereby expressing the explicit desires of the Kwantung Army. The police force in Manchuria was put under Japanese direction; no independent army was to be allowed, and negotiations were to ensue to expand Japanese treaty rights in the region. Soon Henry P'u Yi, heir to the old Manchu dynasty, was installed as "regent," serving as the puppet of Japanese influence. On March 1, 1932, Manchuria was renamed Manchukuo, and its capital was located in Ch'angch'un. Appeals by world leaders to withdraw Japanese forces went unheeded in Tokyo; a year later, Japan withdrew from the League of Nations.[1]

Within this context, Americans were faced with the question of whether to intervene militarily on behalf of Chinese interests, how they might marshal support from other nations, or whether alternative methods of coercion might be chosen. In short, Americans were confronted with the options of *nonintervention, third-party intervention* with or without allied support, or *economic sanctions* against Japan. By what canons of morality could Americans justify the use of force or coercion to affect the course of events on the other side of the globe?

To these questions two of America's most notable Protestant theologians addressed themselves in 1932. Arguing on behalf of nonintervention, H. Richard Niebuhr pointed to the need for repentance by Americans for their own faults and self-interestedness, hoping to prevent the prospect that American action would exacerbate the Manchurian crisis. Defending the option of some form of coercion, Reinhold Niebuhr developed his distinct brand of Christian realism, arguing that struggle was inevitable in human experience, that no relations between individuals or groups would ever be frictionless. Thus, he concluded, repentance at most can only ameliorate the tensions in human experience, but it cannot deliver us entirely from contestations of power. For realists, then, the task was less to eschew confrontation than to determine the ethically proper use of coercive instruments, blunt as they may be.

Yet what is perhaps most important about this famous exchange between these two brothers is how it exposes their theological differences and how such differences translated into different ethical recommendations. Reflecting their Protestant heritage, both authors speak eloquently about the dangers of national self-righteousness and the difficulties of maintaining a disinterested point of view. Yet, operating within this shared perspective, each author compressed a distinctive vision of midtwentieth-century American Protestantism. The first, viewing history as the arena of divine activity, produced an ethic in which human agency is viewed within a complex array of social and natural forces. Accordingly, it emphasized the need for discernment, responsiveness to events, and repentant preparation for a redemptive future. The second, emphasizing the tensions between the ideals of love and the limits of history, viewed divine agape as requiring a form of self-sacrifice. Without supplemental appeals to justice, such a theology was doomed to irresponsibility and ineffectiveness in political affairs. However strange their theological convictions might seem today, together the Niebuhrs clarified many of the terms that would shape subsequent discussions of the ethics of third-party intervention and nonmilitary methods of coercion.

NOTES

1. These events are chronicled in James William Morley, *Japan Erupts: The London Naval Conference and the Manchurian Incident, 1928–32* (New York: Columbia University Press, 1984); Murakami Hyoe, *Japan: The Years of Trial, 1919–52* (Tokyo: Japan Culture Institute, 1982); Takehiko Yoshihashi, *Conspiracy at Mukden: The Rise of the Japanese Military* (New Haven: Yale University Press, 1963).

1

The Grace of Doing Nothing

H. Richard Niebuhr

It may be that the greatest moral problems of the individual or of a society arise when there is nothing to be done. When we have begun a certain line of action or engaged in a conflict we cannot pause too long to decide which of various possible courses we ought to choose for the sake of the worthier result. Time rushes on and we must choose as best we can, entrusting the issue to the future. It is when we stand aside from the conflict, before we know what our relations to it really are, when we seem to be condemned to doing nothing, that our moral problems become greatest. How shall we do nothing?

The issue is brought home to us by the fighting in the east. We are chafing at the bit, we are eager to do something constructive; but there is nothing constructive, it seems, that we can do. We pass resolutions, aware that we are doing nothing; we summon up righteous indignation and still do nothing; we write letters to congressmen and secretaries, asking others to act while we do nothing. Yet is it really true that we are doing nothing? There are, after all, various ways of being inactive and some kinds of inactivity, if not all, may be highly productive. It is not really possible to stand aside, to sit by the fire in this world of moving times; even Peter was doing something in the courtyard of the high-priest's house—if it was only something he was doing to himself. When we do nothing we are also affecting the course of history. The problem we face is often that of choice between various kinds of inactivity rather than of choice between action and inaction.

MEANINGFUL INACTIVITY

Our inactivity may be that of the pessimist who watches a world go to pieces. It is a meaningful inactivity for himself and for the world. His world, at all events, will go to pieces the more rapidly because of that inactivity. Or it may be the inactivity of the conservative believer in things as they are. He does nothing in the international crisis because he believes that the way of Japan is the way of all nations, that self-interest is the first and only law of life, and that out of the clash of national, as out of that of individual, self-interests the greater good will result. His inactivity is one of watchful waiting for the opportunity when, in precisely similar manner, though with less loss of life and fortune if possible, he may rush to the protection of his own interests or promote them by taking advantage of the situation created by the strife of his competitors. This way of doing nothing is not unproductive. It encourages the self-asserters and it fills them with fear of the moment when the new competition will begin. It may be that they have been driven into their present conflict by the knowledge or suspicion that the watchful waiter is looking for his opportunity, perhaps unconsciously, and that they must be prepared for him.

The inactivity of frustration and moral indignation is of another order. It is the way today of those who have renounced all violent methods of settling conflicts and have no other means at hand by which to deal with the situation. It is an angry inactivity like that of a man who is watching a neighborhood fight and is waiting for police to arrive—for police who never come. He has renounced for himself the method of forcible interference which would only increase the flow of blood and the hatred, but he knows of nothing else that he can do. He is forced to remain content on the sidelines, but with mounting anger he regards the bully who is beating the neighbor and his wrath issues in words of exasperation and condemnation. Having tied his own hands he fights with his tongue and believes that he is not fighting because he inflicts only mental wounds. The bully is for him an outlaw, a person not to be trusted, unfair, selfish, one who cannot be redeemed save by restraint. The righteous indignation mounts and mounts and must issue at last—as the police fail to arrive—either in his own forcible entry into the conflict despite his scruples, or in apoplexy.

PUZZLED PACIFISTS

The diatribes against Japan which are appearing in the secular and religious press today have a distressing similarity to the righteously indignant utterances which preceded our conflicts with Spain and with Germany. China is Cuba and Belgium over again, it is the Negro race beaten by Simon Legree; and the pacifists who have no other program than that of abstention from the unrighteousness of war are likely to be placed in the same quandary in which their fellows were placed in 1860, 1898 and 1915, and—unless human attitudes have been regenerated in the interim—they are likely to share the same fate, which was not usually incarceration. Here is a situation which they did not foresee when they made their vow; may it not be necessary to have one more war to end all war? Righteous indignation, not allowed to issue in action, is a dangerous thing—as dangerous as any great emotion nurtured and repressed at the same time. It is the source of sudden explosions or the ground of long, bitter and ugly hatreds.

If this way of doing nothing must be rejected the communists' way offers more hope. Theirs is the inactivity of those who see that there is indeed nothing constructive to be done in the present situation, but that, rightly understood, this situation is after all preliminary to a radical change which will eliminate the conditions of which the conflict is a product. It is the inactivity of a cynicism which expects no good from the present, evil world of capitalism, but also the inactivity of a boundless faith in the future. The communists know that war and revolution are closely akin, that war breeds discontent and misery and that out of misery and discontent new worlds may be born. This is an opportunity, then, not for direct entrance into the conflict, nor for the watchful waiting of those who seek their self-interest, but for the slow laborious process of building up within the fighting groups those cells of communism which will be ready to inherit the new world and be able to build a classless international commonwealth on the ruins of capitalism and nationalism. Here is inactivity with a long vision, a steadfast hope and a realistic program of non-interfering action.

But there is yet another way of doing nothing. It appears to be highly impracticable because it rests on the well-nigh obsolete faith that there is a God—a real God. Those who follow this way share with communism the belief that the fact that men can do nothing constructive is no indication of the fact that nothing constructive is being done. Like the communists they are assured that the actual processes of history will inevitably and really bring a different kind of world with lasting peace. They do not rely on human aspirations after ideals to accomplish this end, but on forces which often seem very impersonal—as impersonal as those which eliminated slavery in spite of abolitionists. The forces may be as impersonal and as actual as machine production, rapid transportation, the physical mixture of races, etc., but as parts of the real world they are as much a part of the total divine process as are human thoughts and prayers.

PRELUDE TO JUDGMENT

From this point of view, naively affirming the meaningfulness of reality, the history of the world is the judgment of the world and also its redemption, and such a conflict as the present one is—again as in communism—only the prelude both to greater judgment and to a new era. The world being what it is, these results are brought forth when the seeds of national or individual self-interest are planted; the actual structure of things is such that our wishes for a different result do not in the least affect the outcome. As a man soweth so shall he reap. This God of things as they are is inevitable and quite merciless. His mercy lies beyond, not this side of, judgment. This inactive Christianity shares with communism also the belief in the inevitably good outcome of the mundane process and the realistic insight that that good cannot be achieved by the slow accretion of better habits alone but more in consequence of a revolutionary change which will involve considerable destruction. While it does nothing it knows that something is being done, something which is divine both in its threat and in its promise.

This inactivity is like that of the early Christians whose millenarian mythology it replaces with the contemporary mythology of social forces. (Mythology is after all not fiction but a deep philosophy.) Like early Christianity and like communism today radical Christianity knows that nothing constructive can be done by interference but that something very constructive can be done in preparation for the future. It also can build cells of those within each nation who, divorcing themselves from the program of nationalism and of capitalism, unite in a higher loyalty which transcends national and class lines of division and prepare for the future. There is no such Christian international today because radical Christianity has not arrived as yet at a program and a philosophy of history, but such little cells are forming. The First Christian international of Rome has had its day; the Second Christian international of Stockholm is likely to go the way of the Second Socialist international. There is need of and opportunity for a Third Christian international.

DIFFERENCE FROM COMMUNISM

While the similarities of a radically Christian program with the communist program are striking, there are also great dissimilarities. There is a new element in the inactivity of radical Christianity which is lacking in communism. The Christian reflects upon the fact that his inability to do anything constructive in the crisis is the inability of one whose own faults are so apparent and so similar to those of the offender that any action on his part is not only likely to be misinterpreted but is also likely—in the nature of the case—to be really less than disinterested. He is like a father, who, feeling a mounting righteous indignation against a misbehaving child, remembers that that misbehavior is his fault as much as the child's and that indignation is the least helpful, the most dangerous of attitudes to take; it will solve nothing though it may repress.

So the American Christian realizes that Japan is following the example of his own country and that it has little real ground for believing America to be a disinterested nation. He may see that his country, for which he bears his own responsibility as a citizen, is really not disinterested and that its righteous indignation is not wholly righteous. An inactivity then is demanded which will be profoundly active in rigid self-analysis. Such analysis is likely to reveal that there is an approach to the situation, indirect but far more effective than direct interference, for it is able to create the conditions under which a real reconstruction of habits is possible. It is the opposite approach from that of the irate father who believes that every false reaction on the part of his child may be cured by a verbal, physical or economic spanking.

IN PLACE OF REPENTANCE

This way of doing nothing the old Christians called repentance, but the word has become so reminiscent of emotional debauches in the feeling of guilt that it may be better to abandon it for a while. What is suggested is that the only effective approach to the problem of China and Japan lies in the sphere of an American self-analysis which is likely to result in some surprising discoveries as to the amount of renunciation of self-interest necessary on the part of this country and of individual Christians before anything effective can be done in the east.

The inactivity of radical Christianity is not the inactivity of those who call evil good; it is the inaction of those who do not judge their neighbors because they cannot fool themselves into a sense of superior righteousness. It is not the inactivity of a resigned patience, but of a patience that is full of hope, and is based on faith. It is not the inactivity of the non-combatant, for it knows that there are no non-combatants, that everyone is involved, that China is being crucified (though the term is very inaccurate), by our sins and those of the whole world. It is not the inactivity of the merciless, for works of mercy must be performed though they are only palliatives to ease present pain while the process of healing depends on deeper, more actual and urgent forces.

But if there is no God, or if God is up in heaven and not in time itself, it is a very foolish inactivity.

2

Must We Do Nothing?

Reinhold Niebuhr

There is much in my brother's article on "The Grace of Doing Nothing" with which I agree. Except for the invitation of the editors of The Christian Century I would have preferred to defer voicing any disagreement with some of his final conclusions to some future occasion; for a casual article on a specific problem created by the contemporary international situation hardly does justice to his general position. I believe the problem upon which he is working—the problem of dissociating a rigorous gospel ethic of disinterestedness and love from the sentimental dilutions of that ethic which are current in liberal Christianity—is a tremendously important one. I owe so much to the penetrating thought which he has been giving this subject that I may be able to do some justice to his general position even though I do not share his conviction that a pure love ethic can ever be made the basis of a civilization.

DEALING WITH A SINFUL NATION

He could not have done better than to choose the Sino-Japanese conflict, and the reactions of the world to it, in order to prove the difficulty, if not the futility, of dealing redemptively with a sinful nation or individual if we cannot exorcise the same sin from our own hearts. It is true that pacifists are in danger of stirring up hatred against Japan in their effort to stem the tide of Japanese imperialism. It is true that the very impotence of an individual, who deals with a social situation which goes beyond his own powers, tempts him to hide his sense of futility behind a display of violent emotion. It is true that we have helped to create the Japan which expresses itself in terms of militaristic imperialism. The insult we offered her in our immigration laws was a sin of spiritual aggression. The white world has not only taught her the ways of imperialism but has preempted enough of the yellow man's side of the world to justify Japan's imperialism as a vent for pent up national energies.

It is also true that American concern over Japanese aggression is not wholly disinterested. It is national interest which prompts us to desire stronger action against Japan than France and England are willing to take. It is true, in other words, that every social sin is, at least partially, the fruit and consequence of the sins of those who judge and condemn it, and that the effort to eliminate it involves the critics and judges in new social sin, the assertion of self-interest and the expression of moral conceit and hypocrisy. If anyone would raise the objection to such an analysis that it finds every social action falling short only because it measures the action against an impossible ideal of disinterestedness, my brother could answer that while the ideal may seem to be impossible the actual social situation proves it to be necessary. It is literally true that every recalcitrant nation, like every anti-social individual, is created by the society which condemns it, and that redemptive efforts which betray strong ulterior motives are always bound to be less than fully redemptive.

INACTION THAT IS ACTION

My brother draws the conclusion from this logic that it is better not to act at all than to act from motives which are less than pure, and with the use of methods which are less than ethical (coercion). He believes in taking literally the words of Jesus, "Let him who is without sin cast the first stone." He believes, of course, that this kind of inaction would not really be inaction; it would be, rather, the action of repentance. It would give every one involved in social sin the chance to recognize how much he is involved in it and how necessary it is to restrain his own greed, pride, hatred and lust for power before the social sin is eliminated.

This is an important emphasis particularly for modern Christianity with its lack of appreciation of the tragic character of life and with its easy assumption that the world will be saved by a little more adequate educational technique. Hypocrisy is an inevitable by-product of moral aspiration, and it is the business of true religion to destroy man's moral conceit, a task which modern religion has not been performing in any large degree. Its sentimentalities have tended to increase rather than to diminish moral conceit. A truly religious man ought to distinguish himself from the moral man by recognizing the fact that he is not moral, that he remains a sinner to the end. The sense of sin is more central to religion than is any other attitude.

SHALL WE NEVER ACT?

All this does not prove, however, that we ought to apply the words of Jesus, "Let him who is without sin cast the first stone," literally. If we do we will never be able to act. There will never be a wholly disinterested nation. Pure disinterestedness is an ideal which even individuals cannot fully achieve, and human groups are bound always to express themselves in lower ethical terms than individuals. It follows that no nation can ever be good enough to save another nation purely by the power of love. The relation of nations and of economic groups can never be brought into terms of pure love. Justice is probably the highest ideal toward which human groups can aspire. And justice, with its goal of adjustment of right to right, inevitably involves the assertion of right against right and interest against interest until some kind of harmony is achieved. If a measure of humility and of love does not enter this conflict of interest it will of course degenerate into violence. A rational society will be able to develop a measure of the kind of imagination which knows how to appreciate the virtues of an opponent's position and the weakness in one's own. But the ethical and spiritual note of love and repentance can do no more than qualify the social struggle in history. It will never abolish it.

AN ILLUSORY HOPE

The hope of attaining an ethical goal for society by purely ethical means, that is, without coercion, and without the assertion of the interests of the underprivileged against the interests of the privileged, is an illusion which was spread chiefly among the comfortable classes of the past century. My brother does not make the mistake of assuming that this is possible in social terms. He is acutely aware of the fact that it is not possible to get a sufficient degree of pure disinterestedness and love among privileged classes and powerful nations to resolve the conflicts of history in that way. He understands the stubborn inertia which the ethical ideal meets in history. At this point his realistic interpretation of the facts of history comes in full conflict with his insistence upon a pure gospel ethic, upon a religiously inspired moral perfectionism, and he resolves the conflict by leaving the field of social theory entirely and resorting to eschatology. The Christian will try to achieve humility and disinterestedness not because enough Christians will be able to do so to change the course of history, but because this kind of spiritual attitude is a prayer to God for the coming of his kingdom.

I will not quarrel with this apocalyptic note, as such, though I suspect many *Christian Century* readers will. I believe that a proper eschatology is necessary to a vigorous ethic, and that the simple idea of progress is inimical to the highest ethic. The compound of pessimism and optimism which a vigorous ethical attitude requires can be expressed only in terms of religious eschatology. What makes my brother's particular kind of eschatology impossible for me is that he identifies everything that is occurring in history (the drift toward disaster, another world war and possibly a world revolution) with the counsels of God, and then suddenly, by a leap of faith, comes to the conclusion that the same God, who uses brutalities and forces, against which man must maintain conscientious scruples, will finally establish an ideal society in which pure love will reign.

A SOCIETY OF PURE LOVE IS IMPOSSIBLE

I have more than one difficulty with such a faith. I do not see how a revolution in which the disinherited express their anger and resentment, and assert their interests, can be an instrument of God, and yet at the same time an instrument which religious scruples forbid a man to use. I should think it would be better to come to ethical terms with the forces of nature in history, and try to use ethically directed coercion in order that violence may be avoided. The hope that a kingdom of pure love will emerge out of the catastrophes of history is even less plausible than the communist faith that an equalitarian society will inevitably emerge from them. There is some warrant in history for the latter assumption, but very little for the former.

I find it impossible to envisage a society of pure love as long as man remains man. His natural limitations of reason and imagination will prevent him, even should he achieve a purely disinterested motive, from fully envisaging the needs of his fellowmen or from determining his actions upon the basis of their interests. Inevitably these limitations of individuals will achieve cumulative effect in the life and actions of national, racial and economic groups. It is possible to envisage a more ethical society than we now have. It is possible to believe that such a society will be achieved partly by evolutionary process and partly by catastrophe in which an old order, which offers a too stubborn resistance to new forces, is finally destroyed.

It is plausible also to interpret both the evolutionary and the catastrophic elements in history in religious terms and to see the counsels of God in them. But it is hardly plausible to expect divine intervention to introduce something into history which is irrelevant to anything we find in history now. We may envisage a society in which human cooperation is possible with a minimum amount of coercion, but we cannot imagine one in which there is no coercion at all—unless, of course, human beings become something quite different from what they now are. We may hope for a society in which self-interest is qualified by rigorous self-analysis and a stronger social impulse, but we cannot imagine a society totally without the assertion of self-interest and therefore without the conflict of opposing interests.

THE COST OF HUMAN PROGRESS

I realize quite well that my brother's position both in its ethical perfectionism and in its apocalyptic note is closer to the gospel than mine. In confessing that, I am forced to admit that I am unable to construct an adequate social ethic out of a pure love ethic. I cannot abandon the pure love ideal because anything which falls short of it is less than the ideal. But I cannot use it fully if I want to assume a responsible attitude toward the problems of society. Religious perfectionism drives either to asceticism or apocalypticism. In the one case the problem of society is given up entirely; in the other individual perfection is regarded as the force which will release the redemptive powers of God for society. I think the second alternative is better than the first, and that both have elements which must be retained for any adequate social ethic, lest it become lost in the relativities of expediency. But as long as the world of man remains a place where nature and God, the real and the ideal, meet, human progress will depend upon the judicious use of the forces of nature in the service of the ideal.

In practical, specific and contemporary terms this means that we must try to dissuade Japan from her military venture, but must use coercion to frustrate her designs if necessary, must reduce coercion to a minimum and prevent it from issuing in violence, must engage in constant self-analysis in order to reduce the moral conceit of Japan's critics and judges to a minimum, and must try in every social situation to maximise the ethical forces and yet not sacrifice the possibility of achieving an ethical goal because we are afraid to use any but purely ethical means.

LIFE AS TRAGEDY

To say all this is really to confess that the history of mankind is a perennial tragedy; for the highest ideals which the individual may project are ideals which he can never realize in social and collective terms. If there is a law in our members which wars against the law that is in our minds as individuals, this is even more true when we think of society. Individuals set the goal for society but society itself must achieve the goal and society is and will always remain sub-human. The goal which a sensitive individual sets for society must therefore always be something which is a little outside and beyond history. Love may qualify the social struggle of history but it will never abolish it, and those who make the attempt to bring society under the dominion of perfect love will die on the cross. And those who behold the cross are quite right in seeing it as a revelation of the divine, of what man ought to be and cannot be, at least not so long as he is enmeshed in the processes of history.

Perhaps that is why it is inevitable that religious imagination should set goals beyond history. "Man's reach is beyond his grasp, or what's a heaven for." My brother does not like these goals above and beyond history. He wants religion and social idealism to deal with history. In that case he must not state his goal in absolute terms. There can be nothing absolute in history, no matter how frequently God may intervene in it. Man cannot live without a sense of the absolute, but neither can he achieve the absolute. He may resolve the tragic character of that fact by religious faith, by the experience of grace in which the unattainable is experienced in anticipatory terms, but he can never resolve in purely ethical terms the conflict between what is and what ought to be.

3

A Communication: The Only Way Into the Kingdom of God

H. Richard Niebuhr

EDITOR THE CHRISTIAN CENTURY:

SIR: Since you have given me leave to fire one more shot in the fraternal war between my brother and me over the question of pacifism, I shall attempt to place it as well as I can, not for the purpose of demolishing my opponent's position— which our thirty years' war has shown me to be impossible— but for the sake of pointing as accurately as I can to the exact locus of the issue between us. It does not lie in the question of activity or inactivity, to which my too journalistic approach to the problem directed attention; we are speaking after all of two kinds of activity. The fundamental question seems to me to be whether "the history of mankind is a perennial tragedy" which can derive meaning only from a goal which lies beyond history, as my brother maintains, or whether the "eschatological" faith, to which I seek to adhere, is justifiable. In that faith tragedy is only the prelude to fulfillment, and a prelude which is necessary because of human nature; the kingdom of God comes inevitably, though whether we shall see it or not, depends on our recognition of its presence and our acceptance of the only kind of life which will enable us to enter it, the life of repentance and forgiveness.

For my brother God is outside the historical processes, so much so that he charges me with faith in a miracle-working deity which interferes occasionally, sometimes brutally, sometimes redemptively, in this history. But God, I believe, is always in history; he is the structure in things, the source of all meaning, the "I am that I am," that which is that it is. He is the rock against which we beat in vain, that which bruises and overwhelms us when we seek to impose our wishes, contrary to his, upon him. That structure of the universe, that creative will, can no more be said to interfere brutally in history than the violated laws of my organism can be said to interfere brutally with my life if they make me pay the cost of my violation. That structure of the universe, that will of God, does bring war and depression upon us when we bring it upon ourselves, for we live in the kind of world which visits our iniquities upon us and our children, no matter how much we pray and desire that it be otherwise.

Self-interest acts destructively in this world; it calls forth counter-assertion; nationalism breeds nationalism, class assertion summons up counter assertion on the part of exploited classes. The result is war, economic, military, verbal; and it is judgment. But this same structure in things which is our enemy is our redeemer; "it means intensely and means good"—not the good which we desire, but the good which we would desire if we were good and really wise. History is not a perennial tragedy but a road to fulfillment and that fulfillment requires the tragic outcome of every self-assertion, for it is a fulfillment which can only be designated as "love." It has created fellowship in atoms and organisms, at bitter cost to electrons and cells; and it is creating something better than human selfhood but at bitter cost to that selfhood. This is not a faith in progress, for evil grows as well as good and every self-assertion must be eliminated somewhere and somehow—by innocence suffering for guilt, it seems.

If, however, history is no more than tragedy, if there is no fulfillment in it, then my brother is right. Then we must rest content with the clash of self-interested individuals, personal or social. But in that case I see no reason why we should qualify the clash of competition with a homeopathic dose of Christian "love."

The only harmony which can possibly result from the clash of interests is the harmony imposed by the rule of the strong or a parallelogram of social forces, whether we think of the interclass structure or the international world. To import any pacifism into this struggle is only to weaken the weaker self-asserters (India, China or the proletariat) or to provide the strong with a facade of "service" behind which they can operate with a salved conscience. (Pacificism, on the other hand, as a method of self-assertion, is not pacifism at all but only a different kind of war.)

The method which my brother recommends, that of qualifying the social struggle by means of some Christian love, seems to me to be only the old method of making Christian love an ambulance driver in the wars of interested and clashing parties. If it is more than that it is weakening of the forces whose success we think necessary for a juster social order. For me the question is one of "either-or;" either the Christian method, which is not the method of love but of repentance and forgiveness, or the method of self-assertion; either nationalism or Christianity, either capitalism-communism or Christianity. The attempt to qualify the one method by the other is hopeless compromise.

I think that to apply the terms "Christian perfectionism" or "Christian ideal" to my approach is rather misleading. I rather think that Dewey is quite right in his war on ideals; they always seem irrelevant to our situation and betray us into a dualistic morality. The society of love is an impossible human ideal, as the fellowship of the organism is an impossible ideal for the cell. It is not an ideal toward which we can strive, but an "emergent," a potentiality in our situation which remains unrealized so long as we try to impose our pattern, our wishes upon the divine creative process.

Man's task is not that of building Utopias but that of eliminating weeds and tilling the soil so that the kingdom of God can grow. His method is not one of striving for perfection or of acting perfectly, but of clearing the road by repentance and forgiveness. That this approach is valid for societies as well as for individuals and that the opposite approach will always involve us in the same one ceaseless cycle of assertion and counter-assertion, is what I am concerned to emphasize.

PART II

The Second World War

INTRODUCTION:
THE "GOOD WAR"?

Twenty-five years after the outbreak of war in 1914, Europeans found themselves once again in battle. Yet what began in 1939 as a war on the continent would soon escalate into another world war, extending to the Soviet Union, North Africa, Indochina, and the South Pacific. The result was two separate wars, a European war and a Far Eastern war. After 1941, Britain and the United States were in both while their enemies waged separate wars. The Soviet Union devoted its forces to the eastern front, until the last days when it declared war against Japan.

World War II began with Hitler's aggression into Poland in 1939, which led France and England to enter war following guarantees to Poland. By May 1940, the Germans had advanced into Norway, the Netherlands, and France, after which they attacked Britain by bombing docks, airports, factories, and cities. The German forces succeeded on the continent largely by implementing the theory of blitzkrieg, which involved a rapid division of opposing forces by making deep thrusts of mechanized columns and then enveloping the enemy with speed and maneuver. Only by virtue of England's geographical separation from the continent was it spared of Germany's strength on the ground. Relying on superior air power and aid from the United States, British forces saved the island from invasion.

Axis powers then turned to the invasion of the Balkans, Greece, and North Africa, and in June 1941 embarked upon Operation Barbarossa, a mass attack on the Soviet Union. Six months later, on December 7, 1941, Japanese pilots bombed and sank most of the American fleet in the Pacific in an air raid over Pearl Harbor, Hawaii. United States bases in Guam and Wake were also bombed, as were British bases in Hong Kong and Singapore. The Japanese rapidly spread through

Indonesia, Burma, the Philippines, and North Borneo, and soon extended west to the borders of India. In the summer of 1942, Germans in the Caucasus and Egypt and Japanese forces in the Indian Ocean threatened to join forces at the Suez canal.

In November of 1942, the U.S. victory at Guadalcanal in the Solomons, the British victory at El Alamein in Egypt, the Russian victory at Stalingrad, and Allied landings in North Africa turned the tide in the European theater. Yet it would take three more years and millions of combatant and civilian lives before Allied forces would be able to join hands at the Elbe in April 1945. And, in the course of liberating those living under Germany's occupation, the Allies uncovered the vast machinery with which Nazi forces sought to exterminate millions of non-Aryans, confirming half-believed accounts that had circulated for years.[1]

For a large number of Americans and British citizens, the Second World War was, as Studs Terkel has written, a "good war"—a war whose justification generated little dissension or public debate.[2] The spread of Nazism, the bombing of London, and the aggressive actions of the Japanese could leave little doubt as to the merits of the Allied cause. Toward the end of defeating these enemies, a vast arsenal of military, industrial, and cultural forces were set in motion to propel the Allies into the fray. But, interestingly enough, this public confidence was not always mirrored in ethical commentary. It was rather the case that the war's ambiguity became the focus of much reflection, both in terms of the war's cause and the methods with which it was fought. However tempting it might have been to adopt the rhetoric of absolute justice, given the nature of German and Japanese aggression, at least some of the ethical commentary called attention to the excesses of the Allied effort.

The Second World War transformed the world's political map, eliminating five nations from the ranks of great powers: Germany, England, France, Japan, and Italy. Now only two great powers remained, the United States and the Soviet Union, both deeply divided over ideological issues. For the next forty-five years, these nations sought to extend their respective spheres of influence. Survivors of the Second World War entered into a cold war that would oscillate between mutual suspicion and fragile détente.

NOTES

1. Harry Browne, *The Second World War* (London: Faber & Faber, 1968); Michael Lyons, *The Second World War: A Short History* (Englewood Cliffs, N.J.: Prentice-Hall, 1989); Edgar McInnis, *The War* (Toronto: Oxford University Press, 1940–46); R. A. C. Parker, *Struggle for Survival: The History of the Second World War* (Oxford: Oxford University Press, 1989).

2. Studs Terkel, *The "Good War": An Oral History of World War II* (New York: Pantheon Books, 1984).

4

Why the Christian Church Is Not Pacifist

Reinhold Niebuhr

Whenever the actual historical situation sharpens the issue, the debate whether the Christian Church is, or ought to be, pacifist is carried on with fresh vigor both inside and outside the Christian community. Those who are not pacifists seek to prove that pacifism is a heresy; while the pacifists contend, or at least imply, that the Church's failure to espouse pacifism unanimously can only be interpreted as apostasy, and must be attributed to its lack of courage or to its want of faith.

There may be an advantage in stating the thesis, with which we enter this debate, immediately. The thesis is, that the failure of the Church to espouse pacifism is not apostasy, but is derived from an understanding of the Christian Gospel which refuses simply to equate the Gospel with the "law of love." Christianity is not simply a new law, namely, the law of love. The finality of Christianity cannot be proved by analyses which seek to reveal that the law of love is stated more unambiguously and perfectly in the life and teachings of Christ than anywhere else. Christianity is a religion which measures the total dimension of human existence not only in terms of the final norm of human conduct, which is expressed in the law of love, but also in terms of the fact of sin. It recognizes that the same man who can become his true self only by striving infinitely for self-realization beyond himself is also inevitably involved in the sin of infinitely making his partial and narrow self the true end of existence. It believes, in other words, that though Christ is the true norm (the "second Adam") for every man, every man is also in some sense a crucifier of Christ.

The good news of the gospel is not the law that we ought to love one another. The good news of the gospel is that there is a resource of divine mercy which is able to overcome a contradiction within our own souls, which we cannot ourselves overcome. This contradiction is that, though we know we ought to love our neighbor as ourself, there is a "law in our members which wars against the law that is in our mind," so that, in fact, we love ourselves more than our neighbor.

The grace of God which is revealed in Christ is regarded by Christian faith as, on the one hand, an actual "power of righteousness" which heals the contradiction within our hearts. In that sense Christ defines the actual possibilities of human existence. On the other hand, this grace is conceived as "justification," as pardon rather than power, as the forgiveness of God, which is vouchsafed to man despite the fact that he never achieves the full measure of Christ. In that sense Christ is the "impossible possibility." Loyalty to him means realization in intention, but does not actually mean the full realization of the measure of Christ. In this doctrine of forgiveness and justification, Christianity measures the full seriousness of sin as a permanent factor in human history. Naturally, the doctrine has no meaning for modern secular civilization, nor for the secularized and moralistic versions of Christianity. They cannot understand the doctrine precisely because they believe there is some fairly simple way out of the sinfulness of human history.

It is rather remarkable that so many modern Christians should believe that Christianity is primarily a "challenge" to man to obey the law of Christ; whereas it is, as a matter of fact, a religion which deals realistically with the problem presented by the violation of this law. Far from believing that the ills of the world could be set right "if only" men obeyed the law of Christ, it has always regarded the problem of achieving justice in a sinful world as a very difficult task. In the profounder versions of the Christian faith the very utopian illusions, which are currently equated with Christianity, have been rigorously disavowed.

Nevertheless, it is not possible to regard pacifism simply as a heresy. In one of its aspects modern Christian pacifism is simply a version of Christian perfectionism. It expresses a genuine impulse in the heart of Christianity, the impulse to take the law of Christ seriously and not to allow the political strategies, which the sinful character of man makes necessary, to become final norms. In its profounder forms this Christian perfectionism did not proceed from a simple faith that the "law of love" could be regarded as an alternative to the political strategies by which the world achieves a precarious justice. These strategies invariably involve the balancing of power with power; and they never completely escape the peril of tyranny on the one hand, and the peril of anarchy and warfare on the other.

In medieval ascetic perfectionism and in Protestant sectarian perfectionism (of the type of Menno Simons, for instance) the effort to achieve a standard of perfect love in individual life was not presented as a political alternative. On the contrary, the political problem and task were specifically disavowed. This perfectionism did not give itself to the illusion that it had discovered a method for eliminating the element of conflict from political strategies. On the contrary, it regarded the mystery of evil as beyond its power of solution. It was content to set up the most perfect and unselfish individual life as a symbol of the Kingdom of God. It knew that this could only be done by disavowing the political task and by freeing the individual of all responsibility for social justice.

It is this kind of pacifism which is not a heresy. It is rather a valuable asset for the Christian faith. It is a reminder to the Christian community that the relative norms of social justice, which justify both coercion and resistance to coercion, are not final norms, and that Christians are in constant peril of forgetting their relative and tentative character and of making them too completely normative.

There is thus a Christian pacifism which is not a heresy. Yet most modern forms of Christian pacifism are heretical. Presumably inspired by the Christian gospel, they have really absorbed the Renaissance faith in the goodness of man, have rejected the Christian doctrine of original sin as an outmoded bit of pessimism, have reinterpreted the Cross so that it is made to stand for the absurd idea that perfect love is guaranteed a simple victory over the world, and have rejected all other profound elements of the Christian gospel as

"Pauline" accretions which must be stripped from the "simple gospel of Jesus." This form of pacifism is not only heretical when judged by the standards of the total gospel. It is equally heretical when judged by the facts of human existence. There are no historical realities which remotely conform to it. It is important to recognize this lack of conformity to the facts of experience as a criterion of heresy.

All forms of religious faith are principles of interpretation which we use to organize our experience. Some religions may be adequate principles of interpretation at certain levels of experience, but they break down at deeper levels. No religious faith can maintain itself in defiance of the experience which it supposedly interprets. A religious faith which substitutes faith in man for faith in God cannot finally validate itself in experience. If we believe that the only reason men do not love each other perfectly is because the law of love has not been preached persuasively enough, we believe something to which experience does not conform. If we believe that if Britain had only been fortunate enough to have produced 30 per cent instead of 2 per cent of conscientious objectors to military service, Hitler's heart would have been softened and he would not have dared to attack Poland, we hold a faith which no historic reality justifies.

Such a belief has no more justification in the facts of experience than the communist belief that the sole cause of man's sin is the class organization of society and the corollary faith that a "classless" society will be essentially free of human sinfulness. All of these beliefs are pathetic alternatives to the Christian faith. They all come finally to the same thing. They do not believe that man remains a tragic creature who needs the divine mercy as much at the end as at the beginning of his moral endeavors. They believe rather that there is some fairly easy way out of the human situation of "self-alienation." In this connection it is significant that Christian pacifists, rationalists like Bertrand Russell, and mystics like Aldous Huxley, believe essentially the same thing. The Christians make Christ into the symbol of their faith in man. But their faith is really identical with that of Russell or Huxley.

The common element in these various expressions of faith in man is the belief that man is essentially good at some level of his being. They believe that if you can abstract the rational-universal man from what is finite and contingent in human nature, or if you can only cultivate some mystic-universal element in the deeper levels of man's consciousness, you will be able to eliminate human selfishness and the consequent conflict of life with life. These rational or mystical views of man conform neither to the New Testament's view of human nature nor yet to the complex facts of human experience. In order to elaborate the thesis more fully, that the refusal of the Christian Church to espouse pacifism is not apostasy and that most modern forms of pacifism are heretical, it is necessary first of all to consider the character of the absolute and unqualified demands which Christ makes and to understand the relation of these demands to the gospel.

II

It is very foolish to deny that the ethic of Jesus is an absolute and uncompromising ethic. It is, in the phrase of Ernst Troeltsch, an ethic of "love universalism and love perfectionism." The injunctions "resist not evil," "love your enemies," "if ye love them that love you what thanks have you?" "be not anxious for your life," and "be ye therefore perfect even as your father is heaven is perfect," are all of one piece, and they are all uncompromising and absolute. Nothing is more futile and pathetic than the effort of some Christian theologians who find it necessary to become involved in the relativities of politics, in resistance to tyranny or in social conflict, to justify themselves by seeking to prove that Christ was also involved in some of these relativities, that he used whips to drive the money-changers out of the Temple, or that he came "not to bring peace but a sword," or that he asked the disciples to sell a cloak and buy a sword. What could be more futile than to build a whole ethical structure upon the exegetical issue whether Jesus accepted the sword with the words: "It is enough," or whether he really meant: "Enough of this"? (Luke 22:36)

Those of us who regard the ethic of Jesus as finally and ultimately normative, but as not immediately applicable to the task of securing justice in a sinful world, are very foolish if we try to reduce the ethic so that it will cover and justify our prudential and relative standards and strategies. To do this is to reduce the ethic to a new legalism. The significance of the law of love is precisely that it is not just another law, but a law which transcends all law. Every law and every standard which falls short of the law of love embodies contingent factors and makes concessions to the fact that sinful man must achieve tentative harmonies of life with life which are less than the best. It is dangerous and confusing to give these tentative and relative standards final and absolute religious sanction.

Curiously enough the pacifists are just as guilty as their less absolutist brethren of diluting the ethic of Jesus for the purpose of justifying their position. They are forced to recognize that an ethic of pure non-resistance can have no immediate relevance to any political situation; for in every political situation it is necessary to achieve justice by resisting pride and power. They therefore declare that the ethic of Jesus is not an ethic of non-resistance, but one of non-violent resistance; that it allows one to resist evil provided the resistance does not involve the destruction of life or property.

There is not the slightest support in Scripture for this doctrine of non-violence. Nothing could be plainer than that the ethic uncompromisingly enjoins non-resistance and not non-violent resistance. Furthermore, it is obvious that the distinction between violent and non-violent resistance is not an absolute distinction. If it is made absolute, we arrive at the morally absurd position of giving moral preference to the non-violent power which Doctor Goebbels wields over the type of power wielded by a general. This absurdity is really derived from the modern (and yet probably very ancient and very Platonic) heresy of regarding the "physical" as evil and the "spiritual" as good. The *reductio ad absurdum* of this position is achieved in a book which has become something of a textbook for modern pacifists, Richard Gregg's *The Power of Non-Violence*. In this book non-violent resistance is commended as the best method of defeating your foe, particularly as the best method of breaking his morale. It is suggested that Christ ended his life on the Cross because he had not completely mastered the technique of non-violence, and must for this reason be regarded as a guide who is inferior to Gandhi, but whose significance lies in initiating a movement which culminates in Gandhi.

One may well concede that a wise and decent statesmanship will seek not only to avoid conflict, but to avoid violence in conflict. Parliamentary political controversy is one method of sublimating political struggles in such a way as to avoid violent collisions of interest. But this pragmatic distinction has nothing to do with the more basic distinction between the ethic of the "Kingdom of God," in which no concession is made to human sin, and all relative political strategies which, assuming human sinfulness, seek to secure the highest measure of peace and justice among selfish and sinful men.

III

If pacifists were less anxious to dilute the ethic of Christ to make it conform to their particular type of non-violent politics, and if they were less obsessed with the obvious contradiction between the ethic of Christ and the fact of war, they might have noticed that the injunction "resist not evil" is only part and parcel of a total ethic which we violate not only in wartime, but every day of our life, and that overt conflict is but a final and vivid revelation of the character of human existence. This total ethic can be summarized most succinctly in the two injunctions "Be not anxious for your life" and "love thy neighbor as thyself."

In the first of these, attention is called to the fact that the root and source of all undue self-assertion lies in the anxiety which all men have in regard to their existence. The ideal possibility is that perfect trust in God's providence ("for your heavenly father knoweth what things ye have need of ") and perfect unconcern for the physical life ("fear not them which are able to kill the body") would create a state of serenity in which one life would not seek to take advantage of another life. But the fact is that anxiety is an inevitable concomitant of human freedom, and is the root of the inevitable sin which expresses itself in every human activity and creativity. Not even the most idealistic preacher who admonishes his congregation to obey the law of Christ is free of the sin which arises from anxiety. He may or may not be anxious for his job, but he is certainly anxious about his prestige. Perhaps he is anxious for his reputation as a righteous man. He may be tempted to preach a perfect ethic the more vehemently in order to hide an unconscious apprehension of the fact that his own life does not conform to it. There is no life which does not violate the injunction "Be not anxious." That is the tragedy of human sin. It is the tragedy of man who is dependent upon God, but seeks to make himself independent and self-sufficing.

In the same way there is no life which is not involved in a

violation of the injunction, "Thou shalt love thy neighbor as thyself." No one is so blind as the idealist who tells us that war would be unnecessary "if only" nations obeyed the law of Christ, but who remains unconscious of the fact that even the most saintly life is involved in some measure of contradiction to this law. Have we not all known loving fathers and mothers who, despite a very genuine love for their children, had to be resisted if justice and freedom were to be gained for the children? Do we not know that the sinful will-to-power may be compounded with the most ideal motives and may use the latter as its instruments and vehicles? The collective life of man undoubtedly stands on a lower moral plane than the life of individuals, yet nothing revealed in the life of races and nations is unknown in individual life. The sins of pride and of lust for power and the consequent tyranny and injustice are all present, at least in an inchoate form, in individual life. Even as I write my little five-year-old boy comes to me with the tale of an attack made upon him by his year-old sister. This tale is concocted to escape paternal judgment for being too rough in playing with his sister. One is reminded of Germany's claim that Poland was the aggressor and the similar Russian charge against Finland.

The pacifists do not know human nature well enough to be concerned about the contradictions between the law of love and the sin of man, until sin has conceived and brought forth death. They do not see that sin introduces an element of conflict into the world and that even the most loving relations are not free of it. They are, consequently, unable to appreciate the complexity of the problem of justice. They merely assert that if only men loved one another, all the complex, and sometimes horrible, realities of the political order could be dispensed with. They do not see that their "if" begs the most basic problem of human history. It is because men are sinners that justice can be achieved only by a certain degree of coercion on the one hand, and by resistance to coercion and tyranny on the other hand. The political life of man must constantly steer between the Scylla of anarchy and the Charybdis of tyranny.

Human egotism makes large-scale co-operation upon a purely voluntary basis impossible. Governments must coerce. Yet there is an element of evil in this coercion. It is always in danger of serving the purposes of the coercing power rather than the general weal. We cannot fully trust the motives of any ruling class or power. That is why it is important to maintain democratic checks upon the centers of power. It may also be necessary to resist a ruling class, nation or race, if it violates the standards of relative justice which have been set up for it. Such resistance means war. It need not mean overt conflict or violence. But if those who resist tyranny publish their scruples against violence too publicly the tyrannical power need only threaten the use of violence against non-violent pressure to persuade the resisters to quiescence. (The relation of pacifism to the abortive effort to apply non-violent sanctions against Italy in the Ethiopian dispute is instructive at this point.)

The refusal to recognize that sin introduces an element of conflict into the world invariably means that a morally perverse preference is given to tyranny over anarchy (war). If we are told that tyranny would destroy itself, if only we would not challenge it, the obvious answer is that tyranny continues to grow if it is not resisted. If it is to be resisted, the risk of overt conflict must be taken. The thesis that German tyranny must not be challenged by other nations because Germany will throw off this yoke in due time, merely means that an unjustified moral preference is given to civil war over international war, for internal resistance runs the risk of conflict as much as external resistance. Furthermore, no consideration is given to the fact that a tyrannical State may grow too powerful to be successfully resisted by purely internal pressure, and that the injustices which it does to other than its own nationals may rightfully lay the problem of the tyranny upon other nations.

It is not unfair to assert that most pacifists who seek to present their religious absolutism as a political alternative to the claims and counter-claims, the pressures and counter-pressures of the political order, invariably betray themselves into this preference for tyranny. Tyranny is not war. It is peace, but it is a peace which has nothing to do with the peace of the Kingdom of God. It is a peace which results from one will establishing a complete dominion over other wills and reducing them to acquiescence.

One of the most terrible consequences of a confused religious absolutism is that it is forced to condone such tyranny as that of Germany in the nations which it has conquered and now cruelly oppresses. It usually does this by insisting that the tyranny is no worse than that which is practiced in the so-called democratic nations. Whatever may be the moral ambiguities of the so-called democratic nations, and however serious may be their failure to conform perfectly to their democratic ideals, it is sheer moral perversity to equate the inconsistencies of a democratic civilization with the brutalities which modern tyrannical States practice. If we cannot make a distinction here, there are no historical distinctions which have any value. All the distinctions upon which the fate of civilization has turned in the history of mankind have been just such relative distinctions.

One is persuaded to thank God in such times as these that the common people maintain a degree of "common sense," that they preserve an uncorrupted ability to react against injustice and the cruelty of racial bigotry. This ability has been lost among some Christian idealists who preach the law of love but forget that they, as well as all other men, are involved in the violation of that law; and who must (in order to obscure this glaring defect in their theory) eliminate all relative distinctions in history and praise the peace of tyranny as if it were nearer to the peace of the Kingdom of God than war. The overt conflicts of human history are periods of judgment when what has been hidden becomes revealed. It is the business of Christian prophecy to anticipate these judgments to some degree at least, to call attention to the fact that when men say "peace and quiet" "destruction will come upon them unaware," and reveal to what degree this overt destruction is a vivid portrayal of the constant factor of sin in human life. A theology which fails to come to grips with this tragic factor of sin is heretical, both from the standpoint of the gospel and in terms of its blindness to obvious facts of human experience in every realm and on every level of moral goodness.

IV

The gospel is something more than the law of love. The gospel deals with the fact that men violate the law of love. The gospel presents Christ as the pledge and revelation of God's mercy which finds man in his rebellion and overcomes his sin.

The question is whether the grace of Christ is primarily a power of righteousness which so heals the sinful heart that henceforth it is able to fulfill the law of love; or whether it is primarily the assurance of divine mercy for a persistent sinfulness which man never overcomes completely. When St. Paul declared: "I am crucified with Christ; nevertheless I live, yet it is no more I that live but Christ that dwelleth in me," did he mean that the new life in Christ was not his own by reason of the fact that grace, rather than his own power, enabled him to live on the new level of righteousness? Or did he mean that the new life was his only in intention and by reason of God's willingness to accept intention for achievement? Was the emphasis upon sanctification or justification?

This is the issue upon which the Protestant Reformation separated itself from classical Catholicism, believing that Thomistic interpretations of grace lent themselves to new forms of self-righteousness in place of the Judaistic-legalistic self-righteousness which St. Paul condemned. If one studies the whole thought of St. Paul, one is almost forced to the conclusion that he was not himself quite certain whether the peace which he had found in Christ was a moral peace, the peace of having become what man truly is; or whether it was primarily a religious peace, the peace of being "completely known and all forgiven," of being accepted by God despite the continued sinfulness of the heart. Perhaps St. Paul could not be quite sure about where the emphasis was to be placed, for the simple reason that no one can be quite certain about the character of this ultimate peace. There must be, and there is, moral content in it, a fact which Reformation theology tends to deny and which Catholic and sectarian theology emphasizes. But there is never such perfect moral content in it that any man could find perfect peace through his moral achievements, not even the achievements which he attributes to grace rather than the power of his own will. This is the truth which the Reformation emphasized and which modern Protestant Christianity has almost completely forgotten.

We are, therefore, living in a state of sorry moral and religious confusion. In the very moment of world history in which every contemporary historical event justifies the Reformation emphasis upon the persistence of sin on every level of moral achievement, we not only identify Protestant faith with a moralistic sentimentality which neglects and obscures truths in the Christian gospel (which it was the mission of the Reformation to rescue from obscurity), but we even neglect those reservations and qualifications upon the theory of sanctification upon which classical Catholicism wisely insisted.

We have, in other words, reinterpreted the Christian gospel in terms of the Renaissance faith in man. Modern pacifism is merely a final fruit of this Renaissance spirit, which has pervaded the whole of modern Protestantism. We have interpreted world history as a gradual ascent to the Kingdom of God which waits for final triumph only upon the willingness of Christians to "take Christ seriously." There is nothing in Christ's own teachings, except dubious interpretations of the parable of the leaven and the mustard seed, to justify this interpretation of world history. In the whole of the New Testament, Gospels and Epistles alike, there is only one interpretation of world history. That pictures history as moving toward a climax in which both Christ and anti-Christ are revealed.

The New Testament does not, in other words, envisage a simple triumph of good over evil in history. It sees human history involved in the contradictions of sin to the end. That is why it sees no simple resolution of the problem of history. It believes that the Kingdom of God will finally resolve the contradictions of history; but for it the Kingdom of God is no simple historical possibility. The grace of God for man and the Kingdom of God for history are both divine realities and not human possibilities.

The Christian faith believes that the Atonement reveals God's mercy as an ultimate resource by which God alone overcomes the judgment which sin deserves. If this final truth of the Christian religion has no meaning to modern men, including modern Christians, that is because even the tragic character of contemporary history has not yet persuaded them to take the fact of human sinfulness seriously.

V

The contradiction between the law of love and the sinfulness of man raises not only the ultimate religious problem how men are to have peace if they do not overcome the contradiction, and how history will culminate if the contradiction remains on every level of historic achievement; it also raises the immediate problem how men are to achieve a tolerable harmony of life with life, if human pride and selfishness prevent the realization of the law of love.

The pacifists are quite right in one emphasis. They are right in asserting that love is really the law of life. It is not some ultimate possibility which has nothing to do with human history. The freedom of man, his transcendence over the limitations of nature and over all historic and traditional social situations, makes any form of human community which falls short of the law of love less than the best. Only by a voluntary giving of life to life and a free interpenetration of personalities could man do justice both to the freedom of other personalities and the necessity of community between personalities. The law of love therefore remains a principle of criticism over all forms of community in which elements of coercion and conflict destroy the highest type of fellowship.

To look at human communities from the perspective of the Kingdom of God is to know that there is a sinful element in all the expedients which the political order uses to establish justice. That is why even the seemingly most stable justice degenerates periodically into either tyranny or anarchy. But it must also be recognized that it is not possible to eliminate the sinful element in the political expedients. They are, in the words of St. Augustine, both the consequence of, and the remedy for, sin. If they are the remedy for sin, the ideal of love is not merely a principle of indiscriminate criticism upon all approximations of justice. It is also a principle of discriminate criticism between forms of justice.

As a principle of indiscriminate criticism upon all forms of justice, the law of love reminds us that the injustice and tyranny against which we contend in the foe is partially the consequence of our own injustice, that the pathology of modern Germans is partially a consequence of the vindictiveness of the peace of Versailles, and that the ambition of a tyrannical imperialism is different only in degree and not in kind from the imperial impulse which characterizes all of human life.

The Christian faith ought to persuade us that political controversies are always conflicts between sinners and not between righteous men and sinners. It ought to mitigate the self-righteousness which is an inevitable concomitant of all human conflict. The spirit of contrition is an important ingredient in the sense of justice. If it is powerful enough it may be able to restrain the impulse of vengeance sufficiently to allow a decent justice to emerge. This is an important issue facing Europe in anticipation of the conclusion of the present war. It cannot be denied that the Christian conscience failed terribly in restraining vengeance after the last war. It is also quite obvious that the natural inclination to self-righteousness was the primary force of this vengeance (expressed particularly in the war guilt clause of the peace treaty). The pacifists draw the conclusion from the fact that justice is never free from vindictiveness, that we ought not for this reason ever to contend against a foe. This argument leaves out of account that capitulation to the foe might well subject us to a worse vindictiveness. It is as foolish to imagine that the foe is free of the sin which we deplore in ourselves as it is to regard ourselves as free of the sin which we deplore in the foe.

The fact that our own sin is always partly the cause of the sins against which we must contend is regarded by simple moral purists as proof that we have no right to contend against the foe. They regard the injunction "Let him who is without sin cast the first stone" as a simple alternative to the schemes of justice which society has devised and whereby it prevents the worst forms of anti-social conduct. This injunction of Christ ought to remind every judge and every juridical tribunal that the crime of the criminal is partly the consequence of the sins of society. But if pacifists are to be consistent they ought to advocate the abolition of the whole judicial process in society. It is perfectly true that national societies have more impartial instruments of justice than international society possesses to date. Nevertheless, no impartial court is as impartial as it pretends to be, and there is no judicial process which is completely free of vindictiveness. Yet we cannot dispense with it; and we will have to continue to put criminals into jail. There is a point where the final cause of the criminal's anti-social conduct becomes a fairly irrelevant issue in comparison with the task of preventing his conduct from injuring innocent fellows.

The ultimate principles of the Kingdom of God are never irrelevant to any problem of justice, and they hover over every social situation as an ideal possibility; but that does not mean that they can be made into simple alternatives for the present schemes of relative justice. The thesis that the so-called democratic nations have no right to resist overt forms of tyranny, because their own history betrays imperialistic motives, would have meaning only if it were possible to achieve a perfect form of justice in any nation and to free national life completely of the imperialistic motive. This is impossible; for imperialism is the collective expression of the sinful will-to-power which characterizes all human existence. The pacifist argument on this issue betrays how completely pacifism gives itself to illusions about the stuff with which it is dealing in human nature. These illusions deserve particular censure, because no one who knows his own heart very well ought to be given to such illusions.

The recognition of the law of love as an indiscriminate principle of criticism over all attempts at social and international justice is actually a resource of justice, for it prevents the pride, self-righteousness and vindictiveness of men from corrupting their efforts at justice. But it must be recognized that love is also a principle of discriminate criticism between various forms of community and various attempts at justice. The closest approximation to a love in which life supports life in voluntary community is a justice in which life is prevented from destroying life and the interests of the one are guarded against unjust claims by the other. Such justice is achieved when impartial tribunals of society prevent men "from being judges in their own cases," in the words of John Locke. But the tribunals of justice merely codify certain equilibria of power. Justice is basically dependent upon a balance of power. Whenever an individual or a group or a nation possesses undue power, and whenever this power is not checked by the possibility of criticizing and resisting it, it grows inordinate. The equilibrium of power upon which every structure of justice rests would degenerate into anarchy but for the organizing center which controls it. One reason why the balances of power, which prevent injustice in international relations, periodically degenerate into overt anarchy is because no way has yet been found to establish an adequate organizing center, a stable international judicatory, for this balance of power.

A balance of power is something different from, and inferior to, the harmony of love. It is a basic condition of justice, given the sinfulness of man. Such a balance of power does not exclude love. In fact, without love the frictions and tensions of a balance of power would become intolerable. But without the balance of power even the most loving relations may degenerate into unjust relations, and love may become the screen which hides the injustice. Family relations are instructive at this point. Women did not gain justice from men, despite the intimacy of family relations, until they secured sufficient economic power to challenge male autocracy. There are Christian "idealists" today who speak sentimentally of love as the only way to justice, whose family life might benefit from a more delicate "balance of power."

Naturally the tensions of such a balance may become overt; and overt tensions may degenerate into conflict. The center of power, which has the function of preventing this anarchy of conflict, may also degenerate into tyranny. There is no perfectly adequate method of preventing either anarchy or tyranny. But obviously the justice established in the so-called democratic nations represents a high degree of achievement; and the achievement becomes the more impressive when it is compared with the tyranny into which alternative forms of society have fallen. The obvious evils of tyranny, however, will not inevitably persuade the victims of economic anarchy in democratic society to eschew tyranny. When men suffer from anarchy they may foolishly regard the evils of tyranny as the lesser evils. Yet the evils of tyranny in fascist and communist nations are so patent, that we may dare to hope that what is still left of democratic civilizations will not lightly sacrifice the virtues of democracy for the sake of escaping its defects.

We have a very vivid and conclusive evidence about the probable consequences of a tyrannical unification of Europe. The nature of the German rule in the conquered nations of Europe gives us the evidence. There are too many contingent factors in various national and international schemes of justice to justify any unqualified endorsement of even the most democratic structure of justice as "Christian." Yet it must be obvious that any social structure in which power has been made responsible, and in which anarchy has been overcome by methods of mutual accommodation, is preferable to either anarchy or tyranny. If it is not possible to express a moral preference for the justice achieved in democratic societies, in comparison with tyrannical societies, no historical preference has any meaning. This kind of justice approximates the harmony of love more than either anarchy or tyranny.

If we do not make discriminate judgments between social

systems we weaken the resolution to defend and extend civilization. Pacifism either tempts us to make no judgments at all, or to give an undue preference to tyranny in comparison with the momentary anarchy which is necessary to overcome tyranny. It must be admitted that the anarchy of war which results from resistance to tyranny is not always creative; that, at given periods of history, civilization may lack the resource to fashion a new and higher form of unity out of momentary anarchy. The defeat of Germany and the frustration of the Nazi effort to unify Europe in tyrannical terms is a negative task. It does not guarantee the emergence of a new Europe with a higher level of international cohesion and new organs of international justice. But it is a negative task which cannot be avoided. All schemes for avoiding this negative task rest upon illusions about human nature. Specifically, these illusions express themselves in the failure to understand the stubbornness and persistence of the tyrannical will, once it is fully conceived. It would not require great argumentative skill to prove that Nazi tyranny never could have reached such proportions as to be able to place the whole of Europe under its ban, if sentimental illusions about the character of the evil which Europe was facing had not been combined with less noble motives for tolerating Nazi aggression.

A simple Christian moralism is senseless and confusing. It is senseless when, as in the World War, it seeks uncritically to identify the cause of Christ with the cause of democracy without a religious reservation. It is just as senseless when it seeks to purge itself of this error by an uncritical refusal to make any distinctions between relative values in history. The fact is that we might as well dispense with the Christian faith entirely if it is our conviction that we can act in history only if we are guiltless. This means that we must either prove our guiltlessness in order to be able to act; or refuse to act because we cannot achieve guiltlessness. Self-righteousness or inaction are the alternatives of secular moralism. If they are also the only alternatives of Christian moralism, one rightly suspects that Christian faith has become diluted with secular perspectives.

In its profoundest insights the Christian faith sees the whole of human history as involved in guilt, and finds no release from guilt except in the grace of God. The Christian is freed by that grace to act in history; to give his devotion to the highest values he knows; to defend those citadels of civilization of which necessity and historic destiny have made him the defender; and he is persuaded by that grace to remember the ambiguity of even his best actions. If the providence of God does not enter the affairs of men to bring good out of evil, the evil in our good may easily destroy our most ambitious efforts and frustrate our highest hopes.

VI

Despite our conviction that most modern pacifism is too filled with secular and moralistic illusions to be of the highest value to the Christian community, we may be grateful for the fact that the Christian Church has learned, since the last war, to protect its pacifists and to appreciate their testimony. Even when this testimony is marred by self-righteousness, because it does not proceed from a sufficiently profound understanding of the tragedy of human history, it has its value.

It is a terrible thing to take human life. The conflict between man and man and nation and nation is tragic. If there are men who declare that, no matter what the consequences, they cannot bring themselves to participate in this slaughter, the Church ought to be able to say to the general community: We quite understand this scruple and we respect it. It proceeds from the conviction that the true end of man is brotherhood, and that love is the law of life. We who allow ourselves to become engaged in war need this testimony of the absolutist against us, lest we accept the warfare of the world as normative, lest we become callous to the horror of war, and lest we forget the ambiguity of our own actions and motives and the risk we run of achieving no permanent good from this momentary anarchy in which we are involved.

But we have a right to remind the absolutists that their testimony against us would be more effective if it were not corrupted by self-righteousness and were not accompanied by the implicit or explicit accusation of apostasy. A pacifism which really springs from the Christian faith, without secular accretions and corruptions, could not be as certain as modern pacifism is that it possesses an alternative for the conflicts and tensions from which and through which the world must rescue a precarious justice.

A truly Christian pacifism would set each heart under the judgment of God to such a degree that even the pacifist idealist would know that knowledge of the will of God is no guarantee of his ability or willingness to obey it. The idealist would recognize to what degree he is himself involved in rebellion against God, and would know that this rebellion is too serious to be overcome by just one more sermon on love, and one more challenge to man to obey the law of Christ.

5

War as the Judgment of God

H. Richard Niebuhr

It is a healthy sign that Christians of all groups are giving increasing attention to the question of God's action in this war. For too long a time we have concentrated on human action in international as in other conflicts and the disagreements among us have been at least partly due to this fact. Pacifists have approached war as an action of the lower human self—the angry, hating self—and have tried to respond to it with the action of the ideal, rational self. Coercionists have looked on war as the action of aggressive nations and have summoned men of good will to resist those of ill will.

These human actions are doubtless present in all war but Christian like Jewish interpretation of history centers in the conviction that God is at work in all events and the ethics of these monotheistic communities is determined by the principle that man's action ought always to be response to divine rather than to any finite action. Hence it is a sign of returning health when God rather than the self or the enemy is seen to be the central figure in the great tragedy of war and when the question, "What must I do?" is preceded by the question, "What is God doing?" To attend to God's action is to be on the way to that constructive understanding and constructive human reaction which the prophets initiated and Jesus set forth in its fullness.

I

To see the act of God in war is to stand where Isaiah stood when he discerned that Assyria was the rod of divine anger and where Jesus stood when he saw in the crucifixion not Pilate's or the Jews' activity but that of the Father who gave Pilate the power to crucify and whose will rather than Pilate's or Jesus' was being done.

The consequent action of Isaiah and Jesus was constructive because it was response to divine action rather than to Assyrian or Roman. It was constructive in that it built new community in the midst of tragedy, cleaned selves and society of egoism, fear and hatred, and opened up a productive future in which the tragedy was made the foundation of a new life. Had Isaiah simply attended to what the Assyrian was doing or Jesus to what the priests and Pilate were doing, it is difficult to see what constructive results could have followed, had they been ever so pacifist or coercionist.

The awareness of Christians that God is acting in the present conflict is still confused and uncertain; hence the reactions are confused. Doubtless much profound searching of soul, mind and Scriptures, much painful intellectual and spiritual labor are required of them, as of the Jews, if they are to learn how to act constructively or, rather, to act as those who are willing instead of unwilling servants of the active God. But something has been gained as a result of the very general recognition that God is judging the nations, the churches and all mankind in this great conflict and crucifixion. The conviction of sin, which the social gospel has brought about, and the old understanding of history, which Marxism has forced Christianity to remember, leave all Christians with a bad conscience in the presence of this struggle and with the recognition that men are reaping what they have sown.

To be sure, there are still parts of the church which think in terms of human rather than of divine judgment. For them the war is an affair of our judgment against the opponents' judgment. Such Christians tend to believe that their judgment on the enemy—both as moral evaluation and as punishment—is really God's judgment and that it is practically unnecessary to inquire what God is doing since they are executing his counsel. Happily these voices are not strong in the church. It must be conceded, of course, that the temptation to make the self the spokesman and lieutenant of the Eternal is never far from any one of us and that a more severe trial than the one we have experienced so far may lead many more of us to fall into this temptation. Still, it remains a cause for gratitude that the churches in the warring nations—on both sides—have so far not tended to confuse divine and human judgment as much as they did a generation ago. It is further a cause for thankfulness that pacifists and coercionists appear to agree on the primacy of God's judgment and its transcendence over all human judgment.

At one point this agreement in interpretation of the situation is leading to a general agreement in ethical decision. All the Christian groups seem to be resolved to exert all their powers to effect a just peace settlement—a peace which will not be based on the interpretation that only one nation is being judged or that the victors are the judges, but rather on the knowledge that all nations have fallen short of simple justice, not to speak of the glory of God. Hence it is demanded that the peace settlement recognize the necessity of sacrifice on the part of all, the limitation of national sovereignty, the claim of all nations to certain political and economic rights. On this the mind of the churches seems to be unified.

Beyond this point, however, there is no agreement and the continued confusion of the churches appears particularly when the question about present rather than future action is raised. It seems that God's judgment on the nations is not so understood as to require a present response, but only a sort of promise that we will try to be good in the future. One group appears to think that besides the action of God in judgment Christians ought to attend to the bad actions of all men who are making war and respond to the latter by refusal to participate in the conflict. Hence many pacifists desire to share in peace-making as those who stand under the judgment of God but to refrain from all participation in war because men, not God, make war.

A second group regards war as judgment of God but also as a defense of our own country against the enemies not of God so much as of our country. Hence it seeks to make a distinction between the response of the Christian to God and the response of the citizen to the enemy. As Christians, then, men do not make war, but as citizens they defend their country.

A third group makes a distinction between the absolute judgment of God to which all men must respond with penitence and the relative judgments of men to which other relative judgments must be opposed. For those who find themselves in this group the war requires the double response of contrition for common sin and of confident assertion of the relative rightness of democracy in opposition to totalitarianism.

In every case there is a dualism: two actions must be responded to, the action of God and the action of the opponent. To be sure, Christians are accustomed to dualism, for their two-worldly life involves them forevermore in the crisis of time and eternity, of this aeon and the future one, of the life in the spirit and the life in the body. But the dualism of double response is an intolerable one; it makes us "double-minded men, unstable in all our ways," ditheists who have two gods, the Father of Jesus Christ and our country, or Him and Democracy, or Him and Peace. Country, Democracy and Peace are surely values of a high order, if they are under God, but as rivals of God they are betrayers of life.

Perhaps further reflection on the nature of divine judgment and on the possibilities of consistent human response to it may be of some help in resolving our confusion and helping us toward the achievement of a common Christian mind.

II

What does it mean to say that this war is a judgment of God on the nations or on all of us? It cannot mean simply that it is the action of a Being who, in primitive human fashion, executes vengeance. Since Hosea's time that interpretation has been rationally impossible. Christians in particular must be convinced by their whole gospel that judgment cannot be separated from redemption, that the harshness of God is not antagonistic to his love but subordinate to it, that divine "penology" is reconstructive and not vindictive in its nature.

The fundamental Christian assumption about divine justice may be stated in another way by saying that it is never merely punishment for sins, as though God were concerned simply to restore the balance between men by making those suffer who have inflicted suffering, but that it is always primarily punishment of sinners who are to be chastened and changed in the character which produced the sinful acts.

Therefore war cannot be interpreted as hell; if it were hell we could not even be aware that God is judging us for we would be without God in war. War as judgment of God is a purgatory, not a hell.

Christians cannot interpret God's action in war as the judgment of vengeance for another and profounder reason: the pains of war do not descend primarily on the unjust but on the innocent. Wars are crucifixions. It is not the mighty, the guides and leaders of nations and churches, who suffer most in them, but the humble, little people who have had little to do with the framing of great policies. Even pacifists in jail have little reason to think of themselves as the martyrs of war when they reflect on all the children, wives and mothers, humble obedient soldiers, peasants on the land, who in the tragedy of war are made an offering for sin.

It is true also in the social sense that the greater burdens of war fall on the relatively innocent and on the weak. The nations which have suffered most in the present conflict are not those which were most responsible for the sins of commission and omission out of which this tragic demonstration of cosmic justice has issued. Czechoslovakia, Norway, the Netherlands, Belgium, Greece, China, the Philippines—these were not the conspicuous egoists, exploiters, self-satisfied and self-righteous among the countries of the earth.

This is not the place, even were the writer competent as he is not, to develop a social theory and application of the atonement. But, surely, Christians know that the justice of God is not only a redemptive justice in which suffering is used in the service of remaking but it is also vicarious in its method, so that the suffering of innocence is used for the remaking of the guilty. One cannot then speak of God acting in this war as judge of the nations without understanding that it is through the cross of Christ more than through the cross of thieves that he is acting upon mankind.

In the second place, if God is judging mankind in this war, as he is, there can be no contention before him about the relative rightness or wrongness of the various groups involved. When we are in the wrong before God we are absolutely in the wrong and no kind of relative rightness can be made the foundation of an appeal to a higher court. When Isaiah saw that Assyria was the rod of God's anger whereby

Israel was chastised he also saw that Assyria was wrong before God and that the axe had no right to boast of itself "against him that heweth therewith."

This truth cuts both ways. It means that if a Hitler is seen to be the rod of God's anger he is not thereby justified, relatively or absolutely; for he does not intend what God intends, "but it is in his heart to destroy and to cut off nations not a few." It means, also, that if the United Nations are the instruments of God's judgment on Germany, Italy and Japan, they are not thereby justified, as though their intentions were relatively or absolutely right. God does not act save through finite instruments but none of the instruments can take the place of God even for a moment, either in their own view or in the view of the one who is being "punished." Whether we speak of nations or of movements, we can be as certain in our day as the prophets were in theirs that our thoughts are not his thoughts and our ways are not his ways. Hence response to divine judgment can never mean justification of either the enemy or of the self. Insofar as such justification is introduced the conviction about God's action is abandoned.

A third point about divine judgment which it seems important to recall again in our time, though it ought to be self-evident, is that it is the judgment of the one and universal God and not the judgment of a Lord of the spiritual life, or of a Lord of religious life, or of a Christian Lord over Christian life. As judgment of a redeemer it cannot be interpreted in the light of revelation, reason and experience as that of a redeemer of the spiritual, the religious or the Christian life. The redeemer is the Father of all things who has created men not only in spiritual society but also in domestic, political and economic society. Hence it is impossible so to separate response to the judgment of God from politically necessary action as to make religious life an affair of repentance while political action remains essentially unrepentant, self-confident action in the defense of our values.

This is what both those groups seem to do who say that in addition to accepting divine judgment we must on the one hand defend our country and, on the other hand, defend democracy. If we do not reform our war-making as well as our peace-making, our defense of values as well as our aggression, our support of democracy as well as our opposition to totalitarianism, this means that we have excluded some part of life from the reign of God or that we have abandoned monotheism, accepting a double standard and a double deity.

III

The interpretation of God's action in this war as redemptive and vicarious, absolute and unified judgment leads to certain consequences for human action.

The first of these is the abandonment of the habit of passing judgments of our own on ourselves and on our enemies or opponents, whether these be national enemies, church enemies or enemies of our ideas. Instead of asking whether we are right people or wrong people we shall simply inquire what duty we have to perform in view of what we have done amiss and in view of what God is doing. If that duty involves, as I believe it does, resistance to those who are abusing our neighbors, we shall not inquire whether our neighbors are not better people than those who are abusing them. In social life our duty frequently requires us to protect neighbors whom we dislike against the injustices of those whom we like and who on the whole seem to us to be better people than their victims are. The same principle applies in the affairs of the society of nations.

If injustice is done to totalitarian countries (as Greece was somewhat totalitarian) or communist countries or the Jewish people, the answer to our question about our duty does not depend on the answer to our question about the relative goodness of the victims and the victimizers. Nor does the answer depend on the reply to our question about our own relative goodness. Duty is duty and no man or nation has a right to excuse the self from doing the dutiful thing now because of past failures. Response to the judgment of God on men who have failed to do their duty in the past consists in the performance of present duty and not in the passing of new judgments on others because they have failed more signally in our view.

A second thing Christians under the judgment of God in war require of themselves, because he requires it of them, is the abandonment of all self-defensiveness, all self-aggrandizement, all thinking in terms of self as central. The judgment of God in this war appears to be less a judgment on past selfish acts than one on the self-centered character of nations, churches, classes and individual men; as redemptive it holds the promise of deliverance from this imprisonment in self. It is a judgment on our nation which in its actions, sentiments and omissions has demonstrated its profound preoccupation with its own prosperity, safety and righteousness, so that in its withdrawal from international political responsibilities, in its tariff, monetary and neutrality legislation, it has acted always with a single eye to its own interests rather than to those of its neighbors in the commonwealth of nations. It is a judgment on the churches which have indicated in their conduct how great their anxiety was for their own survival, their own righteousness, prestige and power.

It was apparent long ago—in the crucifixion of the Jews and China—that the Lord was laying the iniquity of us all on the backs of the innocent. Since this vicarious demonstration of our guilt did not move us we are now to be moved by a vicarious suffering which strikes nearer home. How can we respond to this judgment by persisting to think in terms of self, of defense of our country, or of our democracy, or of our religion? If we accept God's judgment on our self-centeredness we cannot respond to it by persisting in actions of self-defense and by fighting the war for the sake of protecting our selves or our values instead of for the sake of the innocent who must be delivered from the hands of the aggressor.

To carry on the war under the judgment of God is to carry it on as those who repent of their self-centeredness and who now try to forget about themselves while they concentrate on the deliverance of their neighbors. It is to wage war as those do who will not withdraw when their own interests are no longer apparently imperiled while their weaker neighbors remain in danger, who will not wash their hands of the affair if the peace is not to their liking, but who, on the contrary, accept continuous, never ending responsibility for their neighbors. It is also to wage war in such a way that a decent—a just endurable if not a just and durable—peace can come out of it.

If the war is fought with nothing but ideas of self-defense, or defense of our values, in mind, the peace will be a self-defensive peace, however much inconsistent idealists may seek to reverse the processes of their own and of national thinking at that time. It must be emphasized also that for those who refuse to participate in war either by physical or spiritual action such abstention can be response to divine judgment only if it be part of a total action in which concern for others has been given preeminence over concern for self and its values. If non-participation by individuals or by churches is self-centered, as it often is, it is as destructive in the long run as self-centered participation.

Finally, response to God's action in war is hopeful and trusting response. It never gives up the one whom we must oppose, as though he were too depraved for redemption or for restoration to full rights in the human community. It does not accept the counsel of despair in the midst of fighting, allowing vindictive measures because by "fair fighting" our cause might be lost. It trusts that if we do our duty no evil can befall us in life or in death. The response is hopeful in that it regards the time of judgment as also time of redemption and looks in the midst of tragedy for the emergence of a better order than any which has been realized before. Nothing is regarded as beyond the scope of redemption—not the political life of men, nor the economic, nor the spiritual; neither the crucified brigand nor the crucified righteous one are regarded as forsaken by God and far from Paradise. Even should death come to them hope wraps their broken bodies in fine linen, conserving what it can, preparing on Good Friday for an Easter miracle of divine action.

To recognize God at work in war is to live and act with faith in resurrection. If God were not in the war life would be miserable indeed. It would mean that the cosmos had no concern with justice. But if God were in the war only as judge, man's misery would be only slightly assuaged since before the judge all are worthy of death. To see God in the war as the vicarious sufferer and redeemer, who is afflicted in all the afflictions of his people, is to find hope along with brokenheartedness in the midst of disaster.

These are but general reflections which do not presume to say to anyone what his particular duty in response to God's judgment must be. They seek however to describe in what spirit and context Christians in varying vocations and with conflicting political convictions may meet the divine judgment and maintain fellowship with each other.

6

Is God in the War?

Virgil C. Aldrich and H. Richard Niebuhr

Professor H. Richard Niebuhr was given the opportunity of commenting on the following letter to the editor which is directed equally toward an article of his, "War as the Judgment of God," which appeared in these pages (issue of May 13), and a Christian Century editorial, "A Theology of the War" (issue of June 3).

EDITOR THE CHRISTIAN CENTURY:

SIR: I am disturbed by the picture which you and Professor H. Richard Niebuhr give us of the war "from God's point of view." It leaves me trembling with questions that I am going to ask candidly—a bewilderment you can alleviate by answering them clearly in the same spirit.

It appears that both of you are half-consciously entertaining analogies that do not hold, in your position that this war is God's judgment on us—that he "is punishing us for our sins" (editorial, "A Theology of the War"). Consider a father with a large family of children. Now, I can see how, if some of his ruffian sons started a brawl, there might be paternal wisdom and goodness in his sadly standing by and letting them have it out as punishment, in the hope that they will learn from bitter experience. But suppose that some of the little tots also are caught against their will in the mêlée and are getting their skulls bashed in. Would a wise and good father stand by and call this just punishment?

Perhaps you are also toying with the analogy of group

punishment such as a teacher's punishing a whole class for the misdeeds of a few members because she cannot find out who the offenders are. In such cases, the whole class is justly held responsible and punished. But Christian theology would hardly permit God's position to be likened to that of the uninformed teacher.

A third analogy (my main concern) has to do with "vicarious suffering" and "wars as crucifixions." Crucifixion has profound religious and moral significance when the crucified has, by the grandeur of a firm Christian stand against evil, suffered martyrdom for the Cause. The death of such an individual has about it the glory of the cross, and (I believe) is compatible with God's goodness and wisdom towards his creatures. But be pleased to notice two things:

1. A simple God-fearing peasant who knows only his acre of soil, and nurses the living things on it, and wants only to be left in peace, and sickens and weeps at the sight of killed people, is by no means "crucified" for a Christian cause or a "vicarious sufferer" for humanity, when a bomb out of the blue blows him and his family to bits. About such death, there is much more of the air of getting caught in the murderous cross fire between two gangs fighting it out with tommy-guns, than of just "punishment for our sins," or of standing up to die for the Cause, or of "vicariously suffering" for others.

2. Jesus was alarmingly earthy and common-sensical. (That is why he got killed, or was crucified and suffered vicariously for humanity in the straightforward Christian sense of those terms.) What would he say if he were to appear in person and were asked, What "really" and "ultimately" is this war? God punishing us? God's judgment on us? I suspect he would start off with something like the following:

"A pox on your theological dramatizations of the consequences of social mismanagement. What is the war really? It is Tom, Dick and Harry using armed force to get or keep more than they need. It is also a consequence of simple peace-loving Jack and Jill's allowing them to maneuver nations into a position which makes fighting the only way to save anything. God is the spirit of fatherhood and brotherhood. I feel it concentrated and exemplified in my life and, in relation to the war, that spirit is not a punitive agency or judgment, but only one of ineffable sorrow. God in this war is the spirit of universal sadness that catches at our hearts when we see humanity, so full of the milk of human kindness under the right incentive or management, getting into such a tragic predicament. The very notion of punishment is primitive and has only a precarious place in the theology of a Christian. God is love, and his Spirit is trying to love and ache us out of the impasse which is the man-instituted nemesis that has overtaken you. You punish one another. God does not punish."

I realize I have made Jesus say a mouthful, not all of which is compatible with certain traditional theological conceptions of God's relation to man (his absolute omnipotence, etc.). But I must say, frankly, that your dramatized dialectical subtleties look almost pathological to me alongside the above simple statement as to what the war "really" is. You spin speculative systems which are catching you, the spinner, in a network of artificial difficulties. The intellect is known to operate beautifully as an escape mechanism for people who can't stomach simple, hard facts and the kind of action that would really solve the practical problem. (In your case, I believe it is an *inherited* theological tradition you are laboring with.) The Christian Century is eminently practical in most of its proposals, but just now you need a Jeremiah to howl down your growing propensity to treat simple realities in the grand theological manner.

Department of Philosophy, The Rice Institute, Houston, Tex. — VIRGIL C. ALDRICH.

Dr. Neibuhr's Comment

Thank you for giving me the opportunity to reply to Professor Aldrich's letter, for it seems to contain all the main points raised in other communications published in The Christian Century or received by me in answer to the article on war as divine judgment. I shall attempt in my reply to clarify issues rather than to convince dissenters. If such an attempt seems to involve us in "dialectical subtleties" I can only plead in extenuation of my fault that the simplicity of "gospel truth" is a virtue exceedingly difficult to acquire and not an attribute to be assigned to ideas we take for granted.

I. Four main issues appear to me to underlie the present discussion. The first one is a matter of definition. Professor Aldrich, like many others who have written, seems to take for granted that the word "judgment" means punishment and that "punishment" means "expression of vindictive, or at least disapproving, emotion." Hence he refused to use the term in connection with God. If judgment means just that I am inclined to agree with our critic. I was concerned to point out in the article in question that judgment in the Scriptures meant the corrective action of a God who is loyal to his creatures. The idea of emotionally motivated vengeance has little if any place in any effort to think straight on the subject. If then Professor Aldrich does not like the word "judgment" because it is too solidly associated in his mind with the primitive, sentimental conception, I am content to drop it, substituting some other symbol for the experience, if he will provide it. But I am sure that judgment by any other name will hurt as much.

It appears, however, that much more than a difference over words is involved, for the corrective action of a God who stands over against us has as slight a place in the arguments of most of our critics as has the notion of vengeance to which they reduce it, in order—one sometimes thinks—to dispose of it most easily.

2. That brings me to the second point. Professor Aldrich assumes that both the editor and I are trying to understand the war "from God's point of view." I will not try to speak for the editor, but so far as the position I attempted to present is concerned I categorically reject the charge. I am trying to think about war and peace from the only point of view available to me, which is that of a man whose thoughts are very far from being divine; but it is that of one who has been persuaded that if he is to make any sense out of his experience and life he must always try to discover the universal in every particular and respond to it. Further, it is the point of view of one who has been required to seek in every particular that universal being and action which Jesus called Father. Hence my problem is not that of looking with God on the world but of finding God in the world, or rather that of understanding how to stand in the presence of God as I stand in the presence of every individual event, good or evil.

GOD AN OBJECTIVE REALITY

I would say that it is Professor Aldrich who tries to see things from God's point of view. For him Jesus is one who can say of himself that God's spirit is "concentrated" in him; God moreover is a "spirit of universal sadness that catches at our hearts"; God, in other words, is within us; we find him in our sentiments or emotions; he feels in us and looks out through our eyes. This appears to be the real issue in the present discussion: subjectivism versus objectivism in religion. For me, as for all nominalists, the inner world is suspect and God must be objective before he can be subjective. I note in the sadness that is also in my heart a tendency towards the old vice of accidie, and perhaps an emotional substitute for anger. My pious feelings are suspect also; they are more easily aroused by soft music than by the "bitter ballad of the slums."

I must not enter here into a discussion of the meaning of Jesus save to say that I cannot begin, as religious subjectivism does, with the Fourth Gospel, but must start with the Synoptics and with a Jesus who finds God's action not within himself but in objective, natural and historical events. Here is an issue which goes very deep. Whether we approach the war as religious subjectivists or as religious objectivists makes a profound difference to action as well as to thought. As objectivists, we must begin with the initial assumption that there is no event in which divine reason and will are not involved, which must not be understood with the aid of the grand Christian postulate, no matter how difficult the inquiry, and in which we are not required to respond to the universal, no matter how revolutionary for thought and action that demand may be. As subjectivists, we shall look for God's action within, and will judge the world *with* him rather than be placed under the judgment of objective reality.

3. The third issue is closely connected with the preceding one. It is a perennial and a very critical issue for Christianity. At all times of crisis, Christians have been tempted to become dualists who deny the fundamental unity of the world asserted in their monotheism. But radical monotheism must meet everything that happens with the faith that God is one and universal. A scientist is not permitted by his fundamental faith to relinquish the search for an intelligible pattern in events because what he finds does not fit into his hypothesis, but is required to revise his hypothesis; likewise, the monotheist cannot abandon his search for God's will and way in the events of history because these events do not fit into his theological or common-sense hypothesis. To deny that God is

in war is for the monotheist equivalent to the denial of God's universality and unity—to the denial that God is God.

Dr. Aldrich and those who with him refuse to look for divine action in such events as war seem to me to have surrendered to dualism. There is in the world a great pity and love, a universal sadness, and then there is—what? A spirit of evil? An irrational something? At least there is an actuality in which God is not, and there are therefore situations and events in life which do not allow a rational, meaningful response on the part of men. To look for God's judgment is to affirm as radical monotheists that there is no person, no situation, no event in which the opportunity to serve God is not present. It means that we do not relinquish hard and difficult situations to the reign of irrationality and irreligiousness. The fight for the interpretation of war as divine judgment is, to my mind, a fight for rationality in religion and for consistency in man's ethical response to his environment.

VICARIOUS SUFFERING

4. The fourth point Professor Aldrich raises concerns the conception of vicarious suffering. Once more the issue is whether Christian faith is a method of understanding and responding constructively to objective events or a spiritualistic epiphenomenon, perhaps a utopian program for recreating the world according to our desires. If we begin, as Professor Aldrich and other critics do, with the notion that suffering in order to be vicarious must be consciously so—that God acts in men only insofar as their ideas and sentiments are Godlike—we shall need to come to his conclusion: there is little actual vicarious suffering.

But if we must begin with the fact of experience that "simple God-fearing peasants" who want only to be left in peace do suffer and are killed for no apparent fault of their own, and yet maintain our faith that the world is not an accident and a whirl of atoms, but a meaningful process, then we are required to use the idea of vicariousness in order to understand that peasant's crucifixion. Then we need to say, because we see it to be true, that whether they do so willingly or unwillingly, the innocent suffer for our sins; then we need to respond to our understanding of human tragedy as those who turn away with loathing from their own sin and who try to strike off the shackles they have laid on the victims before and while they deal with the chains that other evil men have placed on the sufferers.

Here again is a profound issue. Pacifists and coercionists alike who can get along without the concept of vicarious suffering ought to get together; they think alike though they quarrel about the messianic means whereby to save the world from evil spirits. But pacifists and coercionists who rest under the common conviction of their personal and social sin inspired by the view of the contemporary cross must get together also. They have a hard, continuous labor before them, bringing forth the fruits of repentance.

7
War as Crucifixion
H. Richard Niebuhr

Man, being incurably rational, cannot act without some theory of the events in which he is participating. This truth is clearly apparent in the case of war. A blaze of unreasoning emotion may induce men to exchange a few blows but any long conflict, especially between groups, requires propaganda, which at its worst is an effort to supply a theory that will fit the emotions and at its best is an attempt to direct and restrain emotion by understanding of the situation. To be sure, theories of war in general and of any particular conflict in which we are engaged are not the only factors which influence action, but they are nevertheless important elements in any responsible behavior.

Two main theories of the nature of war are being applied to our present struggle and are influencing in various ways the responses of individuals and communities to the situation. They may be named the amoral and the moral theories. The former interprets war as a conflict of powers in which victory with its fruits belongs to the stronger and in which moral words or phrases are nothing but instruments of power by means of which emotions are aroused and men are unified. This view is held both by certain balance-of-power advocates of unlimited participation in war, so long as national self-interest is involved, and by certain pacifists who wash their hands of war because it makes no moral difference which side wins in a conflict of pure power.

MORAL AND AMORAL THEORIES INADEQUATE

The moral view of war, on the other hand, interprets it as an event in a universe in which the laws of retribution hold sway. According to this theory war begins with a transgression of international, or natural, or human, or divine law and continues in the effort of the law's up-holders to bring the offenders to justice. Those who hold this view make a distinction between unjust war—the act of transgression—and just war—the act of retribution and of defense of order. Again, both participants and non-participants in any particular war may use this theory; their differences are largely due to their estimate of this war as just or as unjust.

Both theories are inadequate and misleading, for both fail to account for all the relevant phenomena and must be abandoned at some point in practice, not because emotion is too powerful to submit to their control, but because they appear unreasonable. Since man is a self-interested being and always desires to extend his power, the amoral theory is partly true. But since man is always interested in values beyond the self and desires not only power but also the enjoyment of the good, the amoral theory is wholly inadequate. It forgets that wars are fought by men and that human power cannot be abstracted from human rationality and morality.

Among men, might not only makes right, but the conviction of being right makes might, and it is impossible to reduce such a conviction to an emotional reaction. However much the power realists may regret the fact, it remains true that in war men do not fight simply for their own interests but make great sacrifices for distant values, for their own country, or Poland, or "democracy," or "the new order," or "the Four Freedoms." It may be said that while individuals do this in war, nations always act amorally. But this again is to deal with unreal, wholly abstract beings, since nations and their governments are human, so that the mixture of motives which is discernible in individuals is always present in groups also.

RETRIBUTION FAILS

The moral view of war seems to take into account those elements which the power theory ignores, yet it also remains inadequate and is in some respects more misleading than its rival. Its failure does not necessarily lie at the point in which the power theory is interested, for it may be very much aware of men's love of power and of the necessity for taking this into account in the making of moral judgments. Its inadequacy appears rather in the impossibility of applying the whole scheme of moral judgment and retributive justice to social relations. It has often been observed that a people cannot be indicted, that the question of war-guilt which appears so easily determinable in time of conflict becomes more difficult with longer perspective, that retribution itself is impractical since the community which is to be punished cannot be excluded from the society of nations as an individual can be banished from his community by imprisonment.

The greatest difficulty of all which the moral theory faces is the fact that in war the burden of suffering does not fall on the guilty, even when guilt is relatively determinable, but on the innocent. Retribution for the sins of a nazi party and a Hitler falls on Russian and German soldiers, on the children of Cologne and Coventry, on the Finns and the French. In order that the moral theory may be used it becomes necessary to convict all the common men, the whole opposing nation of guilt. Even if that were possible the theory does not hold since the suffering for guilt is shared by those who are on the side of "justice." Hence those who hold to the moral theory find themselves unable to follow it in practice. If they declare a present war to be just they must participate in inflicting suffering and death on the "just" with the "unjust"; if they regard a present war as unjust they must stand idly by while the "just" are being made to suffer with the "unjust."

IS WAR CRUCIFIXION?

Since neither theory will do for men who want to act reasonably, on the basis of an intelligible interpretation of the facts of experience, the question arises whether there is not some other pattern than that of the survival of the fittest or that of retributive justice by means of which war may be understood and response to it guided. The question must arise for Christians whether that understanding of the nature of cosmic justice which the crucifixion of Jesus Christ discovered to men must not and may not be applied to war, as it must and may be applied to many personal events that are unintelligible save through the cross. Is war, then, crucifixion?

War is at least very much like the crucifixion. In both events there is a strange intermixture of justice and injustice on the side alike of those who regard themselves as the upholders of the right and on the side of the vanquished. Three men were crucified on Calvary, all, it appears, on more or less the same charge of insurrection. Two of them were malefactors who actually desired to overturn the established order, whether for patriotic or personal motives; yet they were not alike since one recognized the at least relative justice of his punishment while the other remained unrepentant. The third cross carried one who was innocent of the charge made against him; yet ambiguously so, since he was establishing a kingdom of a strange sort which held unknown dangers for the Roman order and the Jewish law.

Nor were the crucifiers less mixed in their justice and injustice: soldiers who did their duty in obedience to their oath, priests who acted according to their lights—though their light was darkness—a judge who failed in his duty, citizens who were devoted to the maintenance of the sacred values of Jewish culture, a mob overborne by emotion. They knew not what they did. War is like that—apparently indiscriminate in the choice of victims and of victors, whether these be thought of as individuals or as communities.

CROSS REVEALS GOD'S MORAL EARNESTNESS

A second point of resemblance between war and the crucifixion is no less striking. The cross which will not yield to analysis in terms of retributive justice, will not yield either to analysis in terms of brute power. If the alternative before men were simply either that God is just in the sense that he rewards the good and punishes the guilty, or that the world is indifferent to good and evil, then the cross would be the final demonstration of God's injustice or, rather, of his non-existence. If that were the alternative then men would need to conclude that "Whirl is king and hath dethroned Zeus."

But the cross does not encourage moral indifference; it

requires men to take their moral decisions with greater rather than less seriousness; it demonstrates the sublime character of real goodness; it is a revelation, though "in a glass darkly," of the intense moral earnestness of a God who will not abandon mankind to self-destruction; it confronts us with the tragic consequences of moral failure. It does all this because it is sacrifice—the self-sacrifice of Jesus Christ for those whom he loves and God's sacrifice of his best-loved Son for the sake of the just and the unjust. War is like the cross in this respect. In its presence men must abandon their moral cynicism along with other peacetime luxuries.

We are moved in the presence of war to think more rather than less seriously of the importance of our decisions and of the evil and good possibilities of our existence. For war also is not only a great slaughter but a great sacrifice. It is the moving sacrifice of our youth for the sake of that which they love; the sacrifice by parents of their best-loved sons. In the midst of its cruelties, falsehoods and betrayals there appear sublime examples of human courage and devotion and selflessness that uplift us as we see the greatness of man revealed alongside his depravity. An almost infinite capacity for goodness is reflected in the dark glass of sinfulness. Vicarious suffering shows up dramatically the tragic issue of our wrongdoings and wrong-being in the midst of our human solidarity. War does not make for moral indifference.

THE CROSS IS RELEVANT

The analogy of war and crucifixion suggests that we are dealing with more than analogy. It indicates that the cross is relevant to the understanding of our world and to our social action in ways which neither the sacerdotal nor the moral influence theory of its meanings has made evident. Hence it directs Christians to wrestle with the problem of the cross in new ways so that new light from it may fall upon the scenes of their present social life as well as upon their personal problems and tragedies. It may well be that the meaning of the cross must become apparent to our time in new situations somewhat as the meaning of the spherical nature of the earth has become apparent in a new way to us in recent years.

The knowledge of the fact that we live on a globe has been

a relatively abstract knowledge for hundreds of years. It was found significant for certain purposes, but on the whole men continued to live their daily lives on the practical assumption of the earth's flatness. All the maps translated our spherical relations into relations on a plane, and so we persisted in the thought that Europe lay to the east of us, never to the north, Asia to the west, never to the north or east. What we have known for hundreds of years we now need to learn because the old pattern of the flat earth no longer suffices even for the life of one who never leaves his continent. The existence of this nation, at least, begins to depend on his now taking seriously a known but unappropriated knowledge. Perhaps it is like this with the cross of Christ and war and every social suffering.

What we shall find when we concern ourselves more seriously with the cross and with its meaning for our war cannot be prophesied. There is one point, however, which seems of great importance and to which all efforts to understand war through the cross must give heed. It is the point which Paul made. The crucifixion illuminated many things for him, but in particular it was the revelation of the righteousness of God which was distinct from the righteousness of the law and which, when it became apparent, showed man's righteousness to be as unrighteous as his unrighteousness.

WHAT KIND OF UNIVERSE?

Perhaps we may understand Paul's point like this: The cross of Jesus Christ is the final, convincing demonstration of the fact that the order of the universe is not one of retribution in which goodness is rewarded and evil punished, but rather an order of graciousness wherein, as Jesus had observed, the sun is made to shine on evil and on good and the rain to descend on the just and the unjust. To live in this divine order of graciousness on the basis of the assumption that reward must be merited and evil avenged is to come into conflict with the real order in things. The pattern of retributive justice simply will not work; it is like the effort to translate the global earth into the terms of a plane. To make distinctions between the just and unjust, and to employ for that purpose the standard of good works performed by them, will not work.

If men are to live at all, as souls or as communities, they must begin with the acceptance not of some standard of judgment—not even the standard of graciousness—but of an act of graciousness to which they respond graciously. The cross is not the demonstration of the fact that man has a wrong standard of judgment which he must correct or for which he must substitute a right standard of judgment by means of which to assess goodness and sinfulness, but it shows that the whole effort to assess and judge the goodness and the evil of self and others, and to reward or punish accordingly, is mistaken.

WAR AND GOD'S GRACIOUSNESS

God's righteousness is his graciousness and his grace is not an addition to his justice; hence man's rightness does not lie in a new order of judging justice, but in the acceptance of grace and in thankful response to it. The cross does not so much reveal that God judges by other standards than men do, but that he does not judge; it does not demonstrate that men judge by the wrong standards but that their wrongness lies in trying to judge each other, instead of beginning where they can begin—with the acceptance of graciousness and response to it.

If the cross is not only a historical event but a revelation of the order of reality, then war is not only like the cross but must be a demonstration of that same order of God. How it demonstrates the disorderliness of human righteousness and unrighteousness is apparent enough. How it demonstrates the fundamental ungraciousness of both the apparently righteous and the apparently unrighteous is perhaps also clear. But that it should be the hidden demonstration of divine graciousness is hard for us to understand. The cross in ancient history is acceptable to us; the cross in "religious" history, in the history of man's relation to a purely spiritual God, is also acceptable; but the cross in our present history is a stumbling block and a folly which illustrates human sinfulness, but not divine graciousness.

Yet how the divine grace appears in the crucifixion of war may become somewhat clear when the cross of Christ is used to interpret it. Then our attention is directed to the death of the guiltless, the gracious, and the suffering of the innocent becomes a call to repentance, to a total revolution of our minds and hearts. And such a call to repentance—not to sorrow but to spiritual revolution—is an act of grace, a great recall from the road to death which we all travel together, the just and the unjust, the victors and the vanquished. Interpreted through the cross of Jesus Christ the suffering of the innocent is seen not as the suffering of temporal men but of the eternal victim "slain from the foundations of the world." If the Son of God is being crucified in this war along with the malefactors—and he is being crucified on many an obscure hill—then the graciousness of God, the self-giving love, is more manifest here than in all the years of peace.

It will be asked, If these suggestions, these vague gestures in the direction of the interpretation of war as crucifixion, are followed, what will be the result for action? No single answer can be given since the cross does not impose a new law on man. But one thing will be common to all actions which are based on such an understanding of war: there will be in them no effort to establish a righteousness of our own, no excusing of self because one has fallen less short of the glory of God than others; there will be no vengeance in them. They will also share one positive characteristic: they will be performed in hope, in reliance on the continued grace of God in the midst of our ungraciousness.

8

The Relation of the Church to the War in the Light of the Christian Faith

The Calhoun Commission (1944)

This report is not a pronouncement in the name of the Christian Church, but a word spoken, we trust, in the faith of the Church, to our fellow Christians, and to all our fellow men. It is a statement of what we have found to be some of our common convictions about the concerns of the Church in a time of global war: its gospel, its relations to individual Christians, Christian groups, the various national communities, and the changing world society, and its consequent duties and opportunities in our day.

The ecumenical judgment of the Protestant and Orthodox Churches concerning modern war was pronounced at Oxford in 1937. It has been reaffirmed innumerable times and we affirm it again as our own. But the theological grounds and implications of that judgment need to be worked out more explicitly than Oxford or any other conference has worked them out. If it be true that war is "a defiance of the righteousness of God as revealed in Jesus Christ and Him crucified," that fact involves most urgent problems of life and thought for the whole body of Christian citizens. For war is no longer a contest between sovereign princes and professional armies. Wherever modern democratic government has come into being, a decision to engage in war is made in the name of a whole people; and in the conduct of modern war, no matter what the form of the belligerent governments, civilians as well as members of the armed forces are participants. Willingly or unwillingly, every one is somehow involved. What, then, has the Christian faith to say to the Church and its members when war develops, since uncritical participation in war does violence to a Christian judgment solemnly and repeatedly avowed, while complete detachment is no longer possible? . . .

The Christian Church and its gospel must always stand in a double relation to human history. On the one hand, they are deeply involved at every moment in the actual events that make up the earthly career of human persons and peoples. The gospel is no mere ideal picture of what would be excellent if only it were true. It is a declaration of what has actually happened to men in history through the actual life and death and resurrection of Jesus Christ, and an avowal of faith in the saving Power that was disclosed through him, as a sovereign help in every time of trouble. The Church, likewise, is so embedded in history, for better and for worse, that in every part of it are visible the marks of historic developments and crises now long past, and of the actual fierce pressures that unite and divide men today. The Church and the gospel, then, are involved in every new human situation.

On the other hand, both the Christian gospel and the Church that proclaims it must display in every age the sort of freedom that comes from being oriented not only to present and passing events of human history but to present and permanent reality and truth that are in God. Such freedom from complete entanglement makes the Church and its gospel view history in a different perspective from that of national patriotism, capitalistic or communistic class interest, or any cultural loyalty alone. A living Church is aware of all these secular loyalties, and reflects them in its actual behavior. At the same time, it must see beyond them, criticize them and itself with them, and affirm as an ultimate court of appeal for all human thought and life the sovereign presence of God. In a word, the Church and its gospel must be at every moment both in the midst of human history and beyond it.

This means that to every historic situation, the Church has a dual word to speak. On the one hand, it must try to bring clearly into view the distinctive character of each new situation, neither blurring its uniqueness with generalities, nor losing sight of its continuity with other historic events past and future. The Church must try to speak directly to the actual needs of each new time. On the other hand, it must try to hold clearly before every age, with changing detailed insights but with steady central conviction, what Christian faith believes to be abiding truth concerning God and man, sin and salvation. The Church must try to speak steadily a word of faith that is for all times.

These two phases of its preaching and teaching involve a third. From the effort thus to apprehend a new situation in the light of an abiding faith, specific guiding judgments should emerge that illuminate Christian action. Such judgments are not a code of rules, but a body of working insights in which the meaning of Christian faith for individual and social conduct in the existing historic crisis is made more explicit. What courses of action will then actually be followed by the Church and by individual Christians must still be determined by conscientious conviction. No body of Christians, large or small, can undertake to replace enlightened conscience by prescribed rules.

There are thus three phases of the word the Church must speak to our time: diagnostic, doctrinal, and practical. The three parts of this report attempt to deal successively with these interrelated demands. The first part is diagnostic: an attempt to make clear what seems to us the character of our present situation, and some of the major problems it raises concerning the relation of the Church, its gospel, and its members to the war. The second is doctrinal: a statement of those primary Christian affirmations that seem to us normative for any attempt to deal with the problems of the Church in war time. The third is practical: a glance at the major attitudes toward war, past and present, that have actually been maintained in the Church as fitting expressions of Christian faith, and a summary of the attitudes that seem to us to accord best with that faith in our own day and for the near future. . . .

I. OUR PRESENT SITUATION AND ITS PROBLEMS

The Character of the Present Crisis

A. *There is general agreement that we are in the midst of one of the great transition periods of human history.* The war that broke out in 1914 and has continued, with temporary and local interruptions, to the present moment—a thirty years' war the end of which cannot yet be clearly seen—is the outward and visible sign of a vaster conflict, by no means identical in its battle-lines with the war between Axis and United Nations. Around the globe, in the home of every civilized people, belligerent or neutral, and in places hitherto but little concerned with the modern world, a life and death struggle is going on between various old ways of living and various new ones. Long after the present phase of organized armed warfare has been succeeded by some sort of armistice or declared peace, unorganized struggles both armed and unarmed will continue, until some worldwide equilibrium not yet discernible may be worked out. So inclusive has this pattern of armed warfare and unarmed conflict become that for magnitude there is no close analogy to it in all previous history. By comparison, the fall of the Roman empire in the West or the rise of the Mongol empire in the East were local in scope, however great in cultural import. And surely no lesser events than these, it now appears, can serve as yardsticks to measure the dimensions of our time. It poses problems of unprecedented magnitude, and no small-scale answers can be regarded for a moment as fit to command our assent.

When as Christians, aware in some degree of the extent of the present crisis, we ask what kinds of factors enter into it and give it a distinctive character, we find ourselves at the outset sharing many insights with secular and non-Christian observers. This crisis, including the war and the still larger struggles revealed and sharpened by *the war, is in one aspect a dynamic readjustment of impersonal forces,* not without likeness to an avalanche or an earthquake, of planetary scope. We recognize in it the violent threshing of physical, biological, and economic forces long out of balance—the impersonal tensions of unequal population pressures, unevenly distributed natural resources, accelerating technological advances, undisciplined mass production methods—released in destructive spasms during the past thirty years, after accumulating during a century of comparative quiet. We recognize in it also *a world-wide power struggle* of the familiar type between loose coalitions of nation-states, each seeking its own advantage, putting first its own national interests in security, prosperity, and prestige. We recognize in it *a revolutionary attempt by each of the chief Axis powers to move toward world conquest* and the establishment of a totalitarian "New Order," and *a resolute struggle by their opponents to prevent such totalitarian conquest* and to keep the way open for more humane modes of life. We recognize in it, cutting across the boundaries of national self-interest and of military alliance, *a clash of forces—psychological, cultural, political—that seek strongly to maintain, to restore, or to extend the old patterns* of privileged minority rule, unrestricted national sovereignty, and colonial imperialism, *against other forces that tend, much less deliberately and concertedly, toward a wider distribution of privilege and power, a more effectively and equitably organized world, or both.* Armed civil wars are in progress within the framework of international war. Unarmed economic and social class struggles, racial and cultural conflicts, and political hostilities zig-zag across all the fighting fronts. All these are essential factors in the war and in the underlying struggle. Together they help make the existing situation a revolutionary crisis, confused, dynamic, charged with opportunity and with dire peril for the life of generations to come.

In the confusion of this crisis, two factors appear to us to need especial notice, although neither must be separated, even in thought, from its roots and total setting. One is an apparent reversal, sudden and violent, of a long trend toward political democracy in the West. In less than two decades, popular governments were overthrown in Italy, Germany, and Spain. Under the pressures of Nazi aggression even the French republic collapsed. Reaction was strengthened, parliamentary government destroyed, and popular leaders and parties harried in all of Germany's satellites and in the countries occupied by her power. At the same time, among her opponents the strongest in military force has been the Soviet Union, that began its career by rejecting political democracy virtually without a trial. The case for democratic government, so long regarded as established beyond challenge in the West, has thus suffered a sudden and very destructive assault. But the experience of European peoples with the newer despotisms has already provoked a powerful counter-movement toward political freedom.

Still more dangerous in some respects has been a closely related but distinguishable assault on the growth of social democracy. In Russia, political dictatorship has itself been used to spread economic and social benefits far more widely among the people. There social democracy has made substantial gains under political despotism. But everywhere else, dictatorial control has been devoted to the advantage of a privileged minority at the expense of subjected groups. In Germany this despotism has assumed, of course, a form almost fantastic in its virulence and ruthlessness: the form of a demonic and terrible religion, laying claim to rule every side of the lives of its devotees, bent on military conquest, and ready to treat as subhuman victims the more helpless of those who stand in its way. Resistance, armed or unarmed, to this Nazi cult of intellectual and moral perversion and to the more primitive Japanese militarist despotism has become a major trend in both East and West.

All these insights must contribute to, but they do not constitute, a distinctively Christian understanding of our situation. In such understanding, the war is an event in the providential reign of God whom we know best through Christ crucified and triumphant. For Christian faith the whole cataclysm, having all the characters just noticed, is a tragic moment in God's work of creating and redeeming man, and in man's long struggle with himself and his Creator. In this perspective, the opportunity and obligation implicit in the crisis appear more commanding, and its dangers not less real but less disheartening than they might well seem apart from Christian faith.

Both the promise and the appalling danger of our situation are in important respects new in human history. They are inseparable from our present stage of political and industrial development. On the political side, our most characteristic achievement is the sovereign national state. To a degree unmatched in the ancient and mediaeval world, the great modern nation combines large territory and populace with effective political unity. Its emergence from the localized, personal, insecure political fabrics of feudalism has been a triumph of social unification and a great gain for stability. It provides greatly expanded and more effectively unified arenas for modern men's quest of freedom under law, and powerful new motives in the form of national loyalties that have helped to give both vitality and direction to that quest.

But this very consolidation of national consciousness, government, culture, and trade within national boundaries has tended no less strongly to accentuate the plurality and the diversity of nations. In feudal Europe there was at least in theory an over-all unity of Christendom under the emperor and the pope. Today each nation claims ultimate political sovereignty for itself, as regards its own territory and subjects, with no effective international or supranational authority to which appeal can be made. National interests, i.e. demands for security, prosperity, prestige, territorial and cultural unity, are superior in the actual practice of world politics to every other consideration. There is an extensive body of international law that exists on paper, but there is no political agency to enforce it, and in a serious collision with the national interests of the great powers, international law now stands little chance of having the last word. Even moral and religious principles, that in theory are widely held as binding upon men of different nations, are not now able in practice to hold in check their dynamic and often conflicting self-interest; and as for the national state itself, the sovereign political authority in each nation, much modern theory and practice frankly declares that upon the State, moral principles are not binding. Expediency, it is held, must be the primary guiding principle for the national state in its dealings with other states.

To this patchwork of modern nationalism, a great deal of modern church life and thought conforms. In theory the Christian Church is one over all the earth. In practice, both individual Christians and organized churches, Roman Catholic, Orthodox, or Protestant, have become so deeply involved in national or cultural loyalties that when serious conflicts arise, their loyalty to a universal Church and to fellow Christians of other countries or cultures is often subordinated, if not temporarily extinguished. Indeed, there have been times when organized churches or their clergy have behaved, in practice, as departments of a national community and agencies of its government, rather than as witnesses to a universal gospel for all mankind. Such churches can scarcely speak convincingly about worldwide obligations, and especially about concern for the welfare of enemies, to a nation fighting for its life. And if the churches cannot so speak, there is little chance that any other group in the nation will do so. Modern national states, especially when at war, do not welcome moral challenge from any of their constituent members. Their claim to ultimate sovereignty is jealously maintained.

At the same time that we have developed a vigorous and tenacious political nationalism, our technology and industry have reached a stage at which physical isolation of one people from another is no longer possible. Both in peace and in war, new methods of transport and communication have tied the world inescapably together. New methods of production, moreover, pour out floods of economic wares that cannot under present conditions be dammed up within national boundaries without either violent economic crises, rigid governmental controls, or both. The worldwide depression of 1929–32, and the rise of international cartels and of expansionist totalitarian programs bear eloquent testimony to the inability of nationalism in its traditional form to cope with the expansive pressures of modern industry and finance. These pressures are by no means to be regarded as capable of producing, by themselves, a new world order. They demand it rather than provide it. But they demand it in language that cannot be ignored.

Our present world situation is distinguished, then, by the clash of divisive national interests in a world physically entangled in the web of modern industry and commerce. There is no chance to restore the physical isolation of nations in time past. The only conceivable way out is to seek, by all suitable means, to transform our interlocked society into world community, in which great nations may have contributive rather than destructive roles. The Industrial Revolution has made us involuntarily a world society, tied together by many sorts of physical bonds, natural and manufactured. But a society thus physically united in space and time may be only the body necessary for a living community, a body that is indispensable but not sufficient. Living community needs also spiritual bonds of the sorts that now exist only within limited areas. It needs common interests, laws, loyalties, traditions, standards, goals. These at once presuppose and promote mutual understanding and appreciation, shared language and experience, joint efforts and achievements. World community, in short, needs on a larger scale not only physical but spiritual interrelations comparable to those that now mark national life at its best. . . .

Practical Problems and Problems of Christian Faith

B. Our difficulties are of two sorts. There are grave practical barriers that stand in the way of needed action, and there are problems of faith and reason that must be faced if we are even to see at all clearly what action is demanded of Christians in wartime, and why.

Practical Problems: *First among the practical problems is one rooted deep in the nature of man and of human community, and the character of modern war. Genuine community must be an expression of the common life of free and responsible persons and groups, not a thinly disguised form of paternalism or servitude. But the necessary restraints upon freedom that become habitual in war, and the profound, demoralizing fatigue that a major war brings, make unusually difficult the extension of responsible freedom when organized fighting gives place to the new stresses of victory, defeat, and a struggle for recovery.* The temptations then are exceedingly strong for both victors and vanquished to seek relief from the pains of responsible social life in dictatorial control without clear and present effort to promote freedom, in irresponsible relaxation and self-indulgence, or in recklessly destructive social explosions—the vengeful and unprincipled "revolution of nihilism" that appeals to frustrated, desperate men. This mood of irresponsible craving for escape from the hard way of growth toward community is sure to be widespread and deeply ingrained when the fighting has burned itself out. If it should be permitted again to dominate the decisions of the victors and the reactions of the vanquished, whatever chance our time may have offered for growth in shared freedom will be postponed to an indefinite future.

A second practical difficulty compounds and complicates this first one: present divisions within and among the United Nations. The best pattern for growth toward world community would seem to be some version of social and political democracy. Hitler's totalitarian pattern for "a new order" had obviously failed even before his armies were driven out of conquered territory. Community of peoples is not to be had on such terms, no matter by what power they are proposed or enforced. But the understanding of man and his freedom, of personal integrity and social interrelations, of the role of minorities, and of the social importance of such moral factors as nonpartisan justice and good faith that has developed in the democratic tradition is by its very nature a demand for universal growth in responsible freedom and community. The more democratically organized great powers among the United Nations, then, might be expected to stand out as the most effective champions of such growth. In principle, and to some considerable degree in fact, they do have this role. They have themselves made substantial progress in achieving and maintaining freedom of thought, speech, and worship at home, and in proving that loyal cooperation among diverse groups for social and political ends is feasible on a large scale without totalitarian control. As things now stand, however, their effectiveness as champions of world democracy is hampered by a deep-going ambiguity in their present status and practice. Their history has forced them at this juncture to defend abroad as well as they can the free democratic way of life when they have achieved it very imperfectly at home and in subject territories. Both the popular will and the national governments of the greater democratic powers are inwardly divided between seeking to extend the freedom, security, and opportunity of ordinary people everywhere, and seeking to maintain special privilege for chosen families, classes, and peoples. Refusal of equal opportunity to persons of Negro, Jewish, or Oriental ancestry, to various colonial peoples, to landless farmers, unorganized laborers, and certain social radicals has long marred the domestic behavior and helped mould the foreign policy of even the most democratic of the United Nations. At the same time, their persisting democratic tradition ensures that even in war time the policies of both those who seek and those who distrust the spread of democracy and of international community shall be openly debated. The net result is at present a partial devotion to worldwide community, with inconsistency of apparent aim and uncertainty as to future policy respecting both the domestic affairs of allied, liberated, and vanquished countries and the pattern of world society for years to come. . . .

There is scarcely need to speak here of the multitude of problems—technical, economic, political—that beset the reconversion of a world mostly organized for combat to the pursuits of competitive production and trade, without losing whatever common devotion and mutual trust may be achieved in alliance for war. *But two problems that especially concern us as Christians need at least brief mention. The first is the unprecedented and appalling extent of calculated ruthlessness, both before and during the present phase of the unfinished revolution, and of the hatred engendered thereby.* Terrorist methods of GPU and Gestapo, brutalities of Japanese, Italian, Spanish, and German troops in the field and in conquered territories, food blockades and obliteration bombings by the United Nations in rejoinder, commando tactics and improved flame throwers, mass murders and robot bombs—all these mere incidents in the global struggle—have brought back on a larger scale the hardness and the vengefulness that must have filled numbers of decent people in the seventeenth century, during the earlier Thirty Years' War. The extent of such implacability today, among victims of the Axis powers and among their own peoples, can only be conjectured. It is hard to doubt that it will prove a major obstacle to the making of genuine peace, and there can be no doubt that it is a peculiar concern of the Christian churches everywhere.

The second of these special problems is posed by the divided loyalties, the human weaknesses, and the secular involvements of the churches themselves. It is neither possible nor desirable that they should stand outside the agonies of the peoples to whom they minister. A Church aloof from sinning, suffering men and nations could not be the Church of Jesus Christ. Its life and its ministries must bear the marks of full humanity, and without intense loyalty to a particular place and folk there is no such thing as full human living. The needs, the sorrows, the sins, and the hopes of particular men and nations, not simply of mankind at large, must be woven into the life of a Church that seeks to be the body of Christ. But its ministry to particular men and nations can be performed with faithfulness only if, like its Master, the Church speaks to them unceasingly, by word and deed, of the judgment and mercy of God that are for all men alike. In as far as the Church embodies and proclaims this saving Word, it can serve at once particular men and nations and all mankind, displaying among them imperfectly but genuinely a common life in which acute differences are composed, deep wrongs are judged with the penetrating wisdom of love, human wounds are healed, and the true God of all the world is worshipped. In as far as the human existence of any church denies or distorts this universal Word instead of proclaiming it, in so far that church fails to be the Christian Church or a faithful member thereof. When through self-interest, or fear, or forgetfulness, through preoccupation with nearby human loyalties, a church or its ministers and members becomes so fully identified with the success of any human group or institution—itself, a class, a nation, a civilization—that it cannot speak any save a partisan or a platitudinous word, then the salt has lost its savor. We rejoice that the churches of our day, with a growing awareness of ecumenical membership and mission, and with new understanding of conscientious differences among their members, have come to see this truth with new clarity. Yet we cannot close our eyes to our own failures and those of many fellow Christians in all lands to find and to speak clearly the words of judgment and of reconciliation that hold true at once for our own folk and for all men. Such words are being spoken superbly here and there, in both East and West. They need to be spoken everywhere with more unanimity and power. From this obligation that rests on us and on all Christians there must arise a concerted demand that in our time the way toward world community—not an expanded imperialism and not continued anarchy—be chosen. . . .

Problems of Christian Faith: But to claim thus for Christian faith and for the Church a crucial role in the world struggle is to throw into more vivid relief the problems posed especially for Christian faith and reason by the struggle itself. It is with these primarily that the next part of this report deals.

They fall easily into four main groups. There are questions, first of all, concerning the grounds of Christian faith and knowledge. If there be indeed a distinctive Christian understanding of the war, it is right to ask upon what foundations that understanding can be affirmed, and what measure of authority it may properly claim.

There are questions next concerning the relation of God to the war. In such a time it seems to many that God (if indeed there be a God) is aloof from His tortured world. To others the war seems rather a direct and fearful act of divine judgment upon human wickedness. To still others it may seem a stunning defeat for God's purposes, at the hands of successful human rebels. Which view is right? or is some other view required?

Thirdly, questions arise concerning man's part in the war. Whether fatally bound or free and responsible, men act in this war time as though issues of better and worse are clearly at stake, and as though their own decisions can make a real difference in the working out of God's will and of men's destiny. Acknowledging more freely than in any other recent war the involvement of both sides in blame for the outbreak of armed conflict, they fight or refuse to fight still with some hope that in so doing they serve God and men. Is this belief in human freedom justified?

Lastly, how does all this bear on the place and tasks of the Church, and of its members, in the war-torn world? A whole array of questions here are pressing: the nature of the Church as universal community, the meaning of its ministry of reconciliation, the obligations that lie upon its members. Perhaps above all, this question: Is there any common life in which all Christians in war time can and should take part together as Christians, alike devoted in their several ways to the Kingdom of God and the salvation of mankind? . . .

II. THE CHRISTIAN FAITH AND THE WAR

Grounds of a Christian Understanding of the War

A. *The primary ground for a distinctive Christian understanding of any situation is the revelation of God in Jesus Christ.* This is not to be separated from continuing revelations of God through the work of the Holy Spirit in the history of the Hebrew people and of the Christian Church, recorded in the Old and New Testaments, and in the whole literature of Christian life. Moreover, to the eye of Christian faith and understanding, there is revelation of the same God in the histories of all peoples, in the existence, order, and growth of the whole world of nature and man, in the rise of conscience, and in every struggle for truth and freedom. But revelation of God in Jesus Christ is the crucial disclosure, from whose light these other areas derive new meaning.

Revelation in Jesus Christ: Revelation of God in Jesus Christ takes place whenever and wherever human persons find themselves effectively confronted, through the Gospel record or some spoken word, through personal contact or social heritage, inside or outside the institutional Church, by the person Jesus of Nazareth as an embodiment of unqualified moral judgment and of regenerating power, "God's power and God's wisdom." Effectively confronted: that is to say, compelled to acknowledge him as stubborn reality, as summons to repentance, and as source of drastic spiritual renewal. The person Jesus of Nazareth: the actual subject of that unique actual human life and death and triumph over death from which the Christian Church and the so-called Christian era of history, a new age and a new mode of life for mankind, have their beginnings. An embodiment of God's power and God's wisdom: one in whom, for Christian faith, the initiative of God for man's redemption uniquely assumed individual human form, so that uniquely and definitively "God was in Christ reconciling the world to himself."

In speaking of the revelation of God in Jesus Christ to us, we speak of a situation in which two stages of disclosure are involved. There is first the need that the man Jesus of Nazareth be disclosed to us, men of the twentieth century. This disclosure comes mainly in two ways. On the one hand, there is the written record in the New Testament of his words and deeds. There are recorded also the reactions of others, in his earthly lifetime and later, to the impact of his personal existence in history. As the record of events that are normative for Christian faith, the New Testament, though it must be interpreted by the Christian community, is itself normative for the life of that community. On the other hand, there is the Christian Church, a living community in which his spirit is still present and active. The written record and the living community cannot be separated. Each involves the other and neither can be reduced to simple dependence on, nor to simple parallelism with the other. Through both at once, the person Jesus of Nazareth makes his impress and finds his interpreters in our day, not perfectly but in the manner of all vital communication in history.

There is hidden within this historical disclosure another that gives it an added dimension of meaning and efficacy. In Jesus of Nazareth, known to us through written word and living church, was present, we believe, the redemptive Word and Will of God. Factual evidence for this conviction has been briefly indicated. Human history then and there entered a new era, became subject to divine judgment and mercy in a new way. But the conviction itself involves not only recognition of a publicly observable state of affairs. It involves a personal reorientation of the one who believes. What is meant by saying that God was in Christ is, in essential part, that Jesus Christ has been able through the centuries and is able now to awaken in men the profound personal response we call faith. Herein is made concrete and contemporary the revealing of God in Jesus Christ to us.

Like love, such faith is a personal response too inclusive and profound to be simply an overt act of either thought or will. It is a basic response of the whole self to the presence of a reality that appears overwhelmingly great and good. It is unreserved commitment in response to a Presence from which one cannot hold oneself back, any more than the eye to which light is present can withhold itself from seeing. Through this commitment, and within the personal life pervaded and conditioned by it, both knowledge and will proceed upon lines not open before, yet so related to the past life and the persisting nature of the believer that he finds in his new orientation a powerful expansion and correction of all that he has been. Through faith, as through love, he becomes a new person, in whom new insights and energies come to life, though never in simple escape from the old self nor from essential human limitations.

In a word, Christ crucified can appear as the embodiment of God's power and God's wisdom, the crucial and unique revelation of God, only to those who actually are moved by him to religious faith and who find that faith actually an enduring condition of new insight, devotion, and regenerate life. *For those who are thus responsive, a basis is provided for a distinctive Christian approach to every situation that calls for understanding. As the natural scientist approaches each phenomenon, no matter how distasteful or threatening it may appear to him personally, with the confidence that in it the great regularities of the natural process will be exhibited, so the Christian comes to each event in his or mankind's history with the confidence that he is dealing with something that contains divine meaning, that is intelligible, if not in every detail yet in essence, in terms of the faithful working of God.* As the former expects to have his previous understanding of natural process not only verified but also corrected and enlarged, so the latter anticipates that in each new event, loyally accepted and responded to, his understanding of God's way and will, received first in the revelation of Christ, will be corrected, widened, and particularized while it is being confirmed.

Basis of Christian Confidence: To describe in these terms the nature of revelation and of Christian faith is to make clear at once the basis for confidence and the need for caution in Christian affirmations about God and man in any complex situation, such as this war. The basis for confidence is the discovery that for oneself, for other Christians, and for the Church as enduring and expanding Christian community, the dynamic life of Jesus Christ as revelation of God has become a vital premise for all thought and action that have in view the ultimate significance of human living. Inasmuch as the actual life of Jesus must have had the specific character required to account for the actual historical results that followed and for the present personal regeneration its impact still produces, the more precisely we learn to know these historical and personal realities, their relations to the rest of nature and history, and the demands they lay upon us, the more accurately and profoundly we may hope to discern the truth and the will of God for us men. We are not dealing simply with human ideals, wishes, wistful hopes that shift like cloud-shapes, from culture to culture and from century to century. We are face to face with an actual expanding range of events in history that arise from and bear witness to an actual center, at which we believe a crucial act of God made manifest His presence and essential aspects of His nature. We affirm, then, an actual specific revelation of the abiding truth and goodness that are in God.

The revelation itself, moreover, both as an historical reality uniquely realized in space and time and as a continuing source of regenerative energy and insight for men at grips with evil today, is an ultimate objective factor in human living. As given fact, the impact of Jesus Christ on human history is not derivative from nor dependent upon some more primary presupposition such as a certain culture or a particular philosophy, within which alone it is valid. The personal commitment to which this revelation gives rise, also, is ultimate for each person who finds himself under its sway. Faith in and love for the God and Father of Jesus Christ is an ultimate inner standard, real though not external, to which the believer's life at every moment and in every decision is amenable. He cannot choose at will to be judged now by this standard and now by some other—by the standard, for example, of unqualified obedience to some national sovereign, or ultimate devotion to some racial group. Christian faith affirms that God is absolutely good, just, merciful, and that the revelation of God in Jesus Christ and the commitment which it awakens are ultimate realities and norms for every Christian. It affirms too that all these are realities and norms even for non-Christians, in the sense that human life carried on without acknowledgement of them and participation in their meaning lacks a dimension for which there is no equivalent. Thus far Christians can speak confidently.

Need for Humility: But in two obvious facts there lies a need for clear-headed humility in Christian judgments about God and human affairs. First, our apprehension of the central revelation in Jesus Christ is in many respects conditioned by our own failings. Our very faith itself, though an ultimate inner reality and norm for each of us, is variable and corruptible. Human devotion to God, though life-giving in principle and in truth, is hard to practice. Devotion to oneself is easier, and faith and insight suffer from that fact. Our understanding of the Scriptures and other records and of the living Church is conditioned in all sorts of ways by the time and place in which we live, the traditions we inherit, the lacks in our individual heredity and training, the blind spots made in us by special interests, desires, and fears. Furthermore, the written records through which the Word of God is transmitted to us, and the Church as historical community in which the spirit of Jesus Christ is alive, themselves leave room for honest differences of understanding. In the Scriptures, the Word of God is mediated through very diverse witnesses, who wrote in the midst of historical situations, known to us only in part, that helped to shape their insights and their words. The institutional Church has come to be not one community but many, and its witness in both word and deed is often confused and contradictory.

Secondly, the specific implications of the revealed truth for human understanding and conduct in a particular present situation can be discerned only by processes of thought that are liable at every step to the risk of error. Sincere Christians who agree on the primary demand of love for neighbors and enemies can disagree on its meaning for statesmen, citizens, and victims of belligerent powers. Too confident assertions about the details of Christian duty, as though human judgment could ever claim the infallibility of God, are presumptuous and self-refuting. There is need then for humility on the part of every Christian.

But to recognize clearly these limitations, and to welcome rather than to evade or suppress the criticisms they invite, can hold the way open for correction of human errors and for emergence of fresh visions of the truth. . . . Though our faith can never be made perfect in this life, it can by just such persistent correction become less bound by our cravings for safety or self-justification, and more responsive to the truth that is in God. . . .

God's Relation to the War

B. *In this mood, we venture to affirm next our belief that God's relation to the war is defined in broad terms by His essential unitary activity as Creator, Redeemer, Life-Giver.* These are not three activities, but one, as the Father, Son, and Holy Spirit of Christian teaching are not three Gods but one. . . .

God as Creator: The doctrine of God as Maker of heaven and earth forbids any assertion that He is aloof from the war. In the first place, that doctrine holds that the existence of every situation depends on the creative energy of God's will, put forth not merely in some past moment of time but throughout all time. In the next place, it holds that as God's energy transcends and pervades all time, all history, so likewise it transcends and pervades all that we call space, in such wise that from no portion of the existing world is God absent. He is the living and present Creator of all men and all nations. Thirdly, it holds that the presence of God is never static but always active presence, not merely form or law but energy. God then is present, active, creative, in every part of nature and history, and so in this war.

But the manner of God's omnipresence as Creator is further defined by the fact that what He creates is existent as other than Himself. God is not identical with the world, nor with any part of it. If there is no event from which God is absent, equally there is no event in which God alone is present. In as far as creation is effective, it brings into existence and maintains in existence subordinate centers and fields of energy that are at once yielding and resistant to the continuing energy of their Creator, as well as embodying attraction and repulsion, partial harmony and partial discord among themselves.

This comment applies with especial pertinence to human history, and to the war, in which natural and impersonal forces are complicated in their working by the continuous cross fire of personal human decisions, and by the consequences of past decisions. The latter may go on long after the initial act, in large part as impersonally as widening and mingling ripples in a pool, so that there is always some temptation to regard them simply as natural entities devoid of moral significance. Slums can look much like swamps, caste systems like terraced hillsides, wars like hurricanes; and both popular and learned opinion has often regarded them as facts of nature or "acts of God." In protest against such easy reduction of important segments of history to natural mechanisms, other interpreters have insisted that slums, caste systems, and wars are all moral realities through and through, the direct and continuous manifestations of human choices and especially of human sins. *The truth as it seems to us is that the war is neither simply a natural fact nor an act of God nor a sinful choice of man. It is a complex event in which all of these factors are present and need to be duly recognized.* God, then, acts in the war as the creative ground that continuously keeps the warring world and its members in existence, and enables them to act in accordance with their respective natures or decisions. God does not act as an all-inclusive "One-and-All," nor in any way that excludes or nullifies decision and action by His creatures. Moreover, God does not act as a world Ruler who has willed the outbreak of the war, nor all those specific antecedent conditions that made the war inescapable. Some of these conditions God directly wills, we believe—the freedom and the interdependence of men, the inseparability of moral decisions from natural consequences, and the like. Others are the resultants of natural forces that operate in relatively uniform causal networks, perhaps without complete mechanical fixity but presumably without the foresight or decision characteristic of persons: natural forces that operate, then, often in ways that enhance or destroy values, even perhaps in ways that further or hamper the will of God, but that are not themselves amenable to moral judgment. Some are the personal decisions of men, together with their antecedents and consequences, some personal, others more or less impersonal, but all identified more directly with responsible human action than with the irresponsible forces of extra-human nature, and all involving a crucial factor of human difference from, and often of opposition to, the will of God.

We notice next another aspect of God's creative action in the war. As Creator He is not only the source of existence in all creatures. He is the ground also of their respective actual natures and primary relationships. His world is a world of order, not caprice. . . . There is indeed a divinely established "order of creation," a universal "law of nature" that has both natural and moral aspects, though as we have seen it will not do to assign to this order without more ado such human institutions as slums, caste systems, slavery, claims of racial inequality, or any particular social, political, or ecclesiastical pattern in history. War is not divinely ordained, any more than these other historical emergents. But in war, as in all of these, divine law and order are present and in the long run controlling, even when human law and order are damaged or demolished by human action.

Lastly, God as Creator "is good, and the Author only of good to men," as Greek wisdom affirmed long ago. His creative will and His providential rule are set to favor not all sorts of action equally, but those that make for the realization of truth, beauty, justice, mercy, good faith, devoted love, and all else that accords with His perfection whether it be known to us or not. The God revealed in Jesus Christ is not a neutral Force but the infinitely perfect Father. His goodness is indeed of a different order from that of most good men. He cares for the unthankful and the evil. He gives sun and rain alike to the just and the unjust, and lets the tares grow along with the wheat. His valuations often are puzzling to sincerely righteous men, who not unnaturally suppose that unequal work in the vineyard deserves unequal pay and that gold pieces in the alms box weigh more than a widow's coppers. He lets His best beloved Son be crucified between two men of violence because He loves them. But in spite of all appearances, He is a God of order and righteousness, who makes even the wrath of men to praise Him. For He is God above all other gods.

In this war, then, He is not neutral, and not helpless. He is maintaining invincibly an order that men cannot overthrow. Moreover, He is taking sides throughout the struggle, not with the Axis powers nor with the United Nations, nor with any government nor any institutional church or churchman, but with the impulses toward good and against the impulses toward evil in every man and every group in both camps. God is not a combatant, nor a neutral onlooker, nor a helpless victim. First of all, He is, in war as in peace, the Creator and Sovereign whose power sustains and governs, but does not annul, the activities of nature and of men.

God as Redeemer: At the same time and for the same reason, His own perfect goodness, God is in the war as Redeemer. Divine redemption of the world appears to us men under two aspects, that can be distinguished but never separated. Redemption embraces both judgment and forgiveness. So we speak of divine justice and mercy, and we seek both in this war, remembering that nowhere ought we expect to find the one without the other. As Calvin wisely noted, even a human judge cannot pronounce an equitable sentence without mercy; nor can mercy work in opposition to justice, nor wait until merciless judgment is first wreaked upon the offender, and be redemptive. No doubt in human action, because it is imperfect, what is called justice is often separated from what is called mercy; but in the perfect redemptive love of God, the two are inseparable at every moment of time. . . .

Divine judgment in the war can be plainly seen at two levels. First, as we have noted, *there is a natural and moral order of creation that God maintains against all man's wayward efforts* in peace and in war. For human persons, that order has especial significance in these respects: that every man is in his essential nature a responsible person, as well as a natural being; that all men are interdependent, as well as dependent upon their natural environment with its network of causal processes; and that the primary demand upon every man in this situation is love, for God, for men as children of God, and for nature as man's temporal home. Man may act, in both peace and war, as though these primary conditions of his life did not exist, but they hold fast and his denials in thought and act bring calamity upon himself, his fellows, and his natural home. *Divine judgment is not vengeful. It is inexorable. And in war, more vividly than in quieter times, men can see its fearful majesty.* In times when human conflict operates below the threshold of armed warfare, men sow with busy hands the winds of private and public aggression or negligence, of headstrong ignorance or cunning treachery. In times of open warfare, they reap the hurricane of outraged human life and divine power. In a terrible way, the fury of war vindicates the existence and inescapability of divine law.

Secondly, God's judgment in war time negates not merely the selfish conduct of men, but also their inadequate ideals for living. There are many of our accustomed ways of action that we are ready to acknowledge to be wrong, even though usually we hope that the fitting penalty for them may somehow be escaped. But other ways of ours seem to us surely right, and the ideals we hold often seem to us beyond criticism. It is hard not to think we know what is right even when we do otherwise. Service to one's country, or to one's church, for example, seems surely right, and the ideal of patriotism or of church loyalty that moves us in our most devoted moments seems wholly good. Precisely at these points of human self-confidence the judgment of God cuts deep. The very group loyalty in which we take pride and find a basis for self-righteousness is shown up in the fierce light of warfare to be tinctured with deadly poison. For uncritical group loyalty is a potent source of war, it helps to intensify hatred while war goes on, it is most characteristic of the more aggressive and tyrannous nations in the present war, and it can retard for generations our attempts to establish a peaceful world when this war has run its course. The judgment of God writ large in war time says: "Patriotism is not enough." Human righteousness at any level thus far achieved is not enough. That is true in times of comparative quiet. It becomes glaringly evident in times of war.

Is then war itself to be called "a divine judgment," or an instrument thereof? Does God decree war to punish the waywardness of men? We have said no. War is not divinely ordained, any more than slums or slavery. God's will is always that men shall live at peace with one another and with Him. This is true at all times and without any exception. This refers not simply to armed warfare. It is not God's will that men shall carry on covert strife with one another, and with Him, under the name of peace. When that is done, His will is already being violated, and the outbreak of open war makes that fact plain. It is not God's will that war shall come upon mankind, at any time, nor that it be regarded as a suitable instrument for good. It is God's will that the primary order of natural and human life be maintained, and in presence of that order some sorts of human conduct bring war. The order itself is confirmed and vindicated. The specific decisions that make war break out are man's decisions, not God's. . . . War is not, then, "a judgment of God" in the sense that God wills it as a punishment for men. It serves to reveal and vindicate the judgment of God that upholds inexorably the order of His world even though in the presence of that order some combinations of human decision and natural causation, in resistance to God's will for peace, bring war.

God's judgment, in a word, is never merely punitive. Man brings down punishment when he acts in violation of God's law made dynamic by God's will. Yet that very law is even in its rigor a gift without which neither natural nor personal life could go on, and the will that maintains it is even in its unyieldingness a will to more abundant life. Divine judgment is redemptive in purpose, and it becomes so in effect, as far as men are brought by its unceasing pressures to respond in repentance and faith.

To make this clear to ourselves, *we seek in the war for evidences also of divine mercy. First, we find such evidence in the fact that in the midst of the terrifying bitterness and hatred, deceit and disruption of war, there are signs of recreative forces at work it would seem continuously.* In part these have a character so drastic that mercy may seem a strange word for them. If that be true, there is need to remind ourselves that divine mercy means not softness but healing, not passivity but regeneration. If divine judgment is not without mercy, divine mercy is not without rigor. Its distinctive character lies in its positive purging, renovating, and reconciling power. This power is discernible in war, on the social side, in the successive breaking down of refuges for human self-sufficiency, and the positive affirmation of interdependence. Every country at war is compelled to seek internal unity, even at the cost of many vested privileges. This is not by the will of men. Self-interest is not displaced in war time. Willful resistance to rationing laws and pressure group tactics for winning private advantages, sharpening of racial, regional, and class jealousies, and departmental factionalism bear witness to the contrary. Likewise, competition and distrust between allied nations even in the face of a dangerous foe make it clear that war does not wholly purge men and nations of divisive self-interest. Yet in spite of these symptoms of continuing illness, the very necessities of war time compel the redoubling of efforts to extend the scope of effective cooperation. Old barriers give way here and there. The self-confidence of a ruling class or the provincialism of a self-satisfied folk group is shaken by new contacts. A new sense of the meaning of wastage of natural resources for human life takes shape. So halting, reluctant, but inescapable awareness of the fact of human and natural interdependence and the need for better cooperation is forced upon men by their very struggles. This is not the purpose of warfare, but it happens in time of war and by reason of some of the special conditions of such a time. Similarly, the pressures of belligerent needs help to stimulate intellectual and technical enterprise, and to force pooling of information and resources, in such fashion that results are quickly achieved (in medicine, in the mechanical arts, in communication, and in social organization) that may be of great value when more peaceable life is resumed. These achievements may be morally neutral in themselves, but the devoted effort spent in reaching them and the new patterns of human cooperation they make possible are not neutral. And in so far as knowledge is better than ignorance, such discoveries have worth that cannot be denied a place among the gifts of God.

Secondly, to some individual men in war time there come searching insights into the meaning of human life and the will of God. Undisciplined wastrels may find new responsibility, snobbish aristocrats or proletarians new respect for their fellows, complacent worldlings a new humility in the presence of engulfing tragedy. Such change may come to men either in or out of uniform, and find expression in words and acts that long outlast the fighting. Particular episodes can be highlighted in the prevailing darkness of war so that they become more effective witnesses to the perpetual beauty of righteousness than the routine of more peaceable living is likely to provide. There must be no exaggeration of these gleams of light, and no minimizing of the horrors against which they are visible. There must be no hint that war is justifiable as a source of human betterment. The point here is rather that, for all its ghastliness, war bears the marks of a Power that works in it for good.

Underlying the two sets of detailed evidence just reviewed, and more impressive than all of them together, we are able to discern what may be called *a residual health of mankind that resists and survives the fevers of war.* Herein is the active mercy of God to be seen, quietly and invincibly at work. We affirm in this specific sense Augustine's judgment, "Nothing can be evil except something which is good." Disease can exist only in a living body, and the very forces of life work to resist disease and to restore health. It is so in national societies, when a despot more powerful than any Caesar cannot prevent Germans from reading the Old Testament or befriending Jews. It is so in international warfare, when the exigencies of war itself cannot altogether prevent men from acting humanely and applauding decency. This we affirm is good evidence that God is in the midst of the struggle as healing power.

Shall we say also as the victim of a new crucifixion? Is war itself a Golgotha, and suffering humanity a new embodiment of the crucified Redeemer? In particular, can we say that the men killed in battle, or the refugees driven out to wander and starve, or the children who die in bomb shelters or blockaded famine areas are vicarious redeemers of our time? We share deeply in the desire of bereaved parents and comrades, and of chaplains and pastors to say these things, but they must not be said carelessly. *War is in a general sense a crucifixion of both man and God, but it is not the crucifixion of Jesus Christ, and it is not a chief source of man's salvation. What made the tragedy on Calvary uniquely redemptive was the Man on the middle cross, and the unmixed revelation of love and power that was in him.* There were crosses on either side of him, and there have been many before and after. In a sense men have been crucifying one another, and in a different sense crucifying God, from the beginning of human history. But only one crucifixion has become a central spring of light and grace for mankind. Let the Church, then, say that in the light of that Crucifixion we see more deeply and clearly the meaning of this present struggle. We see that in our world, the burden of suffering is not distributed according to guilt and innocence, but that all suffer, even the best. We see that the spirit in which suffering and death are confronted can make them vehicles of life for many rather than merely of loss. We see that as the cross of Jesus Christ demonstrated the power of God to overcome evil in its very moment of victory, there is good ground to hope for a like conquest continuing today and tomorrow. We and our brothers are not the saviors of mankind. The Savior is God, who suffers for us, with us, at our own hands, yet in such a way that the outcome is life perpetually made new. Our part is to bear witness to this saving work of God.

God as Holy Spirit: One more dominant role must be ascribed to God in the war, as in all human history: His special work as Holy Spirit, Sanctifier, Sustainer, Life-Giver. This aspect of His presence and action, once more, is not to be thought of as separate from His presence as Creator and as sovereign Redeemer. God is one, and His work is indivisible. Hence, in what has already been said of universal creation and providence, divine judgment and mercy, the work of God as Holy Spirit has been often in view. Yet it is right to recognize along with these more general activities a special range of peculiarly personal relationship between God and those men who actually respond to His presence in conscious trust. Through such men, God is able to perform works of power that are not possible in lives ruled by unbelief. This is in a special way the distinctive work of the Holy Spirit.

The chief of such miracles has already been referred to in the discussion of divine mercy: the actual remaking of persons hard hit by the war, yet quickened into faith and devotion so that they become new and better men and women. This is the Spirit's work of sanctification, springing from God's redemptive love, and issuing in human life transformed, redirected, with new dimensions in which to grow. Nurturing such growth, likewise, toward the full stature of the manhood whose norm is Jesus Christ is the work of the same Spirit, whose impulse is one and whose gifts are many. The impulse is devoted love for God and man, for all that is good, true, and right. Among the gifts are reinforced strength and courage, sharpened insight and self-forgetfulness, steadfast patience and serenity and joy, invincible security, and others too many to name. Including them all is an abiding experience of heightened, deepened, broadened fellowship with men and nature, and with God.

The undivided Source of such new life, and the abiding Sustainer of communion among men and communion of men with God, the Holy Spirit is the living Ground of community as personal fellowship and as corporate life. Where the Spirit works, there diversity becomes enrichment of a common good rather than mere conflict or mutual destruction. We see this Spirit working wherever men are faithful to one another and to the best they know, wherever recognition of human kinship is maintained in spite of separation and strife, and especially wherever men are united in devotion to the one eternal God of heaven and earth. . . .

A striking way in which this divine work comes to be affirmed in war time, with varying degrees of Christian insight, is the report from many quarters of a new sense, that comes to sorely tried men, of the fellowship of the Holy Spirit in hardship and peril, a sense often of supernatural help and protection. In this war, as in earlier wars, there is first-hand testimony, much of it startling, some of it very moving, with respect to the survival of hard-pressed pilots or mariners through unforeseen and powerful aid beyond known human powers. To the minds of many, these are palpable miracles in our time, like the "mighty works" that first century Christians took as signs and gifts of the Holy Spirit. Our problem now, like St Paul's then, is to keep clear the right lines of Christian conviction across an area in which human cravings and emotions are uncommonly strong. It seems to us right to affirm that to every devoted person in war time, Christian or non-Christian, combatant or non-combatant, the presence of God offers an accessible source of power and spiritual security. Especially through genuine prayer, however inarticulate, a human spirit is opened toward God who is never absent, and strengthened to bear rightly whatever burden must be borne. That fresh energies, beyond the shallows drawn upon in ordinary living, can be tapped under conditions of great stress has long been known, and fresh testimony to the fact is welcome. Such energies, and such guidance as the hidden perceptions within men's bodies and minds may provide in times of extreme peril or exhaustion, can indeed manifest the watchful care of the God who neither slumbers nor sleeps.

But as in St. Paul's day, so in ours it is vital to insist that no marvel of force nor of physical guidance, not even a rescue from impending bodily death, is in itself a sufficient evidence of a special working of the Holy Spirit. The crucial test is still the old one: Is the spirit of man, in the presence of these marvels, brought closer to the pattern of the spirit of Jesus Christ? Of two men confronted by the same event, one may be moved to self-searching, humility, and new devotion, the other to self-satisfaction and arrogance. It seems not too rash to say that one has heard in rescue from peril the voice of God, the other only a magnified echo of his own.

The difference becomes very clear in the differing attitudes of those who pray in war time. It is good that men are moved to pray in times of especial stress, far better if they pray continually in good times and bad, both in words and in unspoken cravings and grateful impulses. We believe that the half-involuntary, unaccustomed cry for help and the calm reaffirmation of a lifelong trust are alike understood and accepted by an infinite Father. But they can scarcely be answered alike. Prayer is a mutual relationship between personal spirits and its significance and results are necessarily dependent on the characters, attitudes, and actions of both participants. We are assured that God will unfailingly provide, in answer to every one who turns to Him sincerely in prayer, the utmost of good that the attitude of the petitioner and the whole situation permit. But that good will often be very different from what the petitioner seeks. In particular, there is no warrant for expecting that God will protect from physical harm all those who call upon Him however sincerely, nor that prayers are enough to assure military victory or avert another war. Prayers for all these things can be offered, with or without Christian insight and faith. The one kind of petition, we believe, that God cannot accept as genuine prayer at all is a presumptuous and self-righteous effort to use Him and His power for human ends, chosen without regard to His will. Humble prayer for safety or for bread can be real prayer. Yet we believe that those soldiers pray best who pray in the spirit of the young officer who wrote to his family from Bataan: "My prayer each night is that God will send you His strength and peace. During the first few days of the war, I prayed also for personal protection from physical harm, but now, that I may be given strength to bear whatever I must bear, and do whatever I must do, so that those men under me will have every reasonable chance." The models for prayer in time of trial are still the prayers in Gethsemane and on the cross: "Abba, Father, all things are possible unto thee; take away this cup from me; nevertheless not what I will, but what thou wilt." "Father, forgive them; for they know not what they do." "Father, into Thy hands I commend my spirit."

Man's Part in the War

C. In speaking of God's action in the war, we have spoken continually of man's action also. This is neither accidental nor avoidable. No sharp line can be drawn through the world nor through any part of it with God's acts on one side, man's on the other. In every historical event, both God and man are actively present though neither can at any point be simply identified with the other. Now we seek to view the same war situation from another angle, and ask what man is doing to himself and in relation to God in the struggle. In Christian terms, our concern here is man as creature, as sinner, and as subject of redemption.

Man as Creature Enjoying the Status of Responsible Freedom: First, then, we recognize the existence of man as created personal being. We think of man as emergent in the midst of nature, called into being by the creative power of God, to become a personal self. His natural status is not thus denied, but a further range of life is opened out for him: a status we know as responsible freedom. Man's freedom is visible most simply in his ability to judge his environment and himself, intellectually and morally. In perceptual judgment, in memory and anticipation, and in reasoning to new conclusions such as he has never hitherto experienced, man asserts his partial independence of the physical situation in which at any moment he stands. In self-consciousness he brings even his own thinking under review, and in moral self-criticism he compares himself with standards that he neither has attained nor can attain. In making and carrying out practical decisions, he alters what would have been the natural course of events, and makes both the world and himself different from what they would have been. In this sense, *man affirms his freedom in every act of critical awareness, and especially in self-consciousness, moral judgment, and personal decision.*

This freedom is not negated but complemented by the fact that as person, a man is a responsible being. For responsibility is first of all ability to respond to factors for which many living things have no capacity for response. Truth, justice, humbleness are duties for man because the meanings, the patterns of life, for which these words stand are discernible by him and awaken acknowledgment in him. The presence of other persons as persons, moreover, not as means to his pleasure but as ends for his devotion, and the presence of God beyond all natural and human goods—to these also he is capable of appropriate response, and to them he is thence responsible. *Herein is his more-than-animal freedom the more concretely defined. In being thus obligated, as irresponsible creatures are not, he is the more genuinely free—free, as they are not, to be a person intent upon freely chosen good, whose constraint upon him is not compulsion but obligation, that can be denied though not escaped.*

This paradox of freedom and constraint runs throughout man's existence as social being. Not only is he under obligation to the law of God—the ingrained patterns of the world and his own being that require of him willing affirmation of what is true and right—but he is bound up so intimately with the lives of his fellow-men that apart from them he cannot be himself. Only in community can persons be persons. Yet in human community, growing individuals achieve maturity as persons only through both yielding and resistance to the demands of fellowship. Tension between individual and group, between person and person, between group and group is a constant pattern of growing human life. Group loyalty and individual self-assertion are both indispensable to such personal life as we know, even at its best. This dependence of each person upon the social groups in which he is a member obviously limits his freedom by committing him in advance to specific folkways, in which he is nurtured and which enter into him as presuppositions for action. He becomes a child of his people, his nation, his culture, with his decisions partly predetermined by this social parentage; yet without some such determinations he could not achieve the freedom of personal living at all.

In rigidly authoritarian societies or groups, this sort of moulding through conscious training and the pressure of custom can make it extremely hard for individual persons to act, or even to think freely in relation to the nurturing group. So it is in our day for the young people of both Germany and Japan. Among them, group loyalty has been stressed and personal dissent discouraged until the very meaning of critical independence, one may suppose, has still to be learned. Yet even under extreme conditions, there are two ways in which a person can find a new lease of freedom with respect to his nation or people. One way is through human contacts that make him realize that his nation is one member of a world society in which diverse national and cultural patterns exist in a wider human context. He is himself, therefore, a member of that world society as well as of his smaller group, and the scope of his loyalty is widened, the details of it modified, by this realization. He can still be a devoted patriot if the well-being of his nation is clearly seen to be inseparable from the well-being of the wider society and its other members. But this is different from the patriotism of the unawakened nationalist. A second way to such liberation is through direct conscious dependence on God and His universal laws. This is "the liberty of a Christian man," that sets one free from any cultural, political, or secular absolutism, though not from the demands of God.

In still another way man's freedom is restricted: by his dependence upon nature and history through his particular place in space and time. That he can transcend this location in some fundamental respects we have seen. He has power to think his way out beyond any specifiable limits of spatial or temporal extent. But he cannot escape the actual impacts and restraints, the defects and frustrations that are part and parcel of the world-scene into which he is born. In war time, he cannot escape the special impacts and frustrations of such a time; nor in any given age of history can he live as though the conditions that help to bound his life were not real. Attempts to escape from reality, in this sense, can lead indeed to an irresponsibility of weakness and false comfort but not to an increase of personal freedom. On the other hand, loyal acceptance of the actual place in nature and history into which one is born and grows, and at the same time persistent effort to discern the truth and right that are God's law for human living, can extend one's freedom even though one's finiteness is never left behind. . . .

Man who is thus at once finite and free becomes a genuine person, then, growing in wisdom and stature, in awareness and integrity, by accepting his responsible status and willingly affirming as his own good the truth and right that are involved in God's world-order. The law is at once around him and within him. He is summoned to obey God and thus to become more fully himself. Through love toward God and his fellowmen, and appreciation of his natural home, his own life is widened, deepened, and carried on toward fulfillment.

Man as Sinner: *Conversely, man is a sinner when he denies his responsibility to God and men, and so violates his own nature and his own good as personal self.* Such violation is always wrought by personal decision. It is never the automatic result of natural impacts, as bodily injury or disease may be. In these latter instances a person does not actively identify himself with the corrupting change and make it his own. But in asserting his interests without due regard to his neighbor's, in seeking pleasure or profit or power in defiance of equity, in treating persons as things or the will of God as though it were the will of man, a person affirms as his own the falsehoods that such conduct involves. This is sin, and through such commitment to falsehood a person becomes bound in a different way from the ways that mark his finiteness. As sinner he has corrupted his own powers and become less fully a person than before, less able to see truth and right clearly, and less resistant to the pressures of nature and human society that continually threaten his integrity and personal freedom.

What men thus do as individuals, they do also in groups. Human society as we know it is organized on the understanding that both loyalty and disloyalty are to be expected. We build vast credit systems that presuppose general good faith, and parallel them with police courts and prisons to deal with expected violations. We form voluntary associations for business, education, research, communal worship, held together mainly by voluntary ties, and we organize elaborate coercive machinery in the name of the State to keep the peace when quarrels arise. Within the modern nation, most disputes can be settled either by agreement or by legal coercion. But since no effective government yet runs beyond the frontiers of a state, when international disputes arise, with major collisions of national interests, the stresses and conflicts of ordinary times are likely to deteriorate sooner or later into war.

If we ask how man's sinfulness is manifest in this war, our answer can only select from the appalling tangle a few typical threads. Without minimizing the fateful consequences of the policies and decisions of the Axis governments, we can say that war came not because the peoples on both sides deliberately willed it, but because enough people on each side willed, half-gropingly, half-wittingly, their own apparent advantage without due regard to the obligations of human community and divine order. This involved both deep-seated lack of trust in God and neighbor, and faithlessness to promises given or implied, each act of faithlessness itself prompted in part by suspicion of the others' good faith. To this mesh of distrust all peoples have contributed through all history to the present outbreak, and the weaving of the web still goes on. Bad faith between men presupposes, in large part, men's distrust of God. Instead of seeking security and fullness of life through acceptance of His ways, they have tried to seize and hold these good things by defrauding or subjugating other men. And other men have sought to secure themselves against loss by more subtle deceptions or more powerful retaliations.

Add to faithlessness the kindred sins of pride and idolatry. In pride men seek to achieve fulfillment through the exercise of power above their fellows. During ordinary times, the means are economic, intellectual, social, political, ecclesiastical. The unending struggle for preferment, and assertion of superiority, develops in each people a tradition—almost an ethic—of ambition and domination, a half-articulate *Herrenmoral* in which children are reared believing that life can have savor only through the exercise of lordship. In this context, lesser dominations lead to striving for greater ones. Success already won must be protected against the resentful victim and the envious rival. Success for oneself becomes identified with dominance for one's business house, or class, or church, or nation. Small nations fear larger neighbors and make alliances against them. Large nations fear encirclement, build up armaments, and seek to use small neighbors as outposts against larger ones. Trade rivalries grow into diplomatic contests, and irredentist minorities become symbols of inferiority to be put right. And so at last to war, in which there is no self-confessed aggressor but only aggrieved defenders of imperiled security.

Another way of saying much the same thing is to say that in seeking unrivaled dominance and impregnable security, men are seeking for themselves, their church, their country the status of God. Idolatry thus underlies and aggravates human conflict, in peacetime and in war. In the degree to which one's own finite objects of devotion are treated as absolutes, the crusading temper against which Christian insight within the Church has turned, in recent years, tends to reappear on secular grounds. Defense of home and country, of capitalism, imperialism, or democracy, can become defense of "the faith."

The counterpart to pride and self-seeking, present also in all peoples in varying degree, is moral lethargy and that effort to escape irksome responsibility to which we have already referred. The very persons who are jealous of their own security and privilege are too often unconcerned about the security and freedom of others, and unwilling to share with them the task of seeking opportunity for all. *Aggression and irresponsibility, tyranny and anarchy, two major forms of social sin, feed one upon the other. Deliberate wrongdoing and ignorant unconcern are a human soil in which the dragon's teeth take root and grow.*

Wars, then, are not the outcome of wicked acts of particular men, in isolation from a great body of shared social evil. They grow out of that massive moral and religious wrongness which is the seed-bed of all our specific transgressions, and to which all of us and all our forebears have contributed. For in affirming as our own these war-breeding attitudes toward God and men, we have identified ourselves with the drift toward war, whether we have deliberately sought war or simply a more privileged place in the sun.

Once open war begins, under modern conditions, the malignant propagation of sin becomes a kind of perverted virtue. Systematic lying to both foes and friendly peoples becomes an implement of statecraft. Atrocious cruelties are practiced in hot blood and with cold deliberation. Reports of such cruelties are kept on file, and coined at the proper time into righteous fury and support for counter-measures. Young men are schooled in fighting methods derived from the jungle and improved by cool intelligence and careful experiment. Hatred and ruthlessness are approved, mass exterminations of enemy troops are sought and of civilians are practiced, military necessity tends to become the supreme guiding principle of conduct.

What thus comes to horrid fruitage in the war had its roots, once again, in the behavior of men and nations before the war broke out. Hideous brutalities, cold-blooded treacheries, cowardly evasions, callous stupidities—all these and more we must charge against our present enemies, our allies, and ourselves in varying proportions during the years of miscalled peace. There is no warrant for blurring the differences of situation, behavior, and objectives of the various powers during that armed truce. Some were concerned chiefly to keep advantages already won; some were more bent on revenge and the seizure of increased power at the expense of their neighbors. Some were prepared to maintain, chiefly for their own peoples, such measures of freedom and equity as they had inherited and developed; some were intent on destroying both freedom and equity for the sake of greater power at home and abroad. Though all were involved in sin, their ways of sinning were not identical in the sight of God, we believe, nor in their portent for the common life of men. *In the actual course of events, dominance by the Axis powers would have fastened upon their own peoples and upon conquered lands a reign of tyranny and terror full of danger to humane living everywhere. Resistance to such rule, whether by armed force or by more peaceful means, became imperative. We speak here with keen awareness of the confusions of human motives, the mingling of good with bad intents, the differences among striving human groups that mark each new situation in history. We have in view at the same time the certainty that our own judgment of all these matters is biased and incomplete. Yet one judgment concerning the years of uneasy truce seems clear. Every nation then was concerned more for the immediate advantage of self than for the larger welfare of mankind and for the glory of God as Lord of all. Every nation, moreover, thus jeopardized even its own well-being, along with that of its neighbors, since none can long prosper alone.*

To the sins of the pre-war years, also, the conduct of the war itself has added greatly. It is not to be thought that with the outbreak of war, the distinction between sin and suffering temporarily disappears, so that all who are involved become helpless victims of unmoral necessity because all chance for significant decision is ended until hostilities cease. War is not hell, save in metaphor. It displays horrors, indeed, that are worthy of hell, but they are in essential part the results of continuing decisions of men who are at once bound and free in exactly the same sense in which men are bound and free in the intervals before and after a war. The specific decisions open to them are not the same nor, of course, are the specific conditions—the intellectual barriers and social pressures—under which they must decide. These become far more restrictive, and the range of choice more narrow. But as long as persons are living persons, there is no situation in which their decisions cease to be significant before God.

The view that the war is, for the persons involved in it, a morally neutral though spiritually horrible interlude in human history may seem to find a certain plausibility in another consideration: the distortions of human goodness in war as we know it. *On the one hand, spiritual excellences of many sorts are intrinsic, not accidental, to the conduct of war. This war is the outcome and the scene not only of sin and of natural necessity, but also of impulses to good among many plain people.* Besides the faithlessness that leads to the breakdown of peaceable ways, there is the loyalty that keeps men together under fire. There are promises honored at heavy cost as well as promises broken. There is concern for one's own country and children, and also for weaker peoples abroad, with whose security one's own is involved. This kind of faithfulness of men to one another is characteristic of all armies not demoralized into mobs. Without it war could not go on. There is courage of many grades, up to the lambent heroism of soldiers who smother grenades with their bodies in order that the men beside them may live, or the quiet faith of chaplains who give their life-belts to others and go down with a sinking troop ship. There is love and self-sacrifice and generosity—even at times toward the enemy. The spirit of man is not simply bad in war. . . .

Man as a Subject of Redemption: *A practically urgent question arises from all that has been said about man in war: whether war itself is inevitable, by reason of human nature or of the corruption to which it has already been subjected. We believe that it is not.* Particular wars become inevitable only by reason of a particular series of decisions and causal processes within the framework of the divine order. Given the freedom and interdependence of men, either aggression or neglect of obligation by national governments can result in dangerous tensions. In the absence of international community and effective means for maintaining international order, wars eventually result. But in two ways this situation can be changed, by human decisions and divine grace. On the one hand, the human sources from which war-making tensions develop can be altered by the slow processes of personal regeneration and re-education. *It is an essential article of Christian faith that the hearts of men, though corrupted, can be renewed through the power of God; and only because this is so dare we hope for the ultimate elimination of war. But this hope, especially if it be held for the calculable future, requires that personal regeneration go forward in vital union with institutional change.* As in widening areas through mediaeval and modern history, effective government and living community have been developed, the danger of armed conflict within such areas has decreased. For the world society now crowded into an uneasy physical entanglement, a similar need is evident. World society must become world community, and a way must be found to maintain lawful order and equity as a common trust. What men under God have achieved on the smaller but enlarging scale of provincial and national life we believe is not impossible on the international scale required by the conditions of our time.

Meanwhile, one other question demands an answer. Supposing that a more peaceful time for a future generation is not impossible, what shall we say of the men who are killing and being killed now? Is death for them an ultimate frustration, or does the Christian faith see for them some fulfillment?

There is for us no easy answer. We have felt the shock of untimely death, the pain of broken ties, the loss of unique and irreplaceable companions in our human lot. We have known the cruel disappointment and the lingering regret over powers undeveloped, promises unrealized, when young lives are cut short. We grieve with the parents, wives, and children of all countries who are suffering such pangs today. Their sorrow is not to be quieted by words of ours. It will be quieted, we believe, wherever trust in God becomes the basic premise for understanding life and death alike. For some, the death of a beloved may be the first real doorway to such faith. For some, it will long be like a blank wall that only time can dissolve. For some, there is vivid assurance that resurrection or eternal life means restoration and fulfillment of all that has been lost. For all, it is good to be assured that the souls of the righteous are in the hands of God. Christian faith provides no secret knowledge and no promise of immunity from sorrow and loss. It does provide a wisdom and power in whose presence even death can lose its sting. For we are assured that in the everlasting mercy of God, no faithful servant will have died in vain.

The Church in a World at War

D. We come finally to the Church in a world at war. The context within which the Church has its place in history is human society, partly organized into communities of many sorts, of which the Church itself is one. A community, as we understand the term, is a group of persons in dynamic interrelation, who display both unity and diversity of fairly specific sorts. The unity of such a group may be conditioned in part by such external factors as geographic locale and environmental pressures of various kinds. But its more important conditions are internal. There must be a common ethos: a set of common working presuppositions, whether articulate or not, a body of common traditions, and a sense of shared living. There may be common language and literature, rites and festivals, perhaps a common founder or ruler, ancestors or heroes. At all events, the unity of such a group exists in important part in its imaginative life, its memories, feelings, thoughts, and purposes. . . .

The Nature of the State: The State is the seat of political power in a complex community. In it are concentrated the means for making and recording law, and for interpreting and enforcing it. Law and coercive force are the twin pillars of government, and the State is the enduring custodian of both. Its distinctive task is to maintain order, among the diverse members of the inclusive community—for our present purpose, the modern nation. As far as possible, this is to be done by reason and persuasion, by appeal to community loyalty, and by similar measures. But coercive power, greater than that commanded by any member of the community, is always at the disposal of the State (acting at any given time through the government then in office), and such power can be used for the common good, in accordance with the laws understood to be in force for the whole community. *The State as the chief earthly custodian of law is regarded by most Christians as in principle a pattern of life divinely ordained to safeguard social order against anarchy, justice against injustice. On these grounds it has a just claim to the loyal support of Christian citizens in the performance of its proper duties. It has no just claim to absolute or unconditional authority even within its own territorial bounds. In relations both to its own subjects and to other states or persons, it is bound by the demands of that divine order often denoted by the terms natural and moral law, that is binding upon all men and human institutions. The modern secular theory of ultimate sovereignty for each existing state cannot be justified to Christian faith. . . .*

The Character of the Church: The Church is a community of very special character and of complex status at once within and beyond each nation. The indispensable basis for a doctrine of the Church is recognition of the will of God evoking responses among men. The will of God must be thought of, for this purpose, as the steady power of superhuman wisdom and love, the wisdom and love revealed in Jesus Christ, to which all men are at all times subjected, and to which they are at all times responding in divers ways, whether they know it or not. The will of God is not in any simple way coercive, nor the responses of men automatic. Rather, the infinite variety and the intrinsic freedom of personal appeal and response are maintained on both sides. In consequence, though the love of God is constant because God is unchangeable good, the responses of men are highly variable and always fall short of the whole-souled trust and love which God requires. Yet there is a crucial difference between the orientation of life which in fact (not merely in wish or intent) is moving toward such trust and love, and that which in fact is moving away from it. There is a human craving, much more basic than conscious desire or deliberate intent, which is in effect a hunger and thirst for the true God, a seeking above all things His kingdom and His righteousness. *Wherever the presence of God quickens this deep craving into faith and love toward Him, there exists the "commonwealth of God,"* civitas dei . . . .

This living communion of men with God and with one another which defines the true Church must find historical embodiment in appropriate corporate form, the institutional Church, the outward and visible sign of the invisible fellowship of grace. Full Christian life is not to be lived by lone individuals in separation from their fellows. As in other areas of human behavior, so in this, the living movement of spirit frames itself in social patterns and institutions which may be compared with the habit-patterns of individual life. . . .

To define justly the due relation of Church and world is notoriously hard. One may begin, perhaps, by distinguishing between the world and its worships. A sound doctrine of creation, providence, and grace will not fall into the pessimist's frequent error, and despise the world which God so loves. It will give full recognition to the secular orders of life—domestic, economic, and so on—as homes and proving-grounds for life and love. But it will attack with full force the idolatrous worldliness that confuses love and worship, and renders to Caesar the things that are God's. "The devil's commonwealth," *civitas terrena,* is defined not by secular status but by power-lust and pleasure-lust, egoism and irresponsibility. Against "the world" in this sense of *civitas terrena* the true Church does, and the institutional Church should, maintain a struggle of clear-sighted love, to the end that God's world may the more fully acknowledge Him, and have more abundant life.

This means that the Church, in both peace and war time, as we have said more than once, stands in a double relation to the State and to the community of civil affairs. On the one hand, members and constituent bodies of the Church are members also of civil communities and citizens of particular states that have emerged in history, and as such are obligated by the law of God to render loyal service aimed at promoting the welfare of their respective nations. On the other hand, the Church being universal is not a subject of any state, nor a constituent body in any civil community. It is itself, in principle and to an increasing degree in actuality, an ecumenical community having members in all nations and owing direct allegiance to the God and Father of all mankind. Its proper service to civil life can be rendered only while its ultimate and direct obligation to proclaim the Kingdom of God is kept clear. Its service to the world must be a ministry, not a vassalage nor a partnership.

This double relation of the Church and its members to civil society takes on in war time a phase of exceptional tension. For in any war, the Church as ecumenical community has members in both camps, and as a ministry of God must seek the spiritual welfare of all who are involved in the war. In this war, the Protestant Churches alive with a new sense of ecumenical membership and obligation find themselves compelled to realize this status of the Church far more acutely than quasi-national churches in the past have had to realize it. In this war, moreover, as we have seen, a civil issue of desperate moment for human history and spiritual health is at stake: the issue of establishing or failure to establish an effective international community of civil life. In presence of this imperative laid upon all nations by the law of God at this juncture in history, the Church and its members must seek to discern and to perform their duties to God and to mankind.

III. CHRISTIAN ATTITUDES AND DUTIES IN WAR TIME

. . . It is agreed that the perennial task of the Church and of its members is to bear witness incessantly to the judgment and the mercy of God revealed in Jesus Christ, and thus to carry on through peace and war its ministry of reconciliation. There has long been difference of conviction as to whether in war time this primary task calls for renunciation, by the Church and its members, of all voluntary support to the military efforts of any belligerent group. This difference of conviction is represented among the signers of this report, as later paragraphs will make plain. To a far more profound and far-reaching concurrence among us, both those paragraphs and the report as a whole bear witness. . . .

Attitudes Toward Participation in War

A. Three main attitudes toward participation in war have developed in the life of the Christian Church. With some exceptions and qualifications, and for various reasons, the *general attitude of the Christian communities until the time of Constantine seems to have been renunciation by Christians of military service in war time.* When the Church, hitherto a disapproved fellowship within the Roman empire but not of it, now came to have a privileged and more responsible place in the world of Greek and Roman culture, *a second attitude developed: a readiness to distinguish between just and unjust warfare, and to approve active participation by ordinary Christians in a just war.* Monks and clergy still refrained from bearing arms, though not from exhortations and prayers for victory. For other Christians, it came to be regarded as a civic duty to share in armed defense or attack in a just cause. The just war was carefully defined, in such terms that only one side could be regarded as fighting justly, and strict rules were laid down for the treatment of enemies, prisoners, and non-combatants. Still later a third attitude arose alongside the first two. When the empire in the West disintegrated under successive waves of warring barbarian peoples, who became the citizenry of a new mediaeval Christendom, the rules of just warfare became much harder to enforce. After many vain attempts to get them enforced, the Church—now claiming theocratic authority over civil as well as ecclesiastical life—turned the fierce energies of her bellicose children toward the Holy Land and the infidel Muslim who held it. The crusades that resulted were proclaimed not by a secular prince but by the pope, the "vicar of Christ," for defense not of homeland and civic order but of "the faith," as a religious duty to God and the Lord Christ himself. Many monks and clergy, as well as laity, were now in the fighting ranks, the ordinary rules of just warfare were largely disregarded, and religious benefits were proclaimed for all who took part. *A third attitude was here manifested, not supplanting the first two but taking shape alongside them: an attitude of unrestrained commitment, under the Church's auspices, to a divinely ordained war as a religious duty and privilege.*

All three of these attitudes in changing forms continued within the Church during the rise and the struggles of modern nations, the discovery and colonizing of new continents, the massing of new industrial forces, and the arousing of ancient civilizations to dynamic new life. *The most prevalent attitude in the West, in Roman Catholic, Orthodox, and Protestant churches alike, has been approval of combatant service by laymen in wars regarded as just, that is, decreed by lawful authority for good cause, and conducted without official sanction for slaughter of prisoners or non-combatants, or similar barbarities.* Both renunciation of war and religious zeal for war have almost always been minority attitudes in the churches in modern times.

During the present war, a further development seems to be taking place. Crusading enthusiasm seems to be much diminished, if not wholly lacking this time, among Christians. At the same time, in certain important respects Christians willing to fight in a just war and Christian pacifists have drawn closer together. Many Christian pacifists are acutely aware of the monstrous dangers let loose upon the world by the Axis governments, the self-sacrificing heroism of men and women who are giving their lives in an effort to check the spread of such tyranny, and the inescapable ambiguities of their own moral and religious position in war time. Especially in a social order which refuses them most natural outlets for their readiness to work in relief of war-made suffering, the shortcomings of the ways that remain open to them are kept constantly before their eyes. They act as they must under the dictate of conscience, seeking to be guided by God's will yet always conscious of their failure really to fulfill its demands. Many Christians who are willing to support one side in this war are no less clearly aware of the depth of evil both in the conduct of modern war on either side and in the national behavior on all sides that made this war at last inevitable and a stable peace after the war uncertain, the inadequacy of military victory in itself to bring nearer the Kingdom of God on earth, and the grave compromises into which Christians are forced in military service. They know, in short, that there is no such thing as a wholly just war, that decision to fight on either side is at best a choice among mixed evils in the hope of choosing the least. They also seek to follow the will of God in so choosing, but without exultation and often with heavy hearts. *Under such conditions, there can be more profound mutual understanding and community among Christians of both groups, and better hope than ever before that both may contribute to the deepening and widening of the faith and life they share.*

The Present Obligations of the Church

B. Their common faith and life includes some fundamental convictions about the Church and its ministries and present obligations. *First of all, the true Church cannot and the institutional*

Church ought not to act as a belligerent, nor even as an unarmed co-belligerent, in any war. The ecumenical character and the spiritual task of the Church alike forbid today its participation in the war as though it were a civil community, or a constituent part or a partner of such a community. In this sense, "the Church is not at war." *At the same time, since the Church is never simply separate from the civil orders, and its membership largely consists of persons who are citizens or subjects of nations at war, it cannot exclude from its own life the tensions that their divergent or opposing activities as citizens involve. Some of its members fight in the Allied, some in the Axis armies. Some as conscientious objectors are in alternative service or in prison. The Church must keep room for all these its children, not merely tolerating their differences but seeking to understand them more profoundly, to correct them where correction is clearly needed, and to apprehend more concretely through them all the will of God that they all seek to follow. The Church must continually relate them all, with their various special loyalties and personal stresses, to the Kingdom of God in which they all have their heritage and their best hope.*

In Worship of God: *For the Church's primary task, once more, is its ministry of reconciliation. It must continually serve as vehicle for the reconciling of man with God and of man with man. This means, first, the continuing worship of God.* In Christian worship, the way is kept open for all sorts and conditions of men to seek renewal and inward light in God's presence. Through prayer and meditation, through hearing and expounding of the word of God in the Scriptures, and through participation in the sacraments that attest and renew the communion of the faithful with one another and with God, the Church functions for its members and before all men as a true Body through which the Spirit works. In such worship there is no condoning of human wickedness and no forgetting that the God of our Lord Jesus Christ is kind to the unthankful and the evil, that the Lord himself came to call not the righteous but men of sin to repentance. In such worship men are brought before God on one common footing, as wayward children of one Father, so that in all their strength and weakness, their good and their evil, they stand together beneath His judgment and within His everlasting mercy. . . .

In Services to Men—Interpretation: *Its worship of God must issue continually in distinctive services to men. By spoken and written word, the Church must seek to make clear the meaning and urgency of* *divine judgment and the hope of divine mercy in each new situation.* This involves first and always preaching and teaching the principles of Christian faith. Our conception of the way these bear upon the problems posed by the war has been set forth as fully as we can present it in a brief statement. The content of that faith, however it may best be conceived, comprises the primary message of the Church for our time. Yet not the whole message. For, as we have said in the opening paragraphs, the Church is called upon also to interpret in the light of its own faith each historical situation that involves the lives of its members and the well-being of mankind.

Such interpretation includes two phases, explanation and criticism. In seeking to help make clear what each new phase of history involves for both present and future, the Church will not seek to substitute some quite separate account of its own for the analyses of experts in history, government, psychology, or practical affairs. It will seek to bring their findings into the light of its own unique perspective: the history of God's creative, redemptive, and life-giving work with man. In this perspective, the significance of economic or psychological realities is not diminished but rather deepened and made more concrete, in as far as through such realities the working of God can be discerned. Again, our conception of the way in which a human situation can be illuminated by distinctively Christian judgments has been suggested very briefly in the preceding sections. Other Christians will find very much more that needs to be said.

Beside such effort to help explain a current situation, the Church is called upon also to help criticise it, and especially the personal actions that enter into it. There is need to urge in war time the vital import of conscious personal devotion to the will of God and to the common good, as far as Christian faith and reason, manifested in Christian conscience, make each person aware of these controlling ends. The Church must approve such devotion wherever it appears, among soldiers or civilians, and seek to resist the uncritical submergence of personal decision in mass impulses. It must honor courage and faithfulness, patience and fairness, truth-speaking and generosity, especially where they are displayed under the greatest difficulties and at the greatest cost. Such qualities of spirit displayed under fire or in the face of powerful oppressors mark human life at its best. The Church must condemn cruelty, ruthlessness, and power-lust, especially when they are provoked in large part by the very helplessness of potential victims. In such behavior man appears at his worst, and the Church dare not connive at such evil. Its victims must be aided and its perpetrators steadily opposed in all ways appropriate for an ecumenical and spiritual community. At the same time, even while it understands with deep sympathy the rise, among victims and liberators, of hatred for the oppressors and vengefulness toward them, the Church must resist no less steadily the spread of these self-propagating poisons. . . . The Church of Jesus Christ has a primary obligation to voice and to support such generosity toward the peoples of Germany and Japan, in spite of the evil they have done and are doing, as one indispensable factor in restoring the spiritual health of all peoples in the hard days ahead. Forgiveness, we remember, is a Christian duty; and though forgiveness does not exclude severe correction, it does exclude vindictiveness and retaliation.

In like manner, the Church must approve in war time those influences in the shaping of public policy that best keep the way open for community among men and free worship of God. It must resist, by open criticism and persuasion, the theory and the attempted practice of "total war," and its counterpart, a Carthaginian "peace." Total war is suited only for a totalitarian society, which as we have said is irreconcilable in principle with Christian faith in the sovereignty of God and the responsible freedom of man. No matter what the provocation, however great the extremity of military peril—even to the imminence of military defeat—the Church dare not approve a supposition that military expediency or necessity can ever rightfully become the supreme principle of human conduct. We are acutely aware how difficult it is to apply in practice this principle of resistance to claims for the supremacy in war time of military demands and to the elevation of war even temporarily into a status of unconditional domination of human behavior. All of us agree that in war some practices cannot be regarded by the Church as justifiable: the killing of prisoners, of hostages, or of refugees to lessen military handicaps or to gain military advantages; the torture of prisoners or of hostages to gain military information, however vital; the massacre of civilian populations. Some of the signers of the report believe that certain other measures, such as rigorous blockades of foodstuffs essential to civilian life, and obliteration bombing of civilian areas, however repugnant to humane feelings, are still justifiable on Christian principles, if they are essential to the successful conduct of a war that is itself justified. A majority of the commission, moreover, believe that today war against the Axis powers, by all needful measures, is in fact justified. Others among us believe that the methods named are not justifiable on Christian principles, even though they are now practiced or defended by great numbers of sincere Christians and patriotic non-Christians, and even if they be essential to military victory for the United Nations. If it be true that modern war cannot be successfully waged without use of methods that cannot distinguish even roughly between combatants and non-combatants, or between perpetrators and victims, that fact seems to a minority in the commission to raise the question whether in modern war even the more scrupulous side can meet the conditions hitherto generally held by the Church to define a just war. On these specific issues, then, the commission is divided. *On the basic principle that the Church cannot acquiesce in the supremacy of military considerations even in war time, nor in the view that modern war may properly, even in case of extreme peril to nation, church, or culture, become total war, we are agreed.*

In like manner we are agreed that the Church must oppose any plan to deprive the peoples of Germany and Japan of the basis for a normal, peaceable livelihood or of reasonable opportunity for peaceable intercourse with other peoples. We are not competent to judge what methods for ensuring military disarmament in these countries, and what selective restrictions upon their imports of critical materials and development of heavy industry may best aid the difficult transition from war toward a more peaceful world. We are convinced that the doors must not be closed now, by decisions made in war time, upon the chances of young Germans and Japanese to live normally in the post-war world.

Personal Services: Besides its ministries of preaching, teaching, and writing, the Church is committed also to more concrete, personal services to men everywhere in war time. Men in the armed services rightfully look to the Church for help in their hard, unaccustomed tasks. In camps, on their travels, on furlough, and on the fighting fronts the Church must serve them in ways too many to name here. Interpretation of their goals and duties as members of the armed forces, explanation and help in evaluation of the necessities and the opportunities they face, companionship with them in the worship of God and in dangers at home and abroad: these are among the services the Church must seek to provide. It provides them mainly through the chaplains who are its ministers to the men and women in uniform. We rejoice in the record of their devotion to their task and in the evidences they have given of thoughtful concern for the future as well as the present well-being of the men they serve. At the same time, we remember that the *Church is not a partner of any State, however loyal church members may be as citizens, and its ministries are offered not as civil duties but as the Church's witness to a spiritual Lord of all mankind. Hence, we believe the Church must persistently seek, on behalf of its ministers to men in the armed forces, both freedom from military restraints that hinder their work of Christian ministry, and clear recognition that they serve as clergy of the Church Universal rather than as officers of the several belligerent governments.* Many of us believe that from the standpoint of the Church, civilian status would be preferable to military rank for ministers with the armed forces.

To demobilized soldiers, to war victims, and to defeated enemy peoples the Church has obligations to which it has devoted time, energy, and resources from the beginning of the war. There is no need to urge that these obligations must continue to be met long after the fighting stops. The special responsibility of the churches in lands less severely hurt by the war to their fellow Christians in the fighting zones, on both sides of the lines, cannot be discharged without the establishment of new bonds of fellowship within the Church itself. . . .

Counseling: . . . The Church must teach that the primary determinative obligation of every Christian is to the Kingdom of God, which can best find earthly expression through the growth everywhere of community in which the Holy Spirit is at work. Love of one's country and devotion to its well-being is not to be displaced but rather to be validated by alignment with this primary obligation. As far as the two are clearly in accord, the way is plain. If at any point devotion to the Kingdom of God requires dissent from the present policy of a national government, or the present will of a popular majority, the Church must teach that such dissent can be itself a service to the welfare of the beloved country as well as to the

Commonwealth of God. *The principle for each Christian must be: Devotion above all to God and His righteousness; full loyalty to country, friends, and home within the frame of this more ultimate devotion; support of established public policies, obedience to lawful demands of government, and concurrence in the accepted patterns of civic life as far as Christian conscience will permit. . . .*

In war as in peace, the key to all effort by individual Christians to serve the Kingdom of God is Christian conscience. In agreement with the traditional thought of the Church, we recognize in every man both a general tendency to distinguish between right and wrong, and many specific insights into the rightness or wrongness of particular courses of action. We recognize that these specific insights are learned through personal experience, at once individual and communal, that to every Christian the touchstone for such particular responses is given in that revelation that centers in Jesus Christ, and that each Christian must necessarily apprehend and interpret this revelation in the terms made possible by his own individual existence, with all its resources and its shortcomings. Individual insights and decisions will differ because individual persons differ. Yet there is one obvious common requirement: *that each shall follow, in sober sincerity, what really appears to him as the present way toward fulfillment of God's will. In war time, with its drastic narrowing of some sorts of choice, especially for men of military age, one decision that must be made by very many Christian citizens is decision to participate in the war as soldier or war worker, or to bear one's part as conscientious objector in alternative service or in prison. With many representatives of the Church's mind, we recognize that equally earnest Christians may decide for either course.*

There is no disposition among our members to weaken in any way the primary principle that every Christian is in duty bound to decide for that course which really seems to him right. At the same time, there is no disposition among us to hold that any course actually open to men of our day (or of any day) is wholly good. We are agreed that the objectively right course for any Christian in history is that course which actually will most contribute to, and least detract from, the manifestation of God's reign on earth. His duty as Christian is to choose and follow what seems to him to be that objectively right course, the course of his largest possible contribution, and his own conduct is morally right in as far as it does honestly seek to find and follow that way. His judgment as finite human being, however, can be mistaken as to the manner in which his greatest possible contribution might be made. There is room, therefore, in our imperfect human living, for agreement at this point also upon a primary Christian principle and difference as to the specific ways in which that principle may best be put into current practice.

A majority of our members, then, believe that Christian duty today is more adequately conceived by those Christians who voluntarily support the military campaign of the United Nations against the Axis powers. They are clearly aware that successful military action by itself can at best serve the subordinate end of breaking the present military and political dominance of the Axis governments in their own and in occupied lands. The larger ends sought, in terms of justice, freedom, human understanding and cooperation, require measures other than military force. Yet it seems to a majority of the Commission that these ends cannot, in the actual world situation, be hopefully pursued without the use of military force until full victory is achieved.

For those who take the way of the soldier or civilian war worker, and participate voluntarily in active prosecution of the war, we believe there is need for unceasing effort to keep clear the Christian perspective with regard to God and men. We recognize the heart-breaking strains to which men in combat are subjected, and the extreme pressures that may be imposed on every man in military or civilian war service to subordinate all other considerations to the demand for victory. We are mindful of the profound dangers to individual Christian character in a system of military training and service in which many of the accustomed patterns of Christian conduct are replaced by training for ruthless efficiency in destruction. *We are mindful at the same time of the vital need that the Church and all its members resist any temptation to acquiesce in the displacement of the primary Christian goals and standards by any others, in the lives of its young men. Conscience cannot be adjourned in war time without extreme damage to human personality now and to the chance for progress toward world community even in the distant future.*

A minority of our members believe that those Christians are judging more accurately the meaning of Christian duty who in time of peace preach the renunciation of war, and in wartime follow the way of conscientious objection. The dangers of this course also are present to our minds. There is the always obvious danger of inward dishonesty, of spiritual laziness wearing the mask of self-sacrifice, of preference for personal safety above needed service to fellow men. There is the danger of self-righteousness and the unwarranted assumption of superior virtue. There is the danger that in seeking to serve the advance of community among men the conscientious objector may actually lose touch with the larger communities of which he is already a member, and serve the cause of isolationism instead of more vital world fellowship. We cannot ignore the immensely wide influence that present comradeship in arms will have upon future social, political, and spiritual patterns of life. Besides all these risks to the integrity and actual influence of Christian pacifists, there is the social risk that seems to their critics far more important: the risk that such decision as theirs, if practiced by large enough numbers of Christians, would prevent effective military action by the United Nations, and open the way to control of the world by the totalitarian powers. Yet in spite of these dangers, a minority of the Commission, and a proportionately lesser minority in the churches, are committed to the way of Christian pacifism. To them it appears that resistance to the spread of totalitarian modes of life can best be maintained by Christians who renounce voluntary participation in war, and devote their full energies to practicing as consistently as possible the ways of peace. *They believe that widespread, consistent practice of Christian pacifism is the best way to proclaim now the Church's gospel of reconciliation, and therefore the best way that Christians can help to extend the growth of community among men and nations, and the development of methods other than war for dealing with conflicts of interest.*

Upon Christians who choose this course in war time, there rest special responsibilities of at least two sorts. They must assume voluntarily and wholeheartedly a real share of the burden that the war entails. Most Christian conscientious objectors today, we believe, desire to carry a heavier load rather than a lighter one. They cannot willingly support military action, but they could and would most willingly perform many sorts of arduous and dangerous work for relief of suffering, reconstruction of ruined territories, and ministry to human needs that now are closed against them. We believe that they would be actively grateful for more exacting and varied demands upon their personal resources for service, and that the Church that approves the principle on which they are acting should seek to have their devotion given more significant scope in action. *Meanwhile, it goes without saying that both conscientious objectors of military age and other Christian pacifists must make the most of such ways to serve as may be open to them.* A second responsibility, which they share with all Christians, is the maintenance of understanding, mutual appreciation, and profound fellowship among fellow Christians. This need Christian pacifists cannot meet alone. Yet we believe that the especial risk of isolation which they run should call forth in them an especial, persistent avowal of common faith and hope with their brothers in the Church of Jesus Christ. Among all Christians there is one devotion to the quest for justice and peace. They set out from common premises, seek common goals, and even in their differences can experience together the fellowship of the Holy Spirit.

The Church as a Nucleus for World Community

C. *The most important task of the Church in war time is, indeed, just to be as fully as possible the present embodiment of that fellowship. For in fulfilling this role, the Church can be in principle and to some extent in fact, a present nucleus for the world community that must come to birth.*

There is no warrant for overestimating the influence the Church has now, or will have in the post-war world. Secular forces more powerful than any that history has produced hitherto are alternately seeking to use the Church or to disregard it. A majority of men even in the so-called Christian lands pay it lip-service or none. The Church will not rule the war nor write the peace. In the steps already taken by the Allied great powers toward organizing the post-war world, the dominant influence of vested national interests and of traditional power politics is plain. It is inevitable at least in this stage of history that factors like these should have a major place in the effort to establish world order. Stable large-scale community is not to be had in isolation from large-scale economic and political power. But such power by itself will never produce the community we so desperately need. In fact, possession or quest of great temporal power and exercise of vested privilege tend always to distort any effort to achieve more inclusive unity and greater security. Such power, moreover, the Church itself does not and should not wield. For like every other social institution, the organized Church is liable to the corruption of motive and warping of vision that temporal power and privilege bring, and more than any other institution it can forfeit, through such warping and corruption, its effectiveness for its own proper task. *The Church's task in relation to economic and political power is not to exercise rulership. It is rather to help induce the peoples and governments who may properly wield such power to use it less for immediate gain and more to extend the range of justice, peace, and freedom.* The truth, as Christian faith and fully enlightened reason can see it, is that in thus serving mankind, the great powers of our time would be serving also their own essential interests. But this truth can be fully evident neither to unreflective secular enterprise, nor even to the partly enlightened self-interest of secular prudence. The full strength of powerful tendencies to seek first nearby, clearly visible goods for oneself and one's group always operates to deflect human eyes from more distant goals. The Church must here make common cause with spokesmen of social enlightenment and goodwill, in business, education, press, or political life, to urge the vital need for long-range vision and action.

This need and the difficulty of meeting it are augmented in our day by the brevity of time and by the probable aftermath of war. The demand we face is that power impulses be enlisted for the common good, on the huge scale of international society, within the few years' respite on which we may count after this war. Yet the way is thick with the specific hindrances that arise out of the war itself, some of them noticed in preceding sections of this report, many of them too familiar to need mention. The sum is a task far too great for unaided human powers. In effect, we are called upon to restore a shattered world and to transform it from widespread anarchy to ordered community within one generation—before another war, still more devastating, breaks upon us and our children. For such a task all our secular wisdom, strength, and goodness simply are not enough.

Among all existing institutions, the Church is best able to face this sobering truth without despair. For in the course of a long and growing life, it has shared in the collapse and the transforming of more than one civilization—the Roman empire, the Byzantine world, the feudal order of Christendom—and through such experience has been made all the more vividly aware of the sustaining, redemptive power of God. Today once again the Church can see, pervading and transcending the tumult of world-crisis, His invincible judgment and mercy. At the same time, the Church itself is sharing more inclusively than ever before in the crisis of mankind. In its membership today there are people of all nations and cultures. *The Church that began as a handful of unknown disciples has grown, tenaciously and irrepressibly, through the centuries. Its breadth now, around the globe, is undergirded with the depth and power of proved vitality.* The City of the World is mightier than ever in all the weapons of force, but the City of God still manifests in our time, and that more widely than ever, the unconquered Spirit of life.

Today and tomorrow, that Spirit is the best hope of our war-torn peoples. Their wounds of body and mind and heart the Church must acknowledge as its own, and it must seek to provide for them the healing energies that truth, love, and faithfulness alone possess. Their bewilderment, fear, and despair the Church will need to meet with that demonstration of understanding, mutual forgiveness, and common hope that are its own heritage. *Within its walls, men of all races and cultures have their rightful homes. It will need to make their claims to brotherhood more evident and effective.* In a time when the hope of shared and creative life for all mankind is the one light that can lighten a dark future, the Church must hold that hope high.

With all its faults, the Christian Church in our time is an actual massive embodiment of growing community, and the only one whose organized membership is worldwide. Its long divided constituent bodies are astir today with hunger for closer communion. It seeks a new level of common life among its own people, and in the very quest, it finds an ampler unity-in-difference coming to realization in its own corporate life.

Thus it must come to be, too, in the world society now struggling to find a way of peace. *The Church,* with members now in every major part of that society, and with its faith grounded in the Ever-Living God whose Spirit moves still within His half-finished creation, *can by its very existence as faithful Church help the world* to find that way. The Church must seek to realize yet more fully its own growing unity of spirit, to bring into its communion of faith and love an ever more inclusive company of God's children, and to make its own awareness of divine judgment and forgiveness pervade, like widening daylight, the whole tortured life of our time.

Edwin E. Aubrey
Roland H. Bainton
John C. Bennett
Conrad J. I. Bergendoff
B. Harvie Branscomb
Frank H. Caldwell
Robert Lowry Calhoun
Angus Dun
Nels F. S. Ferré
Robert E. Fitch
Theodore M. Greene
Georgia E. Harkness
Walter M. Horton
John Knox
Umphrey Lee
John A. Mackay
Benjamin E. Mays
John T. McNeill
H. Richard Niebuhr
Reinhold Niebuhr
William Pauck
Douglas V. Steere
Ernest Fremont Tittle
Henry P. Van Dusen
Theodore O. Wedel
Alexander C. Zabriskie

9

The Justice of the Present War Examined

G. E. M. Anscombe

INTRODUCTORY

In these days the authorities claim the right to control not only the policy of the nation but also the actions of every individual within it; and their claim has the support of a large section of the people of the country, and of a peculiar force of emotion. This support is gained, and this emotion caused by the fact that they are "evil things" that we are fighting against. That they are evil we need have no doubt; yet many of us still feel distrust of these claims and these emotions lest they blind men to their duty of considering carefully, before they act, the justice of the things they propose to do. Men can be moved to fight by being made to hate the deeds of their enemies; but a war is not made just by the fact that one's enemies' deeds are hateful. Therefore it is our duty to resist passion and to consider carefully whether all the conditions of a just war are satisfied in this present war, lest we sin against the natural law by participating in it.

THE NATURAL MORAL LAW

This idea of natural moral law is one which modern men have lost; but without it they cannot live in peace within themselves, or socially or internationally. For the natural law is the law of man's own nature, showing how he must choose to act in matters where his will is free, if his nature is to be properly fulfilled. It is the proper use of his functions; their misuse or perversion is sin. So, lying is the misuse of speech, and is therefore wicked. So, justice is the proper working out of relations between man and man, and between societies, each having his due.

To those who believe in God it will rightly appear that His law, the eternal law, has its reflection in the ordered activity of Creation, that 'law of nature' which is the truth of things. In man, this activity is not wholly determined, but there is an element of choice. Thus far, "to him the law is proposed; it is not imposed upon him."[1] But it is not less law for that; it binds because it is the law of his nature. And in what it consists he can discover by reason, checked and guaranteed by the divine revelation of Scripture. Aquinas called it "the participation in the eternal law of the rational creature" (Thomas Aquinas, *Summa Theologiae,* 1a 2ae, Q. 91, art. 2 ad 3); the law in him from his creation, which he, making use of the gifts of reason and revelation, will find for his salvation. Thus will he proceed to his eternal destiny in God; but the condition of the love of God is the observance of the natural law; if man does not live according to his proper nature he will not attain his proper end.[2]

With this in mind, let us proceed to consider what is justice in the matter of war, remembering that whatever human hopes for the happiness of mankind may be, the only way to that happiness is an observance of the law of God without any deviation.

THE CONDITIONS OF THE JUST WAR

There are seven conditions which must be all fulfilled for a war to be just:

(1) There must be a just occasion: that is, there must be violation of, or attack upon, strict rights.

(2) The war must be made by a lawful authority: that is, when there is no higher authority, a sovereign state.

(3) The warring state must have an upright intention in

making war: it must not declare war in order to obtain, or inflict anything unjust.

(4) Only right means must be used in the conduct of the war.

(5) War must be the only possible means of righting the wrong done.

(6) There must be a reasonable hope of victory.

(7) The probable good must outweigh the probable evil effects of the war.[3]

For this present war there is a just occasion; the rights of Poland have been infringed. The war was declared by a lawful authority. There is, so far as we can tell, a reasonable hope of victory. And though we may suspect that war could have been averted by a more intelligent policy up to a very short time before war broke out, yet at the time when war was declared it is possible that the wrong done could not have been righted by peaceful means. But there remain three conditions to be fulfilled: the intentions of our government must be upright, both (1) as to means, and (2) as to ends, and (3) the probable good effects of the war must outweigh the probable evil. If these conditions are not fulfilled, *this* war is rendered wrong, however just the occasion, however desirable that we should fight *a* war. Nor, if we know that a war is wrong, may we take part in it without sin, however grievous it may seem to stand apart from our fellowcountrymen.

We must note that, if we fight a war, it is the government's war, since, as we have seen, wars can only be made by sovereign states. Therefore we cannot say: "The government's intentions are *vicious;* but the things I am fighting for are just," or "The government intends to use evil means, but I shall do nothing unjust." A private person may not make war; and if he joins in a war, he joins in it as justified or vitiated by the just or unjust intentions of the government under which he fights. By "government" we mean the persons holding power in a sovereign state. Another point to note is that a government may succumb to temptation in the course of the war; if this involved departure from any of the seven conditions the justice of the war would be vitiated. But isolated pieces of wickedness, though participation in them would be wrong, would not themselves vitiate the whole war on grounds of intention; the probability of such would simply contribute to the balance of evil effects which must be considered.

ON AIMS

If a war is to be just, the warring state must intend only what is just, and the aim of the war must be to set right certain specific injustices. That is, the righting of wrong done must be a sufficient condition on which peace will be made.

In the present war, we may have grave doubts about our government's sincerity. It may seem that we never cared about Poland, but made the Polish treaty as a pretext for seizing the next opportunity to oppose the German government. Our government was badly frightened; it had been weak; it wanted to take a strong line lest it be utterly discredited; and hence the Polish pact. These beginnings are dubious enough; partly because the injustice done to Poland seems our pretext, not our cause, for entering the war; partly because our government appears to have acted from fear and pride, rather than from a desire for justice. Nevertheless it is not wrong to be afraid of Germany's unjust encroachments and to make war in order to stop them, so long as we feared them because they attacked a just settlement and endangered our just interests. But what is the evidence? After the last war, we made the treaty of Versailles, now condemned by every one. But we have made no attempt to rectify it, even when it became urgently necessary that we should do so. We have not tried to make a just and reasonable settlement with Germany; we have merely allowed Germany to set aside portions of the treaty by force, and with grave injustice. Finally, we have clamoured to negotiate at the last moment, when otherwise Germany would take by force; and our offers have been rejected. Unjustly, it may be; but the evil done by our enemies does not affect our own condemnation.

Our policy, it might be said, is incomprehensible, except as a policy, not of opposing German injustice, but of trying to preserve the status quo and that an unjust one. Some of us may think the case clear enough; yet such argument is likely to lead us into endless controversy. It may be that we could not prove irrefutably that our government's aims are positively vicious. Some might say that the government is not clear enough about its aims for them to be vicious. Yet if this is so, the government's intention in fighting the war must still be condemned. For it is a condition of a just war that it *should* be fought with a *just* intention; not that it should *not* be fought with an *unjust* intention. If the government's intentions cannot be known to be unjust because they are vague, that vagueness itself vitiates them. But the case is even clearer than this. For the truth is that the government's professed intentions are not merely vague, but unlimited. They have not said: "When justice is done on points A, B and C, then we will stop fighting." They have talked about "sweeping away everything that Hitlerism stands for" and about "building a new order in Europe." What does this mean but that our intentions are so unlimited that there is no point at which we or the Germans could say to our government: "Stop fighting; for your conditions are satisfied"[?] It is true that our government has said that it will not consider peace negotiations until certain injustices are set right. But it has made this only a necessary and not a sufficient condition; therefore it is nothing against our argument.

There results a tendency to interpret our government's phrases according to various predilections. A socialist will tell you that he is fighting for social justice and free speech, a Catholic that he is fighting for the Church. We should forget our own desires and consider narrowly what can be deduced from our government's actions, coupled with these vague and inevitable catchwords. There can be only one conclusion: we are fighting against an unjust cause, indeed; but not for a just one.

ON THE MORALITY OF MEANS

Before considering whether or not there are any persons who may not be attacked in war, we must try to elucidate, in however crude a fashion, the doctrine of intention in human acts. For in all actions of rational beings we can distinguish three ends of action: there is the motive or motives of the agent, the proper effect of the act as such, and the completed act itself. These are not always distinct in fact, but they can be; if they do coincide this does not make them less distinct in nature, though the distinction is sometimes subtle. For example, take the action of a carpenter in the stroke of a chisel. His motive may be the glory of God, or the obtaining of wages, or the satisfaction of a completed job, or several or all of these, and more besides. The proper effect of the act as such is the removal of a shaving of wood, and this may also be considered as one of the ends of the agent as well as of the action. The completed act itself is simply the completed successful stroke. Let us apply this analysis to military attack. The motive may be to win the war, or medals, or simply to attack successfully and destroy the enemy who receive the impact of the attack. The proper effect is the weakening, disabling or destruction of those who receive that impact. The completed act itself is the completed attack, or, in the case, let us say, of bombing, the dropping and explosion in the right place of the bomb.

Now as to morals. If an act is to be lawful, it is not sufficient that the motives of the agent should be good, though this is necessary. First, the act itself must not be intrinsically wrong; it must not be such an act as is wrong under any circumstance. Second, the proper effects of the act must be permissible. And unless these conditions are present, the act is wrong. To apply these principles once more in the case of military attack: an attack on men is not intrinsically vicious: is not, that is, a perverted act; it is circumstances that make it right or wrong. The motive of the attackers belongs to a consideration of aims rather than of means; or, if we are considering individual soldiers, it is [a] matter for God at the Last Judgement, not for us here. But what of the proper effects of the completed action? These, as we have seen, consist in the destruction of the persons attacked. If, therefore, the attack is to be lawful, the persons attacked must be persons whom the attackers may legitimately destroy. Our object is to consider whether in warfare these persons include civilians.

ON MEANS

(i) *The prospect of attack on civilians:* It is generally recognized that, in certain circumstances, we shall attack civilians from the air; we are already attacking them by blockade. We have no space to prove these facts in detail: for the first, it suffices to recall the answer made by our government to President

Roosevelt, when he asked for a promise not to attack civilians. We said that we should adhere to international law on the matter, but that we reserved the right "to adopt appropriate measures" if the Germans should break it. If the right to adopt appropriate measures is a reservation to a promise not to attack civilians, then it can only mean that, given certain circumstances, we should attack civilians. The language is veiled, but it can hardly be interpreted in any other way.

(ii) *On blockade:* As for blockade: it has been pretended, in justification, that the blockade is not a blockade; or that it does not attack civilians. But some people, when they are arguing on another subject, when they are assuring us of victory, *then* they tell us that we cannot but win because the Germans cannot survive the blockade, since it prevents things essential to their national life from reaching them. Others, at this point, say that we could not really be responsible for starving the German people, because they divert the supplies to the fighting forces, and therefore are responsible themselves. But this argument admits that civilians do suffer attack and therefore can be dealt with under that head.

(iii) *The 'indivisibility' of modern war and the justification of killing enemies in war:* It is argued that it is just to attack civilians in war because war is now "indivisible." The civilian population is really as much combatant as the fighting forces, for it is their essential backing. The military strength of a country is its whole economic and social strength. Therefore civilians may be attacked as combatants.

Here we must ask two questions: first, what is the justification of killing in war? and, second, in what does the indivisibility of war consist? It is no sin to kill a man in self-defence or in defence of rights, if there is no possibility of appeal to a higher authority. A private person can appeal to the authority of the state, and therefore has no right to choose the death of a man in order to defend his rights; though he commits no sin if his action in resisting attack, at the time of attack, results in the death of the attacker; for such death is accidental. But where there is no higher authority to which to appeal, as in the case of a sovereign state at war, men who are wrongfully attacking rights may be killed in order to defend those rights if they cannot be defended in any other way.

We must notice two things about this doctrine: first that those who are killed are killed as *wrongfully* attacking rights, in virtue of the fact that it is not possible to appeal to any higher authority than the parties in the dispute. In this sense, the justly warring state is 'in the stead of a judge,' having chosen to inflict death on men for the general good. Those men *must* be *wrongfully attacking* rights, or retaining what they have *wrongfully* gained; for it is wrong to slay the innocent for the good of the people. But second, though it proceeds from this quasi-judicial position of the justly warring state, that it can give its ministers authority deliberately to kill its enemies, *yet* they may only kill as a means of self-defence or the defence of rights; the judicial power does not permit them to kill purely punitively; for it is not lawful to kill men simply punitively, except after trial. The justly warring state has to judge of the right or wrong done; but it has no power of judgement on personal guilt or innocence. These two points must therefore be maintained: to quote St. Thomas Aquinas:

> It is unlawful for a man to intend to kill any one in order to defend himself, except for one with public authority; and he, intending to kill a man for his own defence, refers this to the general good, as is plain in the case of a soldier fighting enemies, and the minister of a judge fighting against robbers. (*Summa Theologiae,* 2a 2ae, Q. 64, art. 7)

We have it, then, that no one may be deliberately attacked in war, unless his actions constitute an attack on the rights which are being defended or restored. To deny this will be to assert that we may attack any one anywhere, whose life in any way hinders the prosecution of the war, or in any way assists our enemies; and such a conclusion is as immoral as to be a *reductio ad absurdum* in itself.

Now in what does the 'indivisibility' of war consist? It consists in this, that it would be impossible for the combatant forces to fight, unless they were backed by the economic and social strength of the nation behind them. Therefore, it is argued, the civil population is a military target. To this there is only one reply. The civilian population behind an army does not fulfill the conditions which make it right to kill a man in war. Civilians are not committing wrong acts against those who are defending or restoring rights. They are maintaining the economic and social strength of a nation, and that is not wrong, even though that strength is being used by their government as the essential backing of an army unjustly fighting in the field.

It has been argued that, as accessories to a murder are by law punished equally with the murderer, so the citizens of an enemy country may be killed equally with the fighting forces. But the analogy is false. An accessory is punished as morally guilty of murder. But we have seen that it is not right to kill merely punitively in war; so whatever the guilt of the enemy nation, we cannot arrogate to ourselves the position of a judge, and execute them. A man cannot be judge in his own suit; and we are one of the parties in the quarrel. In default of a higher authority, we may kill those whose actions are an attack on our rights, in order to defend those rights: but the actions must themselves be wrong. The actions of a great mass of the civilian population are not in themselves wrongful attacks on us. Therefore they may not be killed by us, simply as deserving to die, nor yet because their death would be useful to us.

(iv) *A note on reprisals:* It follows from this analysis that no warring state may claim the right to reprisals as such, because the other side deserves them. It is not right to inflict a certain harm on the enemy simply because he has inflicted it on you.[4] The morality of the action itself must be considered before it can be justified.

(v) *On double effect:* It has been argued that it is justifiable to attack civilians because their death is an example of "double effect." But this is no example of double effect, which is exemplified when an action designed to produce one effect produces another as well by accident. If, for example, a military target is being attacked and in the course of the attack civilians are also destroyed, then their destruction is not wicked, for it is accidental. Obviously before their destruction can be passed over on these grounds, it must also be shown that the action is of sufficient importance to allow such grave incidental effects. No action can be excused whose consequences involve a greater evil than the good of the action itself, whether these consequences are accidental or not.[5] Double effect therefore only excuses a grave incidental consequence where the balance of the total effects of an action is on the side of the good.

There is a great distinction between attacking a group of persons directly, and killing them accidentally in the course of attack on others. But yet another distinction must be made. It is a different thing, while making one group of persons a target, to kill others by accident, and to make a group of persons a target, in order—by attacking them all—to attack some members of the group who are persons who may legitimately be attacked. The first case involves no sin; the second involves murder and is not an example of double effect. It has been claimed as such by some who, defending blockade, allow that civilians are not a proper military target, but who argue that attack may be made on a whole group of persons which includes both civilians and combatants. This claim cannot be allowed.

Again, we cannot say with regard to blockade that the starvation of a civilian population by the diversion of supplies to its army is an incidental and unintentional effect of an action intended to demoralize the army. For to do so it would be necessary not only to prove that such an evil effect would in fact be outweighed by the good effects expected, but also that there would be no causal relation between the preceding starvation of a civilian population and the demoralization of an army.[6] This aspect of the problem of double effect is distinct from that treated immediately above. There we were considering whether it is an example of double effect to attack one group of persons as a means of destroying a part of the same group; here, whether an alleged example of double effect is not rather an attack on one group of persons as a means to attacking another and distinct group. Both cases are immoral if a group of, or including, civilians, is made a military target; and neither is a case of double effect.

(vi) *On the balance of good and evil:* It is said that war admittedly produces a number of evil effects, including attacks on civilians, but that these must be balanced against the probable good effects of the war, and if they are outweighed by good, then they can be discounted. It is indeed true that such a balance must be made; but we cannot propose to sin, because that evil will be outweighed by the good effects of the war. That would be to commit sin that good might come; and we may not commit any sin, however small, for the sake of any good, however great; and if the choice lies between our total destruction and the commission of sin, then we must choose to be destroyed.

There is a sense in which it is true to say that the sinful means chosen by the government would not vitiate the whole of a war, on account of the smallness of the sin. Though we could not join in committing the sin, however small, yet if it were very small, it would not, on account of the 'parvity of matter' render the whole war wrong. But unjust deliberate killing is murder and this is a great sin which 'cries to heaven for vengeance'; if, therefore, the warring state intends, under any circumstances, to commit it as a means of prosecuting the war, then the war is made wicked. As we have seen, our government does intend to do that which is unlawful, and it is already blockading Germany with intent to starve the national life. The present war is therefore wrong on account of means.

(vii) *On propaganda:* Europe since the outbreak of war has been comparatively quiet, and in consequence indiscriminate hatred has been far less noticeable than it was during the last war. But as the conflict grows more serious, we cannot expect this state of things to last; already there is less moderation in public speeches and private conversation than at the outset. Worse, there is already suppression and distortion of truth 'in the interests of the state'; and news has become propaganda and advocacy of a case. One man's lies are not justified because they contradict another's. We assert that, on the contrary, to fight for, while not observing, truth, is the same contradiction, madness and unreason which we condemn among the Nazis.

ON THE PROBABLE EVIL EFFECTS OF THE WAR

Finally it remains to consider the last condition. The probable good effects of a war must outweigh its probable evil ones. We hold to the contrary that in this present struggle this condition is not satisfied. We have seen that our government's aims are suspect at the outset; that it is fighting with no desire for justice, so far as we can see, and that it is either ignorant of morals or malicious as far as means are concerned. What is likely to be the end, if we win, if this is what we are like at the beginning? To quote Pope Pius XII in his first encyclical:

> Let us leave the past and turn our eyes to the future which according to those who control the fate and fortune of the peoples, is to consist, once the bloody conflicts have ceased, in a new order, founded on justice and prosperity. Will that future really be different: above all, will it really be better? Will the treaties of peace, will the new international order at the end of the war be animated by justice and equity towards all, by that spirit which frees and pacifies? Or will there be a lamentable repetition of the ancient and recent errors? To hope for a decisive change exclusively from the shock of war and its final issue is idle, as experience shows. The hour of victory is the hour of external triumph for the party to whom the victory falls, but it is, in equal measure, the hour of temptation. In this hour the angel of justice strives with the demon of violence . . . the excited passions of the people, often inflamed by the sacrifices and sufferings they have borne, obscure the vision, even of responsible persons, and make them inattentive to the warning voice of humanity and equity which is overwhelmed and drowned in the inhuman cry 'woe to the conquered.' There is danger lest settlements and decisions born under such conditions be nothing else than injustice under the cloak of justice.[7]

If, therefore, there is little chance of a just and lasting peace, of a "new order in Europe," do not all the inevitable evils which accompany war also condemn this one?

It has been said that the victory of the Allies would at least be better than that of their enemies; for there would be a certain fluidity in the situation which we could scarcely expect if the Germans won. We must repeat that this in itself would supply no justification for the war. And the argument is fallacious. On the one hand no situation is purely static; on the other, a repeated Versailles would determine the future as inevitably and as evilly as the first. The 'preservation of democracy,' the possibility of free speech, and the other such ideals which are valuable only as means, cannot weigh against considerations which belong to the essence of the moral law. The death of men, the curtailment of liberty, the destruction of property, the diminution of culture, the obscuring of judgement by passion and interest, the neglect of truth and charity, the decrease in belief and in the practice of religion—all these are the normal accompaniments of a war. We have, as we have seen, little enough hope of a just settlement to set against such prospects. And finally, there is a widespread tendency to make what our country chooses to do, the criterion of what may be done, and to call this patriotism. So a war against totalitarianism produces a totalitarian tendency; not only are morals lowered, but the very theory of morals is corrupted. If a war lasts a short while, the evils may be slight, but if the war should be engaged in for a long time with a bloody seriousness, then those evil effects will be enormous. Already men are talking of Germany as a pariah nation; they are already saying that she must henceforward be kept down and never allowed to become powerful again. And if they speak thus in England, is it not obvious that our French allies will be even fiercer in this insane determination, which is as foolish as it is immoral? Then after the war, what prospects have we, but of greater poverty, greater difficulties, greater misery than ever, for a space; until just another such war will break out[?]

Such are the probable evil effects; and they greatly outweigh the good effects of putting an end to the injustices of Germany at the present day, since we have so little hope of substituting anything for them but other injustices.

NOTES

1. Sertillanges, quoted "Moral Principles and Practice," Cambridge Summer School (1932), p. 74.
2. For a fuller discussion of the natural law, see Thomas Aquinas, 1a 2ae, 91, 1a 2ae, 94, or any textbook of moral theology.
3. For sources concerning the conditions of the just war, see J. Eppstein, *Catholic Tradition and the Law of Nations* (London, 1935), and, more fully, Regaut, *La Doctrine de la Guerre Juste.*
4. This, of course, does not apply to denunciation or those parts of international law not affected by the natural law.
5. Ctr. Thomas Aquinas, *Summa Theologiae* 2a 2ae, 64, *De Homicidio,* on the example of killing in self-defence. "The force used must be proportioned to the necessity."
6. See any textbook of moral theology.
7. *Summi Pontificatus,* pages 29–30, in the Vatican Latin edition. When quoting from this encyclical we have sometimes made use of the Vatican official English translation, sometimes of the English version of Mgr. Knox; but comparing these with the Latin original we have often found cause to alter the translation ourselves.

10

The Morality of Obliteration Bombing

John C. Ford, S.J.

THE MEANING OF OBLITERATION BOMBING

In general the term obliteration bombing is used as the opposite of precision bombing. In precision bombing very definite, limited targets, such as airfields, munitions factories, railroad bridges, etc. are picked out and aimed at. But in obliteration bombing, the target is not a well-defined military objective, as that term has been understood in the past. The target is a large area, for instance, a whole city, or all the built-up part of a city, or at least a very large section of the total built-up area, often including by design residential districts.

In the early days of the present war the British did not make use of obliteration bombing; the government insisted that only military objectives in the narrow sense were to be aimed at.[1] It was such insistence by the British government that led Canon E. J. Mahoney to justify the Catholic pilot or bombardier ordered by his commanding officers to drop bombs on Continental targets.[2] Churchill, on Jan. 27, 1940, had condemned Germany's policy of indiscriminate bombing as a "new and odious form of warfare."[3] But with the appointment of Sir Arthur Travers Harris to the control of the Bomber Command, on March 3, 1942, the RAF changed its policy and took up obliteration bombing.[4] According to *Time,* the men responsible for the new policy were Sir Arthur Harris, Chief of the RAF Bomber Command, and Major General Clarence Eaker, commander of the United States Eighth Air Force.[5]

The leaders in England acknowledged the new policy. Churchill no longer condemned this "odious form of warfare," and promised the House of Commons on June 2, 1942, that Germany was to be subjected to an "ordeal the like of which has never been experienced by any country." In July, 1943, he spoke of "the systematic shattering of German cities." On Sept. 21, 1943, he said in the House of Commons: "There are no sacrifices we will not make, no lengths in violence to which we will not go."[6] Brendan Bracken, Minister of Information, speaking to the press in Quebec (August, 1943) echoed the leader, saying: "Our plans are to bomb, burn, and ruthlessly destroy in every way available to us the people responsible for creating the war."[7] And when Sir Archibald Sinclair, Secretary of State for Air, was asked in the House of Commons (March 31, 1943) whether on any occasion instructions had been given to British airmen to engage in area bombing rather than limit their attention to purely military targets, he replied: "The targets of Bomber Command are always military, but night bombing of military objectives necessarily involves bombing the area in which they are situated."[8] Area bombing is another name for obliteration bombing.

Leaders in the United States have approved the bombings. President Roosevelt, replying through his secretary, Mr. Stephen Early, to protests against the bombing did not deny that area or obliteration bombing was the present policy, and defended the kind of bombing going on in Germany on the ground that it is shortening the war.[9] A *New York Times* dispatch quotes Chief of Army Air Forces, General H. H. Arnold, as saying that the combined chiefs of staff at the Casablanca Conference had directed American and British Air Forces to destroy the German military, industrial, and economic systems and to undermine the morale of the people. General Arnold is quoted further:

> I remember a day in the summer of 1941, the day a letter from President Roosevelt came to my desk, a letter written to the Secretary of War, asking us to determine what would be required to defeat Germany if we should become involved in the war. The plan drawn up by the air force in response to that letter is in substance the plan we are successfully carrying out right now. (May 23, 1944.)[10]

Because of our bombsight, most of the daytime precision work is assigned to American bombers, while the RAF does the obliteration by night.[11] But the whole strategic plan of wiping out the German cities is agreed on by the leaders of both countries, and the American Air Force on occasion acts interchangeably with the British in obliteration attacks.[12] Accordingly, the moral responsibility for the attacks is shared by both British and American leaders.

I have mentioned the "strategic plan of wiping out German cities"; for the bombing under discussion is strategic as distinct from tactical. The distinction between strategic and tactical operations is not always clear. Sometimes it is said that strategy is the plan of war, tactics the execution of the plan; or, strategy involves the planning and operations which prepare more remotely for the actual combat, the joining in battle. When the battle is joined the operations in support of it are tactical. Thus the bombing of Monte Cassino was clearly a tactical operation, in support of the infantry and artillery. The bombing of the installations along the coast of France on D-Day was clearly a tactical operation in support of the invasion battle. But the bombing of Berlin, Hamburg, and the other eighty-eight industrial centers marked for destruction is clearly a strategic operation. This paper deals only with strategic obliteration bombing. We have nothing to say about the use of tactical bombing as an immediate preparation for battle, or in support of a battle already in progress.[13]

The purpose of this strategic bombing is described by those in charge of it as follows: "The bombing of Germany that is now going on has two main objectives. One is, of course, the destruction of Germany's major industrial cities, with Berlin as the main target because it is the largest as well as the most important of those cities. The other main target is the fighter aircraft factories and all related factories. . . ." Thus [said] Sir Authur Harris, the organizer and chief executive of the obliteration attack.[14] Another purpose is the destruction of railroads and communications generally.[15] And no secret is made of the direct intent to wipe out residential districts where workmen live with their wives and children, so that absenteeism will interfere with industrial production.[16] The leaders have clearly declared their purpose to bomb very large sections of ninety German cities, with the direct intent of wiping out, if possible, not only the industrial but also the residential built-up districts of these cities. In a speech made on November 6, 1943, Sir Arthur Harris said: "We propose entirely to emasculate every center of enemy production, forty of which are centers vital to [this] war effort and fifty that can be termed considerably important. We are well on the way to their destruction."[17] And writing in the *New York Times Magazine*, April 16, 1944, the same leader declares: "There are only thirty industrial towns in Germany with a population over 200,000. . . . Of these thirty major cities there are now only five . . . which have not been seriously damaged. Twelve of them, not including Berlin, . . . now have had their capacity to produce destroyed." He also tells us: "Many cases involve destruction of about half the total built-up area in a city. . . . But many of these industrial towns which have been knocked out of the war are as much as two-thirds or three-quarters devastated." He calls it a "mass destruction of industrial cities."[18]

Charles J. V. Murphy assures us: "In recent months journalists have become aware of the 'blue-book' at Harris' headquarters. . . . In it are vertical maps of every one of the ninety industrial towns and cities of Germany which Harris has marked for 'emasculation'. . . . The industrial areas which include the built-up workers' districts are carefully marked off with a red line. As these are progressively disposed of they are 'blued' out."[19] Murphy also tells us that "Harris' technique . . . is primarily based upon the 'de-housing' of the German worker." And Harris himself reminds us that "in a blitzed town there is at least much loss of production as a result of absenteeism because armament workers have lost their houses and all public transport services are disorganized."[20]

It requires only a little imagination to picture the agonies which this obliteration bombing has inflicted on the civil populations. Since the bombs, including incendiaries, are aimed at whole areas, and aimed at residential districts on purpose, and over these districts are dropped blindly and indiscriminately, deaths of civilians, men, women, and children, have been very numerous. At times the bombs have been dropped through heavy banks of clouds so that the target (that is, the city) could not be seen at all. When the navigation instruments told them they were over the city, they dropped their enormous bomb loads.[21] (According to a press report, the Allies dropped 147,000 tons of explosives on Europe during the month of May, 1944.)

The details of injuries and death to civilians and their property are described at great length by Vera Brittain in the article cited above. She quotes a member of the German Government Statistics Office in Berlin, that over a million German civilians were killed, or reported missing (believed killed) in air raids from the beginning of the war up to October 1, 1943. These figures cannot be verified, and some believe they are unreliable German propaganda.[22] All we can say is that the loss of civilian life has been very great, and that in the interval since October 1, 1943, the combined air forces of Britain and the United States have done much more obliteration bombing than they did before that date. Compared with what we have done, the German blitz over England seems paltry. The words of John Gordon, editor of the *Sunday Express,* in which he welcomed the new policy of obliteration, have been literally fulfilled: "Germany, the originator of war by air terror, is now finding that terror recoiling on herself with an intensity that even Hitler in his most sadistic dreams never thought possible."[23] . . .

The following discussion of the morality of obliteration bombing does not depend altogether on the truth of the facts alleged by Vera Brittain. . . . I have given these facts and many more . . . in order that the phrase obliteration bombing might be given a definite meaning. That definite meaning (or definition) I couch in the following terms: *Obliteration bombing is the strategic bombing, by means of incendiaries and explosives, of industrial centers of population in which the target to be wiped out is not a definite factory, bridge, or similar object, but a large area of a whole city, comprising one-third to two-thirds of its whole built-up area, and including by design the residential districts of workingmen and their families.* If this kind of bombing is not taking place, so much the better. But we have such compelling reasons for thinking it does, that the following discussion of its morality is necessary.

THE MORAL PROBLEM RAISED BY OBLITERATION BOMBING

I do not intend to discuss here the question: Can any modern war be morally justified? The overwhelming majority of Catholic theologians would answer, I am sure, that there can be a justifiable modern war. And the practically unanimous voice of American Catholicism, including that of the hierarchy, assures us that we are fighting a just war at present. I accept that position. Our question deals rather with the morality of a given means made use of in the prosecution of a war which itself is justified.

However, it cannot be denied that this question leads us close to the more general one as to the possibility of a just modern war; for obliteration bombing includes the bombing of civilians, and is a practice which can be called typical of "total" war. If it is a necessary part of total war, and if all modern war must be total, then a condemnation of obliteration bombing would logically lead to a condemnation of all modern war. With Father Ulpian Lopez, of the Gregorian University, I do not intend to go that far.[24] I believe that it is possible for modern war to be waged within the limits set by the laws of morality, and that the resort to obliteration bombing is not an essential part of it, even when war is waged against an enemy who has no scruples in the matter. But I call attention to the close connection between the two questions to show that I am not unaware of the implications. If anyone were to declare that modern war is necessarily total, and necessarily involves direct attack on the life of innocent civilians, and, therefore, that obliteration bombing is justified, my reply would be: So much the worse for modern war. If it necessarily includes such means, it is necessarily immoral itself.

The morality of obliteration bombing can be looked at from the point of view of the bombardier who asks in confession whether he may execute the orders of his military leaders, or it may be looked at from the viewpoint of the leaders who are responsible for the adoption of obliteration bombing as a recognized instrument of the general strategy of war. The present paper takes the latter viewpoint. It is not aimed at settling difficulties of the individual soldier's conscience.

Of course, there is an unavoidable logical connection between the morality of the whole plan and the morality of the act of the bombardier who executes the plan. If the plan is immoral, the execution of it is immoral. And nobody is allowed to execute orders to do something intrinsically wrong on the plea that he did it under orders. But when the priest in the confessional is presented with a comparatively new problem like this one—a problem which may involve tremendous upheavals in the consciences of many individuals, and on which ecclesiastical authorities have not laid down definite norms—he will necessarily hesitate before refusing absolution. When he has, besides, a well-established rule based on the presumption which favors civil authorities, and which in ordinary cases justifies subordinates in carrying out orders, his hesitation will increase. I believe that as far as confessional practice is concerned, the rule I suggested in 1941 (before we entered the war) is a safe one: "The application of our moral principles to modern war leaves so much to be desired that we are not in a position to impose obligations on the conscience of the individual, whether he be a soldier with a bayonet, or a conscientious objector, *except in the cases where violation of natural law is clear.*"[25] A clear violation of natural law can be known to the ordinary individual soldier in a case of this kind through the definite pronouncement of the Church, or of the hierarchy, or even through a consensus of moral theologians over a period of time. On the question of obliteration bombing we have no such norms. The present article obviously does not supply the need. Hence, I believe the confessor is justified in absolving the bombardier who feels forced to carry out orders to take part in obliteration bombing, unless the penitent himself is convinced (as I am) of the immorality of the practice.

The present paper attempts to deal with the problem on a larger scale. The Popes have condemned as immoral some of the procedures of modern war, but they have abstained, as far as I know, from using terms which would put a clear, direct burden on the conscience of the individual subordinate in a new matter like the present one. Later on I shall attempt to show that obliteration bombing must be one of the procedures which Pius XII has condemned as immoral. But my viewpoint at present is that of one trying to solve the general moral problem, not of teaching confessors at what point they must draw the line and refuse absolution. Incidentally, I do not believe a discussion of probabilism, or of what is probably allowable in this matter of bombing, would be fruitful, once one takes the larger point of view. Probabilism is the necessary resort of those who cannot find the truth with certainty, and yet must act. In confessional practice one must rely on it in some form or other. But to approach a major moral question probabilistically would be to confess at the start that the truth is unattainable. Such a state of mind would not be likely to contribute to the science of morality. My object is to make the small beginning of such a contribution.

The principal moral problem raised by obliteration bombing, then, is that of the rights of non-combatants to their lives in war time. Rights are protected by laws. The laws in question are the international law, the law of humanity, and the natural law. These distinct names are heard continually, especially in the documents of the present Pope.[26] But they do not always stand for distinct things. Sometimes international law coincides with and reinforces natural law, or the laws of humanity. And so of the others. The ideas often overlap. But, insofar as they are distinct from one another, that distinction may be briefly indicated and illustrated as follows.

The rights which are protected by mere international law, are derived from positive compacts or treaties between governments, binding in justice, but ceasing to bind when the other party to the contract has ceased to observe it. For instance, certain laws that deal in detail with the treatment to be accorded prisoners are in this category. (I do not mean to imply that a single breach of an international engagement, or of a part of one, by one of the governments immediately releases the other government from all its contractual obligations to the first.)

The laws of humanity are rather vague norms based on more or less universal feelings of what decency, or fair play, or an educated human sympathy demand, but not based on compacts, and not clearly—as to particulars at any rate—contained within the dictates of the natural law. And sometimes the laws of humanity mean the laws of Christian charity, made known to us through the Christian revelation and exemplified in the life of Jesus Christ. For instance, the use of poison gas, or the spreading of disease germs among enemy combatants, if not forbidden already by international law, would be forbidden at least by the laws of humanity. It is not so clear, though, that such methods of putting the enemy soldiers out of the fight would be against the natural law.

I say that this is an example of what is meant by the law of humanity, insofar as this law is distinct from natural or international law. Actually, when the laws of humanity are mentioned, some precept of natural law is often involved. And it has been the task of international law, too, under the nourishing influence of the Christian religion, to protect the natural rights of combatants and non-combatants alike. International agreements have led to a clarification of natural precepts, and made certain what the laws of humanity would leave uncertain, and made definite and particular what the law of nature contained only in a general way. The widespread abandonment of international law which characterizes the conduct of total war, the retrogression towards barbarism in every direction, is one of the most frightening developments in modern times. It is a disease that can destroy civilization.[27]

The present paper, though not excluding considerations based on international law and the law of humanity, will deal principally with the natural-law rights of non-combatants.[28] And our chief concern will be the right of the non-combatant to life and limb. His right not to have his property taken or destroyed (or his family torn asunder) is also pertinent, but will be mentioned only incidentally. Hence, we can put the moral problem raised by obliteration bombing in the form of the following questions, which the rest of the paper will try to answer:

1) Do the majority of civilians in a modern nation at war enjoy a natural-law right of immunity from violent repression?

2) Does obliteration bombing necessarily involve a violation of the rights of innocent civilians?

COMBATANTS AND NON-COMBATANTS

It is fundamental in the Catholic view that to take the life of an innocent person is always intrinsically wrong, that is, forbidden absolutely by natural law. Neither the state nor any private individual can thus dispose of the lives of the innocent. The killing of enemy soldiers in warfare was justified by older writers on the theory that they were not innocent but guilty. They were guilty of unjust aggression, or of a violation of rights which could be forcibly vindicated. The individual enemy soldiers might be only materially guilty, but it was this guilt, and their immediate cooperation in violent unjust acts that made them legitimate objects of direct killing. As far as I know, this distinction between the innocent and guilty has never been abandoned by Catholic theologians. They still maintain that it is always intrinsically wrong to kill directly the innocent civilians of the enemy country.

But in the course of time the terms innocent and guilty have been replaced by the terms non-combatant and combatant, or by civilian and soldier.[29] And the definitions of these terms have been clarified by conventions of international law.[30] Writing in 1910 Mr. J. M. Spaight said:

> The separation of armies and peaceful inhabitants into two distinct groups is perhaps the greatest triumph of international Law. Its effect in mitigating the evils of war has been incalculable. One must read the history of ancient wars, or savage wars of modern times—such as Chaka's campaigns, by which he made the Zulu name terrible throughout the northern Natal—to appreciate the immense gain to the world from the distinction between combatants and non-combatants.[31]

The contribution of international law has been to make precise the definition of combatant and non-combatant and to determine just who is a legitimate object of lethal attack and who is not. Thus the natural-law distinction between innocent and guilty received the sanction of explicit pacts. Furthermore, the term non-combatant included *all* who were not bearing arms, whether they were strictly "innocent" or not, and so the number of those who were immune from attack was increased. The present immunity from direct violence, which the entire civilian population enjoys (theoretically), is based partly on natural law and partly on international law.

I do not believe any Catholic theologian, in the face of papal and conciliar pronouncements, and the universal consensus of moralists for such a long time, would have the hardihood to state that innocent non-combatants can be put to death without violating natural law. I believe that there is unanimity in Catholic teaching on this point, and that even in the circumstances of a modern war every Catholic theologian would condemn as intrinsically immoral the direct killing of innocent non-combatants. Since the denial of this proposition would be rash, I do not believe it incumbent on me to support it by further argument in a journal of this kind.

The thorny question is rather: *Who are to be considered non-combatants in a war like the present one?*

The same Mr. J. M. Spaight, who in 1910 wrote of the great triumph of international law in separating combatants from non-combatants, has written a book in 1944 called *Bombing Vindicated.* He was formerly Principal Assistant Secretary to the British Air Ministry. His thesis is that modern industrial cities are battlefields, and that British "strategic" bombing is a justifiable form of attack on them. He avoids the term obliteration, and insists that the targets are military. He makes little of the civilian losses, though he gives fully many of the horrifying details. He considers them pitiable, but only incidental to the attack on war production. He says not a word of Sir Arthur Harris' explicit aim of destroying residential districts. He believes the distinction between civilian and soldier is an anachronism in the "battle-towns," and he quotes approvingly one of the most cynical statements made during the war. Mr. Churchill, he tells us, solves the civilian problem thus:

> The civilian population of Germany have an easy way to escape from these severities. All they have to do is to leave the cities where munition work is being carried on, abandon the work [as if the majority were engaged in it] and go out into the fields and watch the home fires burning from a distance. In this way they may find time for meditation and repentance. There they may remember the millions of Russian women and children they [was it they or the German army?] have driven out to perish in the snows, and the mass executions of peasants and prisoners of war which in varying scales they [they?] are inflicting on so many of the ancient and famous peoples of Europe.[32]

Mr. Churchill's target is "the life and economy of that whole guilty organization."[33]

All-out exponents of the theory of total war would go even further than Mr. Spaight. He at least is speaking of civilians who are munitions workers, and distinguishes between them and their wives and children. But others (explicitly or implicitly) proceed on the theory that *all* the inhabitants of the enemy country—men, women, and children—are legitimate objects of direct attack.[34]. . .

THE CONTEMPORARY QUESTION OF FACT

It is obvious . . . that the conditions of modern war are changed, and the change makes it very difficult and sometimes impossible to draw accurately the line which separates combatants from innocent non-combatants according to natural law. Soldiers under arms are obviously combatants. It is not so clear what is to be said of civilian munitions workers, the members of various organized labor battalions not under arms, and so of others. Of these doubtful classes I do not intend to speak. In the end, only new international agreements will effectively and precisely protect the rights of these groups.

But it is not necessary to draw an accurate line in order to solve the problem of obliteration bombing. It is enough to show that there are large numbers of people even in the conditions of modern warfare who are clearly to be classed as innocent non-combatants, and then that, wherever the line is drawn, obliteration bombing goes beyond it and violates the rights of these people. It seems to me that an unnecessary attitude of defeat is betrayed by writers like Dr. McReavy, who seem to think that, because we do not know exactly where to draw the line, therefore we have to act as if there were no line at all between innocence and guilt (and hence find some other ground for protecting civilians from savagery). I think it is a fairly common fallacy in legal and moral argumentation to conclude that all is lost because there is a field of uncertainty to which our carefully formulated moral principles cannot be applied with precision.[35] It seems to me, furthermore, that this mentality is encouraged if one is taking the view of a confessor who thinks in terms of absolution for the individual penitent, and who naturally does not want to deny it unless he is certain that he has to. Finally, in this present matter, I think this defeatist mentality is encouraged in moralists who, as it were, have been put on the defensive by public, "patriotic," and official opinion, and overwhelmed with talk of the radically changed conditions of modern war—as if everything were now changed, and all or almost all civilians now played a direct part in the war, and as if in the past, when the classical formulas were put together, the civilians who were declared untouchable in those formulas had little or nothing to do with the war effort of their countries. Is it not evident that the most radical and significant change of all in modern warfare is not the increased co-operation of civilians behind the lines with the armed forces, but the enormously increased power of the armed forces to reach behind the lines and attack civilians indiscriminately, whether they are thus co-operating or not?

And so the question arises, who has the burden of proof—the civilian behind the lines, who clings to his traditional immunity, or the military leader with new and highly destructive weapons in his hands, who claims that he can attack civilians because modern industrial and economic conditions have changed the nature of war radically and made them all aggressors[?] Do we start with the supposition that the whole population of the enemy is presumably guilty, and that anyone who wants to exempt a group from that condemnation is called upon to prove the innocence of the group? Or do we start with the view that only armed soldiers are guilty combatants and anyone who wants to increase the number of the guilty, and make unarmed civilians legitimate objects of violent repression, has the duty of proving his position? Is it not reasonable to put the burden of proof on those who are innovators? Do we not start from here: "Thou shalt not kill"? Seeing that the wartime rights of civilians to life and property are declared by centuries of tradition to be sacrosanct, what do we presume: a man's right to his life, even in war time, or my right to kill him? his right to his property, or my right to destroy it? Not merely the conscience of humanity, not merely international law, but the teaching of Catholic theologians for centuries, the voice of the Church speaking through her Councils and through her hierarchy and through the Supreme Pontiff down to the present day, uniformly insist on the innocence and consequent immunity of civil populations. It is obviously the burden of those who think that distinction invalid (or, what comes to the same thing, completely impractical) to prove their contention. I can understand how a confessor, with thoughts of probabilism running through his head, would feel that when he refuses absolution he has the burden of showing he has a right to refuse it. But I cannot understand a moralist taking that point of view with regard to the rights of civilians. He has not the burden of proving these rights. On the contrary, those who want to increase the number of combatants, and include large numbers, even the "vast majority," of the civilian population amongst the guilty, must justify themselves.

The principal justifications I have seen are worthless. They say: the enemy did it first; or, military necessity demands it; or, it is justified by way of reprisal; or, the present situation is desperately abnormal (as if there were ever a war which was not); or, nowadays the whole nation takes part in the aggression, whereas formerly it was only army against army. As to this last point, it is true that the number of civilians who contribute immediately to the armed prosecution of the war has increased in modern times, but to say that all or nearly all do so is a grave distortion of the facts, as we shall see. And to imply that in the past the general civilian population co-operated not at all or only negligibly is equally far from the facts. Armies in the past had to be supplied with food, clothing, guns, and ammunition, and it was the civilian population who supplied them. The Church and the theologians in declaring civilians innocent realized very well that even in former times civilian sympathies, their moral support, and their actual physical aid went to further the cause of their country.

Perhaps the governments would like to enlist the active and immediate participation of all civilians in the war itself; but even this is doubtful. And the fact is that they do not succeed in doing so, and from the very nature of the case cannot. Even in a modern war there remains necessarily a vast field of civilian work and activity which is remote from the armed prosecution of the war.

Let us see for a moment what the abandonment of the distinction between combatants and non-combatants would mean in practice; or what it would mean to say that hardly any civilians are innocent in a modern war, because all are co-operating in the aggression. It would mean, for instance, that all the persons listed below are guilty, and deserve death, or at least are fit objects of violent repression. I should not inflict this long list on my readers (though I really believe one can profit by its careful perusal), unless I were convinced that some have been misled by the propaganda of total-war-mongers, or have taken uncritically at their face value statements about "a nation in arms," or "all co-operate in the aggression," or "the enemy has mobilized the whole population," or "nobody is innocent except the infant." Read the list. If you can believe that these classes of persons deserve to be described as combatants, or deserve to be treated as legitimate objects of violent repression, then I shall not argue further. If, when their governments declare war, these persons are so guilty that they deserve death, or almost any violence to person and property short of death, then let us forget the law of Christian charity, the natural law, and go back to barbarism, admitting that total war has won out and we must submit to it. The list:

> Farmers, fishermen, foresters, lumberjacks, dressmakers, milliners, bakers, printers, textile workers, millers, painters, paper hangers, piano tuners, plasterers, shoemakers, cobblers, tailors, upholsterers, furniture makers, cigar and cigarette makers, glove makers, hat makers, suit makers, food processors, dairymen, fish-canners, fruit and vegetable canners, slaughterers and packers, sugar refiners, liquor and beverage workers, teamsters, garage help, telephone girls, advertising men, bankers, brokers, clerks in stores, commercial travelers, decorators, window dressers, deliverymen, inspectors, insurance agents, retail dealers, salesmen and saleswomen in all trades, undertakers, wholesale dealers, meatcutters, butchers, actors, architects, sculptors, artists, authors, editors, reporters, priests, laybrothers, nuns, seminarians, professors, school teachers, dentists, lawyers, judges, musicians, photographers, physicians, surgeons, trained nurses, librarians, social and welfare workers, Red Cross workers, religious workers, theatre owners, technicians, laboratory assistants, barbers, bootblacks, charwomen, cleaners and dyers, hotelmen, elevator tenders, housekeepers, janitors, sextons, domestic servants, cooks, maids, nurses, handymen, laundry operatives, porters, victuallers, bookkeepers, accountants, statisticians, cashiers, stenographers, secretaries, typists, all office help, mothers of families, patients in hospitals, prison inmates, prison guards, institutional inmates, old men and women, all children with the use of reason, i.e., from seven years up. (After all, these latter buy war stamps, write letters of encouragement to their brothers in the service, and even carry the dinner pail to the father who

works in the aircraft factory. They all co-operate in some degree in the aggression.[36])

Do these persons, whom I consider to be, almost without exception *certainly innocent non-combatants according to natural law,* constitute a large proportion of the general civilian population? Here again, though it is impossible to give accurate figures for the proportion, it can be maintained with complete certitude that they constitute the vast majority of the entire civil population even in war time. In an industrial country like the United States they represent at least three-quarters of the total civil population, and probably much more. In other countries the proportion would vary according to the degree of industrialization and militarization, but I am convinced that even in the most totally war-minded country in the world the certainly innocent civilians far outnumber those whose status could be considered doubtful.

This estimate of three-quarters can be arrived at in various ways. For instance, the total estimated population of continental United States in 1944 could be placed roughly at 135 millions. An estimate of the armed forces is 11 millions. This leaves a civilian population of 124 millions. (The government census estimated the civilian population as of March 1, 1943, at more than 128 millions.) Of these 124 millions, it would be a very generous estimate that would place the number of those engaged in war work and essential work (manufacturers immediately connected with the violent prosecution of the war, mining, transportation, communications, and even public offices close to the war) at 31 millions of people, that is, one-quarter of the whole civilian population.

I call this a generous estimate for the following reasons. In 1930, when our total population (continental United States) was about 123 millions, the census showed about 49 million persons over 10 years of age gainfully employed. Of these only about 15 millions at the most could be considered as working in industries, manufacturing, and other occupations, which in case of war would become connected closely with the prosecution of the war. It might be argued that at the present time these occupations have more than doubled their numbers, but this would be to forget that the general population has also increased 12 millions meanwhile, and that furthermore a very large number of the 11 million service men have been recruited from these same manufacturing and war industries.

Another approach is to take the total population in 1945, roughly estimated at 136 millions, and subtract from it, first, an estimated army and navy of 12 millions. Of the 124 million civilians left, 68 millions are women, 16 millions are male children under 14 years of age, and more than four and one-half millions are men over 65 years of age. Thus the civilian population of 124 millions contains 88 millions of women, children, and old men. Of course, some (a few millions perhaps?) of these women make munitions and do other war work, as do also some of the old men. They also take part in transportation and communications and other "essential" work. But many more millions of men are not in war work. And making all due allowance, it still seems to be a very safe estimate that at least three-quarters of the civilian population are in no sense giving such immediate co-operation to the armed prosecution of the war that they can be considered combatants, or guilty of aggression, or deserving of violent repression. Further statistics with regard to industrial cities, which will be given later, will confirm this general estimate.

The conclusion of this section of our paper is an answer to the question: Do the majority of civilians in a modern nation at war enjoy a natural-law right of immunity from violent repression? The answer is an emphatic affirmative. The great majority, at least three-quarters in a country like the United States, have such a right.

Now let us proceed to consider whether obliteration bombing, as carefully defined above, violates the rights of innocent non-combatants.

OBLITERATION BOMBING IMMORAL

I have defined obliteration bombing as follows: *It is the strategic bombing, by means of incendiaries and explosives, of industrial centers of population, in which the target to be wiped out is not a definite factory, bridge, or similar object, but a large section of a whole city, comprising one-third to two-thirds of its whole built-up area, and including by design the residential districts of workingmen and their families.* It is perfectly obvious that such bombing necessarily includes an attack on the lives, health, and property of many innocent civilians. Above I estimated that at the very least three-quarters of the civilian population in a country like the United States must be classed as certainly innocent civilians, and immune from attack. That estimate applied to the general population and was an extremely modest one. But even in industrial cities in war time there is a very large proportion of the civil population which it would be certainly immoral to attack—most women, almost all children under 14 years, almost all men over seventy, and a very large number of men who are engaged neither in war manufactures, transport, communications, nor in other doubtful categories. At least two-thirds and probably more are certainly to be classed among the innocent—an estimate based on figures supplied by statisticians of the War Manpower Commission.

For instance, in July, 1944, the Boston Labor Market Area had a total population of about 1,800,000. Of these, the War Manpower Commission estimates that only about 800,000 are gainfully employed, i.e., much less than fifty per cent. Now I feel sure that very few people who are not gainfully employed at all can be classed as proximate co-operators in the armed prosecution of the war. And of those who are employed, a very large number are only remotely connected with the war effort. A statistician connected with the Commission estimates that out of the 800,000 we should consider only about 300,000 as essential war workers. The other 500,000 have been called "less essential" because their connection with the war is more remote. Even the classification "essential" would probably include many persons, such as textile workers making Army cloth and uniforms, etc., who are far from being engaged in violent warlike action.[37]

Making due allowance for government officials, semimilitary personnel, such as air-raid wardens, WAVES, WACS, etc., it is very conservative to say that at least two-thirds of the total population of the Boston area is so remotely connected with the violent prosecution of the war that no stretching of terms or principles could make them legitimate objects of violent repression.

If Boston were subject to obliteration attack, not all the area would become a target. But the principal, more densely populated parts of it would, e.g., North End, South End, West

End, East Boston, South Boston, Dorchester, Charlestown, Everett, Chelsea, Brighton, parts of Brookline, Cambridge, Hingham, Quincy, etc. Perhaps the number of munitions workers and "warlike" workers in these districts forms a higher percentage. It is impossible to find out. (Nor would the Germans bother to find out if they could take up obliteration bombing against us, as we have against them.) In any event, to say that two-thirds of the civil population liable to this kind of bombing is innocent is to make a conservative estimate. . . .

And lest anyone be surprised at this result, we should always remember that fifty per cent of the population throughout the United States is female, and about fifteen per cent are male children and old men. Facts and common sense tell us to guard carefully against the total-war fallacy that the whole nation is arrayed in arms against the whole enemy nation.

These figures are for typical centers of industry in the United States. What the figures would be in Germany no one can tell. But even in Germany in 1939 only about one-half of the total population was listed by the census as gainfully employed. And of these almost one-half were engaged in agriculture, trade, and domestic service. Allowing for higher percentages in the industrial centers (comparable to Boston), now that the war has been going on five years, we are still safe in estimating that the majority of the inhabitants even in the centers of war production marked for devastation and obliteration are innocent civilians.[38]

The Principle of the Double Effect

And so the immorality of obliteration bombing, its violation of the rights of these innocent civilians to life, bodily integrity, and property would be crystal clear, and would not be subject to dispute, at least amongst Catholics, were it not for the appeal to the principle of the double effect. This principle can be worded as follows: The foreseen evil effect of a man's action is not morally imputable to him, provided that (1) the action in itself is directed immediately to some other result, (2) the evil effect is not willed either in itself or as a means to the other result, (3) the permitting of the evil effect is justified by reasons of proportionate weight.

Applying the principle to obliteration bombing, it would be argued: The bombing has a good effect, the destruction of war industries, communications, and military installations, leading to the defeat of the enemy; it also has an evil effect, the injury and death of innocent civilians (and the destruction of their property). The damage to civilian life (and property) is not intentional; it is not a means to the production of the good effect, but is merely its incidental accompaniment. Furthermore, the slaughter, maiming, and destruction can be permitted because there are sufficiently weighty excusing causes, such as shortening the war, military necessity, saving our own soldiers' lives, etc. This viewpoint, therefore, would find a simple solution to the moral problem merely by advising the air strategist to let go his bombs, but withhold his intention. In what follows I shall attempt to show that this is an unwarranted application of the principle of the double effect.

The principle of the double effect, though basic in scientific Catholic morality, is not, however, a mathematical formula, nor an analytical principle. It is a practical formula which synthesizes an immense amount of moral experience, and serves as an efficient guide in countless perplexing cases. But just because it is called into play to solve the more difficult cases, it is liable to sophistical abuse. Some applications of it can only be called casuistical in the bad sense of that word.[39] It is a truism among moralists that, though the principle is clear in itself, its application requires "sound moral judgment." It seems to me that the following are the points which require a moral, rather than a mathematical or merely verbal, interpretation of the principle, when it is applied in practice.

First, when is it possible, psychologically and honestly, for one to avoid the direct willing of an evil effect immediately consequent upon one's action; or to put it another way, when can an action, estimated morally, be considered really twofold in its immediate efficiency? Secondly, when is the evil effect to be considered only incidental to the main result, and not a means made use of implicitly or explicitly to produce it? To arrive at a sound moral estimate in these matters, it is often helpful to consider the physical proximity of the good and evil effects, or the inevitable and immediate character of the evil effect in the physical order, to consider its extent or size by comparison with the good effect immediately produced, and to consider especially whether the evil effect *de facto* contributes to the ultimate good desired, even if not explicitly willed as a means. And, of course, a careful estimate must be made of the proportionate excusing cause, in the light of all the circumstances that have a bearing on the case. Perhaps this is only saying that without common sense the principle of the double effect may lead to casuistical conclusions; but I believe I am saying more than that. I am pointing out that the principle is not an ultimate guide in difficult cases, because it is only a practical formula and has to be applied by a hand well practiced in moral principles and moral solutions.

The Question of Intention

As to obliteration bombing, then, is it possible to employ this procedure without directly intending the damage to innocent civilians and their property? Obviously, the destruction of property is directly intended. The leaders acknowledge it as an objective. And on this score alone one could argue with reason against the morality of the practice. But since the property of civilians is not so absolutely immune as their persons and lives from direct attack in war time, I prefer to deal mainly with the latter.

Looking at obliteration bombing as it actually takes place, can we say that the maiming and death of hundreds of thousands of innocent persons, which are its immediate result, are not directly intended, but merely permitted? Is it possible psychologically and honestly for the leaders who have developed and ordered the employment of this strategy to say they do not intend any harm to innocent civilians? To many, I am sure, the distinction between the material fabric of a city, especially the densely populated residential areas, and the hundreds of thousands of human inhabitants of such areas, will seem very unreal and casuistical.[40] They will consider it merely playing with words to say that in dropping a bomb on a man's house, knowing he is there with his family, the intent is merely to destroy the house and interfere with enemy production (through absenteeism), while permitting the injury and death of the family.

Dr. John K. Ryan of Catholic University wrote on this point as follows (after the present war started, but before we entered it):

> The actual physical situation in great modern cities is not such that they can be subjected to attack on the principle

that only industrial, military, administrative and traffic centers are being attacked directly, while the damage done to non-combatants is only incidental and not an object of direct volition. Modern cities are not as compact and fortresslike as were those of the past. Their residential sections are so extensive, so clearly defined, and so discernible, that it is for the most part idle to attempt to apply the principle of indirection to attacks on these districts. Thus to rain explosives and incendiary bombs upon the vast residential tracts of say, Chicago, or Brooklyn, the Bronx, and the suburbs of New York City, on the score that this is only incidental to attack on munition plants and administrative headquarters in other parts of the city, cannot stand the slightest critical examination either moral or logic, as an instance of the principle of the double effect. In such an argument is contained the explicit distinction between groups and sections that may be made the object of direct attack and other groups and sections that are immune from such attack. But incendiary and explosive bombs would hardly respect this distinction, for they destroy with equal impartiality either group. When an entire city is destroyed by such means the military objectives are destroyed indirectly and incidentally as parts of a great civil center, rather than vice versa. It is a case of the good effect coming along with, or better after and on account of the evil, instead of a case where the evil is incidental to the attainment of a good. . . . It is hardly correct to think and speak of the damage done to life and property in such situations as being 'incidental destruction.' Rather it is the realistic interpretation of this situation to hold that any good gained is incidental to the evil, and that the phrase 'wholesale destruction of property and civilian life' indicates the true relation between the good and evil effects involved. The evil effect is first, immediate and direct, while any military advantage comes through and after it in a secondary, derivative, and dependent way. As far as the principle of the double effect is concerned, an attack upon a large city with the weapons of modern warfare is the direct opposite of such an attack with the weapons of earlier days. . . . The general civil suffering from the immediate effects of total war cannot be justified on the score that it is indirect. Justification for the infliction of such suffering must be sought by other means, and it is doubtful if even war-time propaganda can present the new warfare as other than it is—a direct and intended offensive against the non-combatant population of the nations at war, especially as concentrated in large numbers in the great capital and industrial cities.[41]

Obliteration bombing would come squarely under the condemnation of this argument.[42] It is enough to recall that in a single raid on Cologne (according to Mr. J. M. Spaight, one of the most enthusiastic and articulate defenders of the bombing), 5000 acres of the built-up part of the city was wiped out.[43] That means a territory eight miles square. And the American Army Air Forces' official story of the first year of bombing says of Hamburg: "Well over 2200 British and American aircraft dropped more than 7000 tons of high explosive and incendiaries on a city the size of Detroit. To quote an official report: 'There is nothing in the world to which this concentrated devastation of Hamburg can be compared, for an inferno of this scale in a town of this size has never been experienced, hardly even imagined, before.' "[44] The total weight of the bombs dropped on Hamburg in seven days equaled the tonnage dropped on London during the whole of the 1940–1941 blitz.[45] Mr. Spaight informs us: "What the effect was may be inferred from the ejaculations of one German radio commentator (Dr. Carl Hofman): 'Terror . . . terror . . . terror . . . pure, naked, bloody terror.' "[46]

More than nine square miles of Hamburg (77 per cent of its built-up area), including the largest workers' district in the city, were completely wiped out, according to British reports of the raids.[47] An RAF commentator said: "To all intents and purposes a city of 1,800,000 inhabitants lies in absolute ruins. . . . It is probably the most complete blotting-out of a city that ever happened."[48] This kind of thing is still going on. In July, 1944, General H. H. Arnold, commanding general of our Army Air Forces, announced that latest reports indicated that 40 to 50 per cent of the central portion of Berlin is "burned out. . . . Berlin is a ruined city." The bomber chief also stated that the Army Air Force plans to continue its air offensive against Germany, "burning out" its industries and war centers.[49]

If these are the facts, what is to be said of the contention that the damage to civilian property and especially to civilian life is only incidental? Is it psychologically and honestly possible for the air strategist in circumstances like these to let go his bombs, and withhold his intention as far as the innocent are concerned? I have grave doubts of the possibility.

But there is another reason for excluding the possibility of such merely indirect intent. At the Casablanca conference, the combined chiefs of staff ordered a joint British-United States air offensive to accomplish "the progressive destruction and dislocation of the German military, industrial and economic system and *the undermining of the morale of the German people* to the point where their capacity for armed resistance is fatally weakened."[50] *Target: Germany,* an official publication of the air forces, tells us that "the two bomber commands lost no time in setting about the job. To the RAF fell the task of destroying Germany's great cities, of silencing the iron heart-beat of the Ruhr, *of dispossessing the working population, of breaking the morale of the people.* The mission of VIII Bomber Command was the destruction of the key industries by which the German military machine was sustained."[51] This same authoritative publication (presented with a foreword by General Arnold himself) makes it clear that the terrorization of civilians is part of our bombing strategy. "Bombs behind the fighting fronts may rob armies of their vital supplies and make war so terrible that civilian populations will refuse to support the armed forces in the field. . . . *The physical attrition of warfare is no longer limited to the fighting forces.* Heretofore the home front has remained relatively secure; armies fought, civil populations worked and waited. This conflict's early air attacks were the first portents of a changing order." And after saying that we now follow the "bloody instructions" given us by the Nazis, and after describing the destruction of Hamburg and other industrial cities, this official account says: "Here, then, we have *terror and devastation* carried to the core of a warring nation."[52]

Now I contend that it is impossible to make civilian terrorization, or the undermining of civilian morale, an object of bombing without having a direct intent to injure and kill civilians. The principal cause of civilian terror, the principal cause of the loss of morale, is the danger to life and limb which accompanies the raids. If one intends the end, terror, one cannot escape intending the principal means of obtaining that end, namely, the injury and death of civilians.

Both from the nature of the obliteration operation itself,[53] then, and from the professed objective of undermining morale, I conclude that it is impossible to adopt this strategy without having the direct intent of violating the rights of innocent civilians. This intent is, of course, gravely immoral.

On the question of direct intent it is well to remember, too, that it would be altogether naive to suppose that our military and political leaders were thinking in terms of a distinction between direct and indirect. Without impeaching their moral characters in the least, it is only common sense to recognize that their practical guiding norms in a matter of this kind are military necessity and political expediency. This is not to deny that they have consciences and follow them, but it is to doubt whether their consciences are sufficiently delicate to give them any trouble when this type of decision has to be made. When our forces bombed Rome, the officials took extreme care to hit only military objectives. And they took even greater care to broadcast the precautions they had taken, and to get statements from Catholic pilots defending the operation. Now if this solicitude had been due to a sincere regard for the morality of aiming at non-military targets, or for the necessity of avoiding direct intentional injury of the innocent, they would exercise the same care in every city they bombed, or at least in every comparable case. But I do not think it is cynical to believe that they were more interested in religious *feelings* and world reaction than they were in the morality of killing the innocent whether directly or indirectly, and of destroying non-military property. The present bombing of Germany confirms this view. From the moral point of view, the lives of the innocent inhabitants of Germany or any other country are far more precious than the religious monuments of Rome, or the real estate of the Holy Father. But we hear nothing of a week's preliminary briefing to insure the safety of non-military targets in Berlin. We hear just the opposite. We hear the word obliterate.

Furthermore, we continually hear the argument: "They did it first," as a justification of our bombing of Germany. The argument is that since the Germans have attacked our innocent civilian populations on purpose, we can do the same thing to them.[54] Mr. Norman Cousins, editor of the *Saturday Review of Literature*, who has interested himself in the subject of obliteration bombing, apparently believes that any procedure whatever, no matter how brutal, is moral and legitimate for us to adopt once the enemy adopts it: "Once the enemy *starts* it [poison gas, and even, it seems, indiscriminate bacteriological warfare] it becomes no longer a moral but a military question, no longer a matter of argument but a matter of action."[55] Mr. Churchill's appeal to the popular revenge motive has been public.[56] At the present time there are numerous calls for revenge of the robot bombing. An editorial in the *Boston Herald* asks: "Why not go all out on bombings? . . . *Why be nice about the undefended towns and cities?* . . . The time-honored system of tit for tat is the only one which Hitler and his Germans can understand."[57] The *New York Times* had an editorial along the same lines.[58] And in a letter to that paper one Carl Beck demands an ultimatum from the chiefs of the four United Nations, threatening Germany that "for every prisoner murdered we will take ten German lives, for all civilian mass murder we will take an equivalent number of Germans the minute we reach their soil—we ourselves will treat all prisoners according to civilized warfare."[59]

Naturally one does not expect political leaders to assert definitely that they intend to kill women and children.[60] The feelings of the whole civilized world are so completely in accord with the traditional distinction between innocent and guilty, and such a very large number of people (with votes) everywhere consider themselves to be among the innocent, that it would probably be political suicide to announce explicitly such a policy; and even from the military point of view it would provide the enemy with priceless propaganda. Any attack on the innocent civil population will always be covered up by a euphemistic name, like "area" bombing, or simply written off under the general absolution of "military necessity." My point, therefore, is to indicate that we have good grounds for suspecting that the *de facto* intent of the air strategists is not governed by the morality of direct and indirect intent at all, and that it is naive and unrealistic to imagine them conforming themselves to the principle of the double effect on this score.

The Question of a Proportionately Grave Cause

But furthermore, the question of direct or indirect intent is not decisive in the application of the principle of the double effect. There still remains the question of proportionately grave causes to justify the alleged "permission" of the evil. Even if I doubted, therefore, about the abstract possibility of "holding back the intention," I would have no doubt about the immorality of obliteration bombing. When it is carried out on the scale described, I am convinced it lacks all sufficient justification. And though the question of proportionate cause involves military considerations on which the moralist cannot speak with authority, yet it also includes strictly moral elements. And so, leaving aside for the moment the authority of the Pope (whose voice can be effectively appealed to on this question), as well as those principles of charity and humanity which, by law and example, Christ made the very groundwork of our religion, let us see whether the element of proportionate cause is satisfied in the general strategy of obliteration.

The principal reason alleged to justify the infliction of enormous agonies on hundreds of thousands and even millions of innocent persons by obliteration bombing is the reason of military necessity, or of shortening the war. We hear that "it must be done to win the war"; "it will shorten the war and save our soldiers' lives"; "it will liberate Europe and enable us to feed the starving sooner." Major General J. F. C. Fuller, writing long before obliteration bombing was an issue, said: "When however it is realized that to enforce policy, and not to kill, is the objective [in war] and that the policy of a nation though maintained and enforced by her soldiers and sailors is not fashioned by them but by the civil population, surely then if a few civilians get killed in the struggle they have nothing to complain of—'dulce et decorum est pro patria mori!' "[61] Mr. J. M. Spaight makes the amazing claim that the long-range bomber, built for operations like the present one in Germany, is the savior of lives, of civilization, and the cornerstone of future peace.

Now in the practical estimation of proportionate cause it is fundamental to recognize that an evil which is certain and extensive and immediate will rarely be compensated for by a problematical, speculative, future good. The evil wrought by obliteration is certain injury and death, here and now, to hundreds of thousands, and an incalculable destruction of their property. The ultimate good which is supposed to compensate for this evil is of a very speculative character.

When Great Britain first adopted obliteration as a policy, Mr. Churchill called it an experiment. He did not know whether it would work or not.[62] The U. S. Army Air Forces in their account of the first year's work in Germany say: "*Target: Germany* is the story of an experiment," and admit that after a year "the final evaluation is yet to be made," and from the nature of the case cannot be made ahead of time or even at the time of the bombing. The effects on future battles are too far removed—sometimes not felt for six months.[63] To the question, "Will bombing win the war?", *Target: Germany* replies: "To the military logician the question is beside the point. Aerial assault is directed both at the enemy's will to resist and his means to resist. One may collapse before the other; either eventuality is desirable. Bombing will be carried out to the fullest extent in either case."[64] Naturally the authors of *Target: Germany* have confidence in the military effectiveness of their strategy, but they are far from talking in terms of certainty, and they are talking of the whole air strategy, both the British and American assignments. It is well known, besides, that many military men and many air force men doubted the effectiveness of the strategic bombing of industrial centers. The French military officials were against it.[65] According to Mr. Spaight, the Germans have never believed in its military effectiveness for Germany.[66] This is not the time when we can expect the opponents of strategic bombing to voice their views. After all they are in the service, we are at war, and the defenders of the bombing have had their ideas officially endorsed. But on the merits of the question, whether this bombing is a profitable and effective strategy from the military point of view, there is disagreement among the military experts themselves.

We are told by a competent reporter of facts that Churchill had "powerful critics of the British Bomber command inside his own Air Ministry. . . . [Certain] British airmen . . . have come to distrust his bomber strategy. . . . The night attacks on German industrial populations, they think, are too haphazard, the targets too far back in the production sequence, to affect German military strength *now*. They argue that quite aside from ethical considerations Harris' technique . . . is not necessarily shortening the war." The same writer tells us that there is a "small but influential group of British intellectuals who have been arguing privately that the economic and social problems deriving from the wrecking of German communities will prove more disastrous in the end than the immediate problem which bombing is supposed to bypass."[67]

The United States' air leaders, though fully co-operating with British obliteration methods, cannot help betraying their preference for American precision work. And criticism of the general strategy over Germany is not unheard of among military men in this country. In a forthcoming book, Colonel W. F. Kernan, the well-known strategist, will express his opinion that bombing cities is the wrong strategy—this from a purely military point of view.[68]

It remains to be seen, therefore, whether this type of bombing is a military *necessity* in order to win the war sooner and save British and American lives. The bombing of Monte Cassino was called a military necessity in order to save American lives; but the military experts proved to be mistaken. "Military necessity" can become a mere catchword, and a cloak for every sort of excess, especially when the judgment is made entirely on military grounds without taking into account other factors, such as psychology (not to mention morality).[69] Germany's strategic bombing of England was held to be a failure partly because it stiffened the resistance of the English. Who can say to what extent our obliteration will strengthen rather than weaken the German will to resist—or to what excesses of cruel retribution against our soldiers the people will be aroused? There are many military men who still agree with Marshal Foch: "You cannot scare a great nation into submission by destroying her cities."[70] Members of the French hierarchy have warned us that our bombing in France (the argument holds a fortiori for Germany), "by striking blindly at innocent populations, by mutilating the face of our country, might engender between our nations a volume of hatred which not even the peace will be able to assuage."[71] And more than one observer has noted the extreme cautiousness with which Russia has resorted to this type of bombing, in western Europe. Russia is not making enemies unnecessarily, where she intends to govern.

The next argument—that obliteration bombing will hasten the day when our victorious arms will enable us to feed the starving millions abused by the Axis—seems to contain an element of hypocrisy. If we wanted to feed starving Europe, we (the United States and Great Britain) could feed millions of the innocent right now. Mr. Hoover has pointed out the way. It does not become us to omit to feed the millions we certainly could feed now, and adopt obliteration with its immense torture of the innocent on the plea that it *may* enable us to feed the hungry later on; especially when President Roosevelt's personal envoy, Colonel Donovan, spoke as follows to the French ambassador at Ankara in the spring of 1941: "The American people are prepared to starve every Frenchman if that's necessary to defeat Hitler."[72] It would be more forthright to argue as Mr. Spaight does that *since* it is permissible to starve civilians, then why is it not permissible to go on bombing them?[73] At least this points up the moral issues instead of beclouding them.

To all these bizarre claims, that attacks on the civilian population are a humanizing element in modern war, I think the following words of Dr. Ryan are relevant: "From a merely utilitarian standpoint, these attacks cannot be justified, for they would spread destruction rather than restrict it, lengthen a war rather than shorten it, provide bitter causes for future conflicts rather than the conditions of a lasting peace."[74]

I conclude from all this that it is illegitimate to appeal to the principle of the double effect when the alleged proportionate cause is speculative, future, and problematical, while the evil effect is definite, widespread, certain, and immediate.

But my argument can be pressed still further, and on more general grounds. Even if obliteration bombing did shorten this war (and if the war ends tomorrow we shall never know whether it was this type of bombing that ended it), and even if it did save many military lives, we still must consider *what the result for the future will be if this means of warfare is made generally legitimate.*

Can we afford to justify from this time forward obliteration bombing as a legitimate instrument of war? Once it is conceded that this is a lawful means of waging war, then it is equally available to our enemies, present and future. They will have just as much right to use it against us as they have to use guns against our soldiers. I do not believe any shortening of the present war, or any saving of the lives of our soldiers (problematical at best) is a cause sufficient to justify on moral grounds the use of obliteration bombing in the future.

For in practice, though one may adhere verbally to the distinction between innocent and guilty, the obliteration of great sections of cities, including whole districts of workers' residences, means the abandonment of that distinction as an effective moral norm. When the innocent civil population can be wiped out on such a large scale very little is left practically of the rights of the innocent. Each new and more terrifying procedure, with more and more loss of innocent life, can always be defended as a mere extension of the principle, justified by the desperate military necessities of the case. The wiping out of whole cities is a reversion to barbarism as far as civilian rights are concerned. Already there is talk of using gas when we go into the Far East. The present demands of legislators, editors, and others for the indiscriminate bombing of *non-industrial* towns in Germany is a clear example of an inevitable tendency—once you get used to the idea of obliteration, and justify it.

This is another way of saying that the recognition of obliteration bombing will easily and quickly lead to the recognition of total war itself. Some may say, of course, that we recognize total war already and are waging it. But that would be a gross exaggeration. Dr. Guido Gonella tells us: "The totality of war is generally understood in a three-fold sense. It applies to the *persons* by whom and against whom warlike action is exercised, to the *means* which are employed in war, and to the *places* where warlike action takes place. (The term war-like action is taken in the broadest sense, including not only military action but also every form of manifestation of hostility, for example, by economic blockade, by the war of nerves etc. . . .)" And again: "If total war is defended as a war which is fought without regard to any limitations affecting persons, or means of warfare, or places," then it must be condemned as immoral.[75] All Catholics, following the lead of the Pope, the hierarchy, and firmly established moral principles, condemn total war in this, its fullest, sense. To say that war need know no restraint in these matters is equivalent to asserting that men at war are no longer bound by the natural law at all. And so the elimination of total war was one of the main objectives of the Holy Father's Christmas message of 1941.

I do not think any American or British statesman or leader believes we are waging, or should wage war in this utterly unrestrained and barbaric manner. But I do think the theory of total war, proclaimed unashamedly by some of our enemies, has made an impression on leaders and on the popular mind. The phrase has been tossed about like the phrase "military necessity," and it becomes a cover-all to hide and excuse practices which would otherwise be readily recognized as immoral. The false notion that today whole peoples are waging war against whole peoples is insinuated or openly propagated, and the conclusion is drawn that whole peoples are legitimate objects of attack.[76]

Now the air bombardment of civilian centers is a symbol of total war in its worst sense. It is the first thing that comes to mind when the phrase "total war" is heard. The air bombardment of great centers of population lets down the bars, and opens up enormous categories of persons, hitherto immune, against whom war-like action can now be taken; it changes the scene of war-like activity from the battlefield to the city, and not only to the war factories but to the residential districts of the workers; and it uses explosives and incendiaries to a hitherto unheard of degree, leaving only one more step to go to the use of poison gas or bacteriological war. This means that obliteration bombing has taken us a long step in the direction of immoral total war. To justify it, will, I believe, make it exceedingly difficult to draw the line at further barbarities in practice. If the leaders of the world were well educated in moral matters and conscientious in the application of Christian moral principles to the waging of war, the danger might not be so real. But half of them are not Christian at all and worship material force as an ultimate, while almost all of them are immersed in a completely secularized tradition. If *moralists* grant them the vast horrors of obliteration bombing, what will stop them from that point on? If one were merely applying the principle of the double effect to the act of an individual bombardier dropping a bomb, such considerations would not be very much to the point; but when the question is the whole strategy of obliteration, these larger considerations, the thought of future consequences for the whole civilized world, are the most important elements to be remembered in estimating proportionate cause. . . .

CONCLUSION

The conclusion of this paper can be stated briefly. Obliteration bombing, as defined, is an immoral attack on the rights of the innocent. It includes a direct intent to do them injury. Even if this were not true, it would still be immoral, because no proportionate cause could justify the evil done; and to make it legitimate would soon lead the world to the immoral barbarity of total war. . . .

NOTES

1. J. M. Spaight, *Bombing Vindicated* (London: Geoffrey Bles, 1944), p. 67; also Vera Brittain, "Massacre by Bombing," *Fellowship,* X (March, 1944), 51.
2. E. J. Mahoney, "Reprisals," *Clergy Review,* XIX (Dec., 1940), 471.
3. Vera Brittain, *loc. cit.*
4. Vera Brittain, *loc. cit.;* J. M. Spaight, *loc. cit.;* Charles J. V. Murphy, "The Airmen and the Invasion," *Life,* XVI (Apr. 10, 1944), 95.
5. "Highroad to Hell," *Time,* July 7, 1943.
6. A week or two later, Mr. Churchill, in a message to Bomber Command, described the process as "beating the life out of Germany." Also on Sept. 21, 1943, he told the House of Commons: "The almost total systematic destruction of many of the centers of German war effort continues on a greater scale and at a greater pace. The havoc wrought is indescribable and the effect upon the German war production in all its forms . . . is matched by that wrought upon the life and economy of the whole of that guilty organization . . ." (Vera Brittain, *op. cit.,* p. 52); cf. also Charles J. V. Murphy, *op. cit.,* p. 95.
7. Vera Brittain, *op. cit.,* p. 52.
8. *Loc. cit.*
9. *New York Herald Tribune,* Apr. 26, 1944; Vera Brittain's reply to President Roosevelt, "Not Made in Germany," appears in *Fellowship,* X (June, 1944), 106.
10. May 23, 1944.
11. Sir Arthur Travers Harris, "The Score," *New York Times Magazine,* Apr. 16, 1944, p. 35; cf. also *Target: Germany,* The Army Air Force's Official Story of the VIII Bomber Command's First Year over Europe (New York: Simon and Schuster, 1943), pp. 19–20.
12. *Target: Germany, loc. cit.*
13. J. M. Spaight, *Bombing Vindicated,* pp. 24 ff.
14. "The Score," *op. cit.,* p. 35.
15. *Target: Germany,* pp. 19, 115.
16. Charles J. V. Murphy, *op. cit.,* p. 95.

17. Vera Brittain, *op. cit.*, p. 53.
18. Harris, "The Score," *op. cit.*, p. 36.
19. Charles J. V. Murphy, *op. cit.*, p. 105.
20. *Ibid.*, p. 95.
21. *Ibid.*, p. 104.
22. But Vera Brittain, in "Not Made in Germany," *Fellowship*, X (June, 1944), 107, maintains the reliability of her figures against criticism by Shirer.
23. Vera Brittain, "Massacre by Bombing," p. 52.
24. "Los inocentes y la guerra," *Razon y Fe*, CXXVIII (Sept.–Oct., 1943), 183.
25. "Current Moral Theology," *Theological Studies*, II (Dec., 1941), 556.
26. Cf. *Principles for Peace* (Washington: N.C.W.C., 1943), *passim.*
27. On this point Guido Gonella writes eloquently in *A World to Reconstruct* (Milwaukee: Bruce, 1944), Chap. XII.
28. Discussion of the morality of obliteration bombing became widespread in this country with the publication of Vera Brittain's "Massacre by Bombing" in *Fellowship*, X (March, 1944), 50. The article consisted of extracts from a book which appeared in England under the title, *Seed of Chaos.* A similar but much briefer article by R. Alfred Hassler, "Slaughter of the Innocent," had appeared in *Fellowship*, Febr., 1944. The reception accorded Vera Brittain's sober recital of facts, and moral arguments, is described by James M. Gillis in "Editorial Comment," *Catholic World*, CLIX (May, 1944), 97, who believes that obliteration, on Catholic principles, is clearly immoral. But both the facts and the moral *status quaestionis* of Miss Brittain's article were almost universally ignored or misrepresented by the press. There was an almost complete evasion of the moral issues involved. Even the President's reply, made through Mr. Early, is well characterized by the author herself as "irrelevant, unjustified, and destructive of the very ideals with which the American people went to war" ("Not Made in Germany," *Fellowship*, X, June, 1944, 106). Other discussions of her article, or of the subject of obliteration bombing from the moral point of view: *Saturday Review of Literature*, X (June, 1944), 106; *Christian Century*, March 15, 1944; March 22, 1944; *The Nation*, March 18, 1944; *Newsweek*, March 20, 1944; Nicholson, "Bombing Civilian Centres," *Spectator*, June 4, 1943; W. Johnstone, "Obliteration Bombing," *Spectator*, Sept. 24, 1943; *Commonweal*, March 17, 1944; March 31, 1944 (flatly condemning obliteration bombing as murder); *America*, May 27, 1944 (urging precautions but abstaining from judgment); Thos. H. Moore, S.J., "Obliteration Bombing," *The Founder* (239 Fingerboard Road, Staten Island, N. Y.), April, 1944; *The London Tablet*, May 20, 1944; *The Labor Leader* (New York), Apr. 30, 1944.

Bombing Vindicated (London: Bles, 1944), by J. M. Spaight, is written mostly from the military point of view, but touches on morality, and is a most important book on the subject of the strategy of obliteration bombing and its implications. The Catholic hierarchy of the United States have not offered any joint opinions that I know of on the morality of our present bombing strategy, but they condemn indiscriminate bombing. Individual bishops have spoken in terms that condemn obliteration, e.g., Most Reverend Gerald Shaughnessy, D.D., S.M., of Seattle (cf. *The Catholic Worker,* May, 1944). The Australian hierarchy, protesting the threat to Rome, condemned indiscriminate bombing. . . . John L. Bazinet, S.S., has given excellent arguments against obliteration bombing, which have appeared in the Catholic press.

29. E. J. Mahoney, "Reprisals," *Clergy Review* XIX (Dec., 1940), 471. Canon Mahoney holds that the terms combatant and non-combatant must now be replaced by the terms military and non-military objective; and he believes that it is absolutely essential to allow a very wide latitude in defining what is a military objective in modern warfare. Cf. also J. K. Ryan, *Modern War and Basic Ethics* (Milwaukee: Bruce, 1940), p. 35, who cites A. Pillet, *La guerre et le droit* (Louvain, 1922), p. 14.

30. Louis le Fur, *Précis de droit international public* (Paris; Dalloz, 1939), nn. 889–91. "Belligerents and non-belligerents. The distinction between these two classes of persons is, or at least for centuries has been, a fundamental principle of the law of nations in time of war. Non-belligerents are the civilian population; belligerents those who form a part of the armed forces. . . . Before the war [World War I] the distinction . . . was admitted unanimously and considered essential."

31. *War Rights on Land* (London, 1910), p. 37, cited by Ryan, *op. cit.,* p. 98.

32. *Bombing Vindicated,* p. 95; Mr. Churchill spoke these words in a broadcast on May 10, 1942.

33. Vera Brittain, "Massacre by Bombing," *Fellowship,* X (March, 1944), 52; Mr. Churchill was speaking to the House of Commons. On May 19, 1943, Mr. Churchill said, speaking in the Congress of the United States: "Wherever these centers [of war industry] exist or are developed they will be destroyed, and *the munitions population will be dispersed*" (my italics; cited by Spaight, *op. cit.,* p. 95). What Churchill effectively said to the "munitions-civilians" of the centers marked for obliteration was, in Mr. Spaight's words: "Get out while the going is good. If you don't, we'll bomb you out." Neither Mr. Spaight nor Mr. Churchill suggests any practical means of evacuating all innocent civilians from at least ninety German cities. When

the robot bombing started, London authorities had great difficulty in evacuating a small part of the public.

34. We have had examples of this theory in the mass executions by the Reds in Spain and in Poland, and by the Nazis in Poland, France, and elsewhere.

35. We do not talk this way in the matter of the absolutely grave sum, even though it is impossible to draw the line with precision. Even in philosophy, when determining what is a miracle, we admit we do not know how far nature can go, but we are sure of some things that are beyond her powers.

36. Note also that the civilian populations of neutral countries are also aggressors on this theory—for they supply food and raw materials to the enemy—and so on *ad infinitum.* Another point to be remembered is that when strategic air blows are struck at the very beginning of a war, the populations that feel their heavy weight have not had time to become guilty aggressors.

37. The above estimate does not take into account Army and Navy personnel within the area. Statistics on that point are naturally unavailable, but we should remember that only about 8% of the total U. S. population is in uniform, and that the above area has no large troop concentrations included in the rough estimate of its total population.

38. I have seen the statement made that 10% of the population of the Ruhr is engaged at least part time in air defence work. This would include, I suppose, both the military personnel and the civilian passive defence services. Spaight, *Bombing Vindicated,* p. 115, says: "All the civilians enrolled in the service of passive defence—the fire-fighters, the fire-watchers, the rescue parties, the demolition squads—cannot be classed otherwise than as warriors," and hence are liable to direct lethal attack. The logic of total war is inexorable. I can set fire to your house. When your wife tries to put the fire out, she becomes a "warrior" and I can kill her. Spaight claims immunity for civilians who are not engaged in definitely warlike activities (p. 112), but in practice he extends warlike activity to include fire-watching and rescuing of the wounded.

39. Even St. Thomas has been accused repeatedly of defending the subtle proposition: When you kill an unjust aggressor you merely permit his death while intending to save your own life. Vincente Alonso, *El principio del doble efecto en los comentadores de Santo Tomas* (Rome: Gregorian University Dissertation, 1937), has shown that in II-II, q. 64, a. 7, St. Thomas merely held that the killing of an unjust aggressor must be willed only as a means, not as an end in itself. St. Thomas did not know the principle of the double effect as we formulate it.

40. "When the Germans launched their blitz on the English

cities in 1940 there was a widespread and intense moral indignation at the volume of wholly indiscriminate slaughter and ruin which was only remotely and casuistically to be associated with attacks on ports or factories," says an editorial in *The London Tablet,* CLXXXIII (May 20, 1944), 243. The editorial goes on to say that conditions made it necessary for the British in their bombing to "widen the definition of the target to cover industrial areas and the dwellings of those who worked in the factories." *The Tablet* does not approve this, neither does it condemn it. I consider such "widening the definition of the target" to be a casuistical device.

41. John K. Ryan, *Modern War and Basic Ethics,* pp. 105 ff.

42. But I do not know Dr. Ryan's opinion on this present problem, which arose after he had written the above. To the casual, or even the careful reader of his book, it would appear that he did not believe in the possibility of a just modern war at all. But we know from his later repudiation of this thesis that it had never been his intention to defend it; cf. *Ecclesiastical Review,* CVIII (May, 1943), 350.

43. Spaight, *op. cit.,* p. 96.

44. *Target: Germany,* p. 19.

45. *Loc. cit.*

46. Spaight, *op. cit.,* p. 89.

47. Vera Brittain, "Massacre by Bombing," *Fellowship,* X (March, 1944), 57.

48. *Loc. cit.* Another RAF commentator said that "the greatest destruction from these raids has been to business and residential property, especially in the built-up area." Estimates of those killed varied from 65,000 to 200,000 but these figures have been questioned. Owing especially to phosphorus and incendiaries, Hamburg experts in charge of salvaging bodies believed that in the fire district only a very small percentage of the population, even those in shelters, escaped death.

49. *New York Times,* July 4, 1944.

50. *Target: Germany,* p. 117 (italics added).

51. *Loc. cit.*

52. *Ibid.,* p. 19 (italics added). Charles J. V. Murphy denies the terror motive, saying that the real motive as to civilians is "to hound him with the multiplying incidents of catastrophe . . ." (*op. cit.,* p. 95).

53. Mr. Spaight's description of obliteration technique inadvertently confirms the view that a great deal more than the so-called target is really aimed at. Because precision work was not effective, "it was necessary to bring into use projectiles of such destructive capacity that when launched from great heights on the estimated target area they could be counted upon to wreck the target as well as

(unfortunately) much else besides. The justification of the method must rest on military necessity." Actually this means that one aims at a whole area in order to get at a target. The destruction of the target is incidental to the destruction of the *estimated target area (Bombing Vindicated,* p. 98). On p. 97 he describes the terrible "bomb-splash"; we do not know yet how devastating it is.

54. Mr. Spaight does not argue thus, however, in *Bombing Vindicated.* He claims that Germany never had a strategic bomber command and was seriously opposed to this kind of bombing in the present war, for reasons of self-interest (pp. 30, 41, 42, 47, 72, 74). England started building her strategic force in 1936 (p. 30). (Charles J. V. Murphy, "The Airmen and the Invasion," *Life,* Apr. 10, 1944, p. 95, says the English air force "has been painstakingly assembled since 1940 to do area bombing." General Arnold [see above, note 10] says that the general plans for our present bombing of Germany were laid in the summer of 1941.) Mr. Spaight thinks that England would inevitably have gone bombing in Germany even if Germany had never bombed England (p. 149). "We began to bomb objectives on the German mainland before Germans began to bomb objectives on the British mainland. That is a historical fact which has been publicly admitted" (p. 68). But Germany was the first to bomb towns in the present war, e.g., in Norway (p. 150). Warsaw and Rotterdam were different because there the bombing was tactical—in immediate support of the invading army (p. 43, 149). Mr. Spaight's contention is that to Great Britain belongs the credit and honor of adopting long ago the strategy now being applied (pp. 73, 143). [At the Disarmament Conference of 1932, Italy proposed the abolition of the bombing airplane and was supported by Germany, Russia, and the United States. Great Britain blocked the proposal because she wanted to reserve the use of the bomber for "police work," i.e., for bombing unruly native populations in India. According to *Time,* July 7, 1943, it was Sir Arthur Harris who introduced this technique.] Mr. Spaight is in doubt as to whether the English reservation killed the 1932 proposal at Geneva, but thinks we should at least say: "They [Eden and Lord Londonderry] did not kill the proposal to abolish bombing. If they had done so they would have done something of inestimable value to our national interests and the cause of civilization."

55. "The Non-Obliterators," *Saturday Review of Literature,* Apr. 8, 1944, p. 14.

56. On July 15, 1941, Churchill approved this sentiment: "We will mete out to the Germans the measure and more than the measure that they have meted out to us." He also made revengeful statements before the United States Congress regarding Japan

(Vera Brittain, "Not Made in Germany,"*Fellowship,* X, June, 1944, 108). Mr. Churchill gave the Golden Rule a new twist in a speech broadcast on May 10, 1942. He said that Bomber Command had done a great thing in teaching "a race of itching warriors that there is something after all in the old and still valid Golden Rule" (Spaight, *Bombing Vindicated,* p. 103).

57. *Boston Herald,* July 4, 1944 (italics added).

58. *New York Times,* June 1, 1944.

59. *New York Times,* July 20, 1944. The question of revenge does not constitute any theoretical problem for the moralist. Such a motive includes hatred and is clearly immoral. It violates the Gospel law. But reprisals, as that term is used in international law, must be distinguished from revenge. When used as a last resort and with due regard for the moral law, they can be legitimate; cf. Louis le Fur, *Précis de droit international public* (Paris: Dalloz, 1939), nn. 873, 908. But their use is always dangerous, because it leads to a grim competition of frightfulness; cf. A. Messineo, S.J., "Le rappresaglie e la guerra," *Civiltà Cattolica,* Anno 92 Vol. I (March 15, 1941), p. 420.

60. The statement of Mr. Stanley Baldwin quoted by Fr. Joseph Keating is exceptional: "The only defence is offence which means that you have to kill more women and children more quickly than the enemy [can] if you want to save yourselves" (quoted in "The Ethics of Bombing," *The Catholic Mind,* XXXVI, July 22, 1938, 279, note 3); the speech was made in the House of Commons on Nov. 10, 1932.

61. Quoted by John K. Ryan, *Modern War and Basic Ethics,* p. 115, note. Dr. Ryan gives many references to writers who hold the theory that attacking civil populations is a humanizing element in war.

62. According to *Time,* July 7, 1943, Churchill "stated the reaction of the global strategists when he said, 'The experiment is well worth trying so long as other measures are not excluded.' " This was after Harris and Eaker had given assurances that Germany could be bombed out of the war in 1943. Seven months later this had not taken place.

63. *Target: Germany,* p. 19.

64. *Target: Germany,* p. 118; also p. 115; "The purpose of this book has been factually to record the testing of a new concept of vertical warfare."

65. Spaight, *Bombing Vindicated,* pp. 70–71.

66. *Loc. cit.* Mr. Spaight himself has no doubt about the policy.

67. Charles J. V. Murphy, "The Airmen and the Invasion," *Life,* Apr. 10, 1944, p. 95.

68. Col. Kernan is the author of *Defense Will Not Win This War*

(Boston: Little, Brown, 1942), and *We Can Win This War* (Boston: Little, Brown, 1943). His forthcoming book will be called *Let's Be Heroic,* and it is in Chapter V that he expresses his views on the strategy used over Germany.

69. Vera Brittain, "Not Made in Germany," *Fellowship,* X (June, 1944), 108, answers the President's argument that bombing, in the opinion of an overwhelming percentage of military authorities, is shortening the war. She says: "It is, however, well known that most military authorities possess expert minds which are necessarily limited to their own sphere. With rare exceptions they are apt to perceive only one aspect of the present and little of the future, and their judgments tend to be based on mathematical calculations rather than on human reactions."

70. Quoted by John K. Ryan, *Modern War and Basic Ethics,* p. 117, note.

71. *London Tablet,* CLXXXIII (May 20, 1944), 246.

72. Quoted in *America,* LXX (June 10, 1944), 279.

73. *Bombing Vindicated,* p. 120.

74. *Modern War and Basic Ethics* (1st. ed.; Washington, D.C., 1933) p. 101.

75. *A World to Reconstruct,* Chap. XII.

76. See S. L. A. Marshall, *Blitzkrieg* (New York: Wm. Morrow, 1940), especially pp. 32, 111, 145, 149; George Fielding Eliot, *Bombs Bursting in Air* (New York: Reynal and Hitchcock, 1939), pp. 23–25; Lt. Col. Harold E. Hartney, *What the Citizen Should Know about the Air Forces* (New York: Norton, 1942), p. 205; Fletcher Pratt, *America and Total War* (New York: Smith and Durell, 1941); Cyril Falls, *The Nature of Modern Warfare* (New York: Oxford University Press, 1941); E. J. Kingston-McCloughry, *Winged Warfare* (London: Jonathan Cape, 1937); General Wladyslaw Sikorski, *Modern Warfare* (New York: Roy Publishers, 1943); Giulio Douhet, *The Command of the Air* (New York: Coward McCann, 1942).

[illegible] Van Til [illegible]
[illegible]
[illegible] he expresses his views on the
[illegible]

[illegible]
[illegible]
[illegible]
[illegible]
[illegible] points which [illegible]
[illegible] With rare exceptions [illegible]
[illegible]
[illegible]
[illegible]

[illegible]

[illegible]

[illegible]

[illegible]

[illegible]

[illegible]

[illegible]

[illegible] New York [illegible]
[illegible]
[illegible]
[illegible]

PART III

Vietnam and Its Aftermath

INTRODUCTION:
Doubt and Individual Decision

American involvement in Vietnam began well before the first U.S. combat battalions came ashore at Da Nang in March 1965. Those troops were preceded by over a decade of financial and political support of Ngo Dinh Diem, who rose to power in Saigon soon after the defeat of French forces at Dien Bien Phu in May 1954 and the subsequent partitioning of Vietnam. In July of that same year, agreements in Geneva called for an end of hostilities in Vietnam, Cambodia, and Laos, and provisionally divided Vietnam along the 17th parallel, pending national elections to be held two years later. In 1956, Diem rejected this international settlement and, supported by the United States, continued a widely unpopular dictatorship until he was overthrown and shot in October 1963. By that time, over twelve thousand American "advisers" were in Vietnam assisting South Vietnamese forces against the Vietcong, and hundreds of millions of U.S. dollars had been pledged to the Saigon government.

On August 2, 1964, North Vietnamese forces attacked the USS *Maddox,* a destroyer in the Gulf of Tonkin. A doubtful second incident was reported two days later, leading Congress to pass the Gulf of Tonkin Resolution in order to authorize President Johnson to take extraordinary military initiatives in Southeast Asia. Soon American aircraft bombed targets in North Vietnam; within six months these missions would be coordinated under Operation Rolling Thunder. A month later, two marine battalions landed to defend the Da Nang airfield, commencing a commitment that would take eight long years and would cost 58,000 American lives and hundreds of thousands of Vietnamese lives, not counting civilians.[1]

Although just-war criteria were rarely invoked explicitly in debates about the war, they helped Americans articulate the central moral questions about American involvement. First, there was the question of *just cause*. What events occasioned American involvement in Southeast Asia? What violations of moral and legal conventions justified a military commitment?

These questions were complicated by debates about the kind of war Americans were fighting. Those who adopted the domino theory—the idea that nations in Southeast Asia were progressively falling to communist powers—suggested that the war in Vietnam was indirectly a form of *self-defense*. Those who argued that the Vietcong were being aided and abetted by North Vietnamese forces suggested that American involvement should be seen not in terms of self-defense but as a form of *counterintervention* in a civil war. Such intervention could be justified, so the argument went, as a way to redress the unfair advantage acquired by the Vietcong when North Vietnamese interests entered the war.

Each rationale was subjected to vigorous dispute. The domino theory and its appeal to self-defense found little credibility, and the appeal to redress an unfair advantage in a civil war did little to justify the level of sacrifice that Americans were making.

Second, there was the question of *legitimate authority*. Neither the president nor Congress ever provided a formal declaration of war in Southeast Asia. Since Theodore Roosevelt, presidents have taken extraordinary initiatives toward eventual war, absent congressional authorization. But the Constitution assigns to Congress, not to the president, the final authority to declare war and marshal a defense. Perhaps more than any other reason, this failure to take accountability for the commitment of American troops led to widespread cynicism about leadership in Washington. Making matters more complex, the Diem government was widely perceived to be a puppet of United States political support, lacking political legitimacy. How could a war fought on behalf of an illegitimate authority be justified according to just-war restraints?

Third, many questioned the *intention* of U.S. involvement. What were the purposes that were to be carried out in Southeast Asia? Were purposes ever clear, or did the United States simply "slide" into the quagmire of the Vietnam War? Once U.S. military advisers and troops were sent to the war, did they arrive principally to train and assist South Vietnamese personnel? Were they there to protect the South Vietnamese government from being overthrown? Were they authorized to defeat the Vietcong by attacking vital command and supply centers, in Hanoi or in Cambodia? Or were they to impose an imperialist ideology on the people of Vietnam, advancing a way of life foreign to a peasant culture?

Fourth, there was the question—increasingly urgent as the war wore on and as more troops were committed—about the *proportionality* of the war. Were the values being defended commensurate with the risks that Americans were forced to endure? Was the cause of the Vietnam War, viewed in moral terms, worth sacrificing American lives?

Along these lines, a fifth and related question shaped public debate, especially after the Tet offensive in 1968: Was the war in Southeast Asia winnable? That is, was there a *reasonable hope of success?* Or was it the case that American efforts were increasingly futile, that Ho Chi Minh had time on his side?

Finally, there was the question of war's *means*. Modern communications brought to American homes vivid images of the war's carnage: bloodied bodies in My Lai, children burned by napalm, torched vegetation. Given the nature of guerrilla warfare, it was difficult to draw the kinds of lines implied by *in bello* criteria when forming judgments about noncombatant immunity. The fact that guerrilla warfare itself seemed to require a corruption of traditional Western terms and distinctions led many to conclude that the Vietnamese should be left to themselves to settle their differences, if only as the lesser of two evils.

These questions led many nonpacifists to doubt the merits of American intervention. Thus there emerged some concern about the possibility of *selectively* dissenting from a nation's wars, or selective conscientious objection. Under what conditions, if any, might the voice of conscience allow an individual to abstain from a particular war without adopting an in-principled condemnation of all wars?

NOTES

1. These events are recorded in George McTurnan Kahin, *Intervention: How America Became Involved in Vietnam* (New York: Alfred A. Knopf, 1986); Stanley Karnow, *Vietnam: A History* (New York: Viking Press, 1983); Harry G. Summers, *Vietnam War Almanac* (New York: Facts on File, 1985); George C. Herring, *America's Longest War: The United States and Vietnam 1950–1975,* 2d ed. (Philadelphia: Temple University Press, 1986); Jonathan Mirsky, "Reconsidering Vietnam," *New York Review of Books,* October 10, 1991.

11

Is Vietnam a Just War?

Paul Ramsey

The justifiedness of possible Christian participation in war can be shown because this might well be a requirement of charity—of the light of Christ penetrating man's political existence. It was a work of charity, we would all agree, for the Good Samaritan to give help at some personal cost to the man who fell among thieves on the road to Jericho and who beat him and left him for dead. By one step more, it may have been a work of charity for the innkeeper to hold himself ready to receive wounded and beaten men, and for him to have conducted his business so that he was solvent enough to extend credit to that do-gooder, the Good Samaritan. By another step, it would have been a work of charity, and not of justice only, to maintain and serve in a police force along the Jericho road to prevent such things from happening to travelers. Surely an ambulance theory of Christian charity is not enough, but police action and preventive actions are needed as well. So some may go only so far as to say that it might be a Christian vocation to serve in the military forces of the U.N. on a peace-keeping mission.

But may it not also be a work of charity, by yet another step, and in the absence of effective U.N. peace-keeping, to resist by force of arms any aggression upon the ordering power or nation that maintains a police patrol along the road to Jericho? Ought a Christian to serve in the military forces of a nation in an international system where there is no effective presence of superior authority but mainly a "state of nature" between the nations? We might reformulate that question to read: What should be done where there is no effective presence of a superior political authority but only "a state of nature" *between individuals?* What do you imagine Jesus would have had the Samaritan do if in the story he had come upon the scene when the robbers had just begun their attack and while they were still at their fell work? Would it not then be a work of charity to resort to the only available and effective means of preventing or punishing the attack and resisting the injustice? Is not anyone *obliged* to do this if he can?

Thus do we come to the first fork in the road for Christian conscience. Some at this point will take the path of pacifism, focusing their attention in Christian love upon the enemy. Others at this point will justify participation in war, focusing their attention in Christian love upon the victims of the hostile force that is abroad in the world. In an address to the 1966 Geneva Conference on Church and Society on "Peace in a Nuclear Age," and before espousing "nuclear pacifism" for all Christians today, Professor Helmut Gollwitzer gave a superb statement of this fork in the road for Christian conscience. "The answer given by Christian pacifism," he said, "leaves to non-Christians that very secular task which requires the greatest love and unselfishness, namely, the use of force; and the answer given by the great churches involves Christians so deeply in the conflicts of the world and in the settlement of these conflicts by the use of lethal force, that it is almost impossible for Christians to bear witness to the joyful message of Christ to their adversaries."

One thing seems to me for sure: Jesus would not have told a parable about a band of Good Samaritans who, confronted by this choice between the robbers and their intended victim, "went limp" on the Jericho road *in the belief that* "non-violent resistance" is qualitatively always more righteous than the use of armed force. The infinite qualitative difference is between *resistance* and *non-resisting,* sacrificial love. If then out of this self-same Christian love and responsibility one makes the decision that resistance is the necessary and most loving thing to do for all concerned, if one judges that not to resist is to have complicity in the evil he will fail to prevent, then the choice between violent and nonviolent means is a question of *economy* in the *effective* force to use. The judgment must be one of over-all effectiveness, untrammelled by any prior or absolute decision that non-violent direct action may be moral while violent direct action cannot be.

A Christian who has taken the non-pacifist road must thereafter be concerned with the *morality of war,* and not mix this up with the morality *contra bellum* on which his pacifist brother relies.

He will, first, know something about the intention, direction, and thrust of an act of war if this is ever justifiable. The objective of combat is the incapacitation of a combatant from doing what he is doing because he is this particular combatant in this particular war; it is not the killing of a man because he is this particular man. The latter and only the latter would be murder. From the proper direction of just action in war upon the combatant and not upon the man flows the prohibition of the killing of soldiers who have been captured or who by surrender have taken themselves out of the war and incapacitated themselves from continuing it. The robbers are not to be killed when effective robbery is no longer in them, since it was the robber and not the man who had to be stopped.

From this also flows the cardinal principle governing just conduct in war, namely, the moral immunity of non-combatants from deliberate, direct attack. In this *principle of discrimination* there are two ingredients. One is the prohibition of "deliberate, direct attack." This is the immutable, unchanging ingredient in the definition of justice in war. You have only to get to know the meaning of this in contrast to "aiming indiscriminately." The second ingredient is the meaning of "non-combatancy." This is relativistic and varying in application. "Non-combatancy" is a function of how the nations or the forces are organized for war, and of military technology.

I myself have no hesitation in saying that the counter-insurgency in South Vietnam in its chief or central design falls within the principle of discrimination. It is directed upon combatants as these have organized themselves for war, i.e., among the people like fish in water. No Christian and no moralist should assert that it violates the moral immunity of non-combatants from direct, deliberate attack to direct the violence of war upon vast Vietcong strongholds whose destruction unavoidably involves the collateral deaths of a great many civilians.

Yet this is asserted today by intellectuals and churchmen

who have forgotten if they ever knew the meaning of a *legitimate* military target. With such leadership it is no wonder that people march in the streets with banners proclaiming that they prefer education or a domestic Peace Corps to "murder." They simply do not know the qualitative difference between "murder" and "killing in war." While this is to be expected of a complete pacifist, it is neither expected nor excusable in anyone who does not, like the universal pacifist, propose to withdraw from the political life of his nation insofar as politics in the nation-state system must also be organized for the political use of armed force.

What would be quite inexcusable is for anyone who does not take responsibility for the agonizing decision to withdraw rather largely from the political life of his nation in the present, very imperfect international system, then to continue to berate his government with an indiscriminate requirement that acts of war be discriminating in an abstract sense which the definition of "legitimate" targets, "collateral damage," and justice in the "just conduct" of war never meant, and never could mean. The doctrine of justice in war is not a legalistic device for disqualifying, one by one, all wars in this age of insurgency. Instead, the meaning of noncombatancy is always a function of the current organization of nations and forces for war. The doctrine of justice in war is rather an explanation to statesmen of how within tolerable moral limits they should undertake, if need be, to defend and preserve such politically embodied justice as there is in the world.

II

For the rest, decisions in regard to the political use of violence are governed by political prudence. This is to say, whether a particular war should be fought, or whether it should be fought at a higher level of violence for hopefully a shorter time or be de-escalated and fought for a longer time, and many another question one must ask in justifying a particular political option rather than another, depend on one's count of the costs and the benefits, upon weighing greater and lesser evils in the consequences. In technical language, this is called the *principle of proportion,* which requires that the good achievable or the evil prevented be greater than the values destroyed or the destruction involved in any resort to arms.

A deliberately imprudent act that from inflexibility or bravado or for the sake of "why not victory?" undertakes to do more than we can do without greater harm would certainly be wrong. But so also would an uncharitable exercise of political prudence that in order to get on with our own Great Society would be content to do less than we might do for the just ordering of the world and for the good of other people in coincidence with our own, if these goods can at all be secured by anything we do or do not do. The principle of proportion, or prudence, can be violated by acts of omission as well as commission, while the principle of discrimination in war can be violated only by acts of commission. These are the main limits which the Christian who engages in politics knows to govern the political use of violent means. Then no one should fling around the word "immoral" with any other meaning when he is debating these questions, or when he criticizes the Administration's course of action.

On the matter of weighing the greater and the lesser evil, one can only mean to say that the present policy is prudentially wrong—which may be disastrous enough!—not that it is inherently "immoral." If current policy or his own proposal, either one, were the correct course for a charitable political prudence to take, it would hardly be inherently wrong to do it. On the matter of *discrimination* in acts of war, if one is going to use this assertedly "medieval" notion, he should use it correctly, and he should be able to recognize a medieval fortress when he sees one buried underground in Vietnam—beneath villages.

I can briefly show in a figure the anatomy of a charitable prudence in politics and in the use of force, if the reader will think of the three interlocking circles that are the sign for Ballantine Beer in this culture of ours. In the middle there is a small area where the circles all overlap. Around the edges, there are places where two of the circles overlap. But they are not congruent with one another to the whole extent of each circle; there is an area of each that falls outside of all the others.

Let the three circles in turn represent justice, order, and the legalities; or national security, the common good or values of the nation, and the world common good. In the ideal case, the political use of violence would fall in that area of incidence in the middle of the circles; and of course a just and prudent politics will seek to enlarge this area. Ideally, of course, one should use force only in behalf of justice, order, and the international legal system; or in behalf of national security, the national common good, and the common good of all mankind. Less ideal it would be to use force directly in behalf of only two of these terminal values of politics; to locate one's action in the area of overlap of international law and justice, for example, or of international law with security, or in the coincidence of the national with the world common good, or (and this is the ultimate "reason of state") in the coincidence of national security and the values in the common life of a nation. . . .

In any case, there are no "wandering nations"—nations who, like our father Abraham, abandon their own established interests and go out into a far country. This is not God's call to the nations. In politics we are called rather to wisdom in the embodiment of these terminal political values and their preservation by means of the monopoly of physical power that can be exerted by an organized community. . . .

III

Christians and the churches can very definitely say something about the meaning of discrimination in acts of war. This the Vatican Council did in its central declaration: "Any act of war aimed indiscriminately at the destruction of entire cities or of extensive areas along with their population is a crime against God and man himself. It merits unequivocal and unhesitating condemnation" (Pastoral Constitution on the Church in the Modern World, par. 80).

But then, a Christian today will have to be vigilant in telling what this means intrinsically, and in actual practice. He will have to do some sound thinking in this age when quite a number of people not heretofore noted for their contributions to an understanding of moral principles have begun to use the terms "moral" and "immoral" rather recklessly.

We need to examine carefully the case of insurgency and counter-insurgency warfare in order to show what was always the meaning of "aiming discriminatingly" upon legitimate military targets, and the meaning of this in the case of the newer forms of war the world will face for decades to come.

One must pause to grasp the nature of insurgency's use of violence (whether this is aggression from outside or revolution inside a country, or both). We need to dissect the basic design of insurgency warfare no less than that of counter-insurgency. Only then can we tell how to distribute judgments about the inherent evil of their respective resorts to military force.

One does not justify adultery by saying that it is *selective.* Not even with the additional finding that with one's various mistresses one mainly enjoys the finer things of life and has achieved an orderly domestic economy. Neither does one justify deliberate terror in the conduct of war or revolution by saying that it is selective. Not even with the additional finding that the insurgents win the allegiance of people by many other appeals or also by a program of national liberation. The fact that insurgency resorts to terror, when it does, only minimally or only upon selected people does not qualify it as a discriminating resort to force. That is simply not the meaning of the principle of discrimination in the use of means of violence. It is in fact, morally, the meaning of total war. Decision as to the inherent evil of an act of war or revolution cannot be settled by the body count. There is not a prudent number of villagers, school teachers, or petty local officials and their families that it would be right to disembowel in the village square to dissuade others from allegiance to the existing social processes and institutions, all to the good end of destroying the social fabric of a traditional society and taking over and reforming the country.

Guerrilla war by its main design strikes the civil population (albeit selectively and as rarely as need be) in order to subvert, while striking as few legitimate military targets as possible. This terrible terror, while "selective," is not therefore limited or a rarity. In 1960–61 alone, the Vietcong murdered 6,130 and abducted 6,213 persons, or a total of over 12,000. Proportionately, this is as if the U.S. were under subversive assault in which 72,000 prominent persons, crucial in the life of the nation and its community services, were murdered or abducted annually! This is an inherently immoral plan of war or of revolution, and one that cannot be rendered morally tolerable by reference to the social reforms by which insurgency mainly proposes to succeed.

Without invoking the domino theory, it is a fact of life that the nuclear stalemate has made the world safe for insurgency warfare. *This* is *modern* war! Nor is the threat to just order dependent upon there being an intact worldwide communist conspiracy behind all such resorts to arms. Guatemala recently elected a *left-wing* government that offers some hope of social progress; the next day, a 24-year-old guerrilla leader took to the hills to gain rule or to ruin; and the military made the first "classical" mistake of scorning him as a "bandit."

The question facing the world for decades to come is whether it is possible to oppose these revolutionary wars successfully without joining them in *direct* attacks upon the very people a government may be trying to protect while social progress is secured with liberty. Is counter-insurgency, like insurgency, bound to be warfare over people as a means of getting at the other's forces?

Of course, if the guerrilla lives among the people like a fish in water, he must be opposed mainly by withdrawing the water to see what then happens to the fish. This is to say, insurgency can be finally defeated only by social, economic, and political reformation. But what of the military force that must still be used? If the guerrilla chooses to fight between, behind, and over peasants, women, and children, is it *he* or the counter-guerrilla who has enlarged the legitimate target and enlarged it so as to bring unavoidable death and destruction upon a large number of innocent people?

It is the shape of insurgency warfare that defines the contours of the legitimate combatant destruction and the unavoidably associated civil damage it then may (so far as the principle of discrimination is concerned) be just to inflict in order to oppose evil, subject only to the limitation that this be the proportionately lesser evil. To draw any other conclusion would be like, at the nuclear level, granting an enemy immunity from attack because he had the shrewdness to locate his missile bases in the heart of his cities. It is rather *he* who has deliberately enlarged the extent of foreknowable but collateral civil destruction in the attempt to gain a privileged sanctuary through a military posture that brought more of his own population into range.

The design of insurgency does this to the people of a society it assaults. The onus of the wickedness[1] of placing multitudes of peasants within range cannot be shifted from insurgency to counter-insurgency, any more than it could be called an indiscriminate act of war on the part of some enemy if in the future Omaha, Nebraska, or Colorado Springs,

Colorado, [is] tragically destroyed in the course of destroying the bases and command posts *we* located there.

The principle of discrimination governing the proper conduct of war has no other meaning than this. Some call this a "medieval" notion. One should then be able to recognize a medieval fortress when he sees or hears of one buried underground in South Vietnam—command headquarters, munitions factories, stores of rice and intricate tunnels connecting many villages, with openings into countless peasant huts, or under the water in lakes, streams, and rice paddies, by which the guerrillas may fight and run away and live to fight another day through these same egresses. Plainly, there are here extensive areas subject to the laws of the siege; i.e., "catapults" from as far away as Guam may then not be indiscriminate acts of war. These are unpleasant facts. I did not make them so; originally, Mao Tse-tung did. No Christian or moralist has a right to demand that statesmen or commanders fail to take account of these facts in their policies and plans. This is to suggest, all too briefly, that the main design of the counterinsurgency mounted in Vietnam need not be and likely is *not* an inherently evil or morally intolerable use of armed force—not in any meaning that the distinction between discriminate and indiscriminate conduct in war ever had or should have.

This is not to deny that peripheral to the "central war" against the insurgents there may be taking place many intrinsically wrong actions in this confused and bloody war. (I only say that this is not proved by reference to "the bombing of villages,"[2] etc., that may in fact lie within a vast Vietcong stronghold.) There are those who say that if any of the acts of war violate the canons of justice in war, or if justice is violated by frequent actions that, however, do not or need not fall within the main thrust or design of the war, it is still on the whole unjust and no Christian should support or participate in it. This position is far more to be honored than the indiscriminate use of the principle of discrimination that is current today. Still, to uphold it seems to me to uphold a legalist-pacifist version of the just-war doctrine, as if the purpose of this teaching was to bring peace by discrediting, one by one, all wars. Instead, the just-war doctrine is intended to indicate to political decision makers how, within tolerable moral limits, they are to defend and preserve politically embodied justice in this world.

If by now the reader is alarmed, I can only plead: "Moralists are unhappy people. When they insist on the immutability of moral principles, they are reproached for imposing unlivable requirements on us. When they explain the way in which those immutable principles are to be put into force, they are reproached for making morality relative. In both cases, however, they are only upholding the claims of reason [and, I would add, of a rational explication of Christian ethics] to direct life."[3]

IV

Determining the greater and lesser evil in accord with the *principle of proportion* and the application of the *principle of discrimination* in the face of some new organization of military forces calls for an exercise of political prudence on the part of magistrates and citizens alike. In the particulars of this no Christian can fault the conscience of another. This is especially the case in judgments whether acts of war directed upon *where the guerrillas are* still may not be doing *disproportionate* damage. In this there may certainly be legitimate disagreement. It may be the case that the conflict in South Vietnam has long since been destructive of more values than there is hope of gaining. If this seems to be the case so far as the Vietnamese alone are concerned, one must not forget that there are more values and securities and freedoms to be reckoned in any judgment concerning the proportionately lesser evil. Tragically, or in God's inscrutable providence, neither villagers nor nations are impervious to one another in our fated and fateful togetherness. Again in the particular decision concerning the greater or lesser evil in the whole of Southeast Asia, no Christian can fault the conscience of another. Then in this no Christian can fault the possible correctness of the conscientious estimations made by his government when he states with all urgency his disagreement with it. And no assembly of churchmen should pronounce—as did the 1966 Geneva Conference on Church and Society—that recent U.S. actions in Vietnam "cannot be justified."[4]

At the time of this writing, President Charles de Gaulle has just made his major foreign policy address in Pnompenh, Cambodia, and signed a joint communique with Prince Sihanouk concerning peace in Southeast Asia. One need not—indeed we should not—quibble over the fact that De

Gaulle called for a U.S. time-limit for withdrawal of its forces without calling also for withdrawal of North Vietnamese forces from the South. We may yet need the mediation of France if peace is to be established in Southeast Asia; and in this sense De Gaulle's effort to jostle himself into position for this can only be welcomed. He made the opening of "broad and difficult negotiations" dependent upon "the decision and the commitment America would have wanted to take beforehand to repatriate its forces within a suitable and determined fixed period of time."

The objection, if any, should rather be to the fact that De Gaulle did not tie the timetable (two years has been suggested as what was in his mind) for U.S. withdrawal with progress toward the goal of these negotiations which, the General knows, can alone insure peace, namely, that this would be withdrawal in favor of an "international arrangement" "establishing and guaranteeing the neutrality of the peoples of Indochina and their right to dispose of themselves. . . ." Indeed, we Americans have a great deal to learn from the somber realism with which President de Gaulle greeted his own proposal: the time "is not at all ripe today, assuming that it may ever be," and "in any event, lacking this outcome, no mediation will offer a prospect of success, and that is why France, for her part, has never thought and does not think of proposing one."

If only De Gaulle had clearly acknowledged that the time is not yet ripe either for American withdrawal or for getting an "international arrangement" effectively guaranteeing the neutrality of the peoples of Southeast Asia and their ability to dispose of themselves in independent development as nations! But this is a small matter compared with De Gaulle's effort to nudge the forces involved in this tragic arbitrament of arms in the direction of such an arrangement and such withdrawal.

The point to be made here is simply that such an arrangement has *not* been possible since the decision was made at a meeting of the communist party leaders in North Vietnam to aid and abet the insurgency in the South, and that a tolerably peaceful and just arrangement still eludes attainment. This is what the fighting is all about. If and when the day comes on which negotiations are opened that stand a chance of attaining the internationally *guaranteed* neutralization and protection of the peoples of Southeast Asia, no Christian in the United States should suppose that now at last his government has made peace—a just peace—by peaceful means alone, while before we were doing wrong by fighting. Instead, the present use of armed force, no less than somebody's mediation of the conflict, will *both* have served to make such an arrangement possible.

We Christians should, of course, be the first to acknowledge that such a fragile historical outcome is not in one sense worth a single Vietnamese or American life, nor is a life to be exchanged for the values of an entire, more durable worldly civilization that also passes away in the course of time. We have it on the highest authority that the whole world is not worth a single human soul. But to bring this judgment directly into politics would be to compare incommensurables. It would be to weigh temporal accomplishments against a human life which is a sacredness in the temporal and in the political order. This would be to face what Paul Tillich called the ambiguity of all finite sacrifice. This, however, is not the only assessment to be made of the lives sacrificed and taken in political encounters in this world in which political purposes and the use of force are joined by a tie not lightly broken, nor likely to be broken.

NOTES

1. [Philip Wogaman seems especially offended by this expression ("The Vietnam War and Paul Ramsey's Conscience," *Dialog*, Vol. 6 [Autumn 1967], 294). The distinction is between physical evil and moral evil, between the unavoidable tragedy of war and avoidable wickedness in war. I might have said, "The onus of the *injustice* of placing multitudes of peasants within range cannot be shifted from insurgency to counter-insurgency." If this is "a strange invitation to self-righteousness coming from a Protestant Christian theologian," then we shall all have to stop doing ethics, and there should be no more talk about right and wrong, just or unjustified wars.

While seeming to espouse the just-war tests and only disagreeing with my conscience (my particular judgments on Vietnam), Professor Wogaman in fact abandons the effort to define what is right in war. This is evident from his dismissal of my "strange discussion" distinguishing the sin of murder from killing a combatant in order to incapacitate or stop his combatancy. Here again I am supposed to be "insensitive to the tragedy of all war" and to its ambiguities. Without this distinction (I can only reiterate) there would be no moral ground for prohibiting the killing of prisoners—the possible legitimacy of which Wogaman (strangely) proceeds to draw forth as an entailment of my analysis!]

2. This was the indiscriminate language used by the 1966 Geneva Conference on Church and Society in condemning recent U.S. actions in Vietnam. Report of Section III, par. 131.

3. Jacques Maritain, *Man and the State* (Chicago: The University of Chicago Press, 1951), p. 74.

4. "Structures of International Cooperation: Living Together in Peace in a Pluralistic World Society," Report of Section III, par. 131.

12

The Moral Logic of War

Ralph B. Potter, Jr.

As a professor of social ethics, I wish to speak to the question of the morality of [the Vietnam] war. The ethical analyst as such does not provide policy recommendations, but has the responsibility to ponder what questions ought to be asked in the formulation of policy and to examine critically the cogency of reasons given in support of policy decisions. His duty is to scrutinize the moral logic by which a war may be justified or condemned.

I. WAR AS A RULE-GOVERNED EXCEPTION

All of us are aware that our life together in society depends upon our mutual respect for the principle that we must do no harm to our neighbor. Each of us is extremely vulnerable; our safety and our welfare are secure only so long as the temptation to kill and to commit mayhem, to destroy property and to plunder are suppressed both internally by moral instruction and externally by the severe sanctions of law. In civil society those who inflict severe injuries upon their neighbors are condemned, convicted, and confined.

Our common life is sustained by a strong moral and legal presumption against the use of force. It is remarkable, therefore, that there is a way of thinking and talking that can transmute the act of killing into an act of heroism. By what logic can it happen that a young American gun-lover who kills fourteen strangers from the top of the tower on the University of Texas campus in Austin is summarily slain and denounced as a psychopath, while another young American who kills fourteen strangers in a village in Vietnam is decorated, welcomed at the White House, and acclaimed a model for the youth of the nation?

Clearly some powerful moral logic is at work to enable us to make distinctions and to respond in a strikingly different manner to acts which share many outward characteristics. The term "war" can be used to excuse conduct that would, under other circumstances, be condemned as an inexcusable assault upon the life and property of fellow human beings. It grants to warriors an immunity from punishment and blame. . . .

"War" is not merely a descriptive term employed to inform us that violent deaths are occurring between two organized antagonists. It is also a legal term, indicating a state of hostility in which certain rules and relations ordinarily obtaining between parties or states have been suspended. And it is also a moral term which, when properly applied, is meant to suggest that the bearers of violence are to be considered as acting as officers of the public good and are hence to be judged immune from the ordinary standards of conduct, although perhaps bound still by extraordinary standards appropriate to the state of war. . . .

The logic generally applied by wise critics in thinking about right and wrong in the use of force is admirably simple in its basic structure. First there is a strong presumption against the use of force. The burden of proof rests heavily upon anyone who would take arms against his neighbor. But secondly, it is conceded that certain exceptions must be made for the sake of the common good. There are narrowly definable circumstances which may justify employing force against those who harm the innocent, or refuse to acknowledge the rights of others, or destroy the context of civil society necessary for the nurture of free and stable persons. But the use of force always requires an explanation. It always involves an exception to the rule which forbids us to do harm to our neighbor without due cause.

An Agenda for Ethical Inquiry

Debates about the morality of war are thus to be seen as contentions over the plausibility of claims for allowable exceptions to the general moral ban upon recourse to violence. In such debates three major types of questions recur which will form the agenda of our inquiry. . . .

First, it is possible to ask, "Why should any exceptions be allowed at all?" The question has been posed by pacifists in every age. It demands a justification of the institution of war in general. One must show that it can have some just cause, that it can serve some good purpose, that it may be a necessary device to preserving the common good.

A *second* type of inquiry is, "Upon what conditions should exceptions be made?" If we concede that war may be permissible for certain restricted causes, what acts can and cannot be justified as being appropriate to the tragic, but sometimes justifiable institution of war? What circumstances would disqualify the claim that a particular use of force should be allowed as a permissible exception to the ban on violence?

The *third* type of question is heard most frequently today. "Why should this particular exception be made?" Can this particular war, for instance, the war being waged by U.S. Armed Forces [in] Southeast Asia, be justified under the allowable exceptions we have defined? This calls for the application of the conditions, or standards, or criteria by which we have agreed to assess the legitimacy of all claims for exemptions to the general ban on killing and destruction. It would be crude dishonesty and a denial of reason to persist in using one set of criteria to judge wars in which our own nation engages and another set for the assessment of the conduct of other states. We cannot invoke moral terms capable of justifying our own waging of war apart from a willingness to examine the possibility that their application may reveal that justice rests with our opponents. . . .

II. THREE JUSTIFIABLE CAUSES OF WAR

. . . Three circumstances have perennially been claimed to establish justifiable grounds for resort to war. . . :

A. To protect the innocent from unjust attack

B. To restore rights wrongful[ly] denied

C. To reestablish an order necessary for decent human existence

A just cause of war can only arise out of the necessity to restrain and correct a wrongdoing of others on behalf of the public good. In theological language, war is always a concession to sin, a tragic response to the predatory actions of others. . . .

Every version of [the moral logic of war] begins with a presumption against the use of force. The basis of that presumption may vary. Sometimes it has a shaky foundation in the crass self-interest of individuals prudentially adapting themselves in the presence of equally powerful enemies. For Stoic philosophers, the presumption against the use of force was grounded in a consciousness of the common bond of reason that binds all men together in the family of humanity. For Christians, it is the example of the forbearance and sacrifice of Christ and the content of his teaching that establishes a profound reluctance ever to do injury. Here the tension between spiritual aspiration and apparent political necessity is most severe. When one reflects upon the person of Jesus, his simplicity and gentleness and willingness to suffer, and then surveys the history of military actions conducted by those who claim allegiance to his name, it is impossible to avoid a grotesque sense of incongruity. . . .

A. *The first cause of war* requires the least argument. The institution of war can be justified most plausibly when it is necessary to provide immediate, direct defense of the innocent victims of unjust attack. This commonly accepted case entails certain corollaries which expand the number of those whose participation can be justified. The immediate victim of unjust aggression is entitled not only to repel force by force but also to avail himself of assistance in making his just defense. Those bound to him by treaties and alliances are under strong moral obligation to fulfill their promises by coming to the aid of a nation wrongfully attacked. The right of intervention may be claimed even by other states not bound by treaty or alliance who, nevertheless, perceive that the international community has a common stake in preserving and imposing sanctions against flagrant violations of the rights of others. Failure to intervene, the refusal to give all possible aid to a beleaguered victim, may be viewed as the default of a moral obligation and a disservice to the nascent community of nations.

B. *The second just cause of war* we recognized was to restore a right wrongfully denied. The wrongdoing which occasions such wars may be less visible than a blitzkrieg sweeping across international boundaries. But a war of intervention to correct a flagrant and persistent denial of justice may, nevertheless, be justified as a defense of the innocent. If, for example, in response to revolutionary stirrings among blacks in South Africa, the racist regime of that nation should launch an indiscriminate and deadly assault on the black community within its boundaries, a minimal sense of justice would compel neighboring states to intervene to halt the slaughter. In effect, the international boundary would not only be overlooked but erased. A state which persistently denies equal protection of the laws and as a matter of policy does not seek the consent of the governed or allow participation of the majority in the decision-making processes, is not properly to be considered a sovereign state. It is morally indistinguishable from a band of brigands devoted to exploitation and plunder rather than to the common good. Those who undertake to protect the victims of the brigands are fighting a justifiable war for the defense of the innocent even though their action entails the first crossing of a international boundary.

C. *The third instance in which war may be justified* is when it is the only means of reestablishing an order necessary for decent human existence. Human lives are formed in a social and political context that shapes or misshapes personality. Where oppression and tyranny reign human lives are distorted. Governments are constituted among men "in order to form a more perfect Union, establish justice, insure domestic tranquility, provide for the common defense, promote the general welfare, and secure the blessings of liberty." Where these purposes are not served, a right devolves to the people to reconstitute the political organs of their society, by force, if necessary.

The concept of justifiable revolution is by no means an importation derived from an alien communist ideology. It is the cornerstone of our native political heritage. We cannot deny that armed revolution may on occasion be justifiable without contradicting our own being as a nation and denying the tradition which flows from medieval sources, through the religious and secular political philosophers of sixteenth-century France and seventeenth-century England and Holland, to our own founding fathers in the eighteenth century. . . .

We can hardly deny that the use of force in revolution may, under certain conditions, be justified as a defense of the innocent against the "structural violence" imposed by a despotic and exploitative regime. The assault of established governments upon the innocent can be more subtle and slow and concealed, but it nonetheless demands correction in the name of justice.

Violence as a Faulty Instrument of Enforcement

We have been answering the question, "Why should any exceptions at all be allowed to the general ban upon the use of force in human relations?" The justifications for the institution of war rest upon its presumed utility as a necessary means of serving the common good by protecting the innocent from unjust attack, restoring rights wrongfully denied, or reestablishing a social order necessary for decent human existence. War is always a concession to sin, a restraint upon wrongdoing, a sanction against crime. But it is clearly a clumsy, inefficient, unpredictable, wasteful, and hideous form of sanction, a very faulty instrument of enforcement.

The idea of justifying war as a sanction against wrongdoing rests upon an analogy to conditions within domestic, civil society where the apparatus of government monopolizes the means of violence and enforces the law against those guilty of crimes. Unfortunately, the analogy between civil society and the international system is hardly perfect. Nations live in a state of anarchy in which there is no monopoly upon the use of force. In this international state of nature, it is more difficult to determine when a wrong has been committed and who bears responsibility for its correction. The rules governing the relations between states are less clear than the laws of civil society. Moreover, there is no commonly acknowledged judicial apparatus to assess the justice of claims lodged by and against states. No impartial international tribunal enjoying acknowledged jurisdiction and effective powers of enforcement is available. In the absence of any higher authority able to arbitrate effectively, each nation is forced to be a judge in its own cause. In such circumstances, bias seems inevitable. The cause of justice may be invoked to mask trivial or selfish pretexts for war.

Fair judgments concerning the justice of the cause are difficult to derive. They are even more difficult to enforce.

No police force is available. Nations must rely upon self-help or upon fluctuating arrangements for collective security through which the use of violence may be coordinated. But violence is capricious and unpredictable. There can be no guarantee that the side conscientiously contending for justice will prevail in battle. Villains may gain victory at arms and consolidate their position, increasing their capacity to work mischief. Moreover, violence is a paradoxical means of enforcing justice, for the indiscriminate nature of the processes of violence offends the very justice it may seek to serve. In domestic society, the verdict decreed by a judge and implemented by the police can, with due caution, be applied discriminately and precisely upon the malefactor alone. In war, however, the judgment falls severely upon the innocent child as well as the guilty politician and warrior.

The violence of war always threatens to escape control. The psychological effects of the use of violence are devastating. It engenders ferocity and a spirit of revenge and thus generates a cycle of retaliation. It tends toward relentless escalation beyond the limits originally envisioned. War is, indeed, a very faulty instrument for the enforcement of justice.

War cannot be justified without a just cause. But even with a just cause, the instrument of enforcement is so faulty that further restraints upon the right to wage war must be imposed. Not every just cause is to be prosecuted. There may be situations in which a just cause is undoubtedly present but conditions are such that resort to force would not serve the welfare of the national or international community. Hence, other criteria of the justifiable use of force are required in addition to the certitude of a just cause.

III. THE MORAL LIMITS OF WARFARE

We come, thus, to our second major task of defining the conditions under which it is and is not prudent and permissible to prosecute a just cause. Violence is costly. Once states contemplate the use of armed violence, they suffer under the temptation to recoup some economic, political, territorial, or psychological gain beyond the narrow legitimate benefit of restraining wrongdoers for which the exceptional right to wage war may be conceded. Being aware of such temptations, we can forearm ourselves with specific criteria that will enable us to separate rationalizing pretexts from justifiable causes of war and to detect when the boundary between proper use and improper misuse of force has been passed.

Thus we can justify the institution of war because of its necessity in certain severely limited circumstances but build into our definition of justifiable war rules which prohibit predictable abuses. To revert to the language of philosophers, the institution may be justified by utilitarian reasoning; but the rules inhere in the definition of the institution and cannot be set aside by calculation of immediate advantage. The rules of war are morally binding on all who seek justification for resorting to war. Moral permission for the exceptional use of this exceptionally dangerous device is always conditional upon regard for its right limits.

One way of recounting the basic logic concerning the right and wrong use of force in war would be to say that war can be a justifiable exception to the general ban against doing violence to fellow men only when it is both necessary and effective in serving the public good. . . . Arguments in defense of a particular war must meet all three of these criteria. Arguments against a war must show merely that it fails on one or more counts.

In expounding the criteria to be used in determining when a just cause may be rightfully prosecuted through war, I wish to depart from this tidy formulation and employ the language found in the classical sources provided by those who have elaborated the Augustinian logic through fifteen hundred years.

Criteria Limiting Exceptional Resort to Violence

The *first* criterion that both tests and limits the right to wage war in a just cause is the requirement that there must be a *due proportion* between good to be accomplished through war and the harm predictably to be suffered by all parties. It is clear that war is dangerous: dangerous for every member of a warring state. It is the responsibility of political leaders to see that those placed in their care are not recklessly exposed to danger for trivial reasons. Hence, there must be a proportionality in the gravity of the cause for which war is waged and also a proportionality in the means employed.

A *second* criterion arises out of an appreciation of the psychological effects of wrongdoing and violence and seeks to forestall any resort to war from the motives of vengeance, hatred, ambition, cruelty, greed, or hysteria. War must be waged with just intentions, that is, with a mournful sense of tragic necessity in the service of universal norms of justice. In battle and in victory no other intention can be harbored. . . .

A *third* requirement is that war must always be a *last resort.* Every peaceable means of obtaining redress must have been tried and exhausted. Only strict necessity can legitimate resort to force. Thus, a "preventive war" cannot be justified.

A *fourth* safeguard is the provision that war may be conducted only *by lawful authority.* War is an armed conflict between states, an affair in which the entire political community, every man, woman, and child is brought into severe jeopardy. No one other than the sovereign authority within a state has the right to commit the entire community to undergo the risk of killing and being killed. Members of the community must be protected by clear procedures which focus responsibility for the initiation of war and permit the fullest possible representation of sentiment. If the due processes are not observed, citizens are effectively disenfranchised and war becomes not an act of the political community but an enterprise of a usurping minority upon whom guilt must rest.

The provision that war can be conducted only under lawful authority reinforces the requirement that violence can be justified only when it is politically purposeful, that is, when it can be claimed to serve the public good by establishing or preserving an order of justice in which the impartial application of general laws replaces arbitrary personal rule, and clear canons of equity rather than crude power and fortuity govern the distribution of goods and resources. Thus, the violence of bandits and looters, who serve only their own interest, is to be distinguished from that of would-be patriots organized in guerrilla bands in the service of a provisional government or a government in exile intent upon establishing or reestablishing a political constitution. Bandits and looters who employ violence in their selfish enterprise are punishable under civil law as common criminals. Guerrilla fighters are properly to be treated as prisoners of war acting wrongfully, perhaps, but, nevertheless, in good conscience as officers of a new commonwealth struggling to be born.

A *fifth* condition necessary to justify resort to war is that *a clear declaration* of the causes and aims of war be made generally known at home and abroad. There are three purposes of such a declaration:

A. to indicate to a potential enemy the conditions upon which a settlement might be made and war thereby avoided;

B. to give notice to all other nations so that they may assess the justice of the cause and conduct themselves accordingly;

C. to establish with certainty that war is being waged not on the initiative of a small clique but by the will of the people of the contending states.

A *sixth* condition is that there must be *reasonable hope of success.* This criterion flows from the moral ban upon suicide and the fundamental principle that political leaders are stewards of the welfare of the nation and the life of each citizen. Lives and goods are not to be squandered. War must be a politically purposeful act made barely tolerable by the necessity of defending the innocent. It can never be justified by the vain desire to avoid admitting an error in past judgment, a refusal to acknowledge changed circumstances, or an extravagant and a misplaced sense of heroism. It is immoral to expose other men to death to save one's political face.

All of the above conditions suggest questions that ought to be asked in formulating a response to the question, "When is it permissible to wage war?" These criteria constitute the principles of the *jus ad bellum,* that is, the law governing the just resort to war.

Another basic question may be asked by those contemplating war: "What acts may be committed in the conduct of war?" The principles which determine the response to this question constitute the *jus in bello,* that is, the law governing just conduct of war. A *seventh* condition, then, is that the *jus in bello* must be observed; i.e., only just means must be employed in combat and in conquest.

Scrutinizing the Methods of War

The principles defining *just means* govern the conduct of soldiers during war and relations to vanquished enemies after a war. The principles apply to the treatment of prisoners, hostages, resort to falsehood and torture, espionage, ambush, reparations, pillage, the use of poisons, assassinations and so forth. Reflection upon the just means of war must be guided by the principle of the moral immunity of noncombatants from direct attack. The principle is a simple corollary of the logic we have unfolded. We live by the presumption that men must do no harm to their neighbors. That presumption can be overridden when it is necessary to restrain wrongdoers from inflicting harm. Only the necessity can grant to any man an excuse to kill. It follows that those who need not be restrained must not be killed. This is the heart of the moral logic of war. In seeking to prevent men from doing harm to those who deserve no harm we cannot ourselves rightfully inflict harm upon those who deserve no harm.

We are allowed to use force only to restrain. In this mission we cannot ignore the obligation to respect human life even in the person of our enemy. We must employ only the least amount of force effective to restrain. On occasion, it may be that we cannot prevent a foe from doing injury except by killing him. It is then permissible to do so. But the rightful purpose remains only to restrain. Once that has been accomplished, the right to kill is forthwith revoked.

Only those immediately and actively engaged in the bearing of hostile force in an unjust cause are properly subject to direct attack. Civilians living in the cities of the enemy's homeland or in villages near the scene of battle cannot purposefully be harmed. An enemy soldier who has dropped his weapon to surrender, or has suffered a wound, or is captured unaware, or by any other circumstance is rendered incapable of inflicting harm, reverts immediately to the status of a fellow human being whose life is surrounded by the protection of the principle that we must do no harm to our neighbors. No one can claim an excuse to do him violence. Neither vengeance, nor expediency, nor the need for information, nor the desire to terrorize others, nor fear of future betrayal, nor any other reason can override the restraint embedded in the very logic by which we can barely justify war as itself a measure of restraint. . . .

IV. THE VIETNAM WAR: A PARTICULAR CASE

When we come to our third task of applying the principles we have defined to consideration of the justice of the war in

Vietnam, we discover that they have already been applied. In the debate that has been waged for years between critics and supporters of the war the questions we have raised concerning the just causes of war, due proportion, just intentions, last resort, lawful authority, declaration, hope of success, and just means have been the focal points of controversy. Those who have never been exposed to the tradition of thought on the subject or have never had a [presentation] such as this inflicted upon them, have, by the persistence of their own reasoning, rediscovered the critical moral elements in the situation.

I had intended to recapitulate the debate under the several principles we have defined. The very recitation of the traditional criteria of justifiable war should, however, suffice to bring to mind the arguments underlying the two coherent views evolved by successive administrations and their growing ranks of critics. *Those defending the war* have portrayed it as a heroic defense of the innocent victims of unjust aggression from the north, carried out upon request, with self-sacrificing restraint, as a last resort, to the point of impending success, for the clearly stated purpose of preserving the integrity and safety of "the free world." *Critics of the war* have described it as an unlawful, unnecessary, ineffective, and [indiscriminate] attempt to buttress a series of unrepresentative, oppressive regimes, carried out at disproportionate cost for vague, selfish purposes which continually expand and contract.

The antagonists in the debate disagree in their moral assessment of the war and in their prescriptions for American policy. But they are in agreement concerning the issues that must be considered in constructing an argument for or against the war. Both sides have isolated the morally relevant considerations. They have felt constrained to give some moral justification for resorting to force. In searching for such justification, they have rediscovered the abiding moral relevance of precisely those considerations which imposed themselves upon philosophers and statesmen of earlier generations who have reflected upon the moral logic of war.

Ethics, Casuistry, and Facts

. . . Recognition of the complicated character of policy thought and casuistry, in which empirical, ethical, existential, and quasitheological elements are inevitably intermixed, is a necessary basis for mutual forbearance in debate about

Vietnam and other issues. It must be observed that there can be no purely "non-moral" assessment of policy. There is no way that decisions which affect the welfare of fellow human beings can be reduced to purely technical questions to be presided over by "experts" screened off from public scrutiny by the imposing walls of the Pentagon. Decisions which result in alternative schedules of benefits and harms to human beings are moral decisions. In our nation, such decisions must ultimately be subjected to the judgment of the people.

Conversely, there can be no "purely moral view" of the war. Policy thought inevitably involves factual premises and predictions or hopes concerning the outcome of alternative policy options. You cannot make a significant utterance about the war without making assumptions of fact that may be challenged on the basis of alternative interpretations of military and political realities. Long after the ethicist has done his proper task of specifying what facts would be morally relevant and why, debate can continue concerning [the] present military and political reality in Vietnam and the sources and canons of our knowledge of that reality.

Doubtless, you will be disappointed to be reminded that I am only an ethicist. Concerning the factual ingredient of decisions concerning policy, "all I know is what I read in the papers." I can lay no claim to special competence to deal with the entire range of considerations that properly enter in the formulation of policy. No one can. There is a stalemate among experts; final decision-making power rests with elected generalists trusted to weigh and balance and combine the advice of various sorts of specialists.

My task is not presumptuously to usurp the responsibility of our elected officials to determine national policy hour by hour. But it is clearly my professional and civic duty to inquire into the justice of the policies they ordain, to shape conscientiously my own opinion, and to help form or reform the conscience of the nation. Given my modest definition of the function of ethics, this can best be done by asking questions, questions which probe the moral logic behind alternative courses of policy.

[T]here are four questions I would like to press . . . at this particular moment in the debate.

First, "Is application of the 'domino theory' to legitimate continuation of the war in Vietnam immoral?"

Second, "Could the North Vietnamese be considered to have justifiable cause of war in reaction to wrongful denial of the provisions of the Geneva Accords?"

Third, "How can the President's compromise policy of 'staged withdrawal' be morally justified?"

Fourth, "What actions are appropriate for American citizens convinced that the war is unjust?"

I do not want to impose further upon your patience; but neither do I wish to leave a lovely set of principles floating in the air. I have taken so much time to reach this point because I wanted to show clearly the reasoning by which I have proceeded, in the hope of demonstrating that there can be conscientious and intellectually rigorous members of the "effete corps of impudent snobs." It pains me not to proceed to the point of insuring the happy accolade of being "relevant." But my message is that nothing can be more relevant today than expounding the moral logic of war in the hope that its principles will regain the power to guide and constrain those who contemplate the use of force.

The Ambiguity of Gradual Withdrawal

In order to avoid a truly ludicrous anti-climax, let me at least state baldly my general conclusion that this war must be brought to an end, and that right soon. This conviction arises from the application of the principle of due proportion. The good to be accomplished by prosecuting the war is less than the harm to be inflicted at home and abroad. The conclusion is dependent upon the empirical premise that, acting within the bounds of what a civilized state could do, there is no reasonable hope of achieving the type of "success" sought by successive administrations, that is, the shoring up of the incumbent regime in Saigon so that it could stand alone following the withdrawal of American combat troops, let alone the withdrawal of all American air and logistic support.

The policy by President Nixon in his televised address of November 3, 1969 is appealing but not persuasive. He has, in effect, made two promises: one addressed to the American people promising gradual disengagement, and one to leaders in Saigon promising effective protection from those now in arms against the regime. I fail to see how both promises can be kept, even though the terms of each have been left shamefully vague for the sake of presumed freedom of maneuver. Is the promise of disengagement to be honored, even if the regime in Saigon is threatened with collapse, one, two, three, or four years hence? If so, our pledge to the South Vietnamese will eventually be broken, and every death in the interim will be an utter scandal. Or, are we committed to stay on until it is absolutely certain that the Viet Cong and their allies can never rise again? The only premise that can make both promises certain of fulfillment is that the South Vietnamese will very soon, within a matter of months, be able to defend themselves alone more successfully and justly than they have heretofore been able to do with the assistance of half a million American troops. I find that premise difficult to believe. Apart from it, the promise of disengagement seems devious if not fraudulent.

The President must be urged to clarify the promises he has made. How secure must the Saigon regime be before our troops depart? What level of security is possible in a highly fragmented and volatile context of a developing nation exposed to two alternative patterns of Westernizing influence? The strategy of the insurgents seems clear: avoid heavy losses in contests with the Americans, preserve the political and military structure of the National Liberation Front, and wait; wait a year, two years, five years, a decade or more. Will Americans still be killing and dying in Vietnam? The President can withdraw American troops; he could sustain the present level of engagement or diminish slightly. Or, he could escalate the war and devastate the North. But the one thing he cannot do is guarantee peace in Vietnam. That is a matter the Vietnamese must sooner or later attend to themselves.

My judgment is obviously based upon a prediction of future military and political events; it is derived by extrapolation from secondhand and spotty knowledge of the situation. It can be wrong, just as the judgments of officials who were going to "bring the boys home by Christmas" have been proven wrong for years.

The Native Resources for Protest and Renewal

I cannot be agnostic and tentative enough in stating my opinions on specific and sensitive points of policy. I would like to say much more, but must hasten to conclude with the expression of the deeply held conviction that though the war must be opposed, it must be opposed in a manner that does not destroy the potential for doing great good latent in a chastened America, purged of *hubris,* and revitalized by a renewal of its true heritage.

Protest must continue. Pressure must be sustained. But the most effective expression of dissent from recent American policy in Southeast Asia is a bold reassertion of the fundamentals of the political philosophy and the human values which moved our founding fathers and sustained our forefathers in the pursuit of liberty and justice for all. It is altogether appropriate that citizens young and old should inquire into the purposes for which governments are instituted among men and should be vigilant in insisting that those purposes be served by every act of every administration. The high purposes for which this nation was formed have not always been served well, and too many have been complacent about our broaches of law and morality. With deeds of justice we must reaffirm professions that have a hollow ring to those who have eyes to see and ears to hear the poor, the dispossessed, the bewildered, the aged, the ill-fed, the sick, the illiterate, the victims of prejudice, indifference, and [indiscriminate] violence at home and abroad—all those who seem to be socially invisible to many who enjoy the fat of the land. Beyond or behind the war there is a spiritual and intellectual malaise that can only be overcome by a revival of confidence in the high calling of this first "new nation." The academic and religious community must play a leading role as we purge ourselves of that which is petty and vindictive and challenge that which is superficial and divisive, whether it is foisted upon us by protesting yippies or by presidential cronies.

In bringing the war to a halt, in opening our land once again to those who seek asylum, we must affirm that the sacrifice of 45,000 American lives can be made meaningful not by relentless continuation of futile killing but by the regeneration of our own nation in a new birth of freedom, a new recovery of the moral strength that would enable us to concede that we have made a grim miscalculation concerning our capacity to understand and influence the affairs of other nations.

Only through the renewal of the soul of our nation can we prepare ourselves to be of more certain assistance to the nations of the world. If we have a role in Vietnam, it is not to defend a faction, or to dictate the terms of a political settlement among the splintered segments of that society, or to introduce advanced technology, or to make the nation over in the image of the West. It is to transmit, by deeds of extraordinary political grace, the charitable and tragic sense of Abraham Lincoln, who saw in another civil war the tragedy, the dilemma, the mystery of human sin working itself out in enmity and strife among brothers; but who, near the end of the battle, was able to translate Christian love into a policy of reconciliation. Let America be heard to speak in his words of forgiveness and mercy rather than in vindictive threats to "bomb them back into the stone age." Mr. Lincoln, the President of a nation that had suffered grievous losses in a fratricidal war, ended his second inaugural address with this appeal:

> With malice toward none, with charity for all, with firmness in the right, as God gives us to see the right, let us strive on to finish the work we are in, to bind up the nation's wounds, to care for him who shall have borne the battle and for his widow and his orphan, to do all which may achieve and cherish a just and lasting peace among ourselves and with all nations. (March 4, 1865)

"The work we are in" is pacification, reconciliation, and the nurture of justice for all the people of South Vietnam. The task cannot be promoted in that country today by our prolonged presence and reliance upon our guns. May God grant Richard Nixon the grace and courage to acknowledge that fact soon.

13

A Historical Perspective on Selective Conscientious Objection

LeRoy Walters

During the past six years the question of selective conscientious objection (SCO) has been addressed by a National Advisory Commission on Selective Service, by the Supreme Court, and by numerous legal scholars, political philosophers, and religious ethicists. For the most part, the contemporary debate concerning SCO has been carried on without explicit reference to discussions of SCO by the classic just-war theorists.[1] The few documents which cite the just-war tradition have arrived at apparently contradictory conclusions.

Perhaps the most striking instance of divergence in interpreting the tradition occurred in 1971. John Rohr, in his important study entitled *Prophets Without Honor,* advanced the thesis that, according to the Catholic just-war tradition, conscientious objection to a particular war is seldom a moral obligation.[2] On the other hand, Supreme Court Justice William O. Douglas appealed to the tradition in support of a somewhat different view. Basing his position on a brief prepared by John Noonan and colleagues,[3] Justice Douglas dissented from the majority opinion in the SCO-case *Negre v. Larsen,* arguing that, according to Vitoria and other authorities, "a Catholic has a moral duty not to participate in unjust wars."[4]

The aim of this essay is to survey in systematic fashion the views of the classic just-war theorists concerning SCO. Such an overview will serve to supplement present-oriented discussions of SCO by providing a historical perspective. It may also help to explain seeming contradictions in the interpretation of the just-war tradition.

The essay itself is divided into three parts, which correspond to three major questions discussed by the classic just-war theorists themselves:

1. What is the citizen's presumptive duty, to obey a summons to participate in warfare or to abstain from participation?

2. Under what circumstances, if any, is SCO morally justified?

3. Should governments make legal provision for conscientious objectors to particular wars?

Two clarifications are in order before we examine the first of these three questions. The theorists chosen for inclusion in the survey have been selected on the basis of two criteria: (1) they are regarded by historians of international law and the just-war tradition as the most representative, creative, and influential just-war theorists; and (2) their writings explicitly discuss the question of SCO. On the basis of the first criterion, the large number of theorists in the western tradition can be limited to approximately eight: Cicero, Augustine, Gratian, Thomas Aquinas, Vitoria, Suárez, Gentili, and Grotius.[5] The second criterion excludes Cicero and suggests major concentration on the writings of Vitoria, Suárez, and Grotius, who analyzed the SCO issue most extensively and systematically.

The second preliminary clarification concerns the precise purpose of the essay. In intention at least, the present study concentrates on historical rather than normative ethics. It seeks to examine and compare the views and arguments of several ancient experts, all of whom understood themselves to be within the just-war tradition. A historical gulf separates us from even the most recent of these theorists, Hugo Grotius, who died in 1645. If one recalls that the musket and improved cannons were the ultimate weapons in Grotius' day, that most seventeenth-century soldiers were either professionals or mercenaries, and that the prevalent premodern form of government was monarchical, one begins to sense the depth of that gulf.[6] This historical distance does not render the views of the classic theorists either invalid or irrelevant. It does suggest, however, that any effort to apply their thought concerning SCO to twentieth-century ethical decision-making must take into account a rather significant hermeneutical problem.

THE CITIZEN'S PRESUMPTIVE DUTY

The first question asked by most just-war theorists was *whether* resort to war is ever morally justified. Phrased in the most general terms, their answer was: The prince is permitted to resort to war only as a last resort, after all non-military means of settling a dispute have been tried and have failed. In other words, the prince's *prima facie* duty was to abstain from war.[7]

One might expect the theorists to have argued, analogously, that the presumptive duty of the subject or common citizen was to avoid military action. Generally speaking, however, they did not so argue. In the opinion of most just-war theorists, the prince's decision to wage war carried sufficient moral weight to reverse the presumption. Thus the majority view was that if the prince called to arms, the subject's *prima facie* duty was to obey and participate in warfare. In short, the burden of proof lay with the selective objector.[8]

The theoretical foundations for the majority position were laid by Augustine and Thomas Aquinas. In his work *Contra Faustum* Augustine had written:

> A just man, even if he fights under a sacreligious king, can lawfully fight when the king commands it—as serving the order of peace—if it is certain that what he is commanded to do is not opposed to the precept of God or if it is not certain whether or not it is opposed to the divine precept. Thus the iniquity of the one commanding makes the king guilty, but the order of serving makes the soldier innocent.[9]

This quotation from Augustine found its way into the canon law in the twelfth century and exerted a significant influence on the subsequent just-war tradition.[10]

Although Thomas Aquinas did not explicitly discuss the question of conscientious objection to warfare, he did turn critical attention to an analogous life-and-death issue, namely, the dilemma of an executioner who is ordered by a judge to kill an innocent man.

> He that carries out the sentence of the judge who has condemned an innocent man, if the sentence contains an inexcusable error, he should not obey, else there would be an excuse for the executions of the martyrs: if however it contains no manifest injustice, he does not sin by carrying out the sentence, because he has no right to discuss the judgment of his superior; nor is it he who slays the innocent man, but the judge whose minister he is.[11]

Thomas's example was also cited frequently by later just-war theorists.[12]

Two sixteenth-century Spanish moral theologians, Vitoria and Suárez, most clearly articulated the majority position on the citizen's presumptive duty. In the first place, they argued that the subject had no moral obligation to investigate the cause of a war; rather, he could participate in good conscience provided that the war was not clearly unjust.[13] Vitoria, in fact, distinguished various degrees in the responsibility-to-know. He clearly asserted the duty of the prince, senators, petty rulers, and members of the royal council to examine carefully the alleged grounds for going to war. With typical candor Vitoria explained why ordinary subjects did not share in the same responsibility:

> Other lesser folk who have no place or audience in the prince's council or in the public council are under no obligation to examine the causes of war but may serve in it in reliance on their betters. This is proved, first, by the fact that it is impossible and inexpedient to give reasons for all acts of state to every member of the commonalty. Also by the fact that men of the lower orders, even if they perceived the injustice of a war, could not stop it, and their voice would not be heeded. Therefore, any examination by them of the causes of a war would be futile. Also by the fact that for men of this sort it is enough proof of the justice of war (unless the contrary be quite certain) that it is being waged after public counsel and by public authority. Therefore no further examination on their part is needed.[14]

The majority position on the citizen's presumptive duty was also apparent when Vitoria and Suárez discussed the problem of doubtful cases. Both theorists agreed that as long as the justice of a war was in doubt, the subject was morally obligated to participate.[15] The primary justification for this position was a lesser-of-two-evils, consequentialist argument. If the citizen obeyed his prince in a doubtful cause, Vitoria and Suárez noted, he merely fought with an uncertain conscience. If, on the other hand, the soldier refused to fight merely because of doubts concerning the justice of a war, he exposed his nation to disaster. As Vitoria put it, "The State would fall into grave peril and the door would be opened to wrongdoing."[16] Suárez added that if subjects disobeyed in doubtful situations, "It would be impossible for princes to defend their rights, and this would be a serious and general misfortune."[17]

There was, however, a minority strain in the just-war tradition which, if it did not reverse the citizen's presumptive duty, at least severely qualified it. The most systematic spokesman for this minority view was the Dutch theorist, Hugo Grotius. In full awareness that he was challenging traditional assumptions, Grotius attacked three pillars of the majority position.

First, Grotius at least implied that potential participants in actions which involve the taking of human life should investigate the situation before taking part in such actions. Alluding to an analogous case which had often been cited to support the opposite view, Grotius commented:

> . . . It is probable that even the executioner, who is going to put a condemned man to death, should know the merits of the case, either through assisting at the inquiry and the trial or from a confession of the crime, in such a degree that it is sufficiently clear to him that the criminal deserves death.[18]

Grotius also differed with his distinguished predecessors on the question of secrecy in wartime. As noted, above, Vitoria and Suárez had argued that expediency often prevented a prince from making public the reasons for his war-policies. Grotius' retort bordered on cynicism:

> Although this may be true of persuasive causes, it is not true of justifiable causes, which ought to be clear and open and, further, should be such as may and ought to be openly set forth.[19]

To this response Grotius appended a polite pragmatic warning: the prince who cannot clearly explain the cause of a war may discover that his skeptical soldiers lack enthusiasm for the war-effort.[20]

Finally, in perhaps his boldest departure from tradition, Grotius launched a frontal assault on the majority view concerning doubtful cases. He began by resurrecting the opinion of Adrian, a Dutch theologian, who had stipulated that in cases of doubt the subject should abstain from war. Without unequivocally adopting Adrian's position, Grotius indicated strong sympathy for it.[21] But Grotius went a step further: He stood the traditional lesser-of-two-evils argument on its head. As we have noted, Vitoria and Suárez had argued that in doubtful cases it was morally safer to fight than to risk betraying one's country. Grotius described the moral dilemma differently and came to the opposite conclusion:

> *Disobedience* in things of this kind, by its very nature, is a lesser evil than *manslaughter,* especially than the slaughter of many innocent men.[22]

In summary, according to the majority view in the classic just-war tradition, the citizen's presumptive duty was to obey his prince's call to arms. The primary reason for this presumption against SCO was the theorists' concern for the preservation of the state as a viable agent of justice. Grotius, on the other hand, was the chief spokesman for a minority view which, if it did not reverse the presumption in favor of obedience, at least seemed to provide an expanded theoretical basis for SCO.

THE JUSTIFICATION OF SELECTIVE CONSCIENTIOUS OBJECTORS

A presumption against SCO is precisely not an absolute prohibition of SCO. Implicit in the term "presumption" is the possibility that other considerations will override the presumption. Thus, it is not surprising that several of the major just-war theorists discussed the *Grenzfall,* the situation in which the *prima facie* duty to follow one's prince to war was transcended or reversed.

Generally speaking, the architects of the just-war tradition adopted the standard natural-law position on the question of disobedience to political authority. One of the major theorists, Thomas Aquinas, gave classic expression to the natural-law view in his treatise on law, as well as in numerous other passages of the *Summa theologiae.* Although Thomas did not explicitly relate his analysis of disobedience to the issue of military service, he set clear ethical limits on the citizen's general obligation to obey temporal rulers.

> Man is bound to obey secular princes insofar as this is required by the order of justice. Wherefore if [the prince] . . . commands what is unjust, his subjects are not bound to obey him, except perhaps accidentally, in order to avoid scandal.[23]

The later theorists applied this general doctrine of justifiable civil disobedience to the specific problem of participation in war. Without exception they regarded SCO as a possible response to the call to military service. In the case of Suárez and Gentili the SCO-option was described in rather perfunctory fashion. Suárez noted that if the justice of a war was "extremely doubtful," the subject was morally obligated to investigate the situation before participating. In addition, Suárez implied that SCO was justified if the injustice of a war was "clear," "evident," or "manifest."[24] Gentili, an English contemporary of Suárez, observed that no soldier could be held legally accountable for fighting in an unjust war. Apparently not entirely satisfied with this juridical solution, Gentili went on to acknowledge that a subject could offend in the internal forum of conscience by participating in a war which he knew to be unjust.[25]

It was left to Vitoria and Grotius, however, to provide a more thoroughgoing analysis of the grounds for SCO. Both theorists clearly regarded selective objection as a moral obligation in certain circumstances. In the writings of both, subjective as well as objective factors were taken into account.

The objective prerequisite for SCO was a clearly-unjust war. Grotius was content to state this condition in a single sentence:

> If those under the rule of another [i.e., subjects] are ordered to take the field, as often occurs, they should altogether refrain from so doing if it is clear to them that the cause of the war is unjust.[26]

Vitoria, on the other hand, explained the objective grounds for SCO in somewhat greater detail. His most comprehensive statement concerning SCO was formulated in the following terms:

> If the injustice of a war is clear to a subject, he ought not to serve in it, even on the command of his prince. This is clear, for no one can authorize the killing of an innocent person. But in the case before us the enemy are innocent. Therefore they may not be killed. Again, a prince sins when he commences a war in such a case. But "not only are they who commit such things worthy of death, but they, too, who consent to the doing thereof" (Romans 1:32). Therefore soldiers are not excused when they fight in bad faith. Again, it is not lawful to kill innocent fellow-citizens at the prince's command. Therefore not foreigners either.[27]

In elaborating his position on SCO Vitoria sought to clarify the meaning of "clear injustice" and to emphasize the citizen's responsibility-to-know.

> . . . The proofs and tokens of the injustice of war may be such that ignorance would be no excuse even to the subjects who serve in it. This is clear because such ignorance [on the part of subjects] might be deliberate and adopted with evil intent toward the enemy.[28]

A passage in Vitoria's commentary on the *Summa theologiae* of Thomas Aquinas helped to dramatize the definition of deliberate ignorance:

> If the ignorance is crass and, so to speak, wilful, it does not serve as an excuse. Accordingly, I hold that if there are indications that a war is not just,—[if, for example,] I am in doubt, but close my eyes, saying, "What do I know of the matter?" because I feel affection for my king—then I will not be acquitted of sin."[29]

To clinch his point that the citizen had a responsibility to recognize and avoid obvious moral evil, Vitoria cited three historical precedents which would undoubtedly have made a deep impression upon his Spanish audience. If subjects were not responsible for participating in the injustice of their leaders, he declared, then

> [Moslem][30] unbelievers would be excused when they follow their leaders to war against Christians. . . . Also, the soldiers

who crucified Christ, ignorantly following Pilate's order, would be excused. In addition, the Jewish mob would be excused, which was led by the elders to shout "Away with Him, crucify Him."[31]

The subjective prerequisite for SCO was a citizen's conviction that a war was unjust. According to Vitoria, such a belief was sufficient to justify SCO, regardless of whether the war was in fact just or unjust. In his words,

> . . . Subjects whose conscience is against the justice of war may not engage in it, whether they be right or wrong. This is clear, for "whatever is not of faith is sin" (Romans 14:23).[32]

Writing about seventy-five years after the death of Vitoria, Hugo Grotius reiterated and endorsed Vitoria's view.[33]

In summary, several of the major just-war theorists discussed the circumstances in which SCO was morally justified. There was general agreement among the theorists that no citizen was obliged to participate in a war that was clearly unjust. Vitoria and Grotius added two refinements to this general consensus. They asserted unequivocally that the subject had a moral duty *not* to take part in a clearly unjust war. Second, according to Vitoria and Grotius, a citizen's sincere conviction that a particular war was unjust obligated him to abstain from military participation.

LEGAL PROVISION FOR SELECTIVE CONSCIENTIOUS OBJECTORS

When we look to the classic just-war tradition for statements concerning SCO and the law, we find that the major theorists wrote comparatively little on the issue. A partial explanation for this relative silence is that the just-war theorists concentrated primary attention on the spheres of morality and international law rather than on the provisions of domestic or intranational law. In the case of the later theorists, the silence can also be traced in part to military recruitment practices of their times. Virtually all soldiers in armies of the sixteenth and seventeenth centuries were volunteers, who fought either as professionals in national standing armies or as mercenaries ready to offer their services to the highest bidder.[34] In a context where voluntary participation in military service predominated, the problem of legal provision for SCO was understandably somewhat less acute.

Of the theorists discussed in this essay, only Hugo Grotius explicitly considered how the state should deal with the question of selective conscientious objection. He recommended that administrative procedures be established to insure that no citizen—whether pacifist or selective objector—would be compelled to participate in war against his conscience. Concretely, he proposed that a special tax should be levied on selective objectors.

> . . . If the minds of subjects cannot be satisfied by the explanation of the cause of a war, it will by all means be the duty of a good magistrate to impose upon them extraordinary taxes rather than military service, particularly where there will be no lack of others who will serve.[35]

At no point did Grotius clearly state the warrant for this policy-recommendation. One can perhaps surmise that the logic of his just-war position impelled him to seek institutional arrangements which would make possible the kind of discriminating ethical judgments which he advocated. In addition, however, one finds evidence that Grotius had been sensitized to the problem of SCO by the experience of contemporary Christian conscientious objectors and by pacifistic emphases within traditional Christian ethical thought. In the passage immediately following his discussion of official provision for SCO, Grotius wrote:

> . . . Even if there can be no doubt respecting the cause of war, still it does not seem at all right that Christians should be compelled to serve against their will; the reason is that to refrain from military service, even when it is permissible to serve, is the mark of somewhat greater holiness, which was long demanded from ecclesiastics and penitents, and recommended in many ways to all other persons.[36]

To summarize, the question of legal provision for SCO was largely ignored by the classic just-war tradition. Grotius, however, recommended the establishment of administrative machinery to accommodate the moral convictions of the selective objector.

In conclusion, we return to two points raised in the introduction to this essay. The apparent disagreement between John Rohr and Justice Douglas seems, in light of the foregoing historical survey, to be readily understandable. Rohr is certainly correct in arguing that, according to the Catholic just-war tradition, SCO is seldom a moral obligation. As we noted in the first part of this essay, the major Catholic theorists accepted the citizen's presumptive duty to go to war and treated conscientious objection to military service as a *Grenzfall,* or limiting-case. However, Rohr fails to accord due emphasis to Vitoria's clear statement that in certain circumstances SCO becomes a moral duty.[37] Justice Douglas, on the other hand, accurately reflects the viewpoint of Vitoria when he asserts that "a Catholic has a moral duty not to participate in unjust wars." As the second part of this essay has demonstrated, Vitoria unequivocally asserted the citizen's obligation to avoid any collaboration in military injustice. Two other facets of Vitoria's thought remain unmentioned in the dissent of Justice Douglas, however—Vitoria's emphasis on the citizen's presumptive duty to obey and his insistence on subjective or objective certainty concerning the injustice of a war.

The divergent conclusions of Rohr and Justice Douglas serve as an additional reminder of the complexities involved in any effort to interpret or update the just-war tradition. This hermeneutical problem has at least three dimensions. First, within a single theorist—for example, Vitoria—differing tendencies and emphases appear which the would-be interpreter must hold in tension. In the second place, on certain issues there is a lack of consensus within the tradition. Such internal contradictions virtually compel the modern interpreter to choose one view—perhaps the majority view—and to reject others. Finally, the contemporary interpreter must seek to apply an ancient tradition to a situation characterized by post-monarchical forms of government, military conscription in wartime, and highly-sophisticated weapons of destruction. In short, it is difficult, but possible, to reconstruct what the major just-war theorists said about SCO within their varied historical contexts. What their views mean for our own attempt to think through an ethic of war and peace is much less clear.[38]

NOTES

1. The following are among the most important recent analyses of the SCO question (documents are listed in chronological order by year and in alphabetical order within each year): *In Pursuit of Equity: Who Serves When Not All Serve?* Report of the National Advisory Commission on Selective Service (Washington, D.C.: U.S. Government Printing Office, 1967), esp. pp. 48–51; James Finn, ed., *A Conflict of Loyalties; The Case for Selective Conscientious Objection* (New York: Pegasus, 1968); Edward LeRoy Long, Jr., *War and Conscience in America* (Philadelphia: Westminster Press, 1968), pp. 106–120; William V. O'Brien, "Selective Conscientious Objection and International Law," *Georgetown Law Journal* 56 (June, 1968), 1080–1131; Ralph Potter, "Conscientious Objection to Particular Wars," in *Religion and the Public Order,* No. 4, edited by Donald A. Giannella (Ithaca, N.Y.: Cornell University Press, 1968), pp. 44–99; Paul Ramsey, "Selective Conscientious Objection," in *The Just War: Force and Political Responsibility* (New York: Charles Scribner's Sons, 1970), pp. 91–137; Michael Walzer, "Conscientious Objection," in *Obligation: Essays on Disobedience, War and Citizenship* (Cambridge, Mass.: Harvard University Press, 1970), pp. 120–145; Kent Greenawalt, "All or Nothing at All: The Defeat of Selective Conscientious Objection," in *The Supreme Court Review: 1971,* edited by Philip B. Kurland (Chicago: University of Chicago Press, 1971), pp. 31–94; John A. Rohr, *Prophets Without Honor: Public Policy and the Selective Conscientious Objector,* Studies in Christian Ethics (Nashville: Abingdon Press, 1971); U.S. Supreme Court, *Gillette v. United States* and *Negre v. Larsen et al., U.S. [Supreme Court] Reports* 401 (October Term, 1970), 437–475 (case decided March 8, 1971); David Malament, "Selective Conscientious Objection and the *Gillette* Decision," *Philosophy and Public Affairs,* I (Summer, 1972), 362–386. For further bibliography see Rohr, *Prophets,* pp. 185–188. While many of the documents listed above refer to the just-war tradition in general terms, discussion of the theorists' views on the specific issue of SCO occurs only in the writings of Long, Rohr, and Malament, and in Justice Douglas's dissent from the majority decision in *Negre v. Larsen.*

2. Rohr, *Prophets,* pp. 109–123.

3. Richard Harrington; Leigh Athearn; Stuart J. Land; and John T. Noonan, Jr., *Negre v. Larsen: Reply Brief on Behalf of Petitioner* (Supreme Court, October term, 1970, No. 325).

4. *Gillette v. United States, U.S. [Supreme Court] Reports* 401 (October Term, 1970), 470–471.

5. For evidence on this point see Robert Regout, *La doctrine de la guerre juste. . .* (Paris: A. Pedone, 1934), pp. 79–93, 152–185,

194–230, and 274–278; Joachim von Elbe, "The Evolution of the Just War in International Law," *American Journal of International Law* 33 (1939), 667–669, 674–680; and Arthur Nussbaum, *A Concise History of the Law of Nations,* revised edition (New York: Macmillan, 1953), pp. 10–16, 79–114.

6. For an attempt to reconstruct the historical setting of sixteenth- and seventeenth-century just-war thought see LeRoy Brandt Walters, Jr., "Five Classic Just-War Theories: A Study in the Thought of Thomas Aquinas, Vitoria, Suárez, Gentili, and Grotius" (Ph.D. dissertation, Yale University, 1971), pp. 205–213, 219–269.

7. Thomas Aquinas, *Summa theologiae* (ST), II-II, 40, 1, objections and answer; Francisco de Vitoria, *De jure belli* (DJB), prolog, 1, and 60; Francisco Suárez, *"De bello"* (DB), I, 1; IV, 1, 5, and 7 (the disputation "On War" is part of the treatise on charity in the work entitled *The Three Theological Virtues*); Alberico Gentili, *De jure belli* (DJB), I, 5 (pp. 27–30); I, 13 (p. 58); I, 17 (p. 79); and Hugo Grotius, *De jure belli ac pacis* (JBP), I, 2, 1–9; II, 24, 8–10. Unless otherwise noted, all citations from the writings of Vitoria, Suárez, Gentili, and Grotius refer to the Classics of International Law (CIL) translations of their works. The CIL volume on Suárez bears the title *Selections from Three Works.*

8. See, for example, Vitoria, DJB, 25, 31; Suárez, DB, VI, 8–9. The late John Courtney Murray reasserted this majority view in his essay "War and Conscience," in *A Conflict of Loyalties,* pp. 26–27; see also Paul Ramsey, "Can a Pacifist Tell a Just War?" in *Just War,* pp. 274–275.

9. *Contra Faustum,* 22, 75; cited by Gratian in the *Decretum,* Pt. II, C. 23, qu. 1, c. 4 (Friedberg edition, I, col. 893; author's translation).

10. Frederick Hooker Russell, "The Medieval Theories of the Just War according to the Romanists and Canonists of the Twelfth and Thirteenth Centuries" (Ph.D. dissertation, Johns Hopkins University, 1969), pp. 211, 277, and 340, n. 61; Vitoria, DJB, 31; Suárez, VI, 8; Gentili, DJB, I, 25 (p. 125); and Grotius, JBP, II, 26, 4, 3.

11. ST, II-II, 64, 6, ad 3 (Dominican Fathers' translation).

12. See, for example, Vitoria, DJB, 22 and 31; Suárez, DB, VI, 8; and Grotius, JBP, II, 26, 4, 9.

13. Vitoria, DJB, 22 and 25; Suárez, DB, VI, 8. Gentili added: "It is not for subjects to inquire too curiously which side took up arms with the better right" (DJB, I, 25 [p. 126; CIL translation]).

14. Vitoria, DJB, 25 (CIL translation).

15. Vitoria, DJB, 31; Suárez, DB, VI, 8. Suárez did stipulate, however, that if the arguments against the justice of a war significantly outweighed the arguments in its favor, the subject was bound to investigate the matter further (DB, VI, 9).

16. DJB, 31 (CIL translation).

17. DB, VI, 9 (CIL translation).

18. JBP, II, 26, 4, 9 (CIL translation); see n. 11 above.

19. JBP, II, 26, 4, 5 (CIL translation).

20. JBP, II, 26, 4, 6–7.

21. JBP, II, 26, 4, 4–8. Adrian, who late in life became Pope Hadrian VI, had expressed his view in a work entitled *Quaestiones quodlibeticae,* II; both Vitoria (DJB, 30–31) and Suárez (DB, VI, 9) had explicitly rejected Adrian's argument.

22. JBP, II, 26, 4, 5 (CIL translation; italics added).

23. ST, II-II, 105, 6, ad 3 (Dominican Fathers' translation).

24. DB, VI, 8–9.

25. DJB, I, 25 (p. 126).

26. JBP, II, 26, 3, 1 (CIL translation).

27. DJB, 22 (CIL translation; slightly revised on the basis of comparison with the Latin original.)

28. DJB, 26.

29. *Commentary* on the *Summa theologiae* of Thomas Aquinas, II-II, 40, 8; translated by Gwladys L. Williams in James Brown Scott, *The Spanish Origins of International Law,* Vol. I: *Francisco de Vitoria and His Law of Nations* (Oxford: Clarendon Press, 1934), p. cxix (translation slightly revised on the basis of comparison with the Latin original).

30. Vitoria's general position was that Indian subjects often fought because of invincible ignorance; he did not usually extend such tolerance to Moslem soldiers. Compare the relatively mild prescriptions of the *De Indis* with the rather harsh measures countenanced in DJB, 26, 48, and 60.

31. DJB, 26 (slightly revised on the basis of comparison with the Latin original). Gentili cited an additional example of a clearly-unjust war; in his opinion, "The [Latin American] Indians were not blameless in fighting for a king who made war unjustly" (DJB, I, 25 [p. 126]). Note also Thomas Aquinas' view that the executioners of the martyrs were morally responsible for their actions (see n. 11 above).

32. DJB, 23.

33. JBP, II, 26, 3, 5.

34. Lynn Montross, *War Through the Ages* (New York: Harper & Row, 1944), pp. 204–205, 266–267; cf. Walters, "Five Classic Just-War Theories," pp. 207–209.

35. JBP, II, 26, 5, 1 (CIL translation; punctuation slightly revised); cf. JBP, II, 26, 5, title.

36. JBP, II, 26, 5, 2 (CIL translation). For a discussion of Grotius' relationship to contemporary Dutch pacifists see Walters, "Five Classic Just-War Theories," pp. 253–255, 283–284.

37. My criticism is not that Rohr's interpretation of the Catholic

just-war tradition is incorrect, but rather that it is one-sided. To illustrate, on p. 112 of *Prophets Without Honor* Rohr quotes Vitoria's "third proposition" concerning SCO (DJB, 25). However, he does not cite Vitoria's "first proposition" and "fourth proposition" (DJB, 22 and 26), both of which clearly assert that SCO can become a moral obligation (see nn. 27 and 28 above).

38. I wish to thank Professors Charles E. Curran and James F. Childress for their helpful comments on an earlier version of this article.

PART IV

Nuclear War and Deterrence

INTRODUCTION:
THE ADVENT OF NUCLEAR ETHICS

On July 16, 1945, the atomic bomb, Trinity, exploded in the desert of Alamogordo, New Mexico, auguring a new chapter in the history of war and international relations. Three weeks later, Little Boy, the first atomic weapon employed in warfare, was detonated over Hiroshima, vaporizing 71,000 people instantly and severely injuring 30,000 more. A shock wave destroyed buildings over a mile away from ground zero, and a fire storm fueled by self-generated winds of over fifty miles per hour consumed the city. Hiroshima was soon showered by a black, oily radioactive rain. Three days later a second bomb was dropped, on the city of Nagasaki, killing 73,000 people and severely injuring that many more. Tens of thousands have died from the lingering effects of radioactivity. Indeed, to this day those who have descended from the survivors of Hiroshima and Nagasaki bear the emotional scars and the genetic effects of these historic explosions.

Compared with what was to come, the atomic weapons used at the end of the Second World War were relatively small—about 12.5 kilotons worth of TNT. Within five years the United States embarked upon the mission of constructing a fusion, or hydrogen, bomb, whose destructive potential would be limited only by the material requirements of delivery. The first fusion bomb to be tested, in November 1952, had the explosive capacity of 10.4 million tons of TNT, one thousand times the destructive capacity of Little Boy. By 1953 the U.S.S.R. tested its first fusion weapon, which in fact was significantly smaller than the fission weapons produced by the United States. But within two years, the Soviets were able to test their first true thermonuclear device, thus ending the U.S. monopoly. Moreover, technical breakthroughs in the early 1950s enabled scientists to create very small fission bombs, less than one-third the size of the weapons used against Japan. Less than a decade after Hiroshima, efforts to develop a nuclear arsenal of tactical and strategic nuclear weapons were well under way.

Within the context of cold war suspicion and competition, nuclear deterrence became the centerpiece of superpower relations. *Nuclear deterrence* denotes the goal of preventing the outbreak of nuclear war and some conventional wars by threatening to use nuclear weapons in response to aggressive military actions. To deter, nations make threats of nuclear reprisal or attack, the outcome of which a potential aggressor would consider a disproportionate price to pay for political or military objectives. Deterrence thus takes the form of a conditional or hypothetical threat: If specified conditions are violated, if cooperation cannot be sustained, then intimidating threats will be carried out. Ideally, the goal is to create a situation in which deterrent threats will not have to be exercised. In theory, those who are threatened will cooperate because alternatives to cooperation include harmful consequences. In this way, deterrence relies on coercive measures to secure a desired state of affairs, or to prevent an undesirable state of affairs, with untrustworthy individuals or groups.

Threats of nuclear attack are premised on two main uses of nuclear weapons: counterpopulation and counterforce attacks. The former refers to the use of nuclear weapons against civilian targets, that is, cities. The latter refers to the use of nuclear weapons against military targets, related industries, and communication facilities. Starting in the 1950s, U.S. policy has included both counterforce and counterpopulation targeting.

With the advent of such weapons of mass destruction, ethicists were forced to ask themselves, Have traditional canons of war become obsolete? If not, how are they pertinent? To these questions there was the added problem of how to evaluate the paradox of deterrence. Moral evaluations of nuclear deterrence have sought to address the question, Can we threaten to do evil that good may come? That is, can we threaten, and perhaps intend, to carry out acts of mass destruction if such threats reduce the likelihood that such acts would be carried out? Among nonpacifists, answers to these questions have varied, depending on how just-war criteria have been interpreted. They have also varied according to how applications of just-war criteria have sought to balance concerns for consequences and principles.[1]

NOTES

1. Lawrence Freedman, *The Evolution of Nuclear Strategy* (New York: St. Martin's Press, 1981); Russell Hardin *et al.*, eds., *Nuclear Deterrence: Ethics and Strategy* (Chicago: University of Chicago Press, 1985); Patrick Morgan, *Deterrence: A Conceptual Analysis* (Beverly Hills, Calif.: Sage Press, 1977); John Newhouse, *War and Peace in the Nuclear Age* (New York: Vintage Books, 1990); Thomas Schelling, *Arms and Influence* (New Haven: Yale University Press, 1966).

14

Mr. Truman's Decree

G. E. M. Anscombe

In 1939, on the outbreak of war, the President of the United States asked for assurances from the belligerent nations that [civilian] populations would not be attacked.

In 1945, when the Japanese enemy was known by him to have made two attempts towards a negotiated peace, the President of the United States gave the order for dropping an atom bomb on a Japanese city; three days later a second bomb, of a different type, was dropped on another city. No ultimatum was delivered before the second bomb was dropped.

Set side by side, these events provide enough of a contrast to provoke enquiry. Evidently development has taken place; one would like to see its course plotted. It is not, I think, difficult to give an intelligible account:

(1) The British Government gave President Roosevelt the required assurance with a reservation which meant "if the Germans do it we shall do it too." You don't promise to abide by the Queensberry Rules even if your opponent abandons them.

(2) The only condition for ending the war was announced to be unconditional surrender. Apart from the "liberation of the subject peoples," the objectives were vague in character. Now the demand for unconditional surrender was mixed up with a determination to make no peace with Hitler's government. In view of the character of Hitler's regime that attitude was very intelligible. Nevertheless some people have doubts

about it now. It is suggested that defeat of itself would have resulted in the rapid discredit and downfall of that government. On this I can form no strong opinion. The important question to my mind is whether the intention of making no peace with Hitler's government necessarily entailed the objective of unconditional surrender. If, as may not be impossible, we could have formulated a pretty definite objective, a rough outline of the terms which we were willing to make with Germany, while at the same time indicating that we would not make terms with Hitler's government, then the question of the wisdom of this latter demand seems to me a minor one; but if not, then that settles it. It was the insistence on unconditional surrender that was the root of all evil. The connection between such a demand and the need to use the most ferocious methods of warfare will be obvious. And in itself the proposal of an unlimited objective in war is stupid and barbarous.

(3) The Germans did a good deal of indiscriminate bombing in this country. It is impossible for an uninformed person to know how much, in its first beginnings, was due to indifference on the part of pilots to using their loads only on military targets, and how much to actual policy on the part of those who sent them. Nor do I know what we were doing in the same line at the time. But certainly anyone would have been stupid who had thought in 1939 that there would not be such bombing, developing into definite raids on cities.

(4) For some time before war broke out, and more intensely afterwards, there was propaganda in this country on the subject of the "indivisibility" of modern war. The civilian population, we were told, is really as much combatant as the fighting forces. The military strength of a nation includes its whole economic and social strength. Therefore the distinction between the people engaged in prosecuting the war and the population at large is unreal. There is no such thing as a non-participator; you cannot buy a postage stamp or any taxed article, or grow a potato or cook a meal, without contributing to the "war effort." War indeed is a "ghastly evil," but once it has broken out no one can "contract out" of it. "Wrong" indeed must be being done if war is waged, but you cannot help being involved in it. There was a doctrine of "collective responsibility" with a lugubriously elevated moral tone about it. The upshot was that it was senseless to draw any

line between legitimate and illegitimate objects of attack. . . . I am not sure how children and the aged fitted into this story: probably they cheered the soldiers and munitions workers up.

(5) The Japanese attacked Pearl Harbor and there was war between America and Japan. Some American (Republican) historians now claim that the acknowledged fact that the American Government knew an attack was impending some hours before it occurred, but did not alert the people in local command, can only be explained by a purpose of arousing the passions of American people. However that may be, those passions were suitably aroused and the war was entered on with the same vague and hence limitless objectives; and once more unconditional surrender was the only condition on which the war was going to end.

(6) Then came the great change: we adopted the system of 'area bombing' as opposed to 'target bombing.' This differed from even big raids on cities, such as had previously taken place in the course of the war, by being far more extensive and devastating and much less random; the whole of a city area would be systematically plotted out and dotted with bombs. "Attila was a Sissy," as the *Chicago Tribune* headed an article on this subject.

(7) In 1945, at the Potsdam conference in July, Stalin informed the American and British statesmen that he had received two requests from the Japanese to act as a mediator with a view to ending the war. He had refused. The Allies agreed on the "general principle"—marvelous phrase!—of using the new type of weapon that America now possessed. The Japanese were given a chance in the form of the Potsdam Declaration, calling for unconditional surrender in face of overwhelming force soon to be arrayed against them. The historian of the Survey of International Affairs considers that this phrase was rendered meaningless by the statement of a series of terms; but of these the ones incorporating the Allies' demands were mostly of so vague and sweeping a nature as to be rather a declaration of what unconditional surrender would be like than to constitute conditions. It seems to be generally agreed that the Japanese were desperate enough to have accepted the Declaration but for their loyalty to their Emperor: the "terms" would certainly have permitted the Allies to get rid of him if they chose. The Japanese refused

the Declaration. In consequence, the bombs were dropped on Hiroshima and Nagasaki. The decision to use them on people was Mr. Truman's.

For men to choose to kill the innocent as a means to their ends is always murder, and murder is one of the worst of human actions. So the prohibition on deliberately killing prisoners of war or the civilian population is not like the Queensberry Rules: its force does not depend on its promulgation as part of positive law, written down, agreed upon, and adhered to by the parties concerned.

When I say that to choose to kill the innocent as a means to one's ends is murder, I am saying what would generally be accepted as correct. But I shall be asked for my definition of "the innocent." I will give it, but later. Here, it is not necessary; for with Hiroshima and Nagasaki we are not confronted with a borderline case. In the bombing of these cities it was certainly decided to kill the innocent as a means to an end. And a very large number of them, all at once, without warning, without the interstices of escape or the chance to take shelter, which existed even in the 'area bombings' of the German cities.

I have long been puzzled by the common cant about President Truman's courage in making this decision. Of course, I know that you can be cowardly without having reason to think you are in danger. But how can you be courageous? Light has come to me lately: the term is an acknowledgement of the truth. Mr. Truman was brave because, and only because, what he did was so bad. But I think the judgement unsound. Given the right circumstances (for example, that no one whose opinion matters will disapprove), a quite mediocre person can do spectacularly wicked things without thereby becoming impressive.

I determined to oppose the proposal to give Mr. Truman an honorary degree here at Oxford. Now, an honorary degree is not a reward of merit: it is, as it were, a reward for being a very distinguished person, and it would be foolish to enquire whether a candidate deserves to be as distinguished as he is. That is why, in general, the question whether so-and-so should have an honorary degree is devoid of interest. A very distinguished person will hardly be also a notorious criminal, and if he should chance to be a non-notorious criminal it would, in my opinion, be improper to bring the matter up. It is only in the rather rare case in which a man is known everywhere for an action, in the face of which it is sycophancy to honour him, that the question can be of slightest interest.

I have been accused of being "high-minded." I must be saying "You may not do evil that good may come," which is a disagreeably high-minded doctrine. The action was necessary, or at any rate it was thought by competent, expert military opinion to be necessary; it probably saved more lives than it sacrificed; it had a good result, it ended the war. Come now: if you had to choose between boiling a baby and letting some frightful disaster befall a thousand people—or a million people, if a thousand is not enough—what would you do? Are you going to strike an attitude and say "You may not do evil that good may come?" (People who never hear such arguments will hardly believe they take place, and will pass this rapidly by.)

"It pretty certainly saved a huge number of lives." Given the conditions, I agree. That is to say, if those bombs had not been dropped the Allies would have had to invade Japan to achieve their aim, and they would have done so. Very many soldiers on both sides would have been killed; the Japanese, it is said—and it may well be true—would have massacred the prisoners of war; and large numbers of their civilian population would have been killed by "ordinary" bombing.

I do not dispute it. Given the conditions, that was probably what was averted by that action. But what were the conditions? The unlimited objective, the fixation on unconditional surrender. The disregard of the fact that the Japanese were desirous of negotiating peace. The character of the Potsdam Declaration—their "chance." I will not suggest, as some would like to do, that there was an exultant itch to use the new weapons, but it seems plausible to think that the consciousness of the possession of such instruments had its effect on the manner in which the Japanese were offered their "chance."...

II

Choosing to kill the innocent as a means to your ends is always murder. Naturally, killing the innocent as an end in itself is murder too; but that is no more than a possible future development for us:[1] in our part of the globe it is a practice that has so far been confined to the Nazis. I intend my formulation to be taken strictly; each term in it is necessary. For killing the innocent, even if you know as a matter of statistical certainty that the things you do involve it, is not necessarily murder. I mean that if you attack a lot of military targets, such as munitions factories and naval dockyards, as carefully as you can, you will be certain to kill a number of innocent people; but that is not murder. On the other hand, unscrupulousness in considering the possibilities turns it into murder. I here print as a case in point a letter which I received lately from Holland:

> We read in our paper about your opposition to Truman. I do not like him either, but do you know that in the war the English bombed the dykes of our province Zeeland, an island where nobody could escape anywhere to. Where the whole population was drowned, children, women, farmers working in the field, all the cattle, everything, hundreds and hundreds, and we were your allies! Nobody ever speaks about that. Perhaps it were well to know this. Or, to remember.

That was to trap some fleeing German military. I think my correspondent has something.

It may be impossible to take the thing (or people) you want to destroy as your target; it may be possible to attack it only by taking as the object of your attack what includes large numbers of innocent people. Then you cannot very well say they died by accident. Here your action is murder.

"But where will you draw the line? It is impossible to draw an exact line." This is a common and absurd argument against drawing any line; it may be very difficult, and there are obviously borderline cases. But we have fallen into the way of drawing no line, and offering as justifications what an uncaptive mind will find only a bad joke. Wherever the line is, certain things are certainly well to one side or the other of it.

Now who are "the innocent" in war? They are all those who are not fighting and not engaged in supplying those who are with the means of fighting. A farmer growing wheat which may be eaten by the troops is not "supplying them with the means of fighting." Over this, too, the line may be difficult to draw. But that does not mean that no line should be drawn, or that, even if one is in doubt just where to draw the line, one cannot be crystal clear that this or that is well over the line.

"But the people fighting are probably conscripts! In that case they are just as innocent as anyone else." "Innocent" here is not a term referring to personal responsibility at all. It means rather "not harming." But the people fighting are "harming," so they can be attacked; but if they surrender they become in this sense innocent and so may not be maltreated or killed. Nor is there ground for trying them on a criminal charge; not, indeed, because a man has no personal responsibility for fighting, but because they were not the subjects of the state whose prisoners they are.

There is an argument which I know from experience it is necessary to forestall at this point, though I think it is visibly captious. It is this: on my theory, would it not follow that a soldier can only be killed when he is actually attacking? Then, for example, it would be impossible to attack a sleeping camp. The answer is that "what someone is doing" can refer either to what he is doing at the moment or to his role in a situation. A soldier under arms is 'harming' in the latter sense even if he is asleep. But it is true that the enemy should not be attacked more ferociously than is necessary to put them *hors de combat.*

These conceptions are distinct and intelligible ones; they would formerly have been said to belong to the Law of Nations. Anyone can see that they are good, and we pay tribute to them by our moral indignation when our enemies violate them. But in fact they are going, and only fragments of them are left. General Eisenhower, for example, is reported to have spoken slightingly once of the notion of chivalry towards prisoners—as if that were based on respect for their virtue or for the nation from which they come, and not on the fact that they are now defenceless.

It is characteristic of nowadays to talk with horror of killing rather than of murder, and hence, since in war you have committed yourself to killing—for example "accepted an evil"—not to mind whom you kill. This seems largely to be the work of the devil; but I also suspect that it is in part an effect of the existence of pacifism, as a doctrine which many people respect though they would not adopt it. This effect would not exist if people had a distinct notion of what makes pacifism a false doctrine.

It therefore seems to me important to show that for one human being deliberately to kill another is not inevitably wrong. I may seem to be wasting my time, as most people do reject pacifism. But it is nevertheless important to argue the point because if one does so one sees that there are pretty severe restrictions on legitimate killing. Of course, people accept this within the state, but when it comes to war they have the idea that any restrictions are something like the Queensberry Rules—instead of making the difference between being guilty and not guilty of murder.

I will not discuss the self-defence of a private person. If he kills the man who attacks him or someone else, it ought to be accidental. To aim at killing, even when one is defending oneself, is murderous. (I fear even this idea is going. A man was acquitted recently who had successfully set a lethal booby trap to kill a thief in his absence.)

But the state actually has the authority to order deliberate killing in order to protect its people or to put frightful injustices right. (For example, the plight of the Jews under Hitler would have been a reasonable cause of war.) The reason for this is pretty simple: it stands out most clearly if we first consider the state's right to order such killing within its confines. I am not referring to the death penalty, but to what happens when there is rioting or when violent malefactors have to be caught. Rioters can sometimes only be restrained, or malefactors seized, by force. Law without force is ineffectual, and human beings without laws miserable (though we, who have too many and too changeable laws, may easily not feel this very distinctly). So much is indeed fairly obvious, though the more peaceful the society the less obvious it is that the force in the hands of the servants of the law has to be force up to the point of killing. It would become perfectly obvious any time there was rioting or gangsterism which had to be dealt with by the servants of the law fighting. . . .

Now, this is also the ground of the state's right to order people to fight external enemies who are unjustly attacking them or something of theirs. The right to order to fight for the sake of other people's wrongs, to put right something affecting people who are not actually under the protection of the state, is a rather more dubious thing obviously, but it exists because of the common sympathy of human beings whereby one feels for one's neighbour if he is attacked. So in an attenuated sense it can be said that something that belongs to, or concerns, one is attacked if anybody is unjustly attacked or maltreated.

Pacifism, then, is a false doctrine. Now, no doubt, it is bad just for that reason, because it is always bad to have a false conscience. In this way the doctrine that it is a bad act to lay a bet is bad: it is all right to bet what it is all right to risk or drop in the sea. But I want to maintain that pacifism is a harmful doctrine in a far stronger sense than this. Even the prevalence of the idea that it was wrong to bet would have no particularly bad consequences; a false doctrine which merely forbids what is not actually bad need not encourage people in anything bad. But with pacifism it is quite otherwise. It is a factor in that loss of the conception of murder which is my chief interest [here].

I have very often heard people say something like this: "It is all very well to say 'Don't do evil that good may come.' But *war* is evil. We all know that. Now, of course, it is possible to be an Absolute Pacifist. I can respect that, but I can't be one myself, and most other people won't be either. So we have to accept the evil. It is not that we do not see the evil. And once you are in for it, you have to go the whole hog."

This is much as if I were defrauding someone, and when someone tried to stop me I said: "Absolute honesty! I respect that. But of course absolute honesty really means having no property at all . . ." Having offered the sacrifice of a few sighs and tears to absolute honesty, I go on as before.

The correct answer to the statement that "war is evil" is that it is bad—for example a misfortune—to be at war. And no doubt if two nations are at war at least one is unjust. But that does not show that it is wrong to fight or that if one does fight one can also commit murder.

Naturally my claim that pacifism is a very harmful doctrine is contingent on its being a false one. If it were a true doctrine, its encouragement of this nonsensical 'hypocrisy of the ideal standard' would not count against it. But given that it is false, I am inclined to think it is also very bad, unusually so for an idea which seems as it were to err on the noble side. . . .

Some people actually praise the bombings and commend the stockpiling of atomic weapons on the ground that they are so horrible that nations will be afraid ever again to make war. "We have made a covenant with death, and with hell we are at an agreement." There does not seem to be good ground for such a hope for any long period of time.

Pacifists have for long made it a point in their propaganda

that men must grow more murderous as their techniques of destruction improve, and those who defend murder eagerly seize on this point, so that I imagine by now it is pretty well accepted by the whole world. Of course, it is not true. In Napoleon's time, for example, the means of destruction had much improved since the time of Henry V; but Henry, not Napoleon, was a great massacrer of civilians, saying when he did particularly atrocious things that the French were a sinful nation and that he had a mission from God to punish them. And, of course, really large scale massacre up to now has belonged to times with completely primitive methods of killing. Weapons are now manufactured whose sole point is to be used in massacre of cities. But the people responsible are not murderous because they have these weapons; they have them because they are murderous. Deprived of atomic bombs, they would commit massacres by means of other bombs. . . .

NOTES

1. This will seem a preposterous assertion; but we are certainly on the way, and I can think of no reasons for confidence that it will not happen.

15

Remarks on the Moral Problem of War

John Courtney Murray, S.J.

There are three distinct standpoints from which it is possible to launch a discussion of the problem of war in this strange and perilous age of ours that has yet to find its name. My initial assertion will be that it is a mistake to adopt any one of them exclusively and to carry the argument on to its logical conclusions. If this is done, the argument will end in serious difficulties.

First, one might begin by considering the possibilities of destruction and ruin, both physical and human, that are afforded by existent and projected developments in weapons technology. Here the essential fact is that there are no inherent limits to the measure of chaos that war might entail, whether by the use of nuclear arms or possibly by the methods of bacteriological and chemical warfare. Carried to its logical conclusion an argument made exclusively from this standpoint leads towards the position that war has now become a moral absurdity, not to be justified in any circumstances today. In its most respectable form this position may be called relative Christian pacifism.[1] It does not assert that war is intrinsically evil simply because it is a use of force and violence and therefore a contravention of the Christian law of love promulgated in the Sermon on the Mount. This is absolute pacifism, an unqualified embrace of the principle of nonviolence; it is more characteristic of certain Protestant sects. The relative pacifists are content to affirm that war has now become an evil that may no longer be justified, given the fact that no adequate justification can be offered for the ruinous effects of today's weapons of war. Even this position, I shall say, is not to be squared with the public doctrine of the Church.

Second, one might begin the argument by considering the present historical situation of humanity as dominated by the fact of Communism. The essential fact here is that Communism, as an ideology and as a power-system, constitutes the gravest possible menace to the moral and civilizational values that form the basis of the "the West," understanding the term to designate, not a geographical entity but an order of temporal life that has been the product of valid human dynamisms tempered by the spirit of the gospel. Arguing from this standpoint alone one could well posit, in all logic, the present validity of the concept of the "holy war." Or one might come to some advocacy of "preventive" war or "preemptive" war. Or one might be led to assert that, since the adversary is completely unprincipled, and since our duty in face of him is success in the service of civilization itself, we must jettison the tradition of civilized warfare and be prepared to use any means that promise success. None of these conclusions is morally acceptable.

Third, one might choose as a starting point the fact that today there exists a mode of international organization that is committed by its charter to the preservation of peace by pacific settlement of international disputes. One might then argue that the validity of war even as a legal institution has now vanished, with the passing of the hypothesis under which its legal validity was once defended, namely, the absence of a juridically organized international community. But this conclusion seems, at very best, too rapid, for several reasons. The United Nations is not, properly speaking, a juridical organization with adequate legal authority to govern in the international community. It is basically a power-organization. And its decisions, like those rendered by war itself, are natively apt to sanction injustice as well as justice. It is not at all clear that the existence of the United Nations, as presently constituted, definitely destroys the hypothesis on which the validity of war as a legal institution has traditionally been predicated. It is not at all clear that the United Nations in its present stage of development will be able to cope justly and effectively with the underlying causes of international conflict today or with the particular cases of conflict that may arise.

If therefore one adopts a single standpoint of argument, and adheres to it narrowly and exclusively, one will not find one's way to an integral and morally defensible position on the problem of war. On the other hand, all of the three standpoints mentioned do derive from real aspects of the problem itself. In consequence, each of them must be exploited, if the problem is to be understood in its full scope. This is my second assertion. It is not possible here to develop it in detail. I shall merely suggest that there are three basic questions that must be explored at length and in detail. Moreover, there is an order among these questions.

The first question concerns the exact nature of the conflict that is the very definition of international life today. This is the first question because it sets the perspectives in which all other questions must be considered.[2]

I would note here that Pius XII fairly steadily considered the problem of war and of the weapons of war, as well as the problem of international organization, within the perspectives of what he called "the line of rupture which divides the entire international community into opposed blocs,"[3] with the result that "coexistence in truth"[4] is not possible, since there is no common acceptance of a "norm recognized by all as morally obligatory and therefore inviolable."[5]

I would further note that the exact nature of the international conflict is not easily and simply defined. The line of rupture is not in the first instance geographic but spiritual and moral; and it runs through the West as well as between East and West. It cannot be a question of locating on "our" side of the rupture those who are virtuous and intelligent, and, over against "us," those who are evil and morally blind. In contrast, it cannot be a question of maintaining that both East and West are so full of moral ambiguities that the line of rupture between them either does not exist or is impossible to discern.[6] In a word, one must avoid both a moral simplism and a moral skepticism in the analysis of the international conflict.

Finally, it is most important to distinguish between the mainsprings of the conflict and its concrete manifestations; or, with Sir David Kelly,[7] between the relatively superficial facts of change in our revolutionary world and the underlying currents of change. Moreover, it is important to relate the two levels of analysis, in so far as this can be done without artificiality.

The tendency of this whole line of analysis, bearing on the

nature of the international conflict, will be to furnish an answer to a complex of questions that must be answered before it is possible to consider the more narrow problem of war. What precisely are the values, in what hierarchical scale, that today are at stake in the international conflict? What is the degree of danger in which they stand? What is the mode of the menace itself—in particular, to what extent is it military, and to what extent is it posed by forms of force that are more subtle? If these questions are not carefully answered, one will have no standard against which to match the evils of war. And terror, rather than reason, will command one's judgments on the military problem. This is the danger to which the seven moral theologians in Germany pointed in their statement of May 5, 1958:

> A part of the confusion among our people has its source in the fact that there is an insufficient realization of the reach of values that are endangered today, and of the hierarchical order among them, and of the degree of danger in which they stand. On the other hand, from the *Unheimlichkeit* of the technical problems [of war itself] there results a crippling of intelligence and of will.[8]

The second basic question concerns the means that are available for insuring the defense of the values that are at stake in the international conflict. This too is a large and complex question. A whole array of means is available, in correspondence with the multi-faceted character of the conflict itself. It is a matter of understanding both the usefulness and the limitations of each of them, from spectacular "summit meetings" across the gamut to the wholly unspectacular work, say, of agricultural experts engaged in increasing the food supply of so-called underdeveloped nations. This whole complex question of the means of conflict must be fully explored antecedently to the consideration of the problem of war. The basic reason is that otherwise one can give no concrete meaning to the concept of war as *ultima ratio.* Moreover, the value of the use of force, even as *ultima ratio,* will be either overestimated or underestimated, in proportion as too much or too little value is attached to other means of sustaining and pressing the international conflict.

The third and final question concerns the *ultima ratio* itself, the arbitrament of arms as the last resort.

Here we confront the third novelty in the total problem. The present historical situation of international conflict is unique. "Never," said Pius XII, "has human history known a more gigantic disorder."[9] The uniqueness of the disorder resides, I take it, in the unparalleled depth of its vertical dimension; it goes to the very roots of order and disorder in the world—the nature of man, his destiny, and the meaning of human history. There is a uniqueness too in the second basic question posited above, scil., the unprecedented scope of the conflict in its horizontal dimension, given the variety of means whereby it may be, and is being, waged. A special uniqueness resides too in the existence of the United Nations, as an arena of conflict indeed, but also as an instrument of peacemaking to some degree. However, the most immediately striking uniqueness comes to view when one considers the weapons for warmaking that are now in hand or within grasp.

There are two subordinate questions under this general heading of the nature of war today. The first concerns the actual state of progress (if it be progress and not a regress to barbarism) in the technology of defensive and offensive weapons of war. The second concerns the military usefulness, for any intelligible military and political purposes, of the variety of weapons developed. This latter question raises the issue of the strategic and tactical concepts that are to govern the use of these various weapons. The facts that would furnish answers to these questions are to a considerable extent hidden from the public knowledge; and, to the extent to which they are known, they have been generative of confusion in the public mind. In any case, these questions must have some reasonably satisfactory answer, if the moral problem of war is to be sensibly discussed.

Here then are three preliminary lines of inquiry to be pursued before the moral issues involved in warfare today can be dealt with, even in their generality.

An initial, not necessarily complete, exploration of these three lines is sufficient to suggest the outlines of a general moral theory. Whether Catholic thought can be content to stop with a moral theory cast simply in the mode of abstractness that characterizes the following propositions will be a further question. In any case, it is necessary in the first instance to state the general propositions. In stating them I am undertaking to render the substance of the thought of Pius XII; but there will be only a minimum of citation, and even of explanation.

1) All wars of aggression, whether just or unjust, fall under the ban of moral proscription.

I use the term "war of aggression" because Pius XII used it.[10] However, he gives no real definition of the term. It seems to stand simply as the contrary of a war of self-defense (whose definition, as we shall see, is more concrete and historical). Expressly, the Pope denies that recourse to force is "a legitimate solution for international controversies and a means for the realization of national aspirations."[11] He seems therefore to be denying to individual states, in this historical moment, the *ius belli* (*compétence de guerre*) of the modern era of the unlimited sovereign state, scil., the right of recourse to war, on the sovereign judgment of the national state, for the vindication of legal rights and legitimate interests. The use of force is not now a moral means for the redress of violated legal rights. The justness of the cause is irrelevant; there simply is no longer a right of self-redress; no individual state may presume to take even the cause of justice into its own hands. Whatever the grievance of the state may be, and however objectionable it may find the status quo, warfare undertaken on the sovereign decision of the national state is an immoral means for settling the grievance and for altering existent conditions.[12]

If this be the correct interpretation of Pius XII's thought, it will be seen that an important modification of the modern Scholastic doctrine of war has been made.[13] The reasons for making it derive from two of the above-mentioned lines of inquiry. First, the immeasurably increased violence of war today disqualifies it as an apt and proportionate means for the resolution of international conflicts and even for the redress of just grievances. Second, to continue to admit the right of war, as an attribute of national sovereignty, would seriously block the progress of the international community to that mode of juridical organization which Pius XII regarded as the single means for the outlawry of all war, even defensive war. In this connection, it would be well to note the observation of M. Gabriel Matagrin:

> The preoccupation of Pius XII seems to be much less to determine what might be just in the actual situation of an

unorganized humanity than to promote a genuine international organization capable of eliminating war, because the juridical reason for the right of war is the unorganized state of international life.[14]

Pius XII clearly stigmatized "aggressive" war as "a sin, an offense, and an outrage against the majesty of God."[15] Should this sin in the moral order also be transposed into the crime in the legal order? Pius expressly said that "modern total war, and ABC warfare in particular," when it is not stringently in self-defense, "constitutes a crime worthy of the most severe national and international sanctions."[16] I should think that the same recommendation would apply to less violent forms of "aggressive" warfare. However, Pius XII did not enter the formidable technical problem, how this legal transcription of a moral principle is to be effected. The problem has hitherto been insoluble.

2) A defensive war to repress injustice is morally admissible both in principle and in fact.

In its abstractness this principle has always formed part of Catholic doctrine; by its assertion the Church finds a way between the false extremes of pacifism and bellicism. Moreover, the assertion itself, far from being a contradiction of the basic Christian will to peace, is the strongest possible affirmation of this will. There is no peace without justice, law, and order. But "law and order have need at times of the powerful arm of force."[17] And the precept of peace itself requires that peace be defended against violation:

> The precept of peace is of divine right. Its purpose is to protect the goods of humanity, inasmuch as they are the goods of the Creator. Among these goods there are some of such importance for the human community that their defense against an unjust aggression is without doubt fully justified.[18]

There is nothing new about these assertions. What is important is their reiteration by Pius XII in today's highly concrete historical context of international conflict. The reiteration of the right of defensive war derives directly from an understanding of the conflict and from a realization that nonviolent means of solution may fail. The Church is obliged to confront the dreadful alternative: "the absolute necessity of self-defense against a very grave injustice that touches the community, that cannot be impeded by other means, that nevertheless must be impeded on pain of giving free field in international relations to brutal violence and lack of conscience."[19]

The harshness of statement in that last phrase marks a new note that came only late (in 1953) into Pius XII's utterances. I think it fair to say that the gentle Pope of Peace brought himself only with great reluctance, and under the unrelenting pressure of events, to focus on the instant possibility of war, as generated by the essential ethos of the Communist system: "brutal violence and lack of conscience." The focus becomes even sharper after the events in Hungary, and in the light of the Soviet threat to use atomic weapons in Europe if the French and English adventure in Suez were not terminated. These words from the Christmas message, 1956, need to be quoted:

> The actual situation, which has no equivalent in the past, ought nevertheless to be clear to everyone. There is no further room for doubt about the purposes and the methods that lie behind tanks when they crash resoundingly across frontiers to distribute death and to force civilized peoples to a form of life that they distinctly abhor. When all the possible stages of negotiation and mediation are bypassed, and when the threat is made to use atomic arms to obtain concrete demands, whether these are justified or not, it becomes clear that, in present circumstances, there may come into existence in a nation a situation in which all hope of averting war becomes vain. In this situation a war of efficacious self-defense against unjust attacks, which is undertaken with hope of success, cannot be considered illicit.[20]

One can almost feel the personal agony behind the labored sentences (more tortured in the original than in the translation). The agony, and utterance itself, are born of the Pope's reluctant realization that, as he had said earlier that same year, there are rulers "who except themselves from the elementary laws of human society."[21] The tragedy in the situation is accented by his further vision that the people over whom these rulers stand "cannot but be the first to feel the need once more to form part of the human family."[22]

There is no indication that this reaffirmation of the traditional principle of defensive warfare, to which Pius XII was driven by the brutal facts of international life, extends only to wars conducted by so-called conventional arms. On the contrary, the Pope extended it explicitly, not only to atomic warfare but even to ABC warfare. One cannot therefore uphold the simple statement that atomic war as such, without further qualifications, is morally unjustifiable, or that all use of atomic weapons in war is, somehow in principle, evil.

There are, however, conditions. The basic condition has been stated: "One cannot, even in principle, raise the question of the liceity of ABC warfare except in the case in which it must be judged indispensable for self-defense in the conditions indicated."[23] These further conditions are simply those found in traditional doctrine. But each of them was sharpened to a fresh stringency by Pius XII in the light of the horrors of destruction and death now possible in war.

Briefly, the war must be "imposed by an obvious and extremely grave injustice."[24] No minor infraction of rights will suffice, much less any question of national prestige. The criterion is high, namely, that the nation should "in all truth have been unjustly attacked and menaced in its vital rights."[25]

The second condition is the familiar principle of war as always the *ultima ratio.* Moreover, it is today the extremity of means in a unique sense, given, on the one hand, the new means of negotiation and arbitration presently available, and on the other, the depths of manifold agony into which recourse to the *ultima ratio* may now plunge humanity as a whole.

The third condition is also familiar, the principle of proportion. It invokes a twofold consideration.

First, consideration must be given to the proportion between the damage suffered in consequence of the perpetration of a grave injustice, and the damages that would be let loose by a war to repress the injustice. Pius XII laid some stress on the fact that the comparison here must be between realities of the moral order, and not sheerly between two sets of material damage and loss. The standard is not a "eudaemonism and utilitarianism of materialist origin,"[26] which would avoid war merely because it is uncomfortable, or connive at injustice simply because its repression would be costly. The question of proportion must be evaluated in more tough-minded fashion, from the viewpoint of the hierarchy of strictly moral values. It is not enough simply to consider the "sorrows and evils that flow from war."[27] There are greater evils than the physical death and destruction wrought in war. And there are human goods of so high an order that immense sacrifices may have to be borne in their defense. By these insistences Pius XII transcended the vulgar pacifism of sentimentalist and materialist inspiration that is so common today.

Second, Pius XII requires an estimate of another proportion, between the evils unleashed by war and what he calls "the solid probability of success"[28] in the violent repression of unjust action. The specific attention he gives to this condition was immediately prompted by his awareness of the restiveness of the peoples who are presently captive under unjust rule and who are tempted to believe, not without reason, that their rescue will require the use of force. This condition of probable success is not, of course, simply the stateman's classical political calculus of success. It is the moral calculus that is enjoined in the traditional theory of rebellion against tyranny. Furthermore, Pius XII was careful to warn that in applying this moral calculus regard must be had for the tinderbox character of our world in which a spark may set off a conflagration.[29]

A fourth principle of traditional theory is also affirmed by Pius XII, the principle of limitation in the use of force. It may be a matter of some surprise that he gave so little emphasis and development to it, at least in comparison to the preponderant place that the problem seems to have assumed in the minds of other theorists, Catholic and non-Catholic. There is one formal text. After asserting the legitimacy of "modern total warfare," that is, ABC warfare, under the set of stringent conditions already stated, he added:

> Even then every effort must be made and every means taken to avoid it, with the aid of international covenants, or to set limits to its use precise enough so that its effects will be confined to the strict exigencies of defense. In any case, when the employment of this means entails such an extension of the evil that it entirely escapes from the control of man, its use ought to be rejected as immoral.

> Here it is no longer a question of defense against injustice and of the necessary safeguard of legitimate possessions, but of the annihilation, pure and simple, of all human life within its radius of action. This is not permitted on any account.[30]

This is a very general statement indeed. And it takes the issue at its extreme, where it hardly needs statement, since the moral decision cannot fail to be obvious. Who would undertake to defend on any grounds, including military grounds, the annihilation of all human life within the radius of action of an ABC war that "entirely escapes from the control of man"?[31] We have here an affirmation, if you will, of the rights of innocence, of the distinction between combatant and noncombatant. But it is an extremely broad statement.

One finds in the earlier utterances of the Pope, when he was demonstrating the first thesis in the traditional doctrine of war (that war is an evil, the fruit of sin), much advertence to "massacres of innocent victims," the killing of "infants with their mothers, the ill and infirm and aged," etc. These tragedies stand high on the list of the evils of war. In the text cited there is no explicit return to this principle of the rights of innocence when it is formally a question of total nuclear war and the use of nuclear weapons. If there is an anomaly here, the reason for it may lie in the fact that the Pope was forcing himself to face the desperate case. And in desperate cases, in which conscience is perplexed, the wise moralist is chary of the explicit and the nice, especially when the issue, as here, is one of social and not individual morality. In such cases hardly more than a *Grenzmoral* is to be looked for or counseled. In fact, the whole Catholic doctrine of war is hardly more than a *Grenzmoral,* an effort to establish on a minimal basis of reason a form of human action, the making of war, that remains always fundamentally irrational.[32]

Two further propositions in the general theory must be mentioned. The first concerns the legitimacy of defense preparations on the part of individual states. Their legitimacy is founded on two actual facts of international life. First, at the moment there does not exist what Pius XII constantly looked forward to as the solution of the problem of war, namely, a constituted international authority possessing a monopoly of the use of armed force in international affairs. Second, there does exist the threat of "brutal violence and lack of conscience." In this factual situation, "the right to be in a posture of defense cannot be denied, even today, to any state."[33] Here again the principle is extremely general; it says nothing about the morality of this or that configuration of the defense establishment of a given nation. The statement does not morally validate everything that goes on at Cape Canaveral or at Los Alamos.

Finally, the Pope of Peace disallowed the validity of conscientious objection. The occasion was the controversy on the subject, notably in Germany, where the resonances of a sort of anticipatory *Fronterlebnis* were giving an alarming impulse to pacifist movements. Particularly in question was the deposit of nuclear weapons on German soil as part of the NATO defense establishment. The Pope's judgment was premised on the legitimacy of the government, the democratic openness of its decisions, and the extremity of the historical necessity for making such defense preparations as would be adequate in the circumstances. He concluded that such a government is "acting in a manner that is not immoral" and that "a Catholic citizen may not make appeal to his own conscience as ground for refusing to give his services and to fulfill duties fixed by law."[34] This duty of armed service to the state, and this right of the state to arm itself for self-defense, are, he added, the traditional doctrine of the Church, even in latter days under Leo XIII and Benedict XV, when the problem of armaments and conscription put a pressing issue to the Christian conscience.

The foregoing may do as a statement, at least in outline, of the traditional doctrine on war in the form and with the modifications given it by the authority of the Church today. It is not particularly difficult to make this sort of statement. The difficulty chiefly begins after the statement has been made. Not that objections are raised, at least not in Catholic circles, against the doctrine itself as stated. What is queried is the usefulness of the doctrine, its relevance to the concrete actualities of our historical moment. I shall conclude with some comments on this issue.

I think that the tendency to query the uses of the Catholic doctrine on war initially rises from the fact that it has for so long not been used, even by Catholics. That is, it has not been made the basis for a sound critique of public policies and as a means for the formation of a right public opinion. The classic example, of course, was the policy of "unconditional surrender" during the last war. This policy clearly violated the requirement of the "right intention" that has always been a principle in the traditional doctrine of war. Yet no sustained criticism was made of the policy by Catholic spokesmen. Nor was any substantial effort made to clarify by moral judgment the thickening mood of savage violence that made possible the atrocities of Hiroshima and Nagasaki. I think it is true to say that the traditional doctrine was irrelevant during World War II. This is no argument against the traditional doctrine. The Ten Commandments do not lose their imperative relevance by reason of the fact that they are violated. But there is place for an indictment of all of us who failed to make the tradition relevant.

The initial relevance of the traditional doctrine today lies in its value as the solvent of false dilemmas. Our fragmentized culture seems to be the native soil of this fallacious and dangerous type of thinking. There are, first of all, the two extreme positions, a soft sentimental pacifism and a cynical hard realism. Both of these views, which are also "feelings," are formative factors in the moral climate of the moment. Both of them are condemned by the traditional doctrine as false and pernicious. The problem is to refute by argument the false antinomy between war and morality that they assert in common, though in different ways. The further and more difficult problem is to purify the public climate of the miasma that emanates from each of them and tends to smother the public conscience.

A second false dilemma has threatened to dominate the argument on national defense in Germany. It sloganized itself thus: "Lieber rot als tot." It has made the same threat in England, where it has been developed in a symposium by twenty-three distinguished Englishmen entitled, *The Fearful Choice: A Debate on Nuclear Policy*. The choice, of course, is between the desperate alternatives, either universal atomic death or complete surrender to Communism. The Catholic mind, schooled in the traditional doctrine of war and peace, rejects the dangerous fallacy involved in this casting up of desperate alternatives. Hidden beneath the fallacy is an abdication of the moral reason and a craven submission to some manner of technological or historical determinism.

It is not, of course, that the traditional doctrine rejects the extreme alternatives as possibilities. Anything in history is possible. Moreover, on grounds of the moral principle of proportion the doctrine supports the grave recommendation of the greatest theorist of war in modern times, von Klausewitz: "We must therefore familiarize ourselves with the thought of an honorable defeat." Conversely, the doctrine condemns the hysteria that swept Washington in August when the Senate voted, eighty-two to two, to deny government funds to any person or institution who ever proposes or actually conducts any study regarding the "surrender of the government of the U.S."[35] "Losing," said von Klausewitz, "is a function of winning," thus stating in his own military idiom the moral calculus prescribed by traditional moral doctrine. The moralist agrees with the military theorist that the essence of a military situation is uncertainty. And when he requires, with Pius XII, a solid probability of success as a moral ground for a legitimate use of arms, he must reckon with the possibility of failure and be prepared to accept it. But this is a moral decision, worthy of a man and of a civilized nation. It is a free, morally motivated, and responsible act, and therefore it inflicts no stigma of dishonor. It is not that "weary resignation,"[36] condemned by Pius XII, which is basic to the inner attitude of the theorists of the desperate alternatives, no matter which one they argue for or accept.

On the contrary, the single inner attitude which is nourished by the traditional doctrine is a will to peace, which, in the extremity, bears within itself a will to enforce the precept of peace by arms. But this will to arms is a moral will; for it is identically a will to justice. It is formed under the judgment of reason. And the first alternative contemplated by reason, as it forms the will to justice through the use of force, is not the possibility of surrender, which would mean the victory of injustice. This is the ultimate extremity, beyond even the extremity of war itself. Similarly, the contrary alternative considered by reason is not a general annihilation, even of the enemy. This would be worse than injustice; it would be sheer folly. In a word, a debate on nuclear policy that is guided by the traditional doctrine of war does not move between the desperate alternatives of surrender or annihilation. If it means simply an honorable defeat, surrender may be morally tolerable; but it is not to be tolerated save on a reasonable calculus of proportionate moral costs. In contrast, annihilation is on every count morally intolerable; it is to be averted at all costs, that is, at the cost of every effort, in every field, that the spirit of man can put forth.

Precisely here the proximate and practical value, use, and relevance of the traditional doctrine begin to appear. Its remote value may lie in its service as a standard of casuistry on various kinds of war.[37] Its remote value certainly lies in its power to form the public conscience and to clarify the climate of moral opinion in the midst of today's international conflict. But its proximate value is felt at the crucial point where the moral and political orders meet. Primarily, its value resides in its capacity to set the right terms for rational debate on public policies bearing on the problem of war and peace in this age,[38] characterized by international conflict and by advanced technology. This is no mean value, if you consider the damage that is being presently done by argument carried on in the wrong terms.

The traditional doctrine disqualifies as irrelevant and dangerous the false dilemmas of which I have spoken. It also rejects the notion that the big problem is to "abolish war" or "ban the bomb." It is true that the traditional doctrine on war looks forward to its own disappearance as a chapter in Catholic moral theology. The effort of the moral reason to fit the use of violence into the objective order of justice is paradoxical enough; but the paradox is heightened when this effort takes place at the interior of the Christian religion of love. In any case, the principles of the doctrine themselves make clear that our historical moment is not destined to see a moral doctrine of war discarded as unnecessary. War is still the possibility, not to be exorcised even by prayer and fasting. The Church does not look immediately to the abolition of war. Her doctrine still seeks to fulfill its triple traditional function: to condemn war as evil, to limit the evils it entails, and to humanize its conduct as far as possible.

In the light of the traditional doctrine and in the no less necessary light of the facts of international life and technological development today, what are the right terms for argument on public policy? These are readily reached by a dialectical process, an alternation between principle and fact. The doctrine asserts, in principle, that force is still the *ultima ratio* in human affairs, and that its use in extreme circumstances may be morally obligatory *ad repellendam iniuriam.* The facts assert that today this *ultima ratio* takes the form of nuclear force, whose use remains possible and may prove to be necessary, lest a free field be granted to brutal violence and lack of conscience. The doctrine asserts that the use of nuclear force must be limited, the principle of limitation being the exigencies of legitimate defense against injustice. Thus the terms of public debate are set in two words, "limited war." All other terms of argument are fanciful or fallacious. (I assume here that the argument is to be cast primarily in political terms, only secondarily in military terms; for armed force is never more than a weapon of policy, a weapon of last resort.)

I shall not attempt to construct the debate itself. But two points may be made. First, there are those who say that the limitation of nuclear war, or any war, is today impossible, for a variety of reasons—technical, political, etc. In the face of this position, the traditional doctrine simply asserts again, "The problem today is limited war." But notice that the assertion is on a higher plane than that of sheer fact. It is a moral proposition, or better, a moral imperative. In other words, since nuclear war may be a necessity, it must be made a possibility. Its possibility must be created. And the creation of its possibility requires a work of intelligence, and the development of manifold action, on a whole series of policy levels—political (foreign and domestic), diplomatic, military, technological, scientific, fiscal, etc., with the important inclusion of the levels of public opinion and public education. To say that the possibility of limited war cannot be created by intelligence and energy, under the direction of a moral imperative, is to succumb to some sort of determinism in human affairs.

My second point is that the problem of limited war would seem to require solution in two stages. One stage consists in the construction of a sort of "model" of the limited war. This is largely a problem in conceptual analysis. Its value consists in making clear the requirements of limited war in terms of policy on various levels.[39] Notably it makes clear that a right order must prevail among policies. It makes clear, for instance, that the limitation of war becomes difficult or impossible if fiscal policy assumes the primacy over armament policy, or if armament policy assumes the primacy over military policy, or if military policy assumes the primacy over foreign policy in the political sense.

The second stage is even more difficult. It centers on a *quaestio facti*. The fact is that the international conflict, in its ideological as in its power dimension, comes to concrete expression in certain localized situations, each of which has its own peculiarities. The question then is, where and under what circumstances is the irruption of violence possible or likely, and how is the limitation of the conflict to be effected in these circumstances, under regard of political intentions, as controlling of military necessities *in situ*. The answer to this question is what is meant by the formulation of policy. Policy is the hand of the practical reason set firmly upon the course of events. Policy is what a nation does in this or that given situation. In the concreteness of policy, therefore, the assertion of the possibility of limited war is finally made, and made good. Policy is the meeting-place of the world of power and the world of morality, in which there takes place the concrete reconciliation of the duty of success that rests upon the statesman and the duty of justice that rests upon the civilized nation that he serves.

I am thus led to one final comment on the problem of war. It may be that the classical doctrine of war needs more theoretical elaboration in order to relate it more effectively to the unique conflict that agitates the world today, in contrast with the older historical conflicts upon which the traditional doctrine sought to bear, and by which in turn it was shaped.[40] In any case, another work of the reflective intelligence and study is even more badly needed. I shall call it a politico-moral analysis of the divergent and particular conflict-situations that have arisen or are likely to arise in the international scene as problems in themselves and as manifestations of the underlying crisis of our times. It is in these particular situations that war actually becomes a problem. It is in the midst of their dense materiality that the *quaestio iuris* finally rises. To answer it is the function of the moralist, the professional or the citizen moralist. His answer will never be more than an act of prudence, a practical judgment informed by principle. But he can give no answer at all to the *quaestio iuris* until the *quaestio facti* has been answered. From the point of view of the problem of war and morality the same need appears that has been descried elsewhere in what concerns the more general problem of politics and morality.[41] I mean the need of a far more vigorous cultivation of politico-moral science, with close attention to the enormous impact of technological developments on the moral order as well as on the political order.

The whole concept of force has undergone a rapid and radical transformation, right in the midst of history's most acute political crisis. One consequence of these two related developments was emphasized by Panel Two, "International Security: The Military Aspect," of the Special Studies Project of the Rockefeller Brothers Fund: "The overall United States strategic concept lags behind developments in technology and in the world political situation."[42] This vacuum of military doctrine greatly troubled the members of the panel. But I know from my own association with the Special Studies Project that they were even more troubled by another vacuum in contemporary thought, scil., the absence of an over-all political-moral doctrine with regard to the uses of force. This higher doctrine is needed to give moral sense and political direction to a master strategic concept. "Power without a sense of direction," they said, "may drain life of its meaning, if its does not destroy humanity altogether."[43] This sense of direction cannot be found in technology; of itself, technology tends toward the exploitation of scientific possibilities simply because they are possibilities. Power can be invested with a sense of direction only by moral principles. It is the function of morality to command the use of power, to forbid it, to limit it; or, more in general, to define the ends for which power may or must be used and to judge the circumstances of its use. But moral principles cannot effectively impart this sense of direction to power until they have first, as it were, passed through the order of politics; that is, until they have first become incarnate in public policy. It is public policy in all its varied concretions that must be "moralized" (to use an abused word in its good sense). This is the primary need of the moment. For my part, I am not confident that it is being met.[44]

NOTES

1. On the style, e.g., of F. Stratmann, *War and Christianity Today* (Westminster, Md., 1956); cf. his earlier book, *The Church and War* (New York, 1928).

2. As a minor contribution to this analysis I attempted a description of the unique character of the Soviet Empire in *Foreign Policy and the Free Society* (New York, 1958) pp. 21–49. In what concerns academic and public opinion in the English-speaking world, a considerable difficulty arises from the fact that there exists no real consensus with regard to the aims and motivations of Communist imperialism in its action on the world scene. There are at least four schools of thought; their major difference arises from their variant estimates of the role of ideology in Soviet behavior.

3. Christmas Message, 1950; *AAS* 43 (1951) 57.

4. Christmas Message, 1954; *AAS* 47 (1955) 25.

5. Allocution to the Ambassador of Ecuador, July 13, 1948; *AAS* 40 (1948) 339.

6. This view exists in a number of forms. There is, for instance, the contextualistic morality of Prof. Hans Morgenthau, revealed in his Introduction to E. Lefever, *Ethics and United States Foreign Policy* (New York, 1957). His basic view, never quite brought to philosophical explicitness, seems to be that all moralities are purely "national"; they cannot be subjected to judgment in terms of universal principles. There are also various types of neo-Lutheran theory which see evil as radical, ubiquitous, and inextricable in all human action. In quite a different category there are those who are confused, as well they might be in this age, by the problem of the relations between morality and power; cf., for instance, an intelligent and earnest thinker, Mr. Kenneth Thompson, "Moral Choices in Foreign Affairs," *Worldview* 1 (1958) 4–7. One of today's characteristically confused debates goes on between the "realists" and the "idealists." One school holds that politics is wholly a matter of morality; the other maintains that politics is wholly a matter of power. Both are wrong. But they agree on a disastrous tenet, that between morality and power a great gulf is fixed.

7. *The Hungry Sheep* (London, 1955).

8. *Herder-Korrespondenz* 12, no. 9 (June, 1958) 396.

9. Christmas Message, 1950; *AAS* 43 (1951) 57.

10. The concept of aggression is undoubtedly a major source of bedevilment in the whole modern discussion of the problem of war. The recent lengthy attempt to reach a satisfactory definition resulted in failure; cf. Julius Stone, *Aggression and World Order* (Berkeley, Calif., 1958). The concept, I think, is a typically modern one; older theories more charateristically spoke in terms of "injustice." I venture the opinion, merely as an opinion, that the modern prominence of the concept derives from the modern theory that there may be "justice" on both sides of a conflict. Hence the issue of "justice" is proximately decided by "aggression," scil., which nation's armed forces first cross the borders of the other nation. But

this military transcription of a basically moral concept is of little, if any, use in our contemporary situation, with its two unique new features. First, today's weapons systems make possible the employment of force at enormous distances without concern for the space between; the concept of "crossing borders" no longer means anything. Second, in view of the striking power of these weapons systems the nation that initiates the attack ("crosses the border") can render the opposing nation defenseless, incapable of exerting a right of self-defense. Consequently, aggression in the older military-moral sense has ceased to be a standard by which to decide the issue of justice in war; it has become simply a technique by which to decide the issue of success. The use of force can no longer be linked to the moral order merely by the concept of aggression, in the modern understanding of the concept. There is urgent need for a thorough moral re-examination of the basic American policy that "we will never shoot first." Under contemporary circumstances, viewed in their entirety, is this really a *dictamen rationis?*

11. Christmas Message, 1944; *AAS* 37 (1945) 18.

12. Modern theory distinguished three reasons for recourse to war by the sovereign state: *ad vindicandas offensiones, ad repetendas res, ad repellendas iniurias.* Pius XII, it seems to me, outlawed the first two categories of "war-aims." The third category is proper to the concept of "defensive" war. At that, the main thrust of his thought on war, viewed in the total context of his dominant concern with international organization, goes against the modern notion of the *ius belli* as an inherent attribute of national sovereignty.

13. For a statement of the modern Scholastic theory, and a critique of it, cf. A. Vanderpol, *La doctrine scolastique du droit de guerre* (Paris, 1919). It would be interesting to have a new study made of this book, which is not without its bias. I also suggest another question. Pius XII seems relatively unconcerned to give an exact definition of aggression. He seems to want to move back into the center of Catholic thought the older, broader Augustinian concept of *causa iusta.* War is not simply a problem of aggression; more fundamentally it is a problem of injustice. It is the concept of justice that links the use of force with the moral order. Would it be correct to say that Pius XII represents an effort to return Catholic thought to more traditional and more fruitful premises? If there is a way out of the present impasse created by the outworn concept of aggression in the modern sense, it can only be a return to the concept of justice. There would still remain the formidable moral and legal problem of translating *iustitia* into *tò iustum.* In politico-moral terms this is today the problem of what is called policy. As a moral problem, war is ultimately a problem of policy, and therefore a problem of social morality. Policy is made by society, especially in

a democratic context; and society bears the moral responsibility for the policy made. As a problem in justice, the problem of war is put to the People, in whom, according to good medieval theory, the sense of justice resides, and from whom the moral judgment, direction, and correction of public policy must finally come. As a moral problem in the use of force, war is not simply, or even primarily, a problem for the generals, the State Department, the technologists, the international lawyers. Here, if anywhere, "the People shall judge." This is their responsibility, to be discharged before the shooting starts, by an active concern with the moral direction of national policy. My impression is that this duty in social morality is being badly neglected in America at the moment.

14. "La légitimité de la guerre d'après les textes pontificaux," *Lumière et vie* 7, no. 38 (July, 1958) 56.

15. Christmas Message, 1948; *AAS* 41 (1949) 13.

16. Allocution to the World Medical Congress, Sept. 30, 1954; *AAS* 46 (1954) 589. The tradition maintains that the highest value in society is the inviolability of the order of rights and justice. If this order disintegrates or is successfully defied, society is injured in its most vital structure and end. Peace itself is the work of justice; and therefore peace is not compatible with impunity for the evil of injustice. It is pertinent to emphasize these truths in an age in which economic and material values have come to assume the primacy.

17. Allocution to the visiting members of the U. S. House of Representatives' Armed Services Committee, Oct. 8, 1947; *Civiltà cattolica* 98/4 (1947) 264. Note that there is question of "injustice," not of "aggression."

18. Christmas Message, 1948; *AAS* 41 (1949) 13.

19. Allocution to military doctors, Oct. 19, 1953; *AAS* 45 (1953) 748.

20. Christmas Message, 1956; *AAS* 49 (1957) 19.

21. Radio Broadcast, Nov. 10, 1956; *AAS* 48 (1956) 789.

22. *Ibid.*

23. Allocution to the World Medical Congress, 1954; *AAS* 46 (1954) 589.

24. *Ibid.;* again the word used is "injustice," not "aggression."

25. Allocution to the World Congress of Women's Organizations, Apr. 24, 1952; *AAS* 44 (1952) 422.

26. Christmas Message, 1948; *AAS* 41 (1949) 13.

27. *Ibid.*

28. *Ibid.*

29. *Ibid.*, pp. 11–12.

30. Allocution to the World Medical Congress, 1954; *AAS* 46 (1954) 589.

31. Around this time (1954) there was a lot of loose and

uninformed talk about weapons that really would go beyond human control; there was talk, for instance, of the so-called "cobalt bomb" and its "unlimited" powers of radioactive contamination. It is impossible to know what were the sources of the Pope's scientific information. To my knowledge, he never adverts to the qualitative distinction and radical discontinuity between low-kiloton and high-megaton weapons. The former are not necessarily weapons of mass destruction. Even the latter do not "escape from the control of man"; their blast and fire effects, and their atmosphere-contamination effects, have been fairly exactly measured.

32. I am not for a moment suggesting, of course, that the principle of the rights of innocent life has become in any sense irrelevant to the contemporary problem of war. Still less am I suggesting that Pius XII modified the traditional doctrine in this respect. I am merely noting what I noted, scil., that this principle receives no sharp emphasis, to say the least, in his doctrine. There may be other reasons for this than the one that I tentatively suggested in the text above.

33. Allocution to the Sixth International Congress of Penal Law, Oct. 3, 1953; *AAS* 45 (1953) 733.

34. Christmas Message, 1956; *AAS* 49 (1957) 19.

35. When "Washington" thinks of "surrender," it apparently can think only of "unconditional" surrender. Thus does the demonic specter of the past hover over us, as a still imperious *rector harum tenebrarum.* Thus patriotism, once the last refuge of the scoundrel, now has become the first refuge of the fool. It is folly not to foresee that the United States may be laid in ruins by a nuclear attack; the folly is compounded by a decision not to spend any money on planning what to do after that not impossible event. There is no room today for the heroic romanticism of the apocryphal utterance, "The Old Guard dies but never surrenders." Even Victor Hugo did not put this line on the lips of Cambronne; he simply had him say, "Merde." For all its vulgarity, this was a far more sensible remark in the circumstances. For my part, I am impressed by the cold rationality of Soviet military thought as described by Raymond L. Garthoff, *Soviet Strategy in the Nuclear Age* (New York, 1958): "The fundamental Soviet objectives which determine political and military strategies may be concisely summarized in one: Advance the power of the Soviet Union in whatever ways are most expedient so long as the survival of the Soviet power itself is not endangered" (p. 5). For the Soviet Union survival is not an issue in war; for us it is the only issue. In Soviet thought military action is subordinate to political aims; with us military action creates its own aims, and there is only one, "victory," scil., unconditional surrender. "The Soviet strategic concept, in the thermonuclear era

as before, is founded on the belief that the primary objective of military operations is the destruction of hostile military forces, and not the annihilation of the economic and population resources of the enemy. Thus the Soviets continue to adhere to the classical military strategic concept, while contemporary American views often diverge sharply from this traditional stand" (pp. 71–72). Finally, Soviet policy envisages the "long war" even after a massive exchange of thermonuclear weapons (pp. 87–91). With us, if deterrence fails, and this massive exchange occurs, that is the end; we have no policy after that, except stubbornly to maintain that it is up to the enemy, and not us, to surrender—unconditionally. There is no little irony in the fact that the Communist enemy seems to understand better than we do the traditional doctrine on the uses of force.

36. Christmas Message, 1948; *AAS* 41 (1949) 13.

37. I use the subjunctive because I do not know how many wars in history would stand up under judgment by the traditional norms, or what difference it made at the time whether they did or not.

38. I am not sure that one should talk today in these categories, "war and/or peace," leaving unexamined the question just what their validity is as moral and political categories. The basic fallacy is to suppose that "war" and "peace" are two discontinuous and incommensurable worlds of existence and universes of discourse, each with its own autonomous set of rules, "peace" being the world of "morality" and "war" being the world of "evil," in such wise that there is no evil as long as there is peace and no morality as soon as there is war. This is a common American assumption. Moreover, it would help greatly to attend to the point made by Mr. Philip C. Jessup that we live today in an "intermediate state" between peace and war; he contends that, "if one were accustomed to the idea of intermediacy, it can be argued that the likelihood of 'total war' could be diminished. . . . The basic question is whether our concepts, our terminology, our law have kept pace with the evolution of international affairs" (*American Journal of International Law* 48 [1954] 98 ff.).

39. The most significant attempt in this direction was made by Henry A. Kissinger, *Nuclear Weapons and Foreign Policy* (New York, 1957). The validity of his theories on limited war (chaps. 5–7) has been contested on technical and other grounds. The more permanent value of the book may lie in its convincing argument that a vacuum of doctrine, military as well as moral, lies at the heart of the whole vast defense establishment of the U.S. (cf. chap. 12 and *passim*).

40. It may be that Jessup's "basic question" (cf. supra n. 36) may legitimately be raised in connection with the theory of the just war

as fashioned by later Scholasticism. There is always room for a respectful inquiry, whether a proposed "doctrine" is really the tradition or only an *opinio recepta.* What troubled Vanderpol now troubles others, scil., the subtle impact on the traditional doctrine exerted by the modern concept of the sovereign national state. It might be argued that the traditional doctrine has not absorbed this impact without damage to itself. (The same argument, incidentally, might be made with regard to the traditional doctrine on Church-State relations.) In this connection cf. J. T. Delos, "A Sociology of Modern War and the Theory of the Just War," *Cross Currents* 8 (1958) 248–66.

41. Cf. F. A. Hermens, "Politics and Ethics," *Thought* 29 (1954) 32–50.

42. New York *Times,* January 6, 1958, p. 20, col. 1.

43. *Ibid.,* col. 2.

44. Bibliographies on the military aspects of the problem may be found in Kissinger (*op.cit.*) and in Garthoff (*op. cit.*); also in R. A. Preston, S. F. Wise, H. O. Werner, *Men in Arms: A History of Warfare and its Interrelationships with Western Society* (New York, 1956). The older Catholic books are still the best, though not good enough: e.g., J. Eppstein, *The Catholic Tradition of the Law of Nations* (London, 1935); L. Sturzo, *The International Community and the Right of War* (New York, 1930). The most significant wartime study of a particular problem was by John C. Ford, "The Morality of Obliteration Bombing," THEOLOGICAL STUDIES 5 (1944) 261–309. The periodical literature in recent years has been rather meager; the following is a selection of the more useful articles: A. Gunther, "Der Papst über den Krieg," *Benediktinische Monatschrift* 34 (1958) 279–86; G. Gundlach, S.J., "Der Papst und der Krieg," *Stimmen der Zeit* 159 (1957) 378–83; L. C., "Le Vatican et la seconde guerre mondiale," *Ami du clergé* 66 (1956) 61–64; A. Tillet, "Guerre et paix," *Ami du clergé* 65 (1955) 290–96, 585–92; A. Tillet, "Pie XII et la paix," *Ami du clergé* 65 (1955) 713–17; M. Vaussard, "L'Eglise catholique, la guerre et la paix," *Nouvelle revue théologique* 75 (1953) 951–64; C. Pepler, O.P., "War in Tradition and Today," *Blackfriars* 35 (1954) 62–69; P. Zamayón, O.F.M. Cap., "Moralidad de la guerra en nuestros dias y en lo porvenir," *Salmanticensis* 2 (1955) 42–79; John C. Ford, S.J., "The Hydrogen Bombing of Cities," *Theology Digest* 5 (1957) 6–9; John R. Connery, S.J., "Morality of Nuclear Armament," *Theology Digest* 5 (1957) 9–12; R. Rémond, "Le conflit et la guerre devant l'histoire," *Vie intellectuelle* 26 (1955) 33–48; A. Messineo, S.J., "La comunità internazionale e il diritto di guerra," *Civiltà cattolica* 106/1 (1955) 72–76; J. M. Todd, "Just Wars and Christian Peace," *Irish Ecclesiastical Record* 83 (1955) 27–40; I. Hislop, O.P., and L. Bright, O.P., "The Morality of Nuclear War,"

Blackfriars 37 (1956) 100–117; T. E. Murray, "Rational Nuclear Armament," *Ordnance* 41 (1956) 220–23; "Statement on Atomic Tests and Disarmament," *Ecumenical Review* 10 (1957) 70–72; J. Moretti, "Les effets des armes atomiques," *Etudes* 296 (1958) 353–60; P. Vogelsanger, "Christlicher Atomstreik? Antwort an Helmut Gollwitzer," *Reformatio* 7 (1958) 503–21, 596–608; J. Thibaud, "Le projet de pool atomique et les Etats-Unis d'Europe," *Angelicum* 33 (1956) 267–86; K. Peters, "Probleme der Atomaufrüstung," *Hochland* 51 (1958) 12–25; W. Sandell, "The Church and Nuclear Warfare," *Church Quarterly Review* 159 (1958) 256–65; T. D. Roberts, "Nuclear Dilemma," *Month* 19 (1958) 282–86; A. Auer, "Atombombe und Naturrecht," *Neue Ordnung* 12 (1958) 256–66; K. Schmidthüs, "Atomwaffen und Gewissen," *Wort und Wahrheit* 13 (1958) 405–24; "Ist die Atomrüstung Sünde?", *Orientierung* 22 (1958) 115–19; J. B. Hirschmann, "Kann atomare Verteidigung sittlich gerechtfertigt sein?", *Stimmen der Zeit* 160 (1958) 284–96; A. Buzzard, "Limiting War," *Cross Currents* 8 (1958) 97–101; "La guerre," *Lumière et vie,* no. 38 (1958) (a symposium with articles by J.-Y. Jolif, O.P., A. Brunet, O.P., G. Matagrin, and M.-D. Chenu, O.P.); H. de Riedmatten, O.P., "Christians and International Instutitions," *Blackfriars* 38 (1957) 498–508; P. M. Zammit, O.P., "The Need of International Society," *Thomist* 18 (1955) 71–87; D. Morton, "Morality in International Relations," *Blackfriars* 36 (1955) 108–13; H. Schwann, "Politische Ethik," *Orientierung* 22 (1958) 87–90.

A comprehensive bibliography on limited war, compiled by the staff of the Army library, was recently published as Department of the Army Pamphlet 20–60.

16

Freedom for Life

Karl Barth

We conclude our discussion of the sixth commandment by turning to the problem of war. . . .

In this case, too, we shall begin by trying to stab our consciences awake in relation to certain illusions which may have been feasible once but cannot be entertained any longer.

1. There was a time when it was possible not only for monks and ecclesiastics but also for very wide circles of secular society to throw the problem of military action wholly on the so-called military classes. The very word "soldier," with its suggestion of a being apart, has its origin in this period. War was a matter for princes and rulers and their relatively small armies. It did not concern others unless they were accidentally involved. . . .

Those days are gone. Today everyone is a military person, either directly or indirectly. That is to say, everyone participates in the suffering and action which war demands. All nations as such, and all their members, have long since become responsible military subjects. It would be ridiculous today to throw the responsibility on the collective body, i.e., the fatherland which calls, the people which rallies, and the state which orders. Each individual is himself the fatherland, the people, the state; each individual is himself a belligerent. Hence each individual must act when war is waged, and each has to ask whether the war is just or unjust. This is the first thing which today makes the problem of war so serious from the ethical standpoint. It is an illusion to think that there can be an uncommitted spectator.

2. It has always been realized that war is concerned with the acquisition and protection of material interests, more specifically the possession of land and property. In times past, however, it was easier to lose sight of the material aspect in all kinds of notions about the honour, justice, freedom and greatness of the nation as represented in its princely houses and rulers, or about the supreme human values at stake, so that something of the character of a crusade, of a religious or cultural war, could be conferred upon the conflict, when in reality the decisive if not the exclusive point was simply the deployment of power for the acquisition of power in the elemental sense. Political mysticism, of course, is still to be found; but it is now much more difficult to believe in it sincerely. Certain fog patches have lifted. . . .

This means, however, that in a way very different from previous generations we can and should realize that the real issue in war, and an effective impulse towards it, is much less man himself and his vital needs than the economic power which in war is shown not so much to be possessed by man as to possess him, and this to his ruin, since instead of helping him to live and let live it forces him to kill and be killed. War reveals the basically chaotic character of the so-called peaceful will, efforts and achievements of man. It exposes his radical inability to be master without becoming not merely a slave but his own destroyer, and therefore fundamentally a suicide. It discloses the flagrant incapacity of man and the judgment which he is always on the point of bringing on himself even in peacetime. This means that in reality it is only superficially that the question of war differs from that of peace, i.e., from the question what we will and do, on what our life is fixed and how we order it, before war comes again with its killing and being killed. Do we possess the power to live, or does it possess us? So long as it possesses us, war will always be inevitable. *Si vis pacem, para bellum,* says the old Roman proverb. But a wiser version would be: *si non vis bellum, para pacem.* We should see to it that peace is better organized. But if we want something like war even in peacetime, how can we prepare for peace? How can we do anything but mobilize for war? How can it be otherwise than that war should break out and be fought? This is the unvarnished truth from which we can no longer escape so easily today as previously.

3. It has always been realized that the main goal in war is to neutralize the forces of the enemy. But it has not always been seen so clearly as one might desire that this goal demands not merely the most skillful and courageous dedication and possible forfeiture of one's own life but also quite nakedly and brutally the killing of as many as possible of the men who make up the opposing forces. In former days this was concealed by the fact that the individual confronted an individual opponent and could thus think of himself as in an unavoidable position of self-defense in which it was his duty and right to kill. Today it is even better concealed by the fact that as a result of recent technical development the individual to a very large extent cannot even see his individual opponents as such. . . .

Today, however, the increasing scientific objectivity of military killing, the development, appalling effectiveness and dreadful nature of the methods, instruments and machines employed, and the extension of the conflict to the civilian population, have made it quite clear that war does in fact mean no more and no less than killing with neither glory, dignity nor chivalry, with neither restraint nor consideration in any respect. The glory of the so-called military profession, which has incidentally become the profession of everybody either directly or indirectly, can now feed only on the relics of ancient illusions long since stripped of their substance. Much is already gained if only we do at last soberly admit that, whatever may be the purpose or possible justice of a war, it now means that, without disguise or shame, not only individuals or even armies, but whole nations as such, are out to destroy one another by every possible means. It only needed the atom and hydrogen bomb to complete the self-disclosure of war in this regard. . . .

In view of these questions we do well to make it clear *praenumerando* that if there can be any question of a just war, if we can describe this undertaking and participation in it as commanded, then it can only be with the same, and indeed with even stricter reserve and caution than have been found to be necessary in relation to such things as suicide, abortion, capital punishment etc. War is to be set in this category, nor is there any point in concealing the fact that the soldier, i.e., the fighting civilian, stands in direct proximity to the executioner. At any rate, it is only in this extreme zone, and in conjunction with other human acts which come dangerously near to murder, that military action can in certain instances be regarded as approved and commanded rather than prohibited.

We must also add that in this particular case the question is indeed to be put far more strictly than in relation to the other possibilities. For (1) war is an action in which the nation and all its members are actually engaged in killing, or in the direct or indirect preparation and promotion of killing. All are involved in this action, either as those who desire or as those who permit it, and in any case, as those who contribute to it in some sector. All are directly responsible in respect of the question whether it is commanded killing or forbidden murder. Again, however, killing in war is (2) a killing of those who for the individuals fighting in the service of the nation can be enemies only in the sense that they for their part have to wage war in the service of their country. The fact that the latter fight with approval on the other side can only make them appear guilty and criminal from this side. But whether the participants are guilty and criminal, and as such about to kill and therefore to murder, is a question which they also from their side might put to those who fight with approval on this side. Finally, killing in war (3), unlike the other possibilities already discussed, calls in question, not merely for individuals but for millions of men, the whole of morality, or better, obedience to the command of God in all its dimensions. Does not war demand that almost everything that God has forbidden be done on a broad front? To kill effectively, and in connexion therewith, must not those who wage war steal, rob, commit arson, lie, deceive, slander, and unfortunately to a large extent fornicate, not to speak of the almost inevitable repression of all the finer and weightier forms of obedience? And how can they believe and pray when at the climax of this whole world of dubious action it is a brutal matter of killing? It may be true that even in war many a man may save many things,—and indeed that an inner strength may become for him a more strong and genuine because a more tested possession. But it is certainly not true that people become better in war. The fact is that war is for most people a trial for which they are no match, and from the consequences of which they can never recover. Since all this is incontestable, can it and should it nevertheless be defended and ventured?

All affirmative answers to this question are wrong from the

very outset, and in Christian ethics constitute a flat betrayal of the Gospel, if they ignore the whole risk and venture of this Nevertheless, and do not rest on an exact calculation of what is here at stake and whether we can and must nevertheless reply in the affirmative. We can also put it in this way. All affirmative answers to the question are wrong if they do not start with the assumption that the inflexible negative of pacifism has almost infinite arguments in its favor and is almost overpoweringly strong. . . .

A first essential is that war should not on any account be recognized as a normal, fixed and in some sense necessary part of what on the Christian view constitutes the just state, or the political order demanded by God. Certainly the state as such possesses power and must be able to exercise it. But it does this in any case, and it is no primary concern of Christian ethics to say that it should do so, or to maintain that the exercise of power constitutes the essence of the state, i.e., its *opus proprium,* or even a part of it. What Christian ethics must insist is that it is an *opus alienum* for the state to have to exercise power. It cannot assure the state that in the exercise of power either the state or its organs may do gaily and confidently whatever they think is right. In such cases it must always confront them with the question whether there is really any necessity for this exercise. Especially the state must not be given *carte blanche* to grasp the *ultima ratio* of organizing mass slaughter in its dealings with other states. Christian ethics cannot insist too loudly that such mass slaughter might well be mass murder, and therefore that this final possibility should not be seized like any other, but only at the very last hour in the darkest of days. The Church and theology have first and supremely to make this detached and delaying movement. If they do not first and for a long time make this the burden of their message, if they do not throw in their weight decisively on this side of the scales, they have become savourless salt, and must not be surprised if they are freely trampled underfoot on every side. It is also to be noted that, if the Church and theology think otherwise, if they do not say this first, if they do not throw their weight on this side, if they speak tediously and tritely of war as a political *opus proprium,* then at the striking of the last hour in the darkest of days they will be in no position to say authentically and authoritatively what they may say at such a time. That is to say, they will be in no position authentically and authoritatively to issue a call to arms, to the political *opus alienum.* For they can do this only if they have previously held aloof, calling for peace right up to the very last moment. . . .

What Christian ethics has to emphasize is that neither inwardly nor outwardly does the normal task of the state, which is at issue even in time of war, consist in a process of annihilating rather than maintaining and fostering life. Nor should it be rashly maintained that annihilating life is also part of the process of maintaining and fostering it. Biological wisdom of this kind cannot serve as the norm or rule in ethics. The state which Christian ethics can and must affirm, which it has to proclaim as the political order willed and established by God, is not in itself and as such the mythological beast of the jungle, the monster with the Janus head, which by its very nature is prepared at any moment to turn thousands into killers and thousands more into killed. The Church does the state no honor, nor does it help it, if in relation to it, it acts on this assumption concerning its nature. According to the Christian understanding, it is no part of the normal task of the state to wage war; its normal task is to fashion peace in such a way that life is served and war kept at bay. If there is a mistake in pacifism, apart from the inadvisable ethical absolutism of its thesis, it consists in its abstract negation of war, as if war could be understood and negated in isolation and not in relation to the so-called peace which precedes it. Our attention should be directed to this relation. It is when a state does not rightly pursue its normal task that sooner or later it is compelled to take up the abnormal one of war, and therefore to inflict this abnormal task on other states. It is when the power of the state is insufficient to meet the inner needs of the country that it will seek an outer safety-valve for the consequent unrest and think it is found in war. It is when interest-bearing capital rather than man is the object whose maintenance and increase are the meaning and goal of the political order that the mechanism is already set going which one day will send men to kill and be killed. Against such a perversion of peace neither the supposed, though already undermined and no longer steadfast, love of the masses for peace, nor the well-meant and vocal declaiming of idealists against war, is of any avail. For the point is that when war does break out it is usually the masses who march, and even the clearest words spoken against war, and the most painful recollections of previous wars, are rendered stale and impotent. A peace which is no real peace can make war inevitable. Hence the first, basic and decisive point which Christian ethics must make in this matter is that the state, the totality of responsible citizens, and each individual in his own conduct should so fashion peace while there is still time that it will not lead to this explosion but make war superfluous and unnecessary instead of inevitable. Relatively speaking, it requires no great faith, insight nor courage to condemn war radically and absolutely, for no one apart from leaders of the armaments industry and a few high-ranking officers really believes that war is preferable to peace. Again, it requires no faith, insight nor courage at all to howl with the wolves that unfortunately war belongs no less to the present world order, historical life and the nature of the state than does peace, so that from the very outset we must regard it as an emergency for which preparation must be made. . . . Pacifists and militarists are usually agreed in the fact that for them the fashioning of peace as the fashioning of the state for democracy, and of democracy for social democracy, is a secondary concern as compared with rearmament or disarmament. It is for this reason that Christian ethics must be opposed to both. Neither rearmament nor disarmament can be a first concern, but the restoration of an order of life which is meaningful and just. When this is so, the two slogans will not disappear. They will have their proper place. They will come up for discussion at the proper time. But they will necessarily lose their fanatical tone, since far more urgent concerns will be up for discussion. And there can always be the hope that some day both will prove to be irrelevant.

It is only against the background of this first concern, and only as the Church has a good conscience that it is doing its best for a just peace among states and nations, that it can and should plead for the preservation of peace among states and nations, for fidelity and faith in their mutual dealings as the reasonable presupposition of a true foreign policy, for solid agreements and alliances and their honest observance, for international courts and conventions, and above all, and in all nations, for openness, understanding and patience towards others and for such education of young people as will lead them to prefer peace to war. The Church can and should raise its voice against the institution of standing armies in which the officers constitute *per se* a permanent danger to peace. It can and should resist all kinds of hysterical or premature war scares. It exists in this aeon. Hence it is not commissioned to proclaim that war is absolutely avoidable. But it is certainly commissioned to oppose the satanic doctrine that war is inevitable and therefore justified, that it is unavoidable and therefore right when it occurs, so that Christians have to participate in it. Even in a world in which states and nations are still in the early stages and never at the end of the long road in respect of that first concern, there is never in practice an absolute necessity of war, and the Church certainly has neither right nor obligation to affirm this necessity either in general or in detail as the occasion may arise. We do not need optimism but simply a modicum of sane intelligence to recognize that relatively if not absolutely, in practice if not in principle, war can be avoided to a very large extent. The Church must not preach pacifism, but it must see to it that this sane intelligence is voiced and heard so long as this is possible, and that the many ways of avoiding war which now exist in practice should be honestly applied until they are all exhausted. It is better in this respect that the Church should stick to its post too long and become a forlorn hope than that it should leave it too soon and then have to realize that it has become unfaithful by yielding to the general excitement, and that it is thus the accessory to an avoidable war which can only be described as mass murder. In excitement and propaganda there lurks already the mass killing which can only be mass murder. On no account, not even *in extremis,* should the Church be found among the agitators or use their language. Deliberate agitators, and those deceived by them, must always be firmly and quietly resisted, whether they like it or not. And this is what the Church can do with its word. Hence its word must never be a howling with the pack.

If only the Church had learned the two lessons (a) of Christian concern for the fashioning of true peace among nations to keep war at bay, and (b) of Christian concern for peaceful measures and solutions among states to avert war; if only these two requirements and their unconditional primacy were the assured possession of all Christian ethics, we might feel better assured both against misunderstandings and also against threatened relapses into the post-Constantinian theology of war, and we might therefore be confident to say that we cannot accept the absolutism of the pacifist thesis, and that Christian support for war and in war is not entirely beyond the bounds of possibility. . . .

This . . . point rests on the assumption that the conduct of one state or nation can throw another into the wholly abnormal situation of emergency in which not merely its greater or lesser prosperity but its very existence and autonomy are menaced and attacked. In consequence of the attitude of this other state, a nation can find itself faced by the question whether it must surrender or assert itself as such in face of the claims of the other. Nothing less than this final question must be at issue if a war is to be just and necessary.

Perhaps a state desires to expand politically, geographically or economically, and therefore to extend its frontiers and dominion. Perhaps it thinks it necessary to rectify its internal conditions, e.g., to bring about political unity, by external adventure. Perhaps it considers that its honour and prestige are violated by the attitude of another state. Perhaps it feels that it is threatened by a shift in the balance of power among other states. Perhaps it thinks it sees in the internal conditions of another state, whether revolutionary or reactionary, a reason for displeasure or anxiety. Perhaps it believes it can and should ascribe to itself a historical mission, e.g., a call to lead and rule other nations. All this may well be so. Yet it certainly does not constitute a valid reason for setting one's own great or little war machine in motion, for sending out one's troops to the battlefield to kill and be killed. Such aims may be well worth striving for. But they are too paltry to be worth the terrible price involved in their realization by war. War for such reasons could always have been avoided. War for such reasons is an act of murder. When such reasons lie on one side of the scale, and the knowledge of war and its necessary terrors on the other, we should have to be either incorrigible romanticists or malevolent sophists even to doubt which side ought to rise and which to fall. The Christian Church has to testify unambiguously that wars waged for such reasons are not just, and therefore ought not to be undertaken.

Even the existence or non-existence of a state does not always constitute a valid reason for war. It can sometimes happen that the time of a state in its present form of existence has expired, that its independent life has no more meaning nor basis, and that it is thus better advised to yield and surrender, continuing its life within a greater nexus of states. There are times when this kind of question has to be raised and answered. As is well-known, Jeremiah did not repeat the message of Isaiah in an earlier situation, but summoned the people to submit rather than resist. We may well imagine a case in which the witness of the Christian Church ought to have a similar material content.

Indeed, it is only in answer to this particular question that there is a legitimate reason for war, namely, when a people or state has serious grounds for not being able to assume responsibility for the surrender of its independence, or, to put it even more sharply, when it has to defend within its borders the independence which it has serious grounds for not surrendering. The sixth commandment is too urgent to permit of the justification of war by Christian ethics on any other grounds.

Why do we have to allow the possibility that in the light of the divine commandment this is a justifiable reason for war, so that a war waged for this reason must be described as a just war in spite of all the horrors which it will certainly entail? The obvious answer is that there may well be bound up with the independent life of a nation responsibility for the whole physical, intellectual and spiritual life of the people comprising it, and therefore their relationship to God. It may well be that in and with the independence of a nation there is entrusted to its people something which, without any claim or pretension, they are commissioned to attest to others, and which they may not therefore surrender. It may well be that with the independence of the state, and perhaps in the form of the legally constituted society guaranteed by it, they would also have to yield something which must not be betrayed, which is necessarily more important to them than the preservation of life itself, and which is thus more important than the preservation of the lives of those who unfortunately are trying to take it from them. It may well be that they are thus forbidden by God to renounce the independent status of their nation, and that they must therefore defend it without considering either their own lives or the lives of those who threaten it. Christian ethics cannot possibly deny that this case may sometimes occur. The divine command itself posits and presents it as a case of extreme urgency.

> I may remark in passing that I myself should see it as such a case if there were any attack on the independence, neutrality and territorial integrity of the Swiss Confederation, and I should speak and act accordingly.

But a similar situation may arise in a different form, e.g., when a state which is not itself directly threatened or attacked considers itself summoned by the obligation of a treaty or in some other way to come to the aid of a weaker neighbour which does actually find itself in this situation. In solidarity with the state which it tries to help, it will then find itself in a position of true emergency. At such a time Christian ethics can no longer be absolutely pacifist. It cannot, therefore, oppose all military action, nor resist all military armament. If it has said all there is to be said about true peace and the practical avoidability of war; if it has honestly and resolutely opposed a radical militarism, it may then add that, should the command of God require a nation to defend itself in such an emergency, or in solidarity with another nation in such an emergency, then it not only may but must do so. It may also add that if this is basically the only reason for war on the basis of its constitution and history and in the minds of all its responsible citizens, then it may and must prepare for it even in peacetime. For even though this preparation has in view the terrible venture of killing and being killed, with all that this entails, the venture itself is inescapably demanded.

A distinctively Christian note in the acceptance of this demand is that it is quite unconditional. That is to say, it is independent of the success or failure of the enterprise, and therefore of the strength of one's own forces in comparison with those of the enemy. . . .

We cannot separate the question of the just war from the two questions of faith on the one side and obedience on the other. And these are reciprocal. If war is ventured in obedience and therefore with a good conscience, it is also ventured in faith and therefore with joyous and reckless determination. And if it is really ventured in the necessary faith, its basis is not found in mere enthusiasm but in the simple fact that, perhaps most unwillingly and certainly with a heavy heart, it has to be waged in obedience and certainly cannot be shirked for the sake of a worthless peace. Conversely, "if ye will not believe, surely ye shall not be established" (Is. 7:9). This means that the Christian Church will have its own part to play in a state which finds itself in this kind of emergency and therefore forced into war. But we can also see in what sense it must stand by this nation, rousing, comforting and encouraging it, yet also calling it to repentance and conversion. There can certainly be no question of howling with the pack, or of enunciating a military code invented *ad hoc,* but only of preaching the Gospel of the lordship of God's free grace and of direction to the prayer which will not consist in the invocation of a pagan god of history and battles, but which will always derive from, and return to, the *dona nobis pacem.* In this form, however, the message of the Church may and should be a call to martial resolution which can be righteous only as an act of obedience but which as such can be truly righteous, which can be powerful only as an act of faith but which as such can be truly powerful. If right up to the last moment the Church has really devoted itself to the inculcation of the first two lessons, it need not be afraid that in a genuine emergency it will not have the right word of help and guidance, i.e., this third lesson. Nor need it be concerned lest it should compromise itself with this word in face of the fact that even the most just of wars might end in defeat. The Church which does not give any easy sanction to war, which constantly seeks to avert it, which is studious to avoid any general or institutional approval in principle, which proclaims peace alone as the will of God both internally and externally, which testifies to the very last against unjust reasons for war—this Church is able in a true emergency, or in the rare case of a just war, to tell men that, even though they now have to kill, they are not murderers, but may and must do the will of God in this *opus alienum* of the state.

We have still to consider, however, the same question with reference to the responsibility and decision of the individual. Thus far we have discussed it in relation to the state, war being an action undertaken by the state as a whole. On the Christian view, however, the state is not a strange, lofty and powerful hypostasis suspended over the individual, dominating him, and thinking, willing and deciding for him. To be sure, individuals are included in its jurisdiction and brought under its authority. Individuals are protected by it and owe allegiance to it. Yet in the very same process it is they who support and maintain it. Enjoying its relative perfections, they also share, even if only by silence or inaction, in its imperfections. They bear responsibility for its condition, and for what is done or not done by it. They are in the same boat with its government, whatever its constitutional form and however acceptable or not. They are in solidarity with the majority of its citizens, whether they belong to this majority or not. The infamous statement attributed to Louis XIV can and should be corrected. Every individual in his own place and function is the state. If the state is a divine order for the continued existence of which Christians should pray, we can also say that, as they themselves are the Church, so they are also the state. Hence the state cannot relieve the individual of any responsibility. On the contrary, the state is wholly a responsibility of the individual. Nor is this any less true of war as a responsibility of the individual. The state wages war in the person of the individual. In war it is he, the individual man or woman, who must prepare for, further, support and in the last analysis execute the work of killing. It is part of the responsibility that in so doing he must risk his own life. But the decisive point is that he must be active in the destruction of the lives of others. . . .

As and because this same question is put to the state, it is also a genuine concern of each individual responsible for it and within it. This means, however, that the individual is asked to consider with the state what the state has to consider, not as a private person in a private affair and from a private standpoint, but as a citizen in an affair of state and from a civic standpoint, yet also personally and in personal responsibility. At a specific point and in a specific way it all applies also and especially to him. He personally is asked whether he hears the commandment and sees war in its terrible reality. He is asked whether he is working for the righteous inner peace which cannot lead to war, or whether he is contributing to a rotten and unjust peace which contains the seeds of war. He is asked whether he is helping on the many positive and restraining measures for the avoidance of war, or perhaps the opposite. He is asked whether in his own conduct and general behavior, his way of thinking and speaking, what he permits or forbids himself to do, what he supports or hinders in others, he is postponing or preventing war. Is he clear that if war comes it will not be vertically up from the kingdom of demons but—demonically enough—through men, and that he himself will be one of the men who are guilty or innocent in relation to it? Again, has he set aside all inadequate and false reasons for war, and is he not only prepared to be but genuinely at work as a public and positive witness that most of the reasons are in fact inadequate and false, and do not justify such a dreadful act? Only when he has faced these questions is he finally asked whether, in the event of a true emergency arising in spite of everything for his nation or state, he is willing and ready *ultima ratione, in extremis,* to accept war and military training, to do so as a Christian, and therefore to do so fearlessly in spite of all that it entails, shouldering personal responsibility not merely for being killed but for the much more horrible act of killing. . . . In all these aspects the question of war must be asked and answered as a personal question. And perhaps the most important contribution that Christian ethics can make in this field is to lift the whole problem inexorably out of the indifferent sphere of general political and moral discussion and to translate it into the personal question: "What hast thou so far done or failed to do in the matter, and what art thou doing or failing to do at this moment?" Killing is a very personal act, and being killed a very personal experience. It is thus commensurate with the thing itself that even in the political form which killing assumes in war it should be the theme of supremely personal interrogation.

In this connexion we may conclude with a consideration of the specific problems of conscription and conscientious objection.

The pacifist demand for the abolition of conscription (cf. J.G. Heering, *Der Sundenfall des Christentums,* pp. 252f.) is shortsighted. For conscription has the salutary effect of bringing home the question of war. War is an affair of the state and therefore of the totality of its subjects, not of a minority or majority of volunteers or militarists. All citizens share responsibility for it both in peace and war. They thus share the burden of this responsibility, and must themselves face the question whether it is right or wrong. This fact is given due expression and brought right home by conscription, whereas it is glossed over in every other type of military constitution. To make military service once again something for mercenary or volunteer armies would be to absolve the individual from direct responsibility for war and to leave both war itself and the resultant "moral odium," as Heering calls it, to others. In other words, non-participation becomes a matter of particular prudence and virtue in the one case, and participation of particular stupidness and wickedness in the other. If anything is calculated to perpetuate war, it is this Pharisaic attitude. Conscription, however, has the invaluable advantage of confronting both the prudent and the stupid, both the peace-loving and less peace-loving, with the problem of the belligerent state as their own personal problem, and conversely of compelling them to express their own personal attitude to war in their responsibility as citizens of the state instead of treating it merely as a matter of private opinion. . . . The abolition of conscription would take the edge off this decision for those not personally affected. It would make it merely political rather than both political and personal. This could not possibly contribute to the serious discussion or solution of the problem of war. Pacifists, therefore, should be the very last to call for the abolition of conscription.

The dignity of an absolute divine command cannot, of course, be ascribed to military service. Although the state must claim it from the individual as a compulsory duty, and although its fulfillment is urgently prompted in the first instance by the relation of the individual to the state, it can finally be understood only as a question which is put to him and which no one can answer but himself. The state is not God, nor can it command as He does. . . . Hence it cannot be denied that in virtue of his relationship to God the individual may sometimes find himself compelled, even with a full sense of his loyalty as a citizen, to contradict and oppose what is thought right and resolved by the government or the majority. He will be aware of the exceptional character of this action. Such insubordination cannot be ventured too easily or frequently. He will also be aware of the risk entailed. He cannot but realize that by offering resistance he renders himself liable to prosecution. He cannot deny to the government or the majority the right to take legal and constitutional proceedings against him. He must not be surprised or aggrieved if he has to bear the consequences of his resistance. . . . The contradiction and resistance to compulsory military service can indeed take the form of the actual refusal of individuals to submit to conscription as legally and constitutionally imposed by the government or the majority, and therefore of their refusal to participate directly either in war itself or preparation for it. . . .

Two formal presuppositions are essential if such refusal of military service by one or more individuals is to be accepted as imperative and therefore legitimate. The first is that the objector must accomplish his act of insubordination in the unity of his individual and personal existence with his existence as a citizen. There can be no question of calming his private conscience by binding his civic conscience. His relationship to God will not absolve him from his obligation to the state; it will simply pose it in a specific way, which may perhaps be this way. Quite apart from less worthy motives, it cannot be merely a matter of satisfying his own personal abhorrence of violence and bloodshed, of keeping his own hands clean. His refusal of military service can have nothing whatever to do with even the noblest desertion of the state, and certainly not with anarchy. He must be convinced and assured that by his opposition he stands and acts for the political community as willed and ordained by God, not denying the state but affirming it by contrast to the government, the majority, the existing law and constitution. . . .

Second, the man who objects to military service must be prepared to accept without murmur or complaint the consequences of the insubordinate form of his national loyalty, the hostility of the government or majority to which he may be exposed, and the penalty of his violation of the existing law and constitution. . . . He cannot ask, therefore, for considerate exceptions in the administration of valid decrees, or even for protective laws of exemption, in the case of those likeminded with himself. He should certainly not try to be drafted to the medical or pioneer corps instead of the infantry. He should not ask for the impossible, claiming on the one hand to act as a prospective martyr, and on the other to be spared from martyrdom after all, or at least to have it made easier for him. He must act honestly and consistently as a revolutionary, prepared to pay the price of his action, content to know that he has on his side both God and the better informed state of the future, hoping to bear an effective witness to it today, but ready at least to suffer what *rebus sic stanibus* his insubordination must now entail. . . .

There is also a material error in conscientious objection, however, if it rests on an absolute refusal of war, i.e., on the absolutism of radical pacifism. In such a case, it is no less rebellion against the command of God than an affirmation of war and participation in it on the basis of radical militarism, i.e., of the superstition of the inevitability of war, of the view that it is an element in the divine world order and an essential constituent of the state. If we are genuinely ready to obey the command of God, we cannot go so far either to the right or to the left as to maintain such absolute ethical tenets and modes of action in loyalty to Him. On the contrary, we shall have to take account of the limitation of even the best of human views, principles, and attitudes. In the national loyalty which is always required, conscientious objection is possible only if it is relative and not absolute, and therefore if it is not tainted by the idea that the state is utterly forbidden in any circumstances either to wage war or to prepare for it. Exercised with political responsibility, it must include the readiness of the conscientious objector in other circumstances and in face of other demands to renounce the insubordination which is commanded in certain concrete conditions, and therefore to do always what he is required to do in a given case. He must never allow his conscientious objection to infringe upon either the freedom of the commanding God or his own freedom, i.e., the freedom of his civic conscience. He must fulfill it as a free person, and as one who wills to remain free, in this twofold sense. . . .

On the other hand, conscientious objection may well be necessary and legitimate in a situation in which one or more persons cannot fail to see that the cause for which the state is arming or waging war is concretely an evil one, that the war in which they are asked to participate is one of the many unjust and irresponsible wars which are not risked out of a genuine emergency but planned and embarked upon deliberately. It is not to be expected that in such a situation this recognition will be a general one, or that it will take a specific form among the people at large. It may often be current as an obscure premonition on the part of many, and official propaganda will naturally do all it can to prevent it breaking through. But in such a situation it will certainly obtrude upon certain individuals in such a definite form that in spite of all official propaganda they cannot conceal the fact, but are taught by the divine command, that they must protest against this war not only in thought and word but also by conscientious objection. This does not mean that they will be released from their responsibility to the state. It means that they will have to discharge this responsibility in such a way that they refuse to fulfill the duty of military service, not in principle, but in relation to the concrete military action now demanded, believing that in so doing they desire the very best for the state, ready to suffer for the fact that what they desire differs from what is desired by the government or the majority, and therefore at peace with God and also in the deepest sense with their own conscience. The fact that in a concrete political situation individuals may have to act like this, and therefore to refuse military service, according to the command of God, is a possibility for which provision can hardly be made in political law but which Christian ethics certainly cannot deny as such. . . . The government or majority in any state has to reckon with the fact that individuals cannot spare themselves but have necessarily to put the personal question of responsibility for the specific war at issue, and that it may happen that they will have to return a negative answer to the question even in practice. It would be a great gain for peace if all governments or majorities in all states knew that they had actually to take this into account.

It is, of course, self-evident that individuals cannot be left to deal with this question alone. Here if anywhere the Church, or at any rate enlightened and commissioned men within it, should be at hand and on the watch to give to the individual in changing political situations guidance and direction which are not legalistic, but evangelical, plain and unequivocal, concerning the understanding and keeping of the command of God which is really at issue. How can the Church be neutral or silent in so important and perilous a matter? How can it override the individual conscience by what it says, as is constantly maintained? For far too long the Church has failed to consider the individual conscience and made military obedience a universal duty—and this in the name of God. . . .

17

A Political Ethics Context for Strategic Thinking

Paul Ramsey

If it is an error to suppose it to be possible ever to replace the inter-state system with a system of trustworthy international actors acting completely trustingly and trustworthily, it is equally an error to suppose the inter-state system to be a system of illimitable animosity to which there are no inherent systemic norms (except the norm of quantifiable rationality) which are applicable to the actors and that govern the achievement of their purposes.

For one thing, animosity and conflict are not, unqualifiedly, the characteristics of the system or its interactions. I do not understand strategic theorists to mean any such thing when they speak of international relations as an opposed-system. While there exists no collectivity in which Cain, the fratricide who founded the earthly city, exists no longer, there exists no collectivity in which Abel, progenitor of the Founder of the heavenly city, does not also exist. Empirically, this means simply that statesmen are called to action in the midst of the *unpredictabilities* of other collectives and their leaders. The nation-state is surrounded by arbitrariness on all sides. That is to say, by autonomous actors; not everywhere by hostility and by enemies. The other is a stranger and a source of independent action affecting outcomes for oneself. Since identification can pass between man and man, between collective and collective, only through structures that must be based on the organic development over time of common heritage and community, never upon social-contracting wills alone, the other in the international system remains a potential enemy. He is only that, but he is that.

Responding to the *unpredictability* of the other collective's action requires, *among other things,* preparedness, threat, and perhaps an actual use of force. This requirement does not assume universal hostility or the universality of conflict. Let us have an end to mongering about stereotyped anticommunism or cold-war mentality or generalized animosity as errors of which the strategists are accused. Let us have an end to simplistic appeals that they should look out on the world with rosier expectations. One should prepare for *some* of the worst *not* because of jaundiced vision, but because of the unpredictability of action in the inter-state system. That cannot be replaced by choosing a better picture of the world; it does not vary with tinted glasses. Public officials must be prepared for the unpredictabilities. This means they have to attend to the *capabilities* of other actors, and not to their hypothetical intentions or even first of all to actual better intentions they may have. The system is characterized by the unpredictability of autonomous actors and reactors. That defines the minimum morality of responsible action within the inter-state system. It is the unpredictability, and not the generalized animosity, in all the action coming upon us that makes another's capability (or some of "the worst") one ingredient among the anticipations of appropriate response.

For another thing, there are demonstrable political ethical "rules of practice" to which action and interaction must conform, or which set its outer limits. Since the actors are peoples (or their governments) who have purposes—the chief of which is to continue to be a people able to effectuate their (however variable and divergent) purposes as a people—these rules of practice are *systemic* rules. An analysis of the opposed international system which abstracted from that purpose would be an incorrect account of the action going on in that system. There is a substantive interpretation of statecraft and of the purposive interactions of nations exhibited and summarized in the "just-war theory." Formulated as statements of the justifications needed for resorts to conflict, this body of teachings also expresses an understanding of the strivings going on among interacting collectives by other political means. For this reason, I describe the criteria of just war as *systemic* requirements, and *not* an external ethics vainly imposed. If the just-war theory was a product of western ethics, it is nevertheless a proposal concerning the very nature of the international system.

The political ethical limits and determination of justice in war's conduct and in deterrence policy I have elaborated elsewhere. Readers who do not know this literature are my loss. That loss cannot be repaired here. I can only summarize certain theses which I have, I believe, proved elsewhere *in extenso.* The following are conclusions which I believe are demonstrable in any sound ethical reasoning about politics and warfare.

1. There are two principles governing determinations of *jus in bello,* the just conduct of war as an instrument of national policy: (a) the principle of discrimination or the moral immunity of non-combatants from intended direct attack, and (b) the principle of proportion or prudence, or the requirement that costs in destruction accepted and exacted be warranted by benefits there is reasonable expectation of gaining. Always and everywhere, of course, there have been violations of both requirements; and, in past wars, only extensive violation of the second caused political resorts to violence, by under- or over-reactions, to lose their objective. I have shown that, apart from peripheral violations (that is, so far as the central design of war is concerned), the principle of discrimination is today—in the nuclear age—equally important in keeping uses of violence related to choiceworthy political objectives. Both the moral immunity of non-combatants from deliberate direct attack and the test of costs/benefits are today clearly—so far as concerns the central war—inherent laws of war as a possible instrument of national policy. So I call them both systemic requirements of encounters of purposeful uses of power in the international system.

2. Still there are *two* principles determining *jus in bello;* these are related but *separate* principles; both apply, and neither subordinates or absorbs or exhaustively interprets the other. A violation of the moral immunity of non-combatants from direct attack need not be in its consequences disproportionate or imprudent or disoriented from political purpose. This is true only of the central war in a nuclear age; there the two "rules of practice" of *jus in bello* converge; an actual war

with our most powerful weapons in violation of the principle of discrimination cannot advance the measured political purposes of any people in the international system. The more common error today, however, is the rhetoric which identifies the principle of discrimination with the principle of proportion, which describes any seeming *or actual* disproportionate destruction as "indiscriminate" destruction. This is loose thinking and loose language. The two principles remain separate ways of assessing *jus in bello.*

3. I have shown that in rightly understanding the "moral immunity of non-combatants from deliberate direct attack" there are at least two terms that must be made clear and kept clear, and which should never be confused, if we are rightly to distinguish discriminate from indiscriminate acts of war. There is, first, the meaning of combatancy/non-combatancy. There is, second, the meaning of deliberate direct attack. Unless these terms are clarified and kept clear, the simple and not so simple physical destruction of non-combatants (past an unspecified number) will erroneously be taken to mean they have been directly attacked; and the principle of discrimination will be regarded as a test that can be quantitatively violated. I have shown that it is *not* possible to violate the principle of discrimination by numbers or amount of destruction. Only the principle of proportion *could* be so violated; and proportionate defense or *protective* justice always concerns more than the *amount* of the costs.

4. The meaning of "combatancy/non-combatancy" is a function in some measure of military technology in any epoch; it is certainly a function of how the nations and their forces are organized for war. The meaning of "non-combatants," those who are morally immune, is *relative* in the sense that it is *objectively* determined by the manner in which the nations are organized for war, the technology with which they can wage war, the contours of war in any epoch. I omit here proofs that the distinction is one that can validly be made under any organizations for war. Suffice it to say that the problem of distinguishing between combatants and non-combatants, between forces and civil life, is tractable whatever an epoch's military technology or posture—under any other assumption than the politicizing and militarizing of everyone in a society, including the inmates of homes for the retarded, as "fighters" in a nation's cause. Only an absolute totalitarian-

ism such as the world has never known could justify total war, or the obliteration of the combatant/non-combatant distinction, even though the latter is *objectively relative* to how the nations are organized for war.

The meaning of "deliberate direct attack" is another matter. It is a matter of the intention of acts of war, of their direction or thrusts in the world, of their targets and objectives, the planned design of the war to be executed. From the *objective relativity* of the meaning of "non-combatancy" it cannot be concluded that the meaning of "deliberate direct attack" is *subjectively relative,* or a mere function of actual or foreseen destruction. One cannot conclude from destruction wrought to what was intended and directly done. A great part of the deaths and damage may be collateral, though foreseen. That could be a violation of proportion, while not of the moral immunity of non-combatants from direct attack; or it may be neither.

This unpacking of the principle of discrimination can be expressed in the carefully drawn language of the Vatican Council, which said: "Any act of war aimed indiscriminately at the destruction of entire cities and of extensive areas along with their population is a crime against God and man himself. It merits unequivocal and unhesitating condemnation" *(Gaudium et Spes,* par. 80). That statement, as such, does *not* condemn as politically immoral actions which physically destroy cities, areas, populations. It rather condemns acts which "aim indiscriminately at" such destruction. To understand the moral immunity of non-combatants from deliberate direct attack, and the possible acceptability of their collateral destruction, one has only to get to know the difference between "aiming indiscriminately" at populations and "aiming discriminately" at legitimate (combatant or military) targets. Discrimination in acts of war never meant *attacking* only combatants, never *attacking* non-combatants. It certainly never supposed they are or could be *separated.* It means rather to forbid *directly* attacking non-combatants, to forbid aiming indiscriminately at everyone alike. To acknowledge the force of this requirement, and abide by it, one does not need to know *who* are non-combatants or *where* they are. One only needs to know *that* there are non-combatants (even only inmates of homes for the retarded) to know that he should limit his targeting to *known* legitimate military targets while limiting circumambient damage as much as possible. So long as to this measure the distinction between combatant/noncombatant is objectively tractable relative to any organization of the nations for warfare, the meaning of the immutable principle that acts of warfare should be aimed discriminately can be given content. So also the meaning of "collateral destruction," permitted but only if what is at stake in the encounter is great enough.

5. . . . The morality of war's conduct and the morality of the deterrence of war cannot be separated. Whatever is wrong to do is wrong also to threaten, if the latter means "mean to do." If aiming indiscriminately in actual acts of war (or in fight-the-war policies) is wrong, so also is threatening indiscriminately aimed action wrong to adopt in deter-the-war policies. While, of course, actually to do an evil deed for the sake of supposed good to come is a different wrong—and, we may allow, a far greater wrong—than simply to threaten seriously to do that action for the sake of good to come (deterrence), still these two things are qualitatively cut from the same cloth. To put the point bluntly, if counter-population warfare is murder, then counter-population deterrent threats are murderous. The question, therefore, of the ethical justification of deterrence depends crucially on a question of fact, or of plannable policy: namely, whether the only *effective* deterrent must be suspended from the meant mutual threat of ultimate indiscriminate destruction. If so, then deterrence is irremediably a political immorality, even though to carry out the threatened indiscriminate destruction would be a different species of murderousness, and of course a far greater wrong *of its kind.*

6. Finally, I have drawn attention to the fact that modern warfare (whether by this we mean nuclear war or subconventional war) becomes disproportionate, that is, disoriented from the capacity to effectuate political purposes that are worth it, sooner than it becomes indiscriminate (since the latter is a matter of the aim and direction of acts of war and varies with military technology and the nations' organization for war). This fact . . . provides grounds for a radically different analysis of a feasible deterrence and consequently of the moral justifiability of a possible deterrence, which I call "graduated" deterrence—in contrast to deterrence that is "suspended" from the ultimate and whose effectiveness is

supposed at all lower levels to be indivisibly connected with a conditional willingness to involve that final political immorality. Since I deny the necessary dependence of the deterrence we need upon seriously threatening the indiscriminate destruction of populations, I argue for the morality of the deterrent possession of nuclear weapons. Of this, more later.

In light of the foregoing we may ask what are the imperatives for strategic thinking for the 1970s. One of the tragic results of our Vietnam agony and of anti-militarism feeding off of increased awareness of the vast funds needed to meet our domestic problems has been that the intellectual energy still needed to subdue the paramount military problems of a nuclear age was drained off; that political scientists' advice to government became as confused as the general public; that, today, nuclear posture is expected to stand unreconstructed until abolished by mutual agreement; and that the slight beginnings in the 1960s toward putting the immoral, anti-population use of nuclear weapons in a class by itself as something never to be done in war or meant for deterrence came to a halt. Instead, graduated and flexible response, and schemes that might be equally or more costly for further decentralizing and putting intended indiscriminate destruction out of commission in war and in deterrence, came to be regarded as efforts to "save war" or to save America's interventionary role in the world. Instead of such moves, we ought rather—it was said—to conclude strategic agreements to stop the costly arms race and so release the resources to save our cities.

The result has been that at the beginning of the 1970s the United States adheres even more firmly to a policy of minimum or finite deterrence. Our power at all other levels of war and deterrence is more and more challenged or outstripped, and even the possible vulnerability of our nuclear forces is tolerated for the sake of strategic disarmament treaties to come. It is difficult to tell the difference between editorials on strategic questions in the *New York Times* over the past two or three years and Dulles's "more bang for a buck" policy. The only significant difference seems to be that, while Dulles believed that nuclear threats could be used at times and places of his own choosing to deter war at all lower levels and as an instrument of particular political policies other than the deterrence of nuclear war, the *Times* seems to believe the costs of keeping up to date in nuclear technology can be stopped by treaties at times and places and under conditions of its own choosing without full reckoning, public acknowledgment, or advocacy of the need for and cost of battle- and deterrence-needs of other sorts at other levels. That Dulles also omitted.

The upshot seems clearly to be a return (if that is the word for it) to the most politically immoral nuclear posture imaginable, namely, Mutual Assured Destruction. That is to say, we are further away than ever before from the abandonment of the intentional anti-population use of nuclear weapons at the heart of deterrence, their likely use at the planned end of the scale of nuclear war, or from the "first use" of nuclears against massive conventional attack. (There is no way to renounce the latter except by conventional sufficiency.) I would say that the major imperative for the 1970s is that these issues must again be addressed with the maximum concern of strategic, moral, and political reasoning, so that—if at all possible—we may reverse the devastating effects of the Vietnam interlude in confirming our policy commitments to total counter-people war and deterrence at the nuclear level. The Vietnam war, plus domestic tumult and the native aversion of the American mind to the steady acceptance and use of political power and the need for strategic thinking, have caused us to become committed to, morally, the most unacceptable defense and deterrence policies.

It seems to me that in the ABM debates a good many strategic analysts have performed well in calling the attention of citizens and government to the necessity of protecting the non-lethal end of our nuclear missiles: the invulnerability of bases and systems. I state this as an opinion, without any particular competence or right to hold it *in my capacity as a moralist.* In that role-function, I do not make technical proposals or *particular* war-designs—neither war-making nor war-stopping judgments (a self-denying ordinance I wish many of my fellow churchmen would impose upon themselves in their offices, whatever be their views as citizens). Still I have about as much personal certitude concerning the need for ABM defense as I am certain that a small group of Britishers were correct when early in the nuclear age they began to worry about the fact that Great Britain's deterrent forces were planes motionless on open airfields, and from that went on to establish what became the Institute for Strategic Analysis at the University of London. (The RAND Corporation's struggle to convince the U.S. Air Force of the same point is a matter of record.) Myself, I am rather proud of the fact that many of the people involved in that first move toward strategic thinking—which has resulted in a center most esteemed for its objectivity and rationality—were Christians who for many years had participated in the international affairs department of the British and the World Council of Churches. That bit of history is, by contrast, evidence of our present plight in which ethical considerations on the one hand and political considerations on the other have come to occupy separate worlds.

Churchmen's abdication of their responsibility for this is not my concern here; the responsibilities of strategistic analysis *are* of present concern. And so I return to the moral and political imperatives upon strategic thinking in the 1970s. This is simply that more attention should be paid to the lethal end of our missiles, to the ethico-political limits governing targeting both in war and for deterrence, and not solely to the question of maintaining the invulnerability of bases.

There is at least as much evidence—I judge there is far more evidence—of a continuing intellectual effort to turn away from indiscriminate warfare and from deterrence founded in principle on the meant targeting of populations among strategic thinkers than there is in public opinion generally, in the press, or among academic or church liberals. The ethico-political imperative I am talking about, therefore, only accents a tendency, a line of thought, that is already there among many who have thought long and hard about the relation of arms and men, between armed forces and a political society, between armaments and the political purposes they are meant to serve.

Thus, Donald G. Brennan of the Hudson Institute points out that the acronym for Mutual Assured Destruction is MAD.[1] We ought not to regard such a policy (today renamed "strategic sufficiency") as the most peaceful, stable, secure, cheap, and generally desirable arrangement. If that commonly accepted doctrine were true, the cheapest and most efficient way to achieve it would be for the nuclear powers to mine each other's cities. Such a system is technically feasible, and far safer and more likely to work than missile deterrence.

Brennan's *reductio ad absurdum* agrument is that, "since a mined-city system is clearly the best way to achieve a MAD posture, it follows that a MAD posture as a goal is itself fundamentally absurd—it is, indeed, mad." A rational posture for providing for the common defense cannot be based on deliberately making us all hostages to enemy weapons; by creating "a system in which millions of innocent civilians would, by intention, be exterminated in a failure of the system." The mined-cities "thought experiment" is enough to show that there must be something wrong with the complete reversal of the relation between arms and the body politic which happens when we institutionalize mutual assured destruction as a way of life. In the structure of Brennan's analysis, it seems to me, it matters little whether "sufficiency" is obtained by few weapons or many; it is the posture, the targeting, that is wrong. Instead of being "busily engaged in forging a permanent Sword of Damocles," to hang forever over our heads, our efforts through SALT talks as well as military systems initiative should be to hold down (and redirect?) offense, reduce (and redirect?) our threat, and to make defense as effective as possible. While Brennan allows that we should be able to do about as badly unto the Soviets as they can do to us, still the Defense Department should be more concerned with assuring live Americans than dead Russians.

Now, it seems clear to me that, although the context of Donald Brennan's argument is the debate over ABM defense, his mind is beginning to follow the lineaments of a sound political ethics in regard to the lethal end of our missiles as well.

Arthur Lee Burns's Adelphi Paper "Ethics and Deterrence: A Nuclear Balance Without Hostage Cities?" is an explicit and stalwart effort to meld together security considerations and the political ethical norms of the just war.[2] My plea is simply that strategic thinking has upon it the imperative to address for the next decade the question of how what is morally right in war and deterrence can be made feasible. This requires rejection of utilitarianism, a rejection of "the old liberalism" which "has extemporized itself into contending unambiguously for peace by nuclear terror" (pp. 1, 2).

Burns, as I understand him, believes shared calculations of "unacceptable damage" to be largely "chimerical" and "mere rationalizations for a policy that, once adopted, came to be valued for its own sake" (p. 24). He proposes instead the rule that military capability must be sufficient to "wreak such destruction on the attacker *that neither its government nor any successor at all acceptable to that government would continue to rule*" (p. 3, italics added).

That already begins to "lower the bid," and to suggest that present deterrence postures may not be beyond human amendment. Even if they should prove—or for the meanwhile prove—to be "beyond human amendment," Burns wants it clearly understood that that fact would not make terrorizing kidnapped hostages "any less evil" (p. 6). Even if *for the present* there is only a choice between different immoralities, we ought not to say that the "least immoral course" now available is "for that reason really moral after all." One ought not "to devalue the moral currency" despite the fact that there may be nothing as yet to spend it on (p. 7). In particular, the meaning of *jus in bello* and in deterrence should not be degraded. "The traditional ethic," Burns writes, "of sparing non-combatants as a prima facie obligation is not reconcilable with making them hostages, and unlike utilitarianism it takes account of the intention and the intrinsic quality of an act of a policy, not *only* of the probable consequences" (p. 12); and he concludes: "I cannot see how a city-targeting strategy can possibly be reconciled with principles of the just employment of armed force, even though the threatened destruction of millions of non-combatants is by no means as evil as would be their actual destruction, and though the threat may deter war" (p. 13).

Burns espouses a policy of threatening to retaliate against armed forces only, including the most vital and vulnerable parts of nuclear forces. He contends that totalitarian regimes would regard the loss of whole armies (supposing they could be reached by the strike forces) as a graver threat to the continued existence of the regime than the destruction of a few cities, and to that state's security against conventional challenges by third powers; "the Soviet Union and China would be prepared to sacrifice some cities and industrial areas in order to preserve their conventional forces in effective strength" (p. 17). What objectives of policy (except, of course, the prevention of nuclear attack itself) could be worth the loss of the larger part of a nation's conventional power?

The same point was recently made by Professor Bruce M. Russett of Yale University, who wrote in defense of the feasibility of a "countercombatant" deterrent: "The Soviet Union's ability to defend itself from its neighbors, even the small and now much weaker states of Eastern Europe, would be destroyed. To make this particularly painful the United States might strike, with particular loving care, Russian bases and armed forces along the Chinese border. In effect, the penalty for a Soviet attack on the West would be Soviet impotence vis-à-vis their Asian neighbor."[3]

I believe, however, that Burns is wrong in seeming to suggest that only totalitarian regimes might be deterred by threats to destroy the greater part of their armed forces, and in perhaps seeming to suggest callousness in a government that would value defense forces higher than a few cities. Nor, earlier, should we interpret Burns's replacing definition of "unacceptable destruction" as "such destruction on the attacker that neither its government *nor any successor at all acceptable to that government* would continue to rule" (p. 3, italics added) to imply a regime's unconscionable desire to preserve itself in power. A perception of national values and an entire order of a society's life would be at stake. Such a government would be serving a people's resolve to be a people continuous through time in the international system. If deterred by a real and grave threat to its armed forces, that government would be preserving a cardinal condition on which the political society depends for its independence and continuous life in the world of move and countermove.

There is good reason for any nation to regard the destruction of a great part of its armed forces as a more serious threat to the political society as a whole than the destruction of some part of the population. There is reason to believe that speculation about an adversary's estimation of unacceptable damage to its armed forces would be less chimerical than speculation about the various estimations different societies and cultures would have of unacceptable damage in cities exchanged. A real threat to an essential ingredient in a nation's capacity for further independent action is a threat to its life in the international system. Even so, John Locke argued for the inalienable right of liberty on the grounds that a real threat to that is tantamount to a threat against the life of an individual in a "state of nature." ". . . [H]e who attempts to get another man into his absolute power," wrote Locke, should be understood to have "a design upon his life. For I have reason to conclude that he who would get me into his power without my consent, would use me as he pleased when he got me there."[4] Similarly, a threat to take away armed forces which are essential to continued independence is a *vital* threat to any actor in the opposed international system. Not only totalitarian regimes or calloused political leaders would so view it. Supposing enough of a nation's forces could be reached by the strike forces to render it deeply vulnerable to less than nuclear attacks, that *would be* a threat as serious to the integrity of a nation's life as, or more serious than, the technical taking of certain hostage cities.

This was in fact the first of several elements in the analysis of a moral, *graduated* deterrent which I proposed in the 1960s. I called it deterrence from anticipated "counter*force* target destruction," plus additional elements of a composite graduated deterrence system to be mentioned in a moment.[5] If Burns is correct in some of his suggestions, and especially Russett in speaking rather of a "counter*combatant* deterrent," my expression was too loosely drawn—suggesting as it does a threatening posture *concentrating* on nuclear forces. But then I am a moralist whose business it is to try to indicate the *outer* limits of a possible moral deterrent if one has to go that far to find a feasible way effectively to limit war in a nuclear age. Just as positive law and civil rights provide closer definitions than natural law or natural rights, so it may be that a countercombatant deterrent (if we will but explore it and mount it) can provide a closer definition of an effective moral deterrent than a counter- nuclear-force deterrent. The latter might still remain "not unlawful" when measured by the principles of justice in war and in deterrence. It is my view that a counter*force* deterrent remains just according to the principle of discrimination; a counter*combatant* deterrent—if that is a feasible alternative or stress—may be required by the principle of proportion, or because it further minimizes destruction and risks.

I'd be happy, also, if strategic thinkers could come up with models or arrangements that do not need the other elements of my scheme of graduated deterrent: deterrence from a shared anticipation of collateral civil damage that is unavoidable, unintended, in no measure enlarged; deterrence from the ambiguity inherent in weapons that *could* be used against populations indiscriminately, or ambiguity in how an opponent *perceives* these weapons may be used; and, finally, deterrence from a "bluffing" manner in which these weapons are possessed. I now think that an input of deliberate ambiguity about the counter-people use of nuclear weapons is not possible unless it is (immorally) meant, and not a very good idea in the first place. But, again, I was marking off the outer limits of justice in deterrence, if this final ingredient were needed in crisis to prevent holocaust. But I gather that few experts today think it is a feasible "performance."[6]

I take it that Burns would not disagree with me that none of these elements of a possible deterrent—and I believe an effective one—would violate the laws of just war by *directly* threatening populations as such. Espousing "an assured second strike counter-resource reprisal only," Burns says of it that "no threats to population need be explicitly uttered, no hostages explicitly taken"; and he concludes that "since, though you have the means, you have no intention of striking at his people, you appear to avoid the ethical dilemma of nuclear weapons" (p. 14).

Burns is modest enough in the claims he makes for what he attempts to demonstrate. A "policy of military-targeting only," he urges, "appears feasible for deterring *less-than-ultimate* attacks and attempted coercion" (p. 18). Repeating what I believe to be an exaggerated distinction between totalitarian regimes and *any* regime responsible for the safety of an entire nation, Burns writes: "If there is anything in my view that totalitarian regimes depend upon their conventional forces and value them no less than some cities, etc.; or if the loss of strategic facilities would threaten their power-political positions *without greatly increasing the risk of major nuclear war* [italics added]: then against a *less-than-ultimate* threat a nuclear response against military targets only may both promise to be effective and also escape the central moral dilemma" (p. 18).

But we must come at last to the question of deterring *ultimate* attacks, which Burns excludes from the effectiveness of his scheme. Here, on the matter of practicality, Burns rightly shifts from the principle of discrimination (non-combatant immunity from direct intended attack and from direct intended threats of direct attack) to the other principle of the just war: the principle of proportion, or the expectation of success, success measured —of course—by the preservation of societal values. ". . . One of the criteria of the justice of an employment of force is that there will be a strong expectation that the employment will *succeed*" (p. 19); there must be "a rational expectation that the means employed would achieve the proposed end" (p.18). While altering *past* applications of that to say that against threats of *ultimate* attack a people today should be resolved still to resist by just means only, even though they perish (p. 19), Burns states his conviction that "no universal theory of global deterrence can pass the test" of final success in preserving societal values (p. 12). One "may not acquiesce in the committing of the certain evil of hostage-taking if it no more than probably averts a greater evil" (p. 25), namely, the destruction of both sets of hostages.[7] He asks for calculations, if such are possible, and that the public in Deterrent States be informed in a rational manner "*by how much* the deterrent effect of our reasonably assured retaliatory nuclear force would be *reduced* if we were to commit it to avoidance of non-combatants," etc. (p. 25, italics added).

I think, by not much; or not demonstrably any at all, in view of the greater incredibility of threats the more destructive they become, given that the destruction is mutual. For these reasons, when first exploring the possible *feasibility* (which does not fall within my competence) of a moral, graduated deterrence (which does), I called attention to and took full advantage of a basic fact about modern warfare, namely, that war today becomes a *disproportionate* means to any substantive political purpose long before it need be judged to have become *indiscriminate* (if non-combatant immunity from direct attack is properly understood). This being so, if one starts from the bottom and moves upward in the scale, there would seem to be sufficiently powerful ways to persuade an opponent by the deterring effects mentioned above that do *not* give and take hostage populations or reverse the relation between arms and society.[8]

This seems to me to follow from an attempt to take seriously the just-war theory as an ethics intrinsic to the nature of politics and to a purposeful use of force, and not as an ethics externally imposed on a neutral and alien realm of behavior.[9] Given the disproportionality of political resorts to violence sooner than their indiscriminateness, there appears to be a solution to the moral dilemma of nuclear deterrence. One need not suppose that deterrence is necessarily *suspended* deterrence, that all persuasive effects are indivisibly a part of and depend upon one's final willingness to threaten and to use the threat of attacks on whole populations.

Graduate deterrence must, indeed, threaten something disproportionate, since its virtue entails issuing a signal that one is willing to go to a level of destruction which is greater than what the cause is worth, politically, to oneself or to an opponent. If it is said that such an actual violation of the principle of proportionate good, threatened to another and accepted by oneself, would also always be a grave political immorality, three things can still be said in reply, while granting the facts to which the argument appeals. The first is that not every threat of something disproportionate is itself a disproportionate threat, certainly not when the good at stake is shared persuasive limits upon the escalation of war in a nuclear age. The second reply is that the issuance of threats of disproportionate destruction is ever the nature of deterrence under any conditions of warfare. One has to reject deterrence in general or in any war in order to reject this account of justifiable deterrence in a nuclear age. At the same time, it must be granted that herein lies in all ages the tragedy of war, namely, that threats of disproportionate damage, although proportionate to the end of deterrence, may in reality be disproportionately actualized, and on both sides (as in the politically disproportionate countercombatant destruction in World War I). But this is a question of the immorality of warfare that has lost its objective or become disoriented from it. It is not a question of the morality of deterrence oriented upon *its* objective. The third reply is that, of course, there is an obligation never to mean to do and accept damage disproportionate to political goals; but I suppose no military commander would calculate on actually doing any such thing. If these rejoinders have force, then graduated nuclear deterrence, based on the issuance of threats that might do disproportionate damage to an opponent's military forces, can promise to escape the moral dilemmas; and, as well, they promise to be effective in preventing all but the *ultimate* destruction—which cannot certainly be prevented by arrangements of military power that deliberately build exactly that into the scheme of deterrence itself.

Deterrence of the *ultimate* threat or destruction had better be left to the simple philosophic consequence of the possession of nuclear weapons (Kahn), the subjectively unintended consequence of the mere possession of these weapons. This is particularly the case since the attempt to do otherwise inevitably skews the planned use of military power in war or for deterrence at lower, justifiable levels, and sickens political resolution at levels of usable power by the thought of its indivisible connection with unusable power and politically purposeless and therefore largely incredible threats. While ordinary political and military encounters may be a matter of "minimax"-ing the outcome, it needs to be said quite honestly that, when it comes to the ultimate threat or destruction in a nuclear age, one cannot min the max or max the min. This is not only because military encounters often are not "zero-sum" games in which one gains what another loses, but because one can readily traverse the range of violence to which proportion (costs-benefits) applies as a criterion and soon comes to the point where there are only costs, no comparable benefits. After that comes not a "mixed motive game" but only "no motive" games. Continued intellectual effort to devise abstractly rational schemes for preventing the ultimate destruction that is finally unpreventable by any force (should the system fail and have to be used) can only skew needed effort to prevent the preventable. If we are to assume as an opponent—which we must do—a minimally rational decision-maker, we should assume that substantive political purposes inform his reason, and not alone "winning" in an abstract sorites of interaction mounting to a level of destruction well beyond the worth of any objectives he may have and which he properly sought by lesser, possibly deterrable or defeatable means.[10]

Arthur Lee Burns's description of the purposeful interaction going on in the international system is risky enough to any of the purposes of statecraft. ". . . It is necessary to all *political* interaction," he writes, "that those who interact put the ordering of their preferences at risk, endeavor to reorder the others' preferences, and remain in a position at any time to create a new object of preference or to apprehend such a new creation."[11] That is an apt account of the world of political move and countermove. But one cannot without systemic violation of the nature of those ongoing interactions imagine that the prefer*ers* (the nations) should put themselves at mutual total risk, and not only the ordering of their preferences. Seriously meant counter-people deterrence can no more be an action within the life of the international system than suicide or meant threats of reciprocal suicide can be an act of life for individual persons. Both can be *done,* of course, as acts or designs; but both are contradictions of the moral terms on which each depends, of the goods such policies were supposed to serve.

NOTES

1. *New York Times,* Op-Ed page, May 24 and 25, 1971.
2. Arthur Lee Burns, "Ethics and Deterrence: A Nuclear Balance Without Hostage Cities?" Adelphi Paper No. 69 (London: Institute for Strategic Studies, July 1970). The following paragraphs contain several quotations from this paper. Page number references are noted in parentheses.
3. Bruce M. Russett, "A Countercombatant Deterrent?: Feasibility, Morality and Arms Control," Conference on the Political Sociology of Arms Control, University of Chicago, December 4, 1971; published under the title "Short of Nuclear Madness," *Worldview,* April 1972, p. 34.
4. John Locke, *Second Treatise on Civil Government* [1690], Ch. III, par. 17.
5. Paul Ramsey, *The Just War: Force and Moral Responsibility* (New York: Charles Scribner's, 1968), pp. 248–258, 285–366; originally published in separate pamphlets by the Council on Religion and International Affairs in 1963 and 1965.
6. On June 14, 1982, *Newsweek* magazine published a feature entitled "What is a 'Just War' Today?", by Walter Goodman. Relevant to the foregoing list of elements of a graduated and possibly moral deterrent is the following letter to the editor (shorter version published by *Newsweek,* July 5, 1982):

I am honored to have my name linked with that of Reinhold Niebuhr, America's greatest twentieth-century political analyst. Permit me, however, to make one important correction in Walter Goodman's account of my views ("What Is a 'Just War' Today?", June 14, 1982).

I did once argue (1965) that it is morally permissible for a statesman to go so far as to "bluff" about his intention to use modern weapons deliberately aimed at an adversary's society, if but only if that was judged necessary to deter the maximum war possible today. My reasoning was that (1) a military commander need not publicize his intention not-to-use weapons *with this aim.* It is no violation of justice for him to keep military secrets (Thomas Aquinas). And (2) *deceitfulness* in any case is a lesser wrong than a *murderous* threat to destroy whole populations indiscriminately.

Those arguments were insufficient, indeed disturbingly insufficient, within the year. The "bluff" was withdrawn from my analysis of a possibly moral deterrence. Again, my reasons were two: (1) one's *real* intentions (*not* to go to such use) will be found out; the "bluff" must fail to deter; and (2) even if our top political and military leaders were pure in heart, they *must* count on thousands of men in missile silos, planes and submarines to be conditionally willing, under some circumstances, to become murderers. One should never occasion mortal sin in another, tempt them to it, or enlist them for it.

The latter was the more important reason. It is never right to do evil, or to intend to do evil, that good may come. Moreover, the fact that an adversary did the wrong *first* by an indiscriminate attack, or may intend to do so, does not justify our doing the same wrong *in the second place.* These have been my unvarying beliefs about justice in the conduct of war or in deterrence.

Proportion is a different and a less basic principle than *discrimination* in the moral governance of the use of violence. A judgment of proportion (or of disproportion) is always a matter of political and military *prudence.* It was in this connection that I observed, "A threat of something disproportionate is not necessarily a disproportionate threat." No way does that suspend the prohibition of threats, seriously meant, aimed at entire populations.

As Luther remarked, war is like fishing with a golden net: you run the risk of losing a net worth more than the fish. *This is true of disarmament as well.* Statesmanship has no place to hide from the risks of disproportionate moves and countermoves. Our leaders are always *about to have been right* in their calculations—or *wrong*—as they go about preparing for defense or for disarmament. This is the essential thing to be said about political prudence (proportion). Nevertheless, a seemingly disproportionate venture in the direction of new structures to insure world peace may not be disproportionate—as I said of threats that deter.

But neither this statement nor the one quoted in your article weakens the prohibition of indiscriminate attacks and of counter-*people* deterrence. We ought never to *do,* or seriously *threaten,* or (by indiscriminately aiming at peace or disarmament) *invite* or occasion another power to "any act of war deliberately aimed at the destruction of whole areas and their populations" (Vatican Council II), or at their subjugation.

7. Here Burns incorrectly puts together in a supposedly quantifiable calculus of probability two separate, incommensurable crite-

ria: the evil of hostage-taking and averting a "greater" evil of actual destruction. He seems to give primacy to the first prohibition only because averting the latter is uncertain. This contradicts his earlier statement that such threats can never be moral "though the threat may deter war" (p. 13). Shall we absolutize the prohibition of deterrent violations of non-combatant immunity? Or should we say that the violation of populations by deterrent threats is wrong only because saving them is not apt to result from that? Today the two principles governing a rational resort to political violence have in actuality (and in experience rehearsed in scenarios) converged on the same point. That is to say, while in past ages we morally should have known that it was never right to do wrong that good might come of it (although undoubtedly sometimes good consequences came of it), at the higher levels of violence in the nuclear age we now know that no good can finally come from doing, in the central war, or planning to do wrong that good may come.

8. To repeat: deterrence from (1) the perceived likelihood of unacceptable combatant or military target or nuclear force destruction, (2) the perceived likelihood of unacceptable collateral damage from quite discriminate acts of war in a nuclear age, (3) from the ambiguous possible uses of nuclear weapons, or from an irremovable perception as to their possible uses.

9. Many people appear to believe that the concept of just war implies some minimum agreement concerning "the moral order" and symmetrical adherence to it on the part of contending states. I should rather say that just war presupposes minimum agreement as to the purpose of states in a contentious system; an awareness that contention is not an end in itself, and may reach limits beyond which there are no substantive political reasons to go. All the just-war theory requires is acknowledgment that "action and reaction" is designed to serve one or the other common weal, that the common weal of either party ought not to be made subordinate to abstract success in moves and countermoves, and that there are limits of destruction beyond which there is no interest in going. That is to say, the just-war theory is an ethics of the opposed system *as such;* within the system there doubtless are also opposed political ethics.

10. One of the most thoughtful comments on the SALT agreements brought up the point about the superpowers' commitment to the MAD policy: "The limits on offensive weapons last only five years, while the treaty limiting defensive weapons is perpetual. Even with withdrawal and review provisions, this probably means the two sides are frozen forever into a system of mutual assured destruction. . . . Mutual assured destruction guarantees the utter devastation of both nations. Mutual assured destruction is probably

the best we can do under present technology, though the pact outlaws defensive arrangements that might make it more stable. But if technological advance permits the defense of populations, might not we want to pick up that option? Are we sure enough to foreclose the question in perpetuity?" "Go Slow on SALT, Review and Outlook," *The Wall Street Journal,* May 30, 1972.

11. Arthur Lee Burns, "Quantitative Approaches to International Politics," in Morton A. Kaplan, ed., *New Approaches to International Relations* (New York: St. Martin's Press, 1968), p. 171.

18

Just-War Doctrine in a Nuclear Context

William V. O'Brien

SOURCES AND FUTURE OF JUST-WAR DOCTRINE

Just-war doctrine is derived from an eclectic mixture of theological, philosophical-ethical, and legal sources. At its core is a theological presumption against the taking of human life. The doctrine provides for defense of the public order when the just-war conditions are met, thereby overcoming this presumption.

The war-decision part of just-war doctrine, the *jus ad bellum,* was essentially philosophical-ethical in its origins. The war-conduct part of the doctrine, the *jus in bello,* was predominantly the product of belligerent practice as reflected in the *jus gentium,* the emerging positive law of war. Both components of just-war doctrine reflected substantially the social environment in which they were developed.[1]

Indeed, many have claimed that just-war doctrine died with the older, limited war practices of earlier periods. However, the issues raised by just-war doctrine continue to confront us. War is still a condition that may be thrust upon us regardless of our peaceful intentions, e.g., Pearl Harbor. We still face situations in which a duty to defend the victims of aggression, repression, and monstrous genocidal extermination may be inescapable. If it is difficult to reconcile the realities of nuclear war with just-war doctrine, there remain conventional and revolutionary/counterinsurgency wars by the dozens that have been fought in the nuclear age. Moreover, the whole international system operates nervously under the nuclear balance of terror. It is logical to say that war in the nuclear age is irrational. However, experience has taught us that, irrational or not, war is still a threat to be deterred and resisted as well, in some cases, as a needed instrument of justice.

Whatever may be said about the formulation of issues in just-war doctrine, the clear teaching of the Church continues to acknowledge the right of legitimate self-defense.[2] There may be better ways of posing the moral issues of defense than those provided by just-war doctrine. Perhaps the continuing debate on modern deterrence and war will elicit them. Nevertheless, the fundamental categories of the permissibility of recourse to armed force and the rules of conduct in war are perennial.

These perennial categories, however, have been explored in our time as never before. Efforts to develop positive international law, both in the realm of war-decision and war-conduct law, have generally been incorporated into the just-war teaching of the Church and of many moralists. Papal thought since Pius XII, the teaching of Vatican II in *Gaudium et spes,* and the work of national conferences of bishops have all contributed greatly to the elaboration of just-war doctrine in the context of modern deterrence and war.

Moreover, the moral challenges of modern deterrence and war have evoked from the scholarly community a response shaped by traditional just-war doctrine. A small ecumenical community of scholars has explored the roots of just-war doctrine to understand the perennial elements in it.[3] As important, they have, after serious study of the material issues of modern deterrence and war, brought fresh insights to the study and practical application of just-war doctrine. Modern just-war scholars have, in effect, sought to do the same thing for contemporary just-war doctrine that St. Thomas, Vitoria, Suárez, and Grotius did for the doctrine in their time, namely, ask the traditional just-war questions in the light of the realities and problems of the present. . . . [4]

There is, as yet, no official definition of the entirely new attitude toward war enjoined by Vatican II. There are, however, some guidelines that partly join and partly distinguish just-war doctrine and the future teaching of the Church on deterrence and war. The element of continuity is the reiteration of the right and duty of self-defense against aggression and repression of human rights. No new approach to security is valid unless it makes adequate provision for legitimate self-defense. Beyond that, the guidelines in recent official Catholic teaching have emphasized (1) the imperative need for serious progress in arms control,[5] (2) development of international law and organization,[6] and (3) international development and progress in the quest for international economic and social justice.[7]

Detailed discussion of the last two elements of this entirely new approach to war is beyond the scope of this paper. However, some general observations, based on our experience since the Second World War, are in order. First, this is a very unpromising time for international law and organization. The revolutionary impact of Third World countries and the generally unhelpful role of the communist states have upset the whole structure of international law. No substitute international order seems to be in prospect within any time frame that would be relevant to alleviation of current issues of deterrence and war. Second, while issues of international economic and social justice are important in their own right, they appear to have little bearing on the central issues of deterrence and war between the superpowers and their allies, the critical element in the current nuclear dilemmas.

This leaves the question of progress in arms control. This very term, as distinguished from "disarmament," emphasizes the integral relationship between security and arms reduction. For this reason, no discussion of arms control is possible without adequate analysis of the requirements of deterrence and defense. Moreover, within Church teaching there is a broad consensus that serious efforts in the field of arms control are, in effect, the price that must be paid for continued moral toleration of the risks of modern deterrence and war. Accordingly, this central component of the "new" attitude toward war will be treated briefly at the end of this paper, which concentrates on the issues of deterrence and defense.

The combination of a traditional just-war approach to deterrence and defense with a related emphasis on arms control could be said to reflect a new attitude toward war. Such an attitude undoubtedly falls short of the "entirely" new attitude demanded by Vatican II. However, many inferences might be derived from this interpretation. One, to which I incline, might be that it is not feasible in the present international system to adopt an entirely new attitude toward deterrence and defense. A better use of just-war guidelines, together with prudent arms-control efforts, may be all that can be practically expected. To repeat, this does not mean that efforts on behalf of international law, organization, development, and economic-social justice should not be pressed. It means that we should not beg the questions of deterrence and war while awaiting the appearance of world law, order, and justice in some distant utopia.

The attitude toward the moral issues of deterrence and defense that I recommend consists of three components. First, it holds that a *serious* effort to apply and abide by just-war conditions and prescriptions is *novel.* Just-war doctrine is old, but honest efforts to adhere to it have been rare. Just-war doctrine is undoubtedly being taken more seriously today because of the shocking character of modern war. Although it may not be an *entirely* new attitude, effective implementation of just-war guidelines in deterrence and defense policies constitutes a *new* attitude.

Second, as indicated, an integral link between deterrence and defense policies and arms control is a new element. It is a striking new development, for example, to have lawyers in the Department of Defense routinely and under legal mandate review proposed new weapons systems to make sure that they comply with our obligations under arms-control agreements and the international law of war.[8]

Third, my new approach to war emphasizes that just-war considerations must be raised at all points in the national-security process, particularly at the early junctures where decisions about basic strategies, weapons systems, force structures, and training are made. This means that just-war doctrine must not always be held outside of the defense processes as a source only of post-factum moral evaluation and criticism. Rather, just-war guidelines in applied practical formulations must be imparted to the decision-makers continually, so that strategies and capabilities consonant with just-war requirements are likely to be developed. All of this requires that the teaching of the Church be practical and persuasive and that our educational efforts far exceed anything that has been done thus far.[9]

JUST-WAR DOCTRINE AND NUCLEAR WAR

It is difficult to separate the discussion of the morality of nuclear deterrence from that of the morality of nuclear war. Since the purpose of nuclear deterrence is to prevent a nuclear war, and perhaps other kinds of war, from occurring, there is an obvious difference in its rationale and in the moral questions it raises from the traditional rationale and moral questions of war itself. However, deterrence turns on the credible threat to go to war if the forbidden aggressions eventuate. No deterrent is likely to suffice for long if it is not based on the capability and will to fight the war threatened as the response to aggression. Logically, then, the moral issues of nuclear war should be discussed before addressing the moral issues of deterrence. No matter how unlikely the contingency, the carrying out of the deterrent threat by recourse to war is the critical point in the analysis of deterrence. Accordingly, the just-war issues of nuclear war will be treated first here. . . .

Curiously, there seems to be little authoritative discussion of the question of the weight and relations of the just-war categories in the process of moral decision. A strict view would require full compliance with all the conditions and prescriptions of all categories. I am inclined to think, in the light of a substantial consensus regarding World War II as a just war, that a more flexible approach may be warranted. It appears that a strong just cause, as in the war against Hitler, and very substantial compliance with the just-war conditions may justify characterization of a war as just even if there are some serious violations of the just-war standards for the conduct of the war, e.g., area bombing of cities in World War II by the Allied forces. However, the war-decision law conditions must certainly be met substantially.[10] Further analysis of this relatively unexplored subject is needed. Of course, the whole enterprise of applying just-war standards to past wars and to the scenarios and plans for possible future conflicts is, after many centuries of just-war theorizing, in a very primitive stage.

NUCLEAR WAR AND THE *JUS AD BELLUM*

In this discussion I will assume a NATO context in which, strategic and theater deterrence having failed, the Soviet/

Warsaw Pact forces have attacked Western Europe. Even a brief analysis reveals the difficulties faced in any effort to mount a just and limited NATO defense in which there is the option to use nuclear weapons and the possibility that they may be used by the aggressor.

Competent Authority

There are serious problems with respect to competent authority. NATO rests on a concept of collective defense: an attack on any member is considered an attack against all. There is no automatic cobelligerency for all NATO members in the event of aggression against one or more members. However, all NATO members are expected to come to the assistance of those attacked. The deterrent and defensive effectiveness of the alliance turns in good measure on the assumption that all will come to the defense of victims of aggression.

This means that a president of the United States would have to decide very quickly what measures the U.S. would take as part of the joint defense were any NATO members attacked. Probably U.S. forces in Europe would already have been attacked in the initial phases of aggression. Although there are constitutional and statutory requirements to be considered, the decision of an American president confronting an attack against NATO would have to be taken primarily on his own authority and judgment.[11] In the nature of things, if the attack were nuclear or of such a nature as to elicit an immediate or early nuclear response, the American president would have to be regarded as having competent authority to order the U.S. response. The issue is, of course, complicated by the international character of NATO decision processes and the possibility of usurpation of authority which NATO safeguards are designed to prevent.[12]

An equally important problem increasingly claims the attention of political-military experts as well as moralists: control of nuclear weapons once they are committed in war. A good part of this problem is properly discussed below under the question of proportion, both in war-decision and war-conduct law. However, a war that escapes effective control may clearly be a war waged without competent authority.

The subject falls under the category designated C^3, command control and communications, in defense terminology. Experts fear that C^3 might be interrupted by the effects of nuclear war. If this were the case, subordinate commanders, e.g., the command of a nuclear submarine, might be left uninstructed and unrestrained, except by antecedent contingency plans and standing operating procedures.[13]

It is hard for those not expert in this matter and not having access to current plans and operations to judge the extent of this problem. A fortiori, it is difficult to evaluate prospects for solution of present C^3 vulnerabilities. Two observations are in order. First, there is no justification for concluding that the C^3 problems are hopelessly and permanently beyond remedy. Second, the greatest threat to C^3 would surely come as the result of a major nuclear war of aggression against the United States. If U.S. responses were not as tightly controlled as we would prefer, responsibility for the consequences would seem to fall more on the aggressors than on the victims.[14]

I conclude that there are serious problems regarding competent authority in nuclear war but that these problems do not preclude the possibility of controlling the initiation and conduct of a nuclear response.

Just Cause

The just-cause category has been neglected in the Church's official pronouncements on war. Not since Pope Pius XII has there been explicit, serious recognition of the threats to peace and human rights that make necessary the deterrence and defense policies maintained in the free world at such cost, with such risks, and with such moral misgivings.[15] One can understand a propensity to believe that *no* just cause would justify nuclear war in any form. However, it is still incumbent upon moralists to acknowledge what would be lost by relinquishment of what may be an indispensable means of deterrence and defense in terms of unchecked aggression, intimidation, and subjugation of peoples by unscrupulous aggressors with nuclear means.

In any event, unless it is argued that any and all recourse to nuclear war is *malum in se,* just-war doctrine requires a calculation of proportionality between the just cause and the cost of its defense. How such a calculation can be attempted without an evaluation of the just cause, the referent of proportionality, is beyond my understanding. Yet the failure to offer a sufficient evaluation of the just cause as it emerges in the contemporary world of conflict is the single greatest deficiency in current official Church teaching on deterrence and war, including that of the American Catholic bishops through the second draft pastoral letter. Papal pronouncements and Vatican II's *Gaudium et spes* address their analysis to "nations" and "men," to anonymous actors in the international system. These actors are not recognized as having vastly different policies with respect to war, peace, and human dignity. The avowed enemies of Western civilization and of the Church itself are by implication addressed equally with the defenders of what is left of Christendom. Appeals for greater emphasis on international law and organization leading to the establishment of a world authority imply that the present world is ripe for such developments, when in fact it is engaged in a life-and-death protracted conflict to determine whether the future will be determined by the principles of Lenin, Stalin, and Mao or on those of Jefferson and Franklin Roosevelt.

The statements of the American bishops since 1968 have been less Olympian than those of Rome. However, they have consistently avoided the issue of the nature of the threat to which deterrence and defense policies respond. As these statements penetrate more and more deeply into the essence of U.S. strategic postures, as they become more "destabilizing" in their potential effects on the balance of terror, it surely ought to occur to Church authorities to say something about the threats, if any are perceived, to the United States and the free world.

A serious discussion of just cause in the contemporary situation would have to assess two questions in particular. First, what is the threat of Soviet and other communist aggression against the United States and the free world? Second, what are the probable implications of a defeat of free-world forces and the imposition of a communist totalitarian regime in the occupied territories? . . .

Proportion; Probability of Success

The calculation of proportionality of deterrence and defense means to the values defended must be made in the light of the probability of success. The need to judge the just cause in terms of values and threats to those values has been reiterated. What needs next to be addressed is the question of proposed means and the projected outcomes and effects of their employment.

Official Church pronouncements have moved slowly from generalized condemnations of "nuclear war" and "weapons of mass destruction" as an undifferentiated category to an occasional specification of "strategic" nuclear war as the proscribed means.[16] There may be good reasons for classifying all nuclear weapons in one category for both practical and moral purposes. However, since in practice significant distinctions are made between strategic weapons systems that can strike reciprocally at the homelands of the superpowers, theater or intermediate nuclear weapons systems that are limited in range to a single theater, e.g., Europe, and tactical or battlefield nuclear weapons, one must distinguish different kinds and combinations of nuclear warfare. It is always possible to conclude, after having explored these distinctions, that they are unlikely to survive actual use of nuclear weapons and that escalation to the worst kind of strategic nuclear exchange is the inevitable result of the use of any nuclear weapons. But it is also possible to contend that some kind of limited nuclear war may be feasible and/or that it must be made feasible if a morally usable deterrent/defense posture is to be maintained.[17]

For purposes of this analysis, the following categories of nuclear warfare may be distinguished: (1) strategic nuclear countervalue attacks on cities as such; (2) strategic nuclear countervalue attacks on political-military command, control, and communication centers, war-related industrial facilities, and military assets; (3) strategic nuclear counterforce attacks against military targets, e.g., missile sites, airfields, military facilities, staging areas, troop concentrations; (4) theater/intermediate nuclear counterforce attacks against military targets (as in 3); (5) tactical/battlefield nuclear counterforce attacks against military targets.[18]

It is widely believed that the present deterrent threat to inflict "unacceptable damage" by a strategic nuclear countervalue attack on enemy cities is the essence of the U.S. deterrence posture under MAD (mutual assured destruction). To the extent that this belief is warranted, the MAD system requires the threatening of acts of war which, if ever carried out, would surely be disproportionate, indiscriminate, and suicidal by any calculation. Certainly, the relation of a MAD countervalue countercity strategic nuclear exchange to the values to be protected from aggression would fail the test of war-decision proportionality. One need hardly add that there would be no significant "probability of success" in such a war.[19]

However, the U.S. government has developed a different kind of countervalue strategic nuclear deterrent posture. Trends in deterrence doctrine and policies to which Secretaries of Defense Schlesinger and Brown contributed have produced a new countervalue strategy that is not targeted on cities as such, although it may well endanger many cities. Since somehow this new strategy has not acquired an official designation, I will refer to it henceforth as the Reagan countervalue strategy.[20] This strategy is based on the conviction that, while "value" for the West means population centers, people, "value" for the Soviet leadership has other meanings. On this assumption, the trend in U.S. strategic nuclear countervalue deterrence policy is to "hold at risk those things that the Soviet leadership values most highly—military and political control, nuclear and conventional military assets, and the industrial capability to sustain war." Targeting of "civilian populations as such" is not U.S. strategic policy, "for moral, political and military reasons."[21]

The Reagan countervalue deterrent will be considered further under war-conduct just-war doctrine and in terms of the morality of deterrence. It is important to introduce it here to make the point that even the extreme case of fighting a strategic nuclear war in response to a nuclear attack on the United States and its allies need not necessarily involve the kind of massive mutual destruction of cities that most of us have assumed to be our fate if MAD ever failed. On its face, the new Reagan countervalue strategy threatens destruction and responses that may in the end come close to the consequences to be feared from execution of the strategic countervalue countercity threat. Still, given the continuing need for deterrence, the possibility of a countervalue strategy that is not totally countercity in character deserves further empirical and normative analysis.

Another form of strategic nuclear war that would be more consonant with just-war requirements is strategic nuclear counterforce war, aimed at military targets, e.g., missile sites, airfields, military facilities, staging areas, troop concentrations. Strategic counterforce nuclear war could conceivably comply with just-war principles of proportion and discrimination (to be discussed below), and it could hold out some possibility of survival and perpetuation of the values embraced in the just cause.

Moreover, counterforce strategies are usually associated with such concepts as flexible response, controlled response, and selected options, connoting a very limited rather than general nuclear exchange. Flexible response also refers to the spectrum of means ranging from conventional to theater/tactical nuclear to strategic nuclear envisaged in deterrence/defense postures of NATO and other collective defense systems.[22]

The issue with any kind of counterforce nuclear doctrine is feasibility. The problems include: (1) concern over C^3 in a nuclear-war environment; (2) uncertainty over the accuracy and penetrability of counterforce weapons; (3) doubts about the extent of collateral damage, including radioactive fallout, related to counterforce strikes; (4) fear that a credible counterforce strategy and capability might be interpreted as a first-strike threat and lead an enemy to develop and use its own first-strike capability, i.e., better counterforce policies may be destabilizing.[23]

The important point to be made about strategic nuclear counterforce deterrence is that, as a war-fighting posture for the contingencies where deterrence has failed, it could offer the greatest hope for conformity to just-war conditions and principles. As in the case of the Reagan countervalue deterrent strategy, nuclear war is not desired but there is a readiness to fight a limited nuclear war if necessary. The United States emphasizes effective deterrence so that nuclear war will not occur. Any strategic nuclear deterrent position, when viewed as a war-fighting strategy, is a last-ditch approach to the dilemmas raised by a failure of deterrence leading to a choice between trying to fight a just and limited war and surrendering. The present deterrent leaves little prospect of observing just-war limitations, although it is an improvement over basic MAD countervalue countercity deterrence. Since deterrence continues to be necessary, possibly effective alternatives to the present strategy must be considered.[24]

The two countervalue strategies here discussed, as well as the strategic counterforce strategy which overlaps the emerging new U.S. countervalue approach, are directed to the mission of retaliating after a Soviet nuclear attack on the United States or, possibly, an ally. These strategies would not be put into effect in response to a conventional Warsaw Pact attack on NATO or even to a mixed limited nuclear-conventional aggression. However, in terms of preferred U.S. options, nuclear strategies in defense of NATO take the form of theater and tactical limited nuclear war.

Discussion of theater and tactical limited nuclear war is difficult. Much of the critical factual material about NATO's plans and capabilities is classified. That is true, of course, with respect to strategic contingencies as well. However, there are more variables in the mix of nuclear and conventional options in theater defense, and the probability of war at this level is more clear and present than at the strategic level. So there are important nuances in theater strategies that are hard to grasp. Moreover, NATO has always relied on "creative ambiguity" as to the definition of the nuclear threshold in its defenses as an important asset.[25] Creative ambiguity regarding introduction of nuclear weapons serves two purposes. First, it adds considerably to the deterrent posture of NATO's conventional forces. Second, it obliges the Warsaw Pact forces to base their strategies and tactical plans on the assumption that they might be resisted with nuclear weapons, thereby necessitating very different troop dispositions and maneuvers than would be the case in a purely conventional war.

Since I believe that creative ambiguity about recourse to nuclear weapons may have outlived its usefulness and that both we and our enemies should be clear about the prospects for nuclear war, I cite the continuation of this nuclear deterrent as a fact to be addressed and, if possible, changed. In any event, creative ambiguity makes it very difficult for those outside the NATO decision process to come to grips with theater and tactical nuclear-war issues. This has been demonstrated recently in the latest phase of the "no-first-use-of-nuclear-weapons" debate.[26]

Another related reason for the difficulty in discussing theater and tactical nuclear war is the sensitivity of the subject to the governments and peoples of the threatened countries, particularly the Federal Republic of Germany. Even a conventional defense of NATO would probably produce destruction exceeding that of hostilities in populated areas in World War II. To combine this conventional destruction with any substantial amount of nuclear damage, including radiation fallout, would obviously go far to destroy the society defended. Accordingly, Germans and other Western Europeans tend to favor an emphasis on deterrence as opposed to war-fighting defense.

Deterrence necessarily means emphasis on nuclear response to any aggression, even conventional. Yet initiation of even tactical battlefield nuclear war risks the dangers of an escalatory spiral to general strategic nuclear war. Sensitivity to contemplation of actual defense of Western Europe is surely reflected in the ebbs and flows of European opinion about modernization of NATO's nuclear forces through the introduction of Pershing II and cruise missiles as agreed in December 1979. Ironically, the debate has taken place in the context of an existing and growing Soviet theater nuclear threat to Western Europe, particularly that posed by the Soviet SS-20s already in place and being reinforced.

There are other, more general, problems of evaluating theater and/or tactical nuclear war in practical and moral terms. Among them are the following: (1) difficulty of distinguishing a "theater" attack on military targets in the Soviet Union from a "strategic" attack that might bring a Soviet escalation to strategic nuclear war directed against the United States; (2) the uncertainty, in any event, as to Soviet willingness to observe nuclear thresholds and tacit rules of conflict in a limited nuclear war, particularly if NATO strategies were successful; (3) doubt as to the capabilities of the NATO and Warsaw Pact high commands to control a war involving thousands of nuclear strikes.[27]

The upshot is that the calculus of *jus ad bellum* proportionality of probable good and evil, in the light of the probability of success, in a theater/tactical nuclear defense of NATO produces conclusions that discourage recourse to such a strategy. Of course, this is also true of a conventional defense of NATO. The difference is that probable destruction within NATO would be greater in a nuclear war, plus the critical fact that escalation might bring devastation to the Soviet Union, the United States, and, to varying degrees, other parts of the world. The calculus of proportionality is complex because it includes neutrals and the world itself in addition to the belligerents.[28]

I conclude that a war fought with theater/tactical nuclear weapons in defense of NATO might be managed within just-war limitations but that the odds against this being the case are considerable. Maximum improvement of conventional defense of NATO is required. This could necessitate, *inter alia,* revival of the draft in the United States and greater rather than less expenditure on defense.[29]

In the preceding brief survey of the principal nuclear war-fighting strategies, I have only indirectly alluded to the general probability of success in the sense of defeating the communist aggressors. I have indicated that, regardless of the course of such wars, prospective damage to the societies defended will tend to be disproportionate by any calculation short of one that literally holds out death and destruction as preferable to defeat and subjugation. The analysis can only be more sobering if one contemplates the probabilities of success in the light of the present strategic and theater balances between the U.S./NATO and Soviet Union/Warsaw Pact forces.[30]

The free world is certainly not in a hopeless military position, but it has placed itself in a vulnerable, disadvantaged posture. Since the prospects for meaningful success in the sense of the just-war war-decision requirement of proportionality are so slim and problematic, it should be evident that more and better defensive means are required, not less, as proponents of freezes and defense rollbacks tend to hold. However, even this brief survey should suffice to make the point that improved defense is not simply a matter of quantitative increases in defense expenditures and military assets. Improved defense consonant with just-war requirements means qualitatively improved means that are either exclusively or primarily directed to counterforce missions and are subject to the greatest possible degree of control.

Wherever possible, conventional strategies and capabilities should take precedence over reliance on nuclear weapons. This conclusion is at odds with Western European approaches but, increasingly, their propensity to rely on nuclear deterrence has become acceptable only on the assumption that there is no clear and present threat. This approaches escapism. Some of the issues raised generally in this overview of problems of proportionality in war-decision law will be considered again in the discussion of war-conduct requirements of just-war doctrine.

Exhaustion of Peaceful Alternatives

The last of the just-war conditions that I include within the larger category of just cause is that of exhaustion of peaceful alternatives to war in pursuit of the just cause. This is difficult to interpret in our present circumstances. Our enemies are dedicated to our defeat and subjugation as a matter of profound ideological necessity and alleged historical inevitability. In the deeper sense, there is nothing to negotiate except for the tactical cease-fires and truces of competitive coexistence that punctuate our protracted conflict. Nevertheless, we are obliged to avoid war as best we can so long as we do not fall into self-defeating appeasement leading to surrender.

In these circumstances the just belligerent should be able to look back on a record of willingness to reach reasonable accommodations with the avowed enemy as regards general relations and arms control in particular. Such a record should be the condition precedent for permissible recourse to armed force. The record of the United States and its allies in this regard is good. However, it must be observed that it is highly unlikely that the United States or its allies would initiate a war with the Soviet Union and/or its allies. Hence, the issue of exhaustion of peaceful remedies would arise for the victim of communist attack only if that state had itself previously engaged in blatantly aggressive and immoral activities inviting military countermeasures, a most improbable contingency.

Once in a war, the just-war requirement to find peaceful alternatives to continuation of the conflict persists. The just belligerent must be alert to possibilities for abating or terminating the conflict, as well as to strengthening any rules of conflict that might mitigate the destructiveness of the hostilities. Such a moral requirement parallels the political-military guidelines of limited war that the belligerent must always hold the military instrument subordinate to the political purposes of the war and the political leadership.[31]

Right Intention

The last of the war-decision just-war conditions is right intention. Right intention requires that the just belligerent confine military operations to pursuit of the just cause, that charity rather than hatred and desire for vengeance motivate his policies toward the enemies, and that a just and lasting peace be the ultimate aim of the war. These conditions are not easily met in modern ideological wars characterized by enormous destruction and suffering. Nevertheless, they are enjoined by just-war doctrine, not only because of their limiting and mitigating effects on the conduct of war but out of concern for the spiritual state of the just belligerent. That observance of the condition of right intention is difficult in modern war is demonstrated by American attitudes toward the "Nazis" and "Japs" in World War II. That such attitudes can eventually be overcome and right intention prevail, leading to a just and lasting peace, is illustrated by the enlightened postwar policies that turned hated enemies into our German and Japanese allies.[32]

The experience of a nuclear war would certainly produce emotions at odds with right intention. The goal of a just and lasting peace might well be hard to reconcile with the devastation and contamination of such a war. On the other hand, such a frightful experience might actually encourage greater charity toward other survivors of the ordeal. There appears to be no intrinsic reason for condemning all forms of nuclear war as necessarily precluding right intention, provided those who possess nuclear weapons view them only as a means of deterrent protection and last-ditch defense rather than as a readily available instrument of power politics.

NUCLEAR WAR AND THE *JUS IN BELLO*

In just-war doctrine the war-conduct law, the *jus in bello,* requires observance of the principles of proportion and discrimination. It also would prohibit any means found to be *mala in se*.

Proportion

The war-conduct concept of proportion is one of legitimate military necessity. The subordination of military necessity (*raison de guerre*) to just cause (*raison d'état*) is a precept of just-war doctrine, international law, and the political-military guidelines of limited war. This is an important issue in nuclear war, since any use of nuclear weapons, no matter how "tactical" or "limited," may have implications for the entire war effort.[33]

Subordination of military necessity to *raison d'état* in the form of just cause is the crucial issue with respect to the military proportionality of nuclear weapons. It is obviously possible to envisage discrete use of tactical, theater, or even strategic counterforce nuclear weapons in circumstances that would satisfy the requirement of proportionality: e.g., tactical nuclear weapons used against advancing tank formations in open country; theater nuclear forces used against a heavy concentration of attacking enemy forces or an enemy airfield; strategic nuclear weapons used against a missile base in the wilderness of Siberia.

The problem is to assess the number of such individual proportionate uses, their cumulative effects and their propensity to engender escalation to levels that would clearly be disproportionate to the military advantages pursued. Although the discussion of strategic nuclear means indicated that some forms of strategic nuclear countervalue war or of theater/tactical nuclear war in heavily populated areas might be prima facie disproportionate, one has to be careful about generalizations when assessing proportionality. The high costs of means do not automatically render them disproportionate. Much depends on the weight given to the ends. We do not consider the costs of defeating Hitler to have been disproportionate, even though they were appalling. One practical and moral option in certain cases may be to hold that an end is so precious that its defenders are justified in going down fighting for it. This option, of course, does not warrant a last-stand defense of the just cause that imperils innocent third parties and the world itself, a serious consideration in nuclear war.[34]

I conclude that it is certainly possible to envisage use of nuclear weapons proportionate to legitimate military necessities but that the proportionality of any intended use of nuclear means must be judged in the full context of contemplated use and of the probable outcomes and effects of each case.

Discrimination

The principle of discrimination has dominated most moral analyses of modern war. The standard of proportionality is hard to generalize about and may be subject to manipulation by extending the ends to justify the means.[35] Discrimination, on the other hand, the principle of noncombatant immunity from direct intentional attack, has the appearance of a firm rule of conduct, perhaps the heart of the limiting effort of just-war *jus in bello.*

Predictably, it has proven very difficult to reconcile the principle of discrimination with modern war at any level of intensity. Indeed, by the end of World War II international-law publicists were confessing that the principle of noncombatant immunity in positive international law had been so universally violated that it was not a reliable source of war-conduct law. Since, historically, the principle of discrimination originated in belligerent practice, in the *jus gentium* or law of nations rather than in theological or philosophical formulations of just-war doctrine, the decline and fall of the principle of discrimination in international-law practice, while not settling the moral issues in question, signaled the difficulties of upholding it in the century of total war.[36]

It must be acknowledged that the official teaching of the Church on war since 1945 has not contributed to the resuscitation of the principle of discrimination. A major flaw of the papal and Vatican II analyses has been their failure to use just-war *jus in bello* concepts explicitly and clearly. Nuclear war, modern war, and weapons of mass destruction have been considered and condemned without specification as to the rationales for the judgments in just-war *jus in bello* terms.

It is understandable that the enormity of the destructiveness of modern war would evoke general statements of moral condemnation. But, given the futility of hopes for world law and order, much less justice, and the continued need for deterrence and defense, it has been necessary for responsible statesmen and citizens to seek the means still permitted by just-war doctrine to protect their countries. This quest for moral policies of deterrence and defense has been hampered by the conspicuous failure of official Church teaching to explain in just-war terms what was clearly prohibited, what might be permissible, and, above all, why. The case of the debate over the meaning of discrimination demonstrates this failure.

Two approaches to the principle of discrimination appear prominently in the modern literature on morality and war. The first approach is that of the literal, unqualified application of the prohibition against direct intentional attacks on noncombatants and civilian targets. While this approach may be practically feasible in direct combat between belligerents, it could not be applied even to the indirect combat of a siege of a target including noncombatants without substantially precluding the conduct of war. The literal application of noncombatant immunity is incompatible with modern war, wherein much of the hostilities are carried out by weapons with great ranges and destructive powers. If discrimination means no direct intentional killing of noncombatants in the sense that no such killing would be foreseeable in using the modern means of war, no warfare waged in an environment including noncombatants and civilian targets would be morally permissible.

This pacifist position is rejected, tacitly but clearly, in the official teaching of the Church when the right of legitimate self-defense is reaffirmed. It would be meaningless to reaffirm this right and bar the means necessary to make it efficacious. At this point the official Church teaching leaves it to moralists and perplexed laymen to determine how to fight a war of legitimate self-defense without violating the principle of discrimination. The agonies of this endeavor are manifest in the noble efforts of Paul Ramsey's work.[37] The dilemmas are not made easier by the fact, previously mentioned, that the official Church teaching generally eschews the use of the term "discrimination" or "noncombatant immunity." A tortured debate among modern just-war scholars finds no parallel in the official Church teaching on war.[38]

A second approach to discrimination qualifies the principle by recourse to the principle of double effect. A complex of issues shrouds this second approach to the interpretation of the principle of discrimination. What is "intentional"? What is "direct"? What is "accidental"? Who is a "noncombatant" or "innocent"?[39] Whatever the better answers may be to these questions within the ranks of theologians and philosophers, the ordinary statesman, military commander, or citizen finds it difficult to understand and accept interpretations of discrimination that hold that a belligerent somehow does not "intend" to kill the noncombatants known to be living in a mixed military-civilian target area. It is hard to view the deaths of civilians killed under collateral damage as "accidental." Michael Walzer has provided humanist reinforcements for this ancient scholastic enterprise, but the ultimate fate of the double-effect approach to discrimination remains in doubt.[40]

I adopt a third approach. Discrimination is not an ironclad principle. It is a relative prescription that enjoins us to concentrate our attacks on military objectives and to minimize our destruction of noncombatants and civilian targets, i.e., in contemporary strategic usage, collateral damage. The standard of judging the sufficiency of the effort to minimize civilian damage is one of proportionality. Destruction of a critical military target, e.g., a nuclear-missile site, justifies a proportionate destruction of noncombatant and civilian targets within or adjacent to the military target. Destruction of a military target of ordinary importance at the expense of disproportionate damage to a primarily civilian area is not justified, e.g., the World War II bombing of Dresden. As in all cases of proportionality, the judgment of permissibility depends on the context.[41]

Literal application of the principle of discrimination is incompatible with nuclear war, as it is with virtually any kind of modern war. Discrimination modified by some form of the principle of double effect may manage to salvage some forms of counterforce nuclear war and of modern conventional war. Neither discrimination qualified by double-effect reasoning nor any concept of discrimination with proportionate collateral damage condones attacks on cities as such. My approach to discrimination would be more likely to accept major collateral damage in essentially counterforce attacks or in countervalue attacks against enemy command, control, and communication centers and industrial complexes (current U.S. policy) than would the approaches that employ double-effect reasoning.

The conclusion is inescapable that even the approaches to discrimination that accept some collateral damage in essentially counterforce nuclear attacks draw a line at the destruction of cities as such and condemn such acts as indiscriminate.

MEANS *MALA IN SE*

Many of the condemnations of nuclear war as a general category that are found in modern official Church pronouncements seem to consider it to be *malum in se.*[42] Since nuclear deterrence is deplored but not clearly condemned, however, it is not so certain that nuclear war has been declared *malum in se.* Certainly, official Church teaching is not yet sufficiently elaborated to make a conclusion that nuclear war is *malum in se* persuasive, much less mandatory.[43]

Given the variety of possible forms of nuclear war and the

great spectrum of circumstances in which it might occur, a finding that it is *malum in se* would be valid only if it could be shown that nuclear war inevitably escapes control. It is impossible to prove today whether or not nuclear war must inevitably escape control. One is then reduced to arguing whether the odds for or against its escaping control are such as to raise a moral and practical presumption against its use. I conclude that there is, indeed, a strong moral presumption against the use of nuclear weapons but that nuclear war is not *malum in se.* The only war-related activity singled out by international law and by the official teaching of the Church as *malum in se* is genocide. Genocide, a much abused and exploited term, is actually not a means of war but of gratuitous extermination and cruelty unrelated to any legitimate military necessity.[44] . . .

JUST-WAR DOCTRINE AND DETERRENCE

Just-war doctrine is mainly about fighting war, not deterring it. If, as I contend, only that which could be done morally should be threatened for deterrence, just-war limits should shape a deterrent posture. However, the overwhelming thrust in modern deterrence theory and practice is to pose a threat so horrendous, so "unthinkable," so disproportionate that it will be effective. As long as such threats are effective, we live under the balance of terror without nuclear war. However, if the deterrent ever fails, we confront the choices of carrying out our disproportionate, unthinkable threat, of substituting some lesser action that might conform to just-war requirements, or of surrender in one form or another.[45]

In just-war terms, the essence of deterrence has tended to be the threat to engage in acts of war that, by any interpretation, would be disproportionate and indiscriminate. Such threats to do immoral damage have been justified by the argument that no nuclear war is far better than a limited nuclear war and that threats of disproportionate, indiscriminate nuclear war prevent the lesser war as well as an all-out nuclear war. Neither official Church teaching nor the efforts of just-war scholars have thus far provided us with satisfactory tools of moral analysis for nuclear deterrence, much less realistic and helpful guidance for policy.

The official teaching of the Church, to be made more explicit than formerly in the American bishops' 1983 pastoral letter, is that the mutual assured destruction (MAD) balance-of-terror deterrence system is immoral.[46] However, cognizant of the difficulties and risks involved in altering the nuclear balance of terror, the Church teaching tolerates this moral evil pending sincere and effective efforts to escape the treacherous trap of the arms race and nuclear deterrence.[47] Clearly, the American Catholic bishops consider that what is now being threatened under MAD would be immoral if carried out. At present, the Church is enjoining us to make progress in arms control and the settlement of international conflicts, as it were, "with all deliberate speed."

I will comment briefly on the problems of achieving this progress in arms control below. The issue here is deterrence, the basis for all contemporary arms control. If the present MAD deterrent is morally unacceptable, does this mean that no other form of nuclear deterrence would be permissible? This is an issue that seems to have placed the bishops and moralists in some disarray. Every instinct is to look to a complete escape from the nuclear treacherous trap through dramatic breakthroughs in arms control and peaceful settlement of conflicts. But surely it is unrealistic to expect such early and drastic progress in these endeavors as to provide early relief from the need to maintain a nuclear deterrent. Deterrence will continue to be a necessity for states such as the United States, and it will be nuclear as long as there are nuclear powers—and the trend is toward more nuclear powers.

Countervalue and Counterforce Deterrents

In these circumstances two positions on deterrence have emerged: (1) Maintain the present MAD deterrent posture and its deterrent benefits while resolving never to carry out the deterrent threat and while making every effort to reduce U.S. contributions to the arms race and the nuclear balance of terror. (2) Replace the present MAD deterrent posture with a flexible-response counterforce strategy that might be morally permissible if translated into a war-fighting strategy.

Paul Ramsey at one point explored the possibility of a kind of moral nuclear bluff.[48] This would involve possession and deployment of nuclear weapons systems as though they were intended for use. From this possession and deployment a deterrent effect would be derived immanently. However, the moral decision-maker in a nuclear power would be constrained by just-war principles, particularly discrimination, from ever carrying out this deterrent threat. The theory held out possibilities ranging from actually making deterrent threats without intention of carrying them out to simply possessing the capability to carry out immanent threats. Ramsey argued that the enemy would not risk calling the moral bluff. The enemy could not be sure that our moral scruples would, in the case of aggression, actually restrain us from nuclear retaliation. The bluff would be too risky to call. Thus one could renounce the intention of using nuclear weapons while benefiting from their possession. Confronted with criticism of this approach, notably by practical men who could not imagine how one would operate an entire national-security system on the basis of a bluff, Ramsey ultimately abandoned this idea.[49]

The idea of a nuclear bluff still persists in the minds of some of the American bishops and their advisers. By condemning nuclear deterrence and war without calling for the dismantlement of the U.S./NATO nuclear capabilities, official Church pronouncements have, in effect, condoned the continued deployment of the nuclear deterrent forces. However, even this has been put in question by statements such as that of Cardinal Krol in 1979 before the Senate Foreign Relations Committee. The formulation now seems to be that it is still morally permissible to *possess* nuclear weapons but that it is not moral to *use* them.[50]

This has encouraged the discussion of possession of nuclear weapons as a discrete part of the problem of deterrence. It is argued that mere possession of nuclear weapons serves deterrent purposes in the period of arms-control negotiations before deterrence somehow ceases to be necessary. It is further asserted that the nuclear weapons in our possession are essential bargaining chips in the arms-control process and should not be relinquished unilaterally. The second reason is plausible, although a weapon that is possessed but not deployed by a party disclaiming on moral grounds any intention of using it is a questionable bargaining chip. It is the first argument that needs to be rejected before further confusion is spread.[51]

Nuclear deterrence is based on the capability and will to

inflict unacceptable damage on an aggressor. Without the credible will to carry out the deterrent threat, there is little potential deterrent effectiveness in weapons lying about like so much hardware. Deterrence is derived from the enemy's knowledge that weapons are deployed and ready, targeted on things the loss of which would be unacceptable. In brief, possession of nuclear weapons cannot meaningfully be separated from ready deployment. Ready deployment cannot be separated from a credible intention to use the weapons if the deterrent fails.

In any event, a nuclear bluff based simply on the possession of nuclear weapons is neither sufficient as a credible deterrent nor practical as a posture for a defense establishment. Thus the first position on deterrence currently being taken in debates within the Church, the present position of the American Catholic bishops, is unrealistic and provides no answer to the problem of maintaining deterrence while working for arms control.

The second position, which I espouse, is to develop flexible-response counterforce deterrent strategies and capabilities sufficient to replace MAD while complying with just-war requirements. I withhold judgment on the possibility that the emerging U.S. countervalue deterrent that does not target cities as such may be compatible with the principles of proportion and discrimination. Deterrence through threat of nuclear response at the theater/local level, e.g., NATO, should be limited to counterforce deterrence against nuclear attack. This means that there is an urgent need to increase conventional capabilities so as to make possible reduction of reliance on nuclear weapons for any purpose other than to deter attacks with nuclear weapons.

The technical difficulties of achieving a morally usable spectrum of flexible-response counterforce deterrents have been mentioned above.[52] It is by no means certain that such an approach is feasible. Moreover, it is problematic whether the thresholds and rules of conflict necessary to maintain such a counterforce strategy could survive a nuclear war. The answer to these objections—and here is where I disagree with the American Catholic bishops' committee—is that there really is no alternative. We need a deterrent, and the kind of MAD countervalue deterrent we have now appears to be morally unacceptable. Counterforce deterrence appears to be the only option whereby effective deterrence might be joined to a just-war war-fighting posture.

It is sometimes argued that "limited nuclear war" approaches discount the horrors of nuclear war and may tend to make war more likely. It is also argued, as mentioned above, that counterforce strategies are destabilizing and may encourage initiatives on the other side to develop first-strike policies and capabilities.[53] The second argument poses a real problem, but it is not sufficiently weighty to preclude efforts to develop counterforce policies needed for an effective and moral deterrence posture against an enemy that is quite capable of developing first-strike policies on his own.

As to the first argument, the American experience, including that of President Reagan, has been that statesmen who fully understand the implications of nuclear war will do everything possible to avoid risking it. The purpose of counterforce deterrence is still deterrence, not war-fighting. As deterrence, however, it has the potential advantage of permitting a just and limited strategy in the event of aggression rather than a choice between unleashing an immoral countervalue response or surrender.

Control of Nuclear War

It appears that the most serious objection to a flexible-response counterforce deterrence policy is the fear that any use of nuclear weapons will inevitably mean that they will "escape control." As mentioned above, there are serious questions about the ability of C^3 systems to survive a nuclear war sufficiently to ensure control of it. There is good reason to believe that this is a priority concern of the U.S. government. While the outcome of efforts to improve C^3 is open to speculation, it does not seem justified to write off the one feasible line of reconciliation between the requirements of deterrence and just-war principles on the assumption that C^3 will not be adequate.[54]

Another objection to flexible-response counterforce policies is that in practice they will inflict collateral damage so great as to make them little less objectionable than outright countervalue strategies. The same argument, a fortiori, can be made regarding the Reagan countervalue strategy. As earlier noted, fear of fallout in counterforce strikes contributes to the argument that there is insufficient control.[55]

There is no immediate, clear-cut answer to these serious objections. Nonexperts cannot easily determine whether the threat of counterforce would be effective as a deterrent strategy operating within the limits of just-war doctrine. Abstractly, one can imagine discrete counterforce attacks on military targets that, if confined to these targets, would not cause excessive collateral damage or escape control. One can also imagine attacks intended to be solely counterforce that did cause excessive collateral damage and did escape control. Much would depend on the location and nature of the targets. There is no doubt that these objections are serious and that, given other choices, it would be better to forgo the effort to reconcile any form of nuclear war with just-war standards, starting with the requirement of control. The real issue, however, is whether there is any alternative to attempting to mount a counterforce deterrence posture that would maximize control in order to comply with the principles of proportion and discrimination.[56]

As acknowledged above, a major and intractable problem for any kind of controlled-response nuclear deterrent and/or war is uncertainty as to the extent to which the enemy would observe tacit thresholds and rules of conflict. There is no answer to this problem except the hope that self-interest would induce the enemy to co-operate in keeping any nuclear war limited.

A final word needs to be said about the concept of control itself. It is not difficult to find statements by experienced statesmen and military commanders despairing of the possibility of controlling a nuclear war.[57] No doubt, the chances that such a war might escape control are substantial. However, some thought needs to be given to the degree of certitude that should be required with respect to control of a nuclear war. Just-war doctrine requires an estimate of probable costs weighed against the probable benefits of a war in the light of the probability of success. A particularly thorough and conservative calculation would be required before ordering the use of nuclear weapons. Beyond that, generalizations are difficult.

I conclude that, following just-war standards, a flexible-response counterforce deterrence strategy should be developed to replace the current modified version of countervalue MAD. I acknowledge that the practical obstacles to the maintenance of a flexible-response counterforce strategy are serious and the reconciliation of such a strategy with just-war requirements is not easy. However, given the just cause of protecting the United States and its allies from nuclear aggression, intimidation, and subjugation by an enemy dedicated to the destruction of our society, our values, and of the Church itself, it seems to me that we have no alternative but to attempt to find a deterrence strategy that will be both practically effective and morally permissible. We should also review all possibilities of defending our own populations, hostages under the MAD system, by active and passive defense measures, including ABM, space defense, and civil defense.[58]

ARMS CONTROL IN A WORLD OF CONFLICT

As indicated above, the contemporary term "arms control" connotes an approach to disarmament that emphasizes the balance of opposing forces so that the security of all remains secure. A just-war approach to arms control should begin with a reaffirmation of the just cause that has led to the development of opposing military policies and capabilities. A state should not endanger through arms-control concessions its ability to protect the just cause—in the case of the United States and its allies, survival as free societies.

If this is understood, it should follow that arms-control agreements must be made with full awareness of their potential effects on stable deterrence. Ironically, the whole existing network of arms-control agreements stands on the foundation of the MAD balance of terror. Indeed, the stability of the nuclear deterrence system has been called the "theology of stability."[59] Yet, just-war analysis of the existing MAD deterrent system reveals that it is based on threats to engage in nuclear war that would almost certainly be immoral if carried out. So there is a paradox. Hopes for arms control, required in an entirely new approach to war, rest at present on nuclear deterrent stability, which in turn depends on an immoral balance of terror that must be changed. But all change, even if morally motivated, is risky and suspect in the charged atmosphere of the delicate balance of terror.

A potential dilemma emerges. It seems likely that the greatest near-to-medium-term progress that could be made in arms-control negotiations would be made in the context of perpetuation of the present MAD system. If we move toward development of the kind of flexible-response counterforce deterrence strategy and capability that would better conform to just-war requirements as a war-fighting posture should deterrence fail, arms-control negotiations might very well become more difficult.[60]

It could be that a move to a strategic posture more in keeping with just-war guidelines would complicate arms-control negotiations with an apprehensive Soviet Union. In the long run, however, arms control must rest on stable deterrence. It is difficult to see how our part of the deterrence system can remain stable when we increasingly agitate to have it condemned as immoral. We must have a morally acceptable deterrence posture in order to pursue arms control with confidence. This requirement must be viewed in the light of the prospects for major problems in the arms-control process with respect to verification issues. Given Soviet attitudes regarding on-site inspection and the prospect that the subjects of future arms-control agreements (e.g., qualitative improvements in existing weapons systems and R & D) may not lend themselves to adequate verification by national technical means of verification (e.g., satellite reconnaissance, seismographic techniques, and remote sensors), stable deterrence based on morally permissible means is the foundation of any realistic progress in arms control.[61] In this connection it must be added that nuclear freezes may not be "steps in the right direction" but rather obstacles to developing counterforce capabilities that would permit counterforce strategies possibly consonant with just-war doctrine. Freezes would tend to freeze us into an immoral and disadvantaged nuclear posture.

This negotiation-from-strength approach is far removed from the total elimination of nuclear weapons and other arms-control goals held out in the Church's recent teaching. It may not be considered by some to be sufficiently informed by "an entirely new attitude" toward war. However, the goals set by the Church's official teaching are very remote at best, and the reality of our present MAD posture casts a shadow over all discussions of just war and arms control. The first steps toward arms control may have to be based not so much on an entirely new attitude as on the revival and serious application of an old approach, that of the just-war doctrine.

NOTES

1. See the excellent historical and analytical studies of James T. Johnson in *Ideology, Reason and Limitation of War* (Princeton, N.J.: Princeton University, 1975), and *Just War Tradition and the Restraint of War* (Princeton, N.J.: Princeton University, 1981).

2. On the right and duty of legitimate self-defense, see John Courtney Murray, S.J., *We Hold These Truths* (New York: Sheed & Ward, 1960) 256–61; Paul VI, "Address to the UN Assembly, October 4, 1965," *The Pope Speaks* 11 (1966) 54–55; Pastoral Constitution on the Church in the Modern World (*Gaudium et spes*) no. 79 (*The Documents of Vatican II,* ed. Walter M. Abbott, S.J. [New York: Guild, 1966] 292–93); John J. O'Connor, *In Defense of Life* (Boston: St. Paul Editions, 1981) 37–96; NCCB Ad Hoc Committee on War and Peace, "New Draft of Pastoral Letter, The Challenge of Peace: God's Promise and Our Response," *Origins* 12 (1982) 311–12 (hereinafter cited NCCB, *Draft Pastoral Letter*).

3. John J. Ford, S.J., "The Morality of Obliteration Bombing," *TS* 5 (1944) 261–309; idem, "The Hydrogen Bombing of Cities," in *Morality and Modern Warfare,* ed. William J. Nagle (Baltimore: Helicon, 1960) 98–103; Murray, *We Hold These Truths* 249–73; Paul Ramsey, *War and the Christian Conscience* (Durham, N.C.: Duke University, 1961); idem, *The Just War* (New York: Scribner's, 1968); Robert E. Osgood & Robert W. Tucker, *Force, Order and Justice* (Baltimore: Johns Hopkins University, 1967); Johnson, *Ideology* and *Just War Tradition* (n. 1 above); Michael Walzer, *Just and Unjust Wars* (New York: Basic, 1977); William V. O'Brien, *Nuclear War, Deterrence and Morality* (New York: Newman, 1967); idem, *War and/or Survival* (Garden City, N.Y.: Doubleday, 1969); idem, *The Conduct of Just and Limited War* (New York: Praeger, 1981).

4. See the insightful comments of James T. Johnson regarding Paul Ramsey's work in "Morality and Force in Statecraft: Paul Ramsey and the Just War Tradition," *Love and Society: Essays in the Ethics of Paul Ramsey,* ed. James T. Johnson & David H. Smith (Missoula, Mont.: American Academy of Religion & Scholars Press, 1974) 93–114.

5. John XXIII, *Pacem in terris: Peace on earth,* nos. 109–19 (Washington, D.C.: NCWC, 1963) 26–28; *Gaudium et spes,* nos. 81–92 (*Documents* 294–97); NCCB, *Draft Pastoral Letter* 313–14, 317–22; John Paul II, "Message to the Second Special Session of the U.N. General Assembly Devoted to Disarmament" (June 1982).

6. *Pacem in terris,* nos. 130–45 (NCWC 26–28); *Gaudium et spes,* no. 84 (*Documents* 298–99); NCCB, *Draft Pastoral Letter* 320–22.

7. *Pacem in terris,* nos. 86–108 (22–26); nos. 12–25 (28–29); *Gaudium et spes,* nos. 85–88 (299–303); Paul VI, *On the Development of Peoples: Populorum Progressio,* Encyclical Letter of March 25, 1967

(Washington, D.C.: USCC, 1967); NCCB, *Draft Pastoral Letter* 320–22.

8. See W. Hays Parks, "The Law of War Adviser," *JAG Journal* 31 (1980) 1–52.

9. See O'Brien, *Conduct of Just and Limited War* 301–60.

10. On the judgmental process in just-war analyses, see James F. Childress, "Just-War Theories," *TS* 39 (1978) 427–45; O'Brien, *Conduct* 35–36.

11. Ibid. 17–18.

12. On the NATO nuclear decision process, see U.S. Congress, Congressional Budget Office, *Planning U.S. General Purpose Forces: The Theater Nuclear Forces* (Washington, D.C.: GPO, 1977); Robert Close, *Europe without Defense? Forty-eight Hours That Could Change the Face of the World* (New York: Pergamon, 1979).

13. Francis X. Winters, S.J., raises this point in his comments on my article, "The Peace Debate and American Catholics," *Washington Quarterly* 5 (1982) 219–22. Winters' comments appear in "Fair Hearing for the Bishops," *Washington Quarterly* 5 (1982) 132–37. I reply ibid. 137–42. Winters cites Desmond Ball, "Can Nuclear War Be Controlled?" *Adelphi Paper* no. 169 (London: Institute for Strategic Studies, 1981).

14. See the assessment of the state of C^3 and prospects for its improvement in The Organization of the Joint Chiefs of Staff, *United States Military Posture for FY 1983* (Washington, D.C: GPO, 1982) 24, 81–83; Caspar W. Weinberger, Secretary of Defense, *Annual Report to the Congress, Fiscal Year 1984* (Washington, D.C.: GPO, 1983) 241–59.

15. See particularly Pius XII's Christmas Message of Dec. 23, 1956, in the wake of the bloody repression of Hungary by the Soviet Union, in *Pattern for Peace,* ed. Harry W. Flannery (Westminster, Md.: Newman, 1962) 170–71. While John Paul II has cited as obstacles to peace and arms control "ideologies which . . . are opposed to the dignity of the human person . . . who see in struggle the motivating forces of history, which see in force the source of rights" ("Dialogue for Peace: A Challenge for Our Time," message for the World Day of Peace, released Dec. 20, 1982) and has alluded to communist repression in Poland, he has not addressed the threat to the free world comprehensively.

16. See *Pacem in terris,* nos. 111, 126–29 (29–30); *Gaudium et spes,* no. 80 (293); testimony of John Cardinal Krol, representing the USCC before the Senate Foreign Relations Committee, Sept. 6, 1979, in *The Nuclear Threat: Reading the Signs of the Times,* ed. Patricia L. Rengel (Washington, D.C.: Office of Justice and Peace/USCC, Oct. 1979) 9. The NCCB *Draft Pastoral Letter,* in contrast, distinguishes various nuclear strategies without accepting any.

17. On limited-nuclear-war options, see O'Brien, *Conduct* 134–41. These options are rejected as too questionable and dangerous in NCCB, *Draft Pastoral Letter* 312–18.

18. O'Brien, *Conduct* 127–29.

19. See Donald M. Snow, *Nuclear Strategy in a Dynamic World: American Policy in the 1980s* (University, Ala.: University of Alabama, 1981) 65–66.

20. See Robert A. Gessert & J. Bryan Hehir, *The New Nuclear Debate* (New York: Council on Religion and International Affairs, 1976); Snow, *Nuclear Strategy* 69–85; Secretary of Defense Harold Brown, *Remarks . . . Prepared for Delivery . . . at the Convocation Ceremonies for the 97th Naval War College Class, August 20, 1980* (DOD Release no. 344–80); Robert A. Gessert, "P.D. 59: The Better Way," and J. Bryan Hehir, "P.D. 59: New Issue in an Old Argument," in *Worldview* 23 (1980) 7–9, 10–12; Colin Gray, "Presidential Directive 59: Flawed but Useful," *Parameters* 11 (1981) 28–57; Thomas Powers, "Choosing a Strategy for World War III," *Atlantic* 250 (1982) 82–100.

21. Quotations are from an unclassified but unpublished document currently in use among U.S. government officials for their guidance and for briefing the public. They reflect formulations made in national-security adviser William Clark's letter to the NCCB committee drafting the pastoral letter, July 30, 1982. See *Draft Pastoral Letter,* n. 40 (327). See Richard Halloran, "Pentagon Draws up First Strategy for Fighting a Long Nuclear War," *New York Times* (May 30, 1982) I, 12.

22. Weinberger, *Annual Report FY 1984* 31–39.

23. Snow, *Nuclear Strategy* 32–33, 205–16, 237–40.

24. Weinberger, *Annual Report FY 1984* 51–58.

25. See Laurence Martin, "Limited Nuclear War," in Michael Howard, ed., *Restraints on War: Studies in the Limitation of Armed Conflict* (Oxford: Oxford University, 1979) 103–21.

26. See McGeorge Bundy, George F. Kennan, Robert McNamara, & Gerard Smith, "Nuclear Weapons and the Atlantic Alliance," *Foreign Affairs* 60 (1982) 756–68; Karl Kaiser, Georg Leber, Alois Mertes, & Franz-Joseph Schulze, "Nuclear Weapons and the Preservation of Peace," ibid. 1157–70; Secretary of State Alexander Haig, Jr., "Peace and Deterrence," Address at the Center for Strategic and International Studies, Georgetown University, Washington, D.C., April 6, 1982 (Washington, D.C.: U.S. Department of State, Current Policy No. 383, 1982).

27. O'Brien, *Conduct* 128–29; 229–30.

28. Ibid. 134–37.

29. See Haig, "Peace and Deterrence."

30. See Weinberger, *Annual Report FY 1984* 19–29; JCS, *Military*

Posture FY 1983 1–50; John M. Collins, *American and Soviet Military Trends since the Cuban Missile Crisis* (Washington, D.C.: Center for Strategic and International Studies, Georgetown Univ., 1978).

31. O'Brien, *Conduct* 31–33.

32. Ibid. 33–35, 76–78.

33. Ibid. 38–42, 223–24.

34. See the analysis of proportion in Johnson, *Just War Tradition* 196–224.

35. See Tucker in Osgood & Tucker, *Force, Order and Justice* 233–38, 266–84, 289–90, 300–301, 319.

36. See, e.g, Myers S. McDougal & Florentino P. Feliciano, *Law and Minimum World Public Order* (New Haven: Yale University, 1961) 79–80 and authorities cited therein.

37. See Ramsey, *Just War* passim.

38. See O'Brien, *Conduct* 44–45, with examples of official Church pronouncements cited in 378, n. 14.

39. See R. A. McCormick, "War, Morality of," *New Catholic Encyclopedia* 14 (1967) 802–7; J. Bryan Hehir, "The Just-War Ethic and Catholic Theology: Dynamics of Change and Continuity," in *War and Peace: The Search for New Answers,* ed. Thomas A. Shannon (Maryknoll, N.Y.: Orbis, 1980) 15–39; Walzer, *Just and Unjust Wars* 151–59; O'Brien, *Conduct* 46–47.

40. Walzer, *Just and Unjust Wars* 151–59; see Tucker's skeptical comments in Osgood & Tucker, *Force, Order and Justice* 311–13.

41. O'Brien, *Conduct* 44–46.

42. *Pacem in terris,* nos. 109–19 (26–28), 126–29 (29–30); *Gaudium et spes,* nos. 79–82 (291–97); Cardinal Krol's 1979 testimony in *New Nuclear Threat* 9–10.

43. The second draft pastoral letter does not totally condemn nuclear weapons as *mala in se,* although it finds no use of them that it can approve as a war-fighting instrument.

44. See the Convention on Genocide, Res. No. 260 (III) A, UN GAOR 3d sess. (I), Resolutions, 174; UN Doc. No. A/810; *U.S. Department of State Bulletin* no. 3416 (1946); *Gaudium et spes,* no. 79 (292); William V. O'Brien, "Genocide," *New Catholic Encyclopedia* 6 (1967) 336–37.

45. See Ramsey, *Just War* 285–313.

46. NCCB, *Draft Pastoral Letter* 315–18. However, while the countercity countervalue destruction threatened by MAD is condemned, the deterrence system that depends on this threat is condoned, leaving the issue uncertain.

47. Ibid., reflecting *Gaudium et spes,* nos. 80–82 (293–97); Krol, *Nuclear Threat* 9–10.

48. See Ramsey, *Just War* 249–58. Hehir appears to adopt

Ramsey's bluff approach in Gessert & Hehir, *New Nuclear Debate* 44, 47–53, 66–69.

49. "I now think that an imput of deliberate ambiguity about the counter-people use of nuclear weapons is not possible unless it is (immorally) meant, and not a very good idea in the first place" (Paul Ramsey, "A Political Ethics Context for Strategic Thinking," in Morton A. Kaplan, ed., *Strategic Thinking and its Moral Implications* [Chicago: University of Chicago Center for Policy Study, 1973] 142). (See this volume, p. 303. —Ed.)

50. See Krol, *Nuclear Threat* 10; NCCB, *Draft Pastorial Letter* 314–18.

51. See my exchange with Winters, *Washington Quarterly* 5 (1982) 132–42.

52. See Victor Utgoff, "In Defense of Counterforce," *International Security* 6 (1982) 44–60.

53. See the differing views of Snow, *Nuclear Strategy* 32–33, 205–16, 237–40, and Utgoff, "In Defense of Counterforce."

54. See the indications of the U.S. government's concern and actions with respect to C^3 problems in the reports cited in n. 14 above.

55. See Snow, *Nuclear Strategy* 32–33.

56. Utgoff, "In Defense of Counterforce."

57. The NCCB *Draft Pastoral Letter* cited a number of authorities on the difficulty, if not impossibility, of controlling nuclear war in notes 27, 28, and 29 (327). See, e.g., John Steinbrumer, "Nuclear Decapitation." *Foreign Policy* 45 (1981–82) 16–28; Desmond Ball, "Can Nuclear War Be Controlled?" See Henry Kissinger's more optimistic view in "Nuclear Weapons and the Peace Movement," *Washington Quarterly* 5 (1982) 31–39.

58. On counterforce and damage limitation, see Keith B. Payne, *Nuclear Deterrence in U.S.-Soviet Relations* (Boulder, Colo.: Westview, 1982).

59. John Newhouse, *Cold Dawn* (New York: Holt, Rinehart & Winston, 1973).

60. Thus violating the guidelines suggested by David Hollenbach, S.J., "Nuclear Weapons and Nuclear War: The Shape of the Catholic Debate," *TS* 43 (1982) 602–5.

61. Snow, *Nuclear Strategy* 166–68, 205–6.

PART V

The Limits of Just-War Criteria

INTRODUCTION:
THE REALIST TEMPTATION

From Augustine to the present day, pacifists and nonpacifists alike have been aware of the uneasy relation between just-war criteria and the exigencies of realism in political ethics. The general suspicion has been that, however much just-war criteria were developed in the effort to discipline our political reasoning, such criteria have been all too easily co-opted by the requirements of military efficiency or *raison d'état.* The need to provide a realistic ethic, it has been alleged, weakens the possibility for crafting a robust vocabulary of social criticism. Instead, appeals to realism provide an easy way to sanctify the decisions made in defense of national self-interest. Recalling that the just-war tradition is rooted in Augustine's effort to accommodate Christian morality to the requirements of statecraft in the waning years of the Roman Empire, critics of nonpacifism insist that it is congenital with an ethics of compromise.

One possible reply might be to argue that just-war criteria constitute a *via media* between the extremes of pacifism and total-war doctrine. By providing a basis for justifying war, just-war ideas differ from the former alternative; by insisting on the proper limits to the use of force, just-war tenets depart from the latter route. In either instance, just-war theory can appeal to the virtue of justice as a basis for its judgements: To allow heedless aggression is unfair to its victims; yet to do anything to win is to inflict unjust harm, creating another set of innocent victims. That just-war ideas have been co-opted and compromised by realism says less about the theory and the virtue of justice than about humanity's ongoing attempt to engage in self-justification.

Yet this reply is giving way to alternative approaches among nonpacifists today. Perhaps it is too simple, obscuring the moral ambiguity that surrounds using lethal force to vindicate a moral principle. Perhaps it suggests that we can divorce theory from application or the history of effects, contrary to the pragmatic instincts of many who embrace some version of nonpacifism.

With these concerns in mind, recent ethicists have sought to strengthen the theoretical resources of just-war criteria, hoping to provide a last line of defense against the danger of co-optation. The general goal is to take up Ralph Potter's suggestion that a presumption against violence, injury, and war helps shape the morphology of just-war tenets, and that such a presumption is meant to resist the kinds of claims made on behalf of necessity or military efficiency. Going hand in hand with this goal is the effort to articulate a vocabulary for chastened civic virtue, one that is tempered in its patriotic allegiances.

Generally, attempts to resist the realist temptation have developed by way of exploring the connections between just-war criteria and pacifism. Although such connections, as they are represented in this anthology, take on various nuances, the main idea is that just-war criteria and pacifism share more in common than do just-war criteria and total-war, or "war is hell," doctrine. The main reason for this view is that just-war criteria and pacifism are wedded to the value of nonviolence and share a strong bias against the use of violence to vindicate justice. Further, just-war tenets are premised on the idea that war is a rule-governed activity, providing a set of conditions that prevent the ends from justifying all possible means in the exercise of force. Seen in this way, just-war criteria cannot be subsumed under utilitarian assumptions. Moreover, just-war criteria require us to explore alternatives to the use of force as a means of settling disputes. In contrast, total-war theory assumes that there are no limits to war beyond the requirement to limit one's force to the most efficient means. Beyond that, the ends justify the means, providing a basis for "doing anything necessary to win." By exploring the connections between pacifism and just-war criteria, recent just-war theorists have in effect sharpened the differences between just-war and total-war doctrine. By their account, then, it would be incorrect to view just-war criteria as constituting a perfect *via media* between two radical alternatives. Rather, such criteria begin with a presumption in favor of nonviolence and against war, and define the conditions according to which such a presumption may be overridden.[1]

NOTES

1. In addition to those materials included in this anthology, I have sought to develop some suggestions from this account of just-war tenets in *Interpretations of Conflict: Ethics, Pacifism, and the Just-War Tradition* (Chicago: University of Chicago Press, 1991).

19

Just-War Criteria

James F. Childress

If the distinction between nonviolence and violence is morally significant and if nonviolence has moral priority over violence, it is important to examine the criteria by which the transition from nonviolence to violence and from peace to war might be justified. In addition, it is important to examine the criteria for the right conduct of war. [Here] I want to offer a general analysis and assessment of just-war criteria. . . .

There are at least two useful approaches to the criteria of just wars. One starts from basic ethical principles and asks what criteria of just wars can be derived from them. The other starts from the just-war criteria that we have inherited and criticizes them in terms of consistency, coherence, and fidelity to fundamental ethical principles and values. Within either approach, we move back and forth between our practices, including our ordinary judgments, and ethical principles and theories.

An example of the first approach is John Rawls's *A Theory of Justice,* which treats just-war criteria within the context of a systematic theory of justice as fairness. Unfortunately, his treatment is very sketchy and mainly reaffirms the traditional criteria without establishing the links between them and his theory of justice. Taking the second approach, several theologians and philosophers appropriate and apply traditional just-war criteria without adequately probing their bases, interrelations, and functions. In a recent article entitled "Just

War Theory: What's the Use?" James Johnson considers the implications and applications of this "broadly defined collection of practical principles" called just-war theory. He takes "classic just-war theory" (which is actually more a tradition than a single theory) as normative, viewing several developments in the last three centuries as dilutions and distortions. Indeed, he uses this classic theory to expose contemporary misunderstandings of just-war criteria. But he offers few arguments for taking particular "classic" formulations as normative and for viewing later developments as decline rather than progress.[1]

We should begin with the historical deposit of just-war criteria, now accessible in a number of fine historical studies.[2] But we should not stop there, especially if just-war criteria are to be defensible and usable for policy-makers and citizens. It is also essential to offer a rational reconstruction of these criteria. I will try to show how the traditional just-war criteria can be reconstructed, explicated, and defended in relation to the prima facie duty of nonmaleficence—the duty not to harm or kill others. Then I will reconstruct their foundations and interrelations before considering their order and strength. Finally, I will examine their function in a pluralistic society and ask what stake, if any, pacifists might have in such criteria.

THE LOGIC OF PRIMA FACIE DUTIES

. . . First, let us consider the notion of a prima facie obligation or duty. (I am using *obligation* and *duty* interchangeably in this context.) W. D. Ross introduced the distinction between prima facie and actual obligations to account for conflicts of obligations, which, he maintained, proved to be "nonexistent" when fully and carefully analyzed. When two or more prima facie obligations appear to come into conflict, we have to assess the total situation, including various possible courses of action with all their features of prima facie rightness and wrongness, to determine what we actually ought to do. The phrase *prima facie* indicates that certain features of acts that have a tendency to make an act right or wrong claim our attention; insofar as an act has those features it is right or wrong. But our actual obligation depends on the act in its wholeness and entirety. For "while an act may well be prima facie obligatory in respect of one character and prima facie forbidden in virtue of another, it becomes obligatory or forbidden only in virtue of the totality of its ethically relevant characteristics."[3] *Prima facie* does not mean "apparent" in contrast to "real," for prima facie duties are real although they are distinguished from "actual" duties. Although some prima facie obligations are more stringent than others (e.g., nonmaleficence is more stringent than beneficence), it is not possible to provide a complete ranking or a scale of stringency of obligations.

To hold that an obligation or duty is prima facie is to claim that it always has a strong moral reason for its performance although this reason may not always be decisive or triumph over all other reasons. If an obligation is viewed as absolute, it cannot be overridden under any circumstances; it has priority over all other obligations with which it might come into conflict. If it is viewed as relative, the rule stating it is no more than a maxim or rule of thumb that illuminates but does not prescribe what we ought to do. If it is viewed as prima facie, it is intrinsically binding, but it does not necessarily determine one's actual obligation.

As individuals or members of institutions, we have a prima facie duty not to injure others. Injury may mean an unwarranted or unjustified harm or violation of rights, or it may mean inflicting actual harm (e.g., shooting someone) that may or may not be warranted or justified. In the first sense, it is, of course, always wrong by definition; an obligation not to injure others wrongfully would be absolute rather than prima facie. In the second sense, it is prima facie. Insofar as an act injures another, it is prima facie wrong and stands in need of justification. Although act-utilitarians imply that killing (which I am treating for the moment under injury) is morally neutral, William Frankena rightly insists that some kinds of action including killing are "intrinsically wrong." For they are "always prima facie wrong, and they are always actually wrong when they are not justified on other moral grounds. They are not in themselves morally indifferent. They may conceivably be justified in certain situations, but they always need to be justified; and even when they are justified, there is still one moral point against them." If the Fifth (or Sixth) Commandment reads "Thou shalt not kill," it is prima facie rather than absolute, for the Hebrews admitted killing in self-defense, capital punishment, and war. If it reads "Thou shalt not commit murder," it can then be taken as absolute, but it leaves open the question which killings are to be counted as murder.[4]

It is not necessary to defend Ross's intuitionism in order to hold that injury and killing are intrinsically prima facie wrong. For Ross, both fall under the obligation of nonmaleficence. For Rawls, there is a "natural duty," that is, a duty owed to persons generally, not to injure or harm others and not to inflict unnecessary suffering; this natural duty can be derived from the original position.[5] Christian theologians might derive this obligation not to injure or kill others from the norm of agape. The claim that injury and killing are prima facie wrong is compatible with a number of philosophical and religious frameworks.

An overridden or outweighed prima facie obligation continues to function in the situation and the course of action one adopts. It leaves what Robert Nozick calls "moral traces." It has "residual effects" on the agent's attitudes and actions. As A. C. Ewing suggests, "If I have a prima facie obligation which I cannot rightly fulfill because it is overruled by another, stronger prima facie obligation, it does not by any means follow that my conduct ought to be unaffected by the former obligation. Even if I am morally bound to do something inconsistent with it, it should in many cases modify in some respect the way in which the act is performed and in almost all it should affect some subsequent action." For example, if I think that a stronger obligation requires me to break a promise, I should at least explain the situation to the promisee, ask him not to hold me to the promise, apologize for breaking it and even try to make it up to him later. At the very least, Ewing goes on to say, the prima facie obligation to keep the promise "should always affect our mental attitude toward the action" to the extent of evoking regret. According to W. D. Ross, "we do not for a moment cease to recognize a prima facie duty to keep our promise, and this leads us to feel, not indeed shame or repentance, but certainly compunction for behaving as we do."[6]

One important difference between many Protestant and Catholic interpretations of just war appears at this point. They differ on the appropriate attitude toward a just war that overrides the prima facie duty not to injure or kill others. In accord with their belief in the universality of sin, many Protestant theologians, such as Reinhold Niebuhr, insist that the decision to wage a just war is "the lesser of two evils," which they understand as "moral" as well as physical evils. Thus, remorse and repentance are proper responses. As Saint Augustine stressed, wars should be both just and mournful. Many Catholic theologians, joined by some Protestants, most notably Paul Ramsey, insist that "an act of self-defense or an act of vindictive justice, although imposed by circumstances which are regrettable, is morally good." For them, "war is not the lesser of two evils, but the lesser of two goods (one of which appears, at the moment of choice, unattainable)."[7]

Whether a war that justly and justifiably overrides the prima facie duty not to injure or kill others should evoke regret or remorse may be debatable, but such a war engenders certain obligations as well as attitudes. The traces or residual effects of the overridden prima facie duty are extremely important, as will be clear in my discussion of such just-war criteria as right intention, proportionality, and just conduct.

Before I develop those criteria, I want to summarize and amplify some implications of the prima facie duty not to injure or kill others. They are actually presuppositions of many just-war theories that include both *jus ad bellum* and *jus in bello*. First, because it is prima facie wrong to injure or kill others, such acts demand justification. There is a presumption against their justification, and anyone who tries to justify them bears a heavy burden of proof. Second, because not all duties can be fulfilled in every situation without some sacrifices (this inability may be understood as natural or as the result of sin), it is necessary and legitimate to override some prima facie duties. Some other duties (for instance, the prima facie duty to uphold justice or to protect the innocent) may be more stringent and thus take priority over the duty not to injure others. War thus can be a moral undertaking in some circumstances. Third, the overridden prima facie duties should affect the actors' attitudes and what they do in waging the war. Some ways of waging war are more compatible than others with the overridden prima facie duties not to injure or kill others. War can be more or less humane and civilized.

War and politics, or war and peace, are not two totally separate realms or periods.[8] Both are subject to moral principles and rules and, indeed, to many of the same principles and rules. War ought to fall within many of the boundaries that are also important to peace.

Theorists and practitioners are commonly tempted to make war merely an extension of politics so that it requires very little to justify waging war; or they are tempted to make politics and war so discontinuous that once one enters the state of war previously important moral, political, and legal considerations become irrelevant. Two points need to be affirmed. On the one hand, war must be justified because it violates some of our prima facie obligations, not because it is totally immoral or amoral or utterly discontinuous with politics. On the other hand, it can be more or less humane insofar as it is conducted in accordance with some standards that derive from the overridden prima facie obligations and other obligations that endure even in war. Furthermore, however much continuity there is between peace and war, peace remains the ultimate aim of a just war.

The model of war as a rule-governed activity stands in sharp contrast to the model of war as hell, which is accepted by most pacifists and by many "realists" who recognize no restraints other than proportionality. Both models are evident in the following passage from Rolf Hochhuth's play, *Soldiers:*

> *Bishop Bell of Chichester:* We denigrate our men if we suggest that they require directives to tell them that the burning of defenseless persons is murder.
>
> *P.M.* (savagely, not looking at Bell): War is murder. The murderer is the man who fires first. That man is Hitler.

According to one view, war is hell, murder, and there is thus only the crime of war, within which anything goes, for "all's fair . . . " According to another view, war is a gamelike (not in a frivolous sense) or a rule-governed conflict, within which one may legitimately injure, kill, and destroy, but not commit war crimes such as injuring or killing defenseless persons who are noncombatants or ex-combatants. For the view that war is "total" and without limits, the only critical moral factor is the decision to wage war, and moral blameworthiness may attach to the side starting the war, sometimes even to the side firing the first shot. For the view that war is a rule-governed activity, the *jus in bello* becomes very important. Any adequate theory, however, should *not* maintain that *jus ad bellum* is unimportant because the difference between war and peace is not all that great since some moral rules and principles persist in war. There is an important difference between them so that the *jus ad bellum* remains indispensable, but this difference is not to be described as that between morality and immorality or amorality. In Paul Ramsey's thought, for example, the emphasis is on the continuity between politics and war. Thus, he concentrates on the *jus in bello*, holding that the "*laws* of war are only an extension, where war is the only available means, of the rules governing any use of political power." Unfortunately, this emphasis on the continuity between politics and war may be excessive, since Ramsey does not pay enough attention to the moral issues in crossing the line between ordinary politics and war—the *jus ad bellum*.[9]

GROUNDS OF JUST-WAR CRITERIA

Most of the criteria traditionally associated with just-war theories emerge because war involves a conflict between prima facie obligations (when it is just and justified) and because the overridden prima facie obligations forbid us to injure and kill others. Many of these criteria apply in other areas, as I have suggested, because of similar conflicts between prima facie obligations, not because the prima facie obligations not to injure or kill others are involved at every point. Nevertheless, the content of the prima facie obligations that are overruled in just wars certainly shapes the criteria, particularly those having to do with *jus in bello*, since the conduct of the war should be as compatible as possible with the overridden prima facie obligations.

The first criterion of a just war is right or legitimate authority, which is really a presupposition for the rest of the criteria. In fact, it determines *who* is primarily responsible for judging whether the other criteria are met. As Quentin Quade indicates, "the principles of Just War become operative only *after* the classic political question is answered: who should do the judging?" Answering the authority question is a precondition for answering the others; it thus cannot be dismissed as a "secondary criterion." James Johnson appears to think that legitimate authority was a secondary criterion for Saint Augustine, but Augustine's writings indicate that the authority of the prince or state or God's direct authorization is indispensable for just war. In his attempt to reconstruct the *jus ad bellum,* Johnson does not address this criterion, except in passing, because he thinks that the current de facto definition of right authority (wherever there is sovereignty, there is right authority) is politically workable, although it has some moral difficulties. Nevertheless, any adequate just-war theory must seriously address this question "who decides?" Even in the use of these criteria for justifying and limiting revolution, surrogates for the established authority are often found in the revolutionary elite or the "people."[10]

After the proper authority has determined that a war is just and justified and thus overrides the prima facie obligation not to injure and kill others, citizens, including subject-soldiers, face a different presumption. Whereas the proper authority has to confront and rebut the presumption against war, the subject-soldier now confronts the presumption that the war is just and justified because the legitimate authority has so decided in accord with established procedures.[11] In all political orders, the subject has a moral right and duty—although not a legal right—not to fight if the war is manifestly unjust. And in a democracy, the citizen is ruler as well as subject and thus has a greater responsibility to apply these criteria to war. As subject, however, his presumption is still that the authorities, if they are legitimate and have followed proper procedures, have decided correctly.

The requirement of a just cause is simply the requirement that the other competing prima facie duty or obligation be a serious and weighty one, e.g., to protect the innocent from unjust attack, to restore rights wrongfully denied, or to reestablish a just order. Because war involves overriding important prima facie obligations not to injure or kill others, it demands the most weighty and significant reasons. These obligations cannot be overridden if there are other ways of achieving the just aim short of war. War is the *ultima ratio,* the last resort, but the requirement that war be the last resort does not mean that all possible measures have to be attempted and exhausted if there is no reasonable expectation that they will be successful. James Johnson does not emphasize the criterion of "last resort" in part because he thinks that it tends to be understood as condemning the first use of force, but this requirement does not necessarily mean that the side that first resorts to armed force should be condemned.[12]

Insofar as a formal declaration is sometimes required, it stems not only from the nature of the political society, but also from the requirement that war be the last resort. Ultimata or formal declarations of war "are the last measures of persuasion short of force itself." Although a formal declaration of war may not be appropriate for various reasons, the significance of this criterion, broadly understood, should not be underestimated. Conceding that the best publicists differed on the necessity of a declaration, Francis Lieber defended it because "decent regard for mankind" and "public good faith" require that a government explain and justify its departure from peace.[13] A failure to announce the intention of and the reasons for waging war is a failure to exercise the responsibility of explaining and justifying exceptional action to those involved. An announcement of intentions and explanation of reasons may be more appropriate than a formal declaration of war.

The requirements of reasonable hope of success and proportionality are closely related. If war has no reasonable chance of success, it is clearly imprudent. But more than a dictate of prudence is involved in the demand for a reasonable hope of success. If none of the just and serious ends, none of the other prima facie obligations, could be realized or fulfilled through the war, a nation should reconsider its policy, which, after all, involves overriding stringent prima facie obligations. Nevertheless, numerous qualifications are in order. This criterion applies more clearly to offensive than to defensive wars. In any war success may be broader than "victory." As Lieber wrote of John Brown's raid: it was irrational, but it will be historical! Success could include witnessing to values as well as achieving goals; for instance, a group might engage in resistance in order to retain self-respect even in its demise. Regarding the limited Jewish resistance in Nazi Germany, some Jewish thinkers have insisted that if the holocaust comes again Jews must not "die like sheep." Although Ralph Potter has derived the criterion of reasonable hope of success from the moral prohibition of suicide and from the fact that statesmen are stewards of a nation, heroic acts such as falling on a grenade to save one's comrades may be fitting for individuals and suicide itself may be justifiable in some cases, particularly if it can be a noble witness to some higher values in the face of certain and imminent death.[14] Even if a nation has good reason to think that it will be defeated anyway, its vigorous resistance may preserve significant values beyond number of lives and retention of territory or sovereignty. Furthermore, what is "reasonable" depends on the situations in which actors have to make responsible decisions; retrospective judgments by others should include only what the actors could and should have foreseen. Finally, this criterion appears only to exclude totally "useless" or "pointless" or self-indulgent warfare, which reasonable people cannot expect to achieve goals or to express values. Such warfare is excluded because it cannot override the prima facie duties not to injure or kill others, duties as binding on states as on individuals.

Regarding proportionality, Ramsey writes: "It can never be right to resort to war, no matter how just the cause, unless a proportionality can be established between military/political objectives and their price, or unless one has reason to believe that in the end more good will be done than undone or a greater measure of evil prevented. But, of all the tests for judging whether to resort to or to participate in war, this one balancing an evil or good effect against another is open to the greatest uncertainty. This, therefore, establishes rather than removes the possibility of conscientious disagreement among prudent men."[15] Here, too, defensive measures are less restricted than offensive ones, but this criterion includes the welfare of all countries and peoples and not merely one's own country. Certainly the weight of the cause and the probability of success enter the discussion of proportionality, but the probable negative consequences must also be considered—even beyond the negative feature of injuring or killing others.

The last major criterion of the *jus ad bellum* is right or just intention, which, along with proportionality, is very important in particular battles, engagements, and acts within war and not merely for the war as a whole. For the war as a whole, right intention is shaped by the pursuit of a just cause, but it also encompasses motives. For example, as Augustine and others have insisted, hatred is ruled out. Some would hold that the dominance, if not the mere presence, of hatred vitiates the right to wage war even if there is a just cause. For example, McKenna holds that a "war which is otherwise just becomes immoral if it is waged out of hatred."[16] Such a contention, however, is difficult to establish, for if all the conditions of a just and justified war were met, the presence of vicious motives would not obliterate the *jus ad bellum,* although they would lead to negative judgments about the agents. Insofar as these vicious motives are expressed in such ways as the use of disproportionate force or the infliction of unnecessary suffering, one may condemn the belligerent for violating the *jus in bello.* Nevertheless, this criterion of right intention, understood not merely as pursuit of a just cause but also as proper motives, remains significant in part because war is conducted between public, not private, enemies. Furthermore, an attitude of regret, if not remorse, is appropriate when a prima facie obligation is overridden.

Another interpretation of right intention focuses on peace as the object or end of war. It too bridges the *jus ad bellum* and *jus in bello,* and I shall emphasize its impact on the conduct of war. Augustine and many others have affirmed that peace is the ultimate object, end, or intention of war. In short, war as injury, killing, and destruction is not an end in itself but a means to another end—a just or better peace. Even apart from the justice that is sought, peace retains its moral claim during war and thus constitutes an ultimate or final objective. There is a duty to restore the "normal" state of affairs as quickly and surely as possible.

It may be dangerous, however, to stress that it is urgent to restore peace, especially if peace is defined as the absence of conflict rather than a specific set of relationships that may include conflict. For such an emphasis may engender support for a quick, brutal, and total war that may undermine the limits set by the *jus in bello.* Paul Ramsey holds that, unless there is a morality that intrinsically limits the conduct of war, "then we must simply admit that war has no limits—since these can hardly be derived from 'peace' as the 'final cause' of just wars." But if one does not misconstrue peace as the total absence of conflict, one can see how the prima facie obligation not to injure or kill others persists even in the midst of war by mandating the ultimate object of peace. And through the object of peace (but not only this way), it imposes other restraints on the conduct of war. Since the aim of war is "a just peace," John Rawls contends, "the means employed must not destroy the possibility of peace or encourage a contempt for human life that puts the safety of ourselves and of mankind in jeopardy." General Orders No. 100 of 1863 insists that "military necessity does not include any act of hostility which makes the return to peace unnecessarily difficult."[17]

If peace does not require mutual goodwill, it at least requires some trust and confidence. Thus, perfidy, bad faith, and treachery are ruled out in part because they are destructive of the ultimate object of peace. If they are prevalent in war, to restore and maintain peace becomes very difficult short of the total subjugation of the enemy. Acceptable ruses of war, according to one commentator on the laws of war, are "those acts which the enemy would have had reason to expect, or in any event had no reason not to expect."[18] Perfidy or treachery involves the betrayal of a belligerent's confidence that is based on moral or legal expectations or both (such as the expected protection of prisoners of war). This requirement of good faith derives not only from the ultimate end of peace but also from the respect for the humanity of the enemy that is expressed in a number of prima facie obligations.

The prima facie obligation not to injure or kill others should also more directly affect the choice of weapons and methods to fight wars than should the ultimate object of peace. Since this prima facie obligation is not cancelled even when it is overruled, its impact can be seen in various restrictions of the *jus in bello*.

First, the immediate object is not to kill or even to injure any particular person, but to incapacitate or restrain him.[19] The enemy soldier is not reduced to his role as combatant, and when he surrenders or is wounded, he ceases to be a combatant because he ceases to be a threat. He becomes an ex-combatant, and as a prisoner of war, he is entitled to certain protections. As a wounded person, he is entitled to medical treatment equal to that of one's own wounded comrades.

Second, to attack certain noncombatants directly is not legitimate. This principle is sound even if the distinction between combatant and noncombatant is contextual and thus is partially determined by the society and the type of war. In the gray areas, noncombatants include those persons whose functions in factories and elsewhere serve the needs of the person *qua* person rather than his or her role as military personnel. Thus, while food is essential for the soldier to function, it is also indispensable for him as a human being. Similarly, chaplains and medical personnel primarily serve the soldier as human being even when their ministrations indirectly aid the war effort. Finally, indiscriminate methods of warfare are prohibited by this principle.

Third, the original prima facie obligation not to injure others also excludes inflicting unnecessary suffering. Thus, cruelty (inflicting suffering for the sake of suffering) and wanton destruction (destruction without a compelling reason) are wrong. Such acts are not essential to the war effort. Acts that appear to fall under these vague categories of "cruelty" and "wanton destruction" are not cruel or wanton if they are "necessary." The relation between military necessity and such categories is a serious problem area in the *jus in bello*. . . . At any rate, certain weapons (such as dumdum bullets and explosive or inflammable projectiles weighing less than four hundred grams) are prohibited because they are calculated to cause "unnecessary suffering" or "superfluous injury." The rationale is simple. An ordinary rifle bullet or projectile weighing less than four hundred grams is designed to incapacitate only one person. To make the bullet or projectile do more damage to that one person is to inflict suffering that is unnecessary or superfluous.[20] That suffering offers no military advantage. (Of course, not all suffering that offers military advantage is necessary and justified.)

Fourth, even the indirect, incidental, or obliquely intentional effects on civilians must be justified by the principle of proportionality.

I have not tried to offer an exhaustive list of the requirements of the *jus in bello*, but rather to show that some restrictions emerge from the continued pressure of the prima facie duty not to injure or kill others even when it is overridden by the *jus ad bellum*. That duty persists and imposes restrictions indirectly through the ultimate object of peace and directly as in the protection of certain classes, avoidance of unnecessary suffering, and care for combatants who are *hors de combat*.

ORDER AND STRENGTH OF CRITERIA

How can these criteria be used to assess particular wars? How can we determine when a war is just and justified or unjust and unjustified? Various applications of just-war criteria have been proposed and used. (1) Some just-war theorists contend that the inability to meet any single criterion, such as last resort, renders a war unjust. Each criterion is necessary and all are collectively sufficient.[21] (2) Under another theory the criteria establish prima facie duties, which follow the logic of such duties, and the criteria should be met unless they are overridden by more stringent duties.[22] (3) Some theorists maintain that no single criterion must be met, but at least several criteria must be satisfied before a war can be justified. A war should approximate the criteria, even though it cannot fully satisfy them. (4) Other theorists contend that the criteria are "rules of thumb" or "maxims" that identify some morally relevant considerations; they illuminate but do not prescribe what we ought to do. (5) Still others arrange the criteria in a serial or lexical order so that some must be met before others can even be considered. For example, if there is no just cause, there is no reason to consider proportionality, for the war cannot be justified.

There are other possible ways to apply just-war criteria, and these five approaches can be combined in various ways. For example, some of the criteria could establish necessary conditions for justified war, or at least prima facie duties, while others could serve as rules of thumb. The fifth approach is especially promising, and one possible serial or lexical order is suggested in my arrangement of the criteria in the previous section. Whether this fifth approach, perhaps in combination with one or more of the others, could be developed is a subject for further reflection. It is unfortunate that philosophers and theologians have not devoted more attention to the order, mode of application, and weight of the various criteria.

Proposals on these matters will depend, in part, on a particular theory's substantive view of justice and other moral principles. But they are not reducible to substantive interpretations of justice, for my tentative order in the preceding section could be justified in terms of the logic of overriding prima facie duties. For the most part, the conception of just-war criteria in this essay is independent of substantive views of justice. It is not purely formal, however, for it hinges on material moral principles or prima facie duties (e.g., the duty not to injure or kill others). But it is intended to be accessible to many different theories of justice.

Paul Ramsey prefers to translate *justum bellum* as "justified war" rather than "just war," in part because he does not think that a substantive theory of justice in relation to ends can be developed or that one side can legitimately claim justice while denying it to the other.[23] Such an approach fits with a formal understanding of these criteria. When a policy-maker raises these formal questions of the *jus ad bellum* and gets affirmative answers, resort to war is "justified," although we cannot say that it is "just." A procedural justification is possible even when we lack a substantive theory of justice. Ramsey is more willing to provide content for *jus in bello* at least in terms of a principle of discrimination that rules out direct attacks on noncombatants. Indeed, he says very little about *jus ad bellum,* concentrating instead on *jus in bello.*

Many classic and contemporary theorists construe "just cause" to include last resort, reasonable chance of success, and proportionality. A nation does not have a just cause unless these other conditions are also met. Nonetheless, one way to use the distinction between just and justified war is to restrict the language of "justice" to war's cause or aim and then to determine whether the war is "justified" by reference to the other criteria, including last resort, reasonable chance of success, and proportionality. While a war may be "unjust," according to this approach, when its cause does not satisfy standards of justice, it is "unjustified" when it does not meet the other criteria. It is important to emphasize, as Joel Feinberg has pointed out, that one and the same act need not be both just and justified.[24] It may be just and unjustified, for example, if it renders various parties their due but violates some other moral principles or results in terrible consequences, or it may be unjust and justified when, for example, an unfair act is required to prevent a disaster. Only when a war is both just and justified does a state have a *jus ad bellum.*

Does the *jus ad bellum* establish only a right or also a duty to go to war, at least under certain circumstances? Because the language of duty can lead to or support crusades and holy wars, it is somewhat suspect. There is no prima facie duty to go to war (i.e., to injure and kill), but because some other prima facie duties, such as the duty to protect the innocent, may override the prima facie duty not to injure or kill, there may be an actual duty to fight, especially in a situation where the language of necessity seems appropriate. To say that war stands in need of justification because it violates certain prima facie duties is not to rule out the language of actual duty or obligation in a particular set of circumstances. To think of some wars as duties does not entail modifying or relaxing the *jus in bello*. Even a policeman who has a duty to try to stop an escaped criminal who has taken hostages still should respect certain moral and legal limits.

Another important distinction is between rights and right conduct or between rights and their exercise.[25] It is useful for construing the relation between *jus ad bellum* and *jus in bello*. For example, perhaps one side could meet most of the conditions of *jus ad bellum* but would have little chance of success without fighting the war unjustly and unfairly. We might say, "You have a right to go to war, but you ought not to exercise that right." Such an approach, however, favors the established military powers. Should a theory of just war make it impossible for one country or revolutionary movement to wage a "successful" war? Ideological bias and the tension between success and moral requirements must be confronted clearly and honestly. . . .

THE FUNCTION OF JUST-WAR CRITERIA

It is important to examine the possible function of just-war criteria in a society that has several competing theories of justice and to determine the pacifist's stake, if any, in such a function. Many recent attempts to restate just-war criteria apparently treat them as questions that policy-makers and others ought to consider. These criteria constitute a formal framework and structure for moral debates about the use of force. They are important and even essential because of the prima facie duty not to injure or kill others, and they identify the kinds of questions that should be answered affirmatively before war and other acts that override prima facie duties can be justified. Perhaps because they are empty, they can serve to organize and orchestrate disputes in the public arena; even pacifists could and did appeal to these criteria to condemn the war in Vietnam. In democratic theory and practice, formal procedures can accommodate conflicts about moral convictions and interests; they do not dictate the material outcome. Similarly, just-war criteria constitute a formal framework within which different substantive interpretations of justice and morality as applied to war can be debated. For example, the formal interpretation holds that it is morally mandatory to determine that one has a "just" cause, but exactly what constitutes a "just" cause will depend on substantive convictions about justice and morality. This formal function of the criteria is hardly what traditional just-war theorists expected, for they developed their criteria within substantive theories of justice and the common good.

Some critics of a formalist interpretation of just-war criteria contend that such an interpretation cannot be accepted or supported because it does not serve, in fact, to restrain and limit war. Nevertheless, one of its manifest functions can be viewed as restraining and limiting war because it holds that only some wars, and only some acts within war, justifiably override the prima facie duty not to injure or kill others. The formalist interpretation fulfills this function, however, in the context of the legitimation of war as an exceptional practice. Its function is both positive (legitimation) and negative (limitation). It justifies but also restrains.[26]

Some critics are not satisfied with this explanation of the dual function of just-war theories.[27] They insist that this formalist interpretation fails to give clear and precise determinations regarding the justification of actual wars. In particular, they contend, it fails to give clear and precise *negative* answers. It fails to specify when particular wars or acts within wars are unjust or unjustified. In short, these critics wonder whether a formalist interpretation of just-war criteria can overcome the emptiness and vacuity that are deficiencies of most formalist theories in ethics. Agreement is possible precisely because they do not involve material content.

What these critics expect of just-war criteria is available only within *substantive* theories. There is no single substantive theory of just war. But these critics ask that the just-war criteria serve the same function now as they served in a different era when (presumably) there were strong shared convictions about justice and accepted arbiters of justice of and in war. This is impossible in a pluralistic society. But even in a pluralistic society, just-war criteria as defined [here] have the important function of serving as a framework for debates about which wars, if any, are justified.

Just-war criteria within a substantive theory should indicate when war is unjust and when it is conducted unjustly. They should define not only just cause, but also such terms as *innocence* and *discrimination.* I have not tried to develop a substantive theory of just war [here], but I have tried to show that just-war criteria are important and even indispensable moral standards apart from any particular theory of justice. They are explicable, I have argued, by reference to the notion of prima facie duties and, specifically, to the prima facie duty not to injure or kill.

If we accept this prima facie duty of nonmaleficence and if we accept the responsibility to think morally about the use of force in a sinful world, we should be committed to a framework and procedure of reasoning that is at least analogous to just-war criteria. Furthermore, it is important to secure support for this formal framework in order to avoid the amoral approaches to power that only appreciate "national interest" (as defined in nonmoral terms) or Machiavellian maneuvers. If the pacifist admits that there will always be "wars and rumors of wars"—an admission that will depend on his theology and anthropology—then he too has an important stake in the moral assessment of wars and acts within wars. He too should provisionally accept something analogous to just-war criteria.

There may be some misunderstanding of the nature and function of just-war criteria. They are not designed to answer the question of the justification of war in general but the question of the justification of particular wars. That is, they do not determine *whether* war as an institution or practice can ever, or in principle, be justified; they rather indicate *when* particular wars can be justified. They presuppose an affirmative answer to the question whether war can ever be justified and then pinpoint the conditions required for the justification of any particular war. Just-war criteria, thus, are not involved in the debate between the pacifist and the just-war theorist over *whether* war can ever be justified. This debate hinges on such general theological, anthropological, and moral convictions as sin, the place and function of the state, and political responsibility. It focuses on whether any moral principles and values, such as justice, can ever outweigh or override the prima facie duty of nonmaleficence.

But if just-war criteria presuppose an affirmative answer to the question whether war can ever be justified, how can the pacifist appeal to these criteria in discourse about a particular war? Sometimes in the moral assessment of particular wars, pacifists are ignored or excluded on the grounds that "we already know their conclusions."[28] Because the pacifist does not accept the premise of just-war theories that war can, in principle, be justified as an exceptional practice, so the argument goes, he cannot participate openly and impartially in the debate. But this argument is not cogent. The pacifist can apply the criteria of just war, as accepted by other groups, to a particular war. He can be sensitive to the implications of the criteria and whether they are satisfied by the factual circumstances, for example. He need not accept the premise of just-war theorists; his premise may be only that "of all possible wars, one that meets these criteria is less evil than one that does not."

In conclusion, pacifists and just-war theorists are actually closer to and more dependent on each other than they often suppose. Just-war theorists sometimes overlook the fact that they and the pacifists reason from a common starting point. Both begin with the contention that nonviolence has moral priority over violence, that violent acts always stand in need of justification because they violate the prima facie duty not to injure or kill others, whereas only some nonviolent acts need justification (e.g., when they violate laws). While pacifists can remind just-war theorists of this presumption against violence, pacifists also need just-war theorists. In a world in which war appears to be a permanent institution, debates about particular wars require a framework and a structure that can be provided by the criteria of the just-war tradition properly reconstructed. In addition, there are degrees of justice and humanity within violence and warfare, and the just-war theorist can emphasize these moral constraints, which the pacifist view of war as hell or murder (shared by some realists) tends to obscure. Even the pacifist has a stake in the integrity of just-war criteria as the coin of the political realm. The pacifist finally cannot be satisfied with that coin, just as the just-war theorist finally cannot be satisfied with the weight pacifism gives to the duty not to injure or kill others. The pacifist may charge that concentration on just-war criteria assumes the inevitability of war and makes war more likely by making it appear acceptable as long as it respects some limits and boundaries. But the just-war theorist may respond that concentration on the avoidance of war may weaken the sense of limits that should prevail even in war. Despite their differences, what the pacifist and the just warrior share—the moral presumption against war—can be neglected only at great peril to all of us.

NOTES

1. John Rawls, *A Theory of Justice* (Cambridge, Mass.: Harvard University Press, 1971), n. 58; James T. Johnson, "Just War Theory: What's the Use?" *Worldview,* XIX (July-August, 1976), 41–47. See Michael Walzer, *Just and Unjust Wars* (New York: Basic Books, 1977), probably the best book on morality of and in war in this century. See also my review of *Just and Unjust Wars* in *Bulletin of the Atomic Scientists,* XXXIV (October, 1978), 44–48, and James T. Johnson's review essay in *Religious Studies Review,* IV (October, 1978), 240–45.

2. See Frederick H. Russell, *The Just War in the Middle Ages* (New York: Cambridge University Press, 1975); James T. Johnson, *Ideology, Reason, and the Limitation of War* (Princeton, N.J.: Princeton University Press, 1975); LeRoy Brandt Walters, Jr., "Five Classic Just-War Theories: A Study in the Thought of Thomas Aquinas, Vitoria, Suárez, Gentili, and Grotius" (Ph.D. diss., Yale University, 1971).

3. W. D. Ross, *Foundations of Ethics* (Oxford: Clarendon Press, 1939), 86. Cf. Ross, *The Right and the Good* (Oxford: Clarendon Press, 1930), Chap. 2.

4. William K. Frankena, *Ethics* (2nd ed.; Englewood Cliffs, N.J.: Prentice-Hall, 1973), 55–56. For some of the issues see J. J. Stamm with M. E. Andrew, *The Ten Commandments in Recent Research* (London: SCM Press, 1967), 98–99, which views what is prohibited as "illegal killing inimical to the community." See also Solomon Goldman, *The Ten Commandments* (Chicago: University of Chicago Press, 1963).

5. Rawls, *A Theory of Justice,* 113–14.

6. Robert Nozick, "Moral Complications and Moral Structures," *Natural Law Forum,* XIII (1968), 1–50; A. C. Ewing, *Second Thoughts in Moral Philosophy* (London: Routledge and Kegan Paul, 1959), 110; Ross, *The Right and the Good,* 28. For a criticism of the view that

prima facie obligations retain their tendency to be binding and thus occasion some measure of moral regret, see Maurice Mandelbaum, *The Phenomenology of Moral Experience* (Baltimore: Johns Hopkins University Press, 1969), 79–81.

7. See Henry Paolucci, ed., *The Political Writings of St. Augustine* (Chicago: Henry Regnery, 1962), 162–83, and Roland H. Bainton, *Christian Attitudes Toward War and Peace* (Nashville: Abingdon Press, 1960), 98; Joseph C. McKenna, S.J., "Ethics and War: A Catholic View," *American Political Science Review,* LIV (1960), 658, cf. 650. For Ramsey's theoretical statement, see *Deeds and Rules in Christian Ethics* (New York: Charles Scribner's Sons, 1967), 187–88. For some trends in recent Catholic moral theology that are similar to the language of prima facie duties proposed in this essay, see Richard McCormick, S.J., "Notes on Moral Theology, 1977: The Church in Dispute," *Theological Studies,* XXXVIII (1978), 103; Albert R. DiIanni, S.M., "The Direct/Indirect Distinction in Morals," *Thomist,* XLI (1977), 350–80.

8. Paul Ramsey, *The Just War: Force and Moral Responsibility* (New York: Charles Scribner's Sons, 1968), 55, 142, 143, 475, et passim.

9. Rolf Hochhuth, *Soldiers: An Obituary for Geneva,* trans. Robert David MacDonald (New York: Grove Press, 1968), 208. The formulation of the ideas in this paragraph is indebted to some lectures on war by Michael Walzer at Harvard University, Fall, 1972. The substance of these lectures appears in Walzer, *Just and Unjust Wars.* See Ramsey, *The Just War,* 144, cf. 475; James T. Johnson, "Toward Reconstructing the *jus ad bellum,*" *Monist,* LVII (1973), 461–88.

10. Quentin L. Quade, "Civil Disobedience and the State," *Worldview,* X (November, 1967), 4–9; Johnson, "Just War Theory," 42; Paolucci (ed.), *Political Writings of St. Augustine,* 163–66, et passim; Johnson, "Toward Reconstructing the *jus ad bellum,*" 487 n. See also Richard Neuhaus' suggestions in Peter L. Berger and Richard J. Neuhaus, *Movement and Revolution* (Garden City, N.Y.: Doubleday, 1970), 164–78.

11. See John A. Rohr, *Prophets Without Honor: Public Policy and the Selective Conscientious Objector* (Nashville: Abingdon Press, 1971), 98; Ramsey, *The Just War,* 98, 274–75, 360, et passim.

12. Johnson, "Just War Theory," 44, and "Toward Reconstructing the *jus ad bellum,*" 487 (where this criterion is not included in the reconstruction).

13. McKenna, "Ethics and War," 650. . . . This quotation comes from Francis Lieber, "Laws and Usages of War," lecture given at Columbia Law School, December 3, 1861.

14. Ralph Potter, "The Moral Logic of War," *McCormick Quarterly* 23 (1970), 219. (See this volume, p. 207. —Ed.)

15. Ramsey, *The Just War,* 195.

16. McKenna, "Ethics and War," 652.

17. Ramsey, *The Just War,* 152; Rawls, *A Theory of Justice,* 379. See James F. Childress, "Francis Lieber's Interpretation of the Laws of War: General Orders No. 100 in the Context of His Life and Thought," *American Journal of Jurisprudence,* XXI (1976), 49, 63–65. On the dangers of an excessive emphasis on the end of peace, see Johnson, "Just War Theory," 43–44.

18. Frits Kalshoven, *The Law of Warfare: A Summary of Its Recent History and Trends in Development* (Leiden: A. W. Sijthoff, 1973), 102.

19. See Ramsey, *The Just War,* 397, 502, et passim.

20. *Weapons That May Cause Unnecessary Suffering or Have Indiscriminate Effects* (Geneva: International Committee of the Red Cross, 1973), 12–13. The quoted passage is from the St. Petersburg Declaration of 1868. See also Morris Greenspan, *Soldier's Guide to the Laws of War* (Washington, D.C.: Public Affairs Press, 1969).

21. See Johnson, "Just War Theory," 42, 46.

22. D. Thomas O'Connor, "A Reappraisal of the Just-War Tradition," *Ethics,* LXXXIV (1974), 167–73.

23. Paul Ramsey, *War and the Christian Conscience: How Shall Modern War Be Conducted Justly?* (Durham, N.C.: Dube University Press, 1961), 15, 28, 31–32.

24. Walters, "Five Classic Just-War Theories," 316–20; William V. O'Brien, "Morality and War: The Contribution of Paul Ramsey," in James Johnson and David Smith (eds.), *Love and Society: Essays in the Ethics of Paul Ramsey* (Missoula, Mont.: Scholars Press, 1974), 181; Joel Feinberg, "On Being 'Morally Speaking a Murderer.' " in Judith J. Thomson and Gerald Dworkin (eds.), *Ethics* (New York: Harper and Row, 1968), 295–97.

25. See A. I. Melden, *Rights and Right Conduct* (Oxford: Blackwell, 1959).

26. For a discussion of legitimating and restraining functions of just-war theories, see Walters, "Five Classic Just-War Theories," 414–418, et passim.

27. Similar criticisms were offered by John Howard Yoder in an exchange in "Can Contemporary Armed Conflicts Be Just?" [Evening Dialogue at the Woodrow Wilson Center of the Smithsonian Institution, Washington, D.C., October 5, 1978]. Yoder, James T. Johnson, and I presented papers, to which Bryan Hehir and Seymour Siegel responded. Since at that time and subsequently John Howard Yoder's similar criticisms emerged in the context of an oral debate, I do not wish to suggest that he holds them in the form they take in this essay.

28. See Ramsey, *The Just War,* Chap. 12: "Can a Pacifist Tell a Just War?"

20

The Challenge of Peace: God's Promise and Our Response

U.S. Catholic Bishops

The Second Vatican Council opened its evaluation of modern warfare with the statement: "The whole human race faces a moment of supreme crisis in its advance toward maturity." We agree with the council's assessment; the crisis of the moment is embodied in the threat which nuclear weapons pose for the world and much that we hold dear in the world. We have seen and felt the effects of the crisis of the nuclear age in the lives of people we serve. Nuclear weaponry has drastically changed the nature of warfare, and the arms race poses a threat to human life and human civilization which is without precedent.

We write this letter from the perspective of Catholic faith. Faith does not insulate us from the daily challenges of life but intensifies our desire to address them precisely in light of the gospel which has come to us in the person of the risen Christ. Through the resources of faith and reason we desire in this letter to provide hope for people in our day and direction toward a world freed of the nuclear threat.

As Catholic bishops we write this letter as an exercise of our teaching ministry. The Catholic tradition on war and peace is a long and complex one; it stretches from the Sermon on the Mount to the statements of Pope John Paul II. We wish to explore and explain the resources of the moral-religious teaching and to apply it to specific questions of our day. In doing this we realize, and we want readers of this letter to recognize, that not all statements in this letter have the same moral authority. At times we state universally binding moral principles found in the teaching of the Church; at other times the pastoral letter makes specific applications, observations and recommendations which allow for diversity of opinion on the part of those who assess the factual data of situations differently. However, we expect Catholics to give our moral judgments serious consideration when they are forming their own views on specific problems. . . .

While this letter is addressed principally to the Catholic community, we want it to make a contribution to the wider public debate in our country on the dangers and dilemmas of the nuclear age. Our contribution will not be primarily technical or political, but we are convinced that there is no satisfactory answer to the human problems of the nuclear age which fails to consider the moral and religious dimensions of the questions we face. . . .

The Presumption Against War and the Principle of Legitimate Self-Defense

71. Under the rubric, "curbing the savagery of war," the council contemplates the "melancholy state of humanity." It looks at this world as it is, not simply as we would want it to be. The view is stark: ferocious new means of warfare threatening savagery surpassing that of the past, deceit, subversion, terrorism, genocide. This last crime, in particular, is vehemently condemned as horrendous, but all activities which deliberately conflict with the all-embracing principles of universal natural law, which is permanently binding, are criminal, as are all orders commanding such action. Supreme commendation is due the courage of those who openly and fearlessly resist those who issue such commands. All individuals, especially government officials and experts, are bound to honor and improve upon agreements which are "aimed at making military activity and its consequences less inhuman" and which "better and more workably lead to restraining the frightfulness of war."[1]

72. This remains a realistic appraisal of the world today. Later in this section the council calls for us "to strain every muscle as we work for the time when all war can be completely outlawed by international consent." We are told, however, that this goal requires the establishment of some universally

recognized public authority with effective power "to safeguard, on the behalf of all, security, regard for justice, and respect for rights."[2] *But what of the present?* The council is exceedingly clear, as are the popes:

> Certainly, war has not been rooted out of human affairs. As long as the danger of war remains and there is no competent and sufficiently powerful authority at the international level, governments cannot be denied the right to legitimate defense once every means of peaceful settlement has been exhausted. Therefore, government authorities and those who share public responsibility have the duty to protect the welfare of the people entrusted to their care and to conduct such grave matters soberly.
>
> But it is one thing to undertake military action for the just defense of the people, and something else again to seek the subjugation of other nations. Nor does the possession of war potential make every military or political use of it lawful. Neither does the mere fact that war has unhappily begun mean that all is fair between the warring parties.[3]

73. The Christian has no choice but to defend peace, properly understood, against aggression. This is an inalienable obligation. It is the *how* of defending peace which offers moral options. We stress this principle again because we observe so much misunderstanding about both those who resist bearing arms and those who bear them. Great numbers from both traditions provide examples of exceptional courage, examples the world continues to need. Of the millions of men and women who have served with integrity in the armed forces, many have laid down their lives. Many others serve today throughout the world in the difficult and demanding task of helping to preserve that "peace of a sort" of which the council speaks. We see many deeply sincere individuals who, far from being indifferent or apathetic to world evils, believe strongly in conscience that they are best defending true peace by refusing to bear arms. In some cases they are motivated by their understanding of the gospel and the life and death of Jesus as forbidding all violence. In others, their motivation is simply to give personal example of Christian forbearance as a positive, constructive approach toward loving reconciliation with enemies. In still other cases, they propose or engage in "active non-violence" as programmed resistance to thwart

aggression, or to render ineffective any oppression attempted by force of arms. No government, and certainly no Christian, may simply assume that such individuals are mere pawns of conspiratorial forces or guilty of cowardice.

74. Catholic teaching sees these two distinct moral responses as having a complementary relationship, in the sense that both seek to serve the common good. They differ in their perception of how the common good is to be defended most effectively, but both responses testify to the Christian conviction that peace must be pursued and rights defended within moral restraints and in the context of defining other basic human values.

75. In all of this discussion of distinct choices, of course, we are referring to options open to individuals. The council and the popes have stated clearly that governments threatened by armed, unjust aggression must defend their people. This includes defense by armed force, if necessary, as a last resort. We shall discuss below the conditions and limits imposed on such defense. Even when speaking of individuals, however, the council is careful to preserve the fundamental *right* of defense. Some choose not to vindicate their rights by armed force and adopt other methods of defense, but they do not lose the right of defense nor may they renounce their obligations to others. . . .

77. None of the above is to suggest, however, that armed force is the only defense against unjust aggression, regardless of circumstances. Well does the council require that grave matters concerning the protection of peoples be conducted *soberly*. The council fathers were well aware that in today's world, the "horror and perversity of war are immensely magnified by the multiplication of scientific weapons. For acts of war involving these weapons can inflict massive and indiscriminate destruction far exceeding the bounds of legitimate defense."[4] Hence, we are warned: "Men of our time must realize that they will have to give a somber reckoning for their deeds of war. For the course of the future will depend largely on the decisions they make today."[5] There must be serious and continuing study and efforts to develop programmed methods for both individuals and nations to defend against unjust aggression without using violence.

78. We believe work to develop non-violent means of fending off aggression and resolving conflict best reflects the call of Jesus both to love and to justice. Indeed, each increase

in the potential destructiveness of weapons and therefore of war serves to underline the rightness of the way that Jesus mandated to his followers. But, on the other hand, the fact of aggression, oppression and injustice in our world also serves to legitimate the resort to weapons and armed force in defense of justice. We must recognize the reality of the paradox we face as Christians living in the context of the world as it presently exists; we must continue to articulate our belief that love is possible and the only real hope for all human relations, and yet accept that force, even deadly force, is sometimes justified and that nations must provide for their defense. It is the mandate of Christians, in the face of this paradox, to strive to resolve it through an even greater commitment to Christ and his message. . . .

79. In light of the framework of Catholic teaching on the nature of peace, the avoidance of war, and the state's right of legitimate defense, we can now spell out certain moral principles within the Catholic tradition which provide guidance for public policy and individual choice.

THE JUST-WAR CRITERIA

80. The moral theory of the "just-war" or "limited-war" doctrine begins with the presumption which binds all Christians: we should do no harm to our neighbors; how we treat our enemy is the key test of whether we love our neighbor; and the possibility of taking even one human life is a prospect we should consider in fear and trembling. How is it possible to move from these presumptions to the idea of a justifiable use of lethal force?

81. Historically and theologically the clearest answer to the question is found in St. Augustine. Augustine was impressed by the fact and the consequences of sin in history—the "not yet" dimension of the kingdom. In his view war was both the result of sin and a tragic remedy for sin in the life of political societies. War arose from disordered ambitions, but it could also be used, in some cases at least, to restrain evil and protect the innocent. The classic case which illustrated his view was the use of lethal force to prevent aggression against innocent victims. Faced with the fact of attack on the innocent, the presumption that we do no harm, even to our enemy, yielded to the command of love understood as the need to restrain an enemy who would injure the innocent.

82. The just-war argument has taken several forms in the history of Catholic theology, but this Augustinian insight is its central premise.[6] In the twentieth century, papal teaching has used the logic of Augustine and Aquinas[7] to articulate a right of self-defense for states in a decentralized international order and to state the criteria for exercising that right. The essential position was stated by Vatican II: "As long as the danger of war persists and there is no international authority with the necessary competence and power, governments cannot be denied the right of lawful self-defense, once all peace efforts have failed."[8] We have already indicated the centrality of this principle for understanding Catholic teaching about the state and its duties.

83. Just-war teaching has evolved, however, as an effort to prevent war; only if war cannot be rationally avoided does the teaching then seek to restrict and reduce its horrors. It does this by establishing a set of rigorous conditions which must be met if the decision to go to war is to be morally permissible. Such a decision, especially today, requires extraordinarily strong reasons for overriding the presumption *in favor of peace* and *against* war. This is one significant reason why valid just-war teaching makes provision for conscientious dissent. It is presumed that all sane people prefer peace, never *want* to initiate war, and accept even the most justifiable defensive war only as a sad necessity. Only the most powerful reasons may be permitted to override such objection. . . .

84. The determination of *when* conditions exist which allow the resort to force in spite of the strong presumption against it is made in light of *jus ad bellum* criteria. The determination of *how* even a justified resort to force must be conducted is made in light of the *jus in bello* criteria. . . .[9]

The Value of Non-violence

111. Moved by the example of Jesus' life and by his teaching, some Christians have from the earliest days of the Church committed themselves to a non-violent lifestyle.[10] Some understood the gospel of Jesus to prohibit all killing. Some affirmed the use of prayer and other spiritual methods as means of responding to enmity and hostility.

112. In the middle of the second century, St. Justin proclaimed to his pagan readers that Isaiah's prophecy about

turning swords into ploughshares and spears into sickles had been fulfilled as a consequence of Christ's coming:

> And we who delighted in war, in the slaughter of one another, and in every other kind of iniquity have in every part of the world converted our weapons into implements of peace—our swords into ploughshares, our spears into farmers' tools—and we cultivate piety, justice, brotherly charity, faith and hope, which we derive from the Father through the crucified Savior. . . .[11]

113. Writing in the third century, St. Cyprian of Carthage struck a similar note when he indicated that the Christians of his day did not fight against their enemies. He himself regarded their conduct as proper:

> They do not even fight against those who are attacking since it is not granted to the innocent to kill even the aggressor, but promptly to deliver up their souls and blood that, since so much malice and cruelty are rampant in the world, they may more quickly withdraw from the malicious and the cruel.[12]

114. Some of the early Christian opposition to military service was a response to the idolatrous practices which prevailed in the Roman army. Another powerful motive was the fact that army service involved preparation for fighting and killing. We see this in the case of St. Martin of Tours during the fourth century, who renounced his soldierly profession with the explanation: "Hitherto I have served you as a soldier. Allow me now to become a soldier of God. . . . I am a soldier of Christ. It is not lawful for me to fight."[13]

115. In the centuries between the fourth century and our own day, the theme of Christian non-violence and Christian pacifism has echoed and re-echoed, sometimes more strongly, sometimes more faintly. One of the great non-violent figures in those centuries was St. Francis of Assisi. Besides making personal efforts on behalf of reconciliation and peace, Francis stipulated that laypersons who became members of his Third Order were not "to take up lethal weapons, or bear them about, against anybody."

116. The vision of Christian non-violence is not passive about injustice and the defense of the rights of others; it

rather affirms and exemplifies what it means to resist injustice through non-violent methods.

117. In the twentieth century, prescinding from the non-Christian witness of a Mahatma Gandhi and its worldwide impact, the non-violent witness of such figures as Dorothy Day and Martin Luther King has had a profound impact upon the life of the Church in the United States. The witness of numerous Christians who had preceded them over the centuries was affirmed in a remarkable way at the Second Vatican Council.

118. Two of the passages which were included in the final version of the *Pastoral Constitution* gave particular encouragement for Catholics in all walks of life to assess their attitudes toward war and military service in the light of Christian pacifism. In paragraph 79 the council fathers called upon governments to enact laws protecting the rights of those who adopted the position of conscientious objection to all war: "Moreover, it seems right that laws make humane provisions for the case of those who for reasons of conscience refuse to bear arms, provided, however, that they accept some other form of service to the human community."[14] This was the first time a call for legal protection of conscientious objection had appeared in a document of such prominence. In addition to its own profound meaning this statement took on even more significance in the light of the praise that the council fathers had given in the preceding section "to those who renounce the use of violence and the vindication of their rights."[15] In *Human Life in Our Day* (1968) we called for legislative provision to recognize selective conscientious objectors as well.[16]

119. As Catholic bishops it is incumbent upon us to stress to our own community and to the wider society the significance of this support for a pacifist option for individuals in the teaching of Vatican II and the reaffirmation that the popes have given to non-violent witness since the time of the council.

120. In the development of a theology of peace and the growth of the Christian pacifist position among Catholics, these words of the *Pastoral Constitution* have special significance: "All these factors force us to undertake a completely fresh reappraisal of war."[17] The council fathers had reference to "the development of armaments by modern science

[which] has immeasurably magnified the horrors and wickedness of war."[18] While the just-war teaching has clearly been in possession for the past 1,500 years of Catholic thought, the "new moment" in which we find ourselves sees the just-war teaching and non-violence as distinct but interdependent methods of evaluating warfare. They diverge on some specific conclusions, but they share a common presumption against the use of force as a means of settling disputes.

121. Both find their roots in the Christian theological tradition; each contributes to the full moral vision we need in pursuit of a human peace. We believe the two perspectives support and complement one another, each preserving the other from distortion. Finally, in an age of technological warfare, analysis from the viewpoint of non-violence and analysis from the viewpoint of the just-war teaching often converge and agree in their opposition to methods of warfare which are in fact indistinguishable from total warfare. . . .

MORAL PRINCIPLES AND POLICY CHOICES

Counter Population Warfare

147. Under no circumstances may nuclear weapons or other instruments of mass slaughter be used for the purpose of destroying population centers or other predominantly civilian targets. Popes have repeatedly condemned "total war" which implies such use. For example, as early as 1954 Pope Pius XII condemned nuclear warfare "when it entirely escapes the control of man," and results in "the pure and simple annihilation of all human life within the radius of action."[19] The condemnation was repeated by the Second Vatican Council: "Any act of war aimed indiscriminately at the destruction of entire cities or of extensive areas along with their population is a crime against God and man itself. It merits unequivocal and unhesitating condemnation."[20]

148. Retaliatory action, whether nuclear or conventional, which would indiscriminately take many wholly innocent lives, lives of people who are in no way responsible for reckless actions of their government, must also be condemned. This condemnation, in our judgment, applies even to the retaliatory use of weapons striking enemy cities after

our own have already been struck. No Christian can rightfully carry out orders or policies deliberately aimed at killing non-combatants.[21]

149. We make this judgment at the beginning of our treatment of nuclear strategy precisely because the defense of the principle of noncombatant immunity is so important for an ethic of war and because the nuclear age has posed such extreme problems for the principle. Later in this letter we shall discuss specific aspects of U.S. policy in light of this principle and in light of recent U.S. policy statements stressing the determination not to target directly or strike directly against civilian populations. Our concern about protecting the moral value of non-combatant immunity, however, requires that we make a clear reassertion of the principle our first word on this matter.

The Initiation of Nuclear War

150. We do not perceive any situation in which the deliberate initiation of nuclear warfare, on however restricted a scale, can be morally justified. Non-nuclear attacks by another state must be resisted by other than nuclear means. Therefore, a serious moral obligation exists to develop non-nuclear defensive strategies as rapidly as possible.

151. A serious debate is under way on this issue.[22] It is cast in political terms, but it has a significant moral dimension. Some have argued that at the very beginning of a war nuclear weapons might be used, only against military targets, perhaps in limited numbers. Indeed it has long been American and NATO policy that nuclear weapons, especially so-called tactical nuclear weapons, would likely be used if NATO forces in Europe seemed in danger of losing a conflict that until then had been restricted to conventional weapons. Large numbers of tactical nuclear weapons are now deployed in Europe by the NATO forces and about as many by the Soviet Union. Some are substantially smaller than the bomb used on Hiroshima; some are larger. Such weapons, if employed in great numbers, would totally devastate the densely populated countries of Western and Central Europe.

152. Whether under conditions of war in Europe, parts of Asia, or the Middle East, or the exchange of strategic weapons directly between the United States and the Soviet Union, the

difficulties of limiting the use of nuclear weapons are immense. A number of expert witnesses advise us that commanders operating under conditions of battle probably would not be able to exercise strict control; the number of weapons used would rapidly increase, the targets would be expanded beyond the military, and the level of civilian casualties would rise enormously.[23] No one can be certain that this escalation would not occur, even in the face of political efforts to keep such an exchange "limited." The chances of keeping use limited seem remote, and the consequences of escalation to mass destruction would be appalling. Former public officials have testified that it is improbable that any nuclear war could actually be kept limited. Their testimony and the consequences involved in this problem lead us to conclude that the danger of escalation is so great that it would be morally unjustifiable to initiate nuclear war in any form. The danger is rooted not only in the technology of our weapons systems but in the weakness and sinfulness of human communities. We find the moral responsibility of beginning nuclear war not justified by rational political objectives.

153. This judgment affirms that the willingness to initiate nuclear war entails a distinct, weighty moral responsibility; it involves transgressing a fragile barrier—political, psychological, and moral—which has been constructed since 1945. We express repeatedly in this letter our extreme skepticism about the prospects for controlling a nuclear exchange, however limited the first use might be. Precisely because of this skepticism, we judge resort to nuclear weapons to counter a conventional attack to be morally unjustifiable.[24] Consequently we seek to reinforce the barrier against any use of nuclear weapons. Our support of a "no first use" policy must be seen in this light.

154. At the same time we recognize the responsibility the United States has had and continues to have in assisting allied nations in their defense against either a conventional or a nuclear attack. Especially in the European theater, the deterrence of a *nuclear* attack may require nuclear weapons for a time, even though their possession and deployment must be subject to rigid restrictions.

155. The need to defend against a conventional attack in

Europe imposes the political and moral burden of developing adequate, alternative modes of defense to present reliance on nuclear weapons. Even with the best coordinated effort—hardly likely in view of contemporary political division on this question—development of an alternative defense position will still take time.

156. In the interim, deterrence against a conventional attack relies upon two factors: the not inconsiderable conventional forces at the disposal of NATO and the recognition by a potential attacker that the outbreak of large scale conventional war could escalate to the nuclear level through accident or miscalculation by either side. We are aware that NATO's refusal to adopt a "no first use" pledge is to some extent linked to the deterrent effect of this inherent ambiguity. Nonetheless, in light of the probable effects of initiating nuclear war, we urge NATO to move rapidly toward the adoption of a "no first use" policy, but doing so in tandem with development of an adequate alternative defense posture.

LIMITED NUCLEAR WAR

157. It would be possible to agree with our first two conclusions and still not be sure about retaliatory use of nuclear weapons in what is called a "limited exchange." The issue at stake is the *real* as opposed to the *theoretical* possibility of a "limited nuclear exchange."

158. We recognize that the policy debate on this question is inconclusive and that all participants are left with hypothetical projections about probable reactions in a nuclear exchange. While not trying to adjudicate the technical debate, we are aware of it and wish to raise a series of questions which challenge the actual meaning of "limited" in this discussion.

—Would leaders have sufficient information to know what is happening in a nuclear exchange?

—Would they be able under the conditions of stress, time pressures, and fragmentary information to make the extraordinarily precise decision needed to keep the exchange limited if this were technically possible?

—Would military commanders be able, in the midst of the destruction and confusion of a nuclear exchange, to maintain a policy of "discriminate targeting"? Can this be done in modern warfare, waged across great distances by aircraft and missiles?

—Given the accidents we know about in peacetime condi-

tions, what assurances are there that computer errors could be avoided in the midst of a nuclear exchange?
—Would not the casualties, even in a war defined as limited by strategists, still run in the millions?
—How "limited" would be the long-term effects of radiation, famine, social fragmentation, and economic dislocation?

159. Unless these questions can be answered satisfactorily, we will continue to be highly skeptical about the real meaning of "limited." One of the criteria of the just-war tradition is a reasonable hope of success in bringing about justice and peace. We must ask whether such a reasonable hope can exist once nuclear weapons have been exchanged. The burden of proof remains on those who assert that meaningful limitation is possible.

160. A nuclear response to either conventional or nuclear attack can cause destruction which goes far beyond "legitimate defense." Such use of nuclear weapons would not be justified.

161. In the face of this frightening and highly speculative debate on a matter involving millions of human lives, we believe the most effective contribution or moral judgment is to introduce perspectives by which we can assess the empirical debate. Moral perspective should be sensitive not only to the quantitative dimensions of a question but to its psychological, human, and religious characteristics as well. The issue of limited war is not simply the size of weapons contemplated or the strategies projected. The debate should include the psychological and political significance of crossing the boundary from the conventional to the nuclear arena in any form. To cross this divide is to enter a world where we have no experience of control, much testimony against its possibility, and therefore no moral justification for submitting the human community to this risk.[25] We therefore express our view that the first imperative is to prevent any use of nuclear weapons and our hope that leaders will resist the notion that nuclear conflict can be limited, contained, or won in any traditional sense. . . .

MORAL PRINCIPLES AND POLICY CHOICES

178. Targeting doctrine raises significant moral questions because it is a significant determinant of what would occur if

nuclear weapons were ever to be used. Although we acknowledge the need for deterrent, not all forms of deterrence are morally acceptable. There are moral limits to deterrence policy as well as to policy regarding use. Specifically, it is not morally acceptable to intend to kill the innocent as part of a strategy of deterring nuclear war. The question of whether U.S. policy involves an intention to strike civilian centers (directly targeting civilian populations) has been one of our factual concerns.

179. This complex question has always produced a variety of responses, official and unofficial in character. The NCCB Committee has received a series of statements of clarification of policy from U.S. government officials.[26] Essentially these statements declare that it is not U.S. strategic policy to target the Soviet civilian population as such or to use nuclear weapons deliberately for the purpose of destroying population centers. These statements respond, in principle at least, to one moral criterion for assessing deterrence policy: the immunity of non-combatants from direct attack either by conventional or nuclear weapons.

180. These statements do not address or resolve another very troublesome moral problem, namely, that an attack on military targets or militarily significant industrial targets could involve "indirect" (i.e., unintended) but massive civilian casualties. We are advised, for example, that the United States strategic nuclear targeting plan (SIOP—Single Integrated Operational Plan) has identified 60 "military" targets within the city of Moscow alone, and that 40,000 "military" targets for nuclear weapons have been identified in the whole of the Soviet Union.[27] It is important to recognize that Soviet policy is subject to the same moral judgment; attacks on several "industrial targets" or politically significant targets in the United States could produce massive civilian casualties. The number of civilians who would necessarily be killed by such strikes is horrendous.[28] This problem is unavoidable because of the way modern military facilities and production centers are so thoroughly interspersed with civilian living and working areas. It is aggravated if one side deliberately positions military targets in the midst of a civilian population. In our consultations, administration officials readily admitted that, while they hoped any nuclear exchange could be kept limited, they were prepared to retaliate in a massive way if

necessary. They also agreed that once any substantial numbers of weapons were used, the civilian casualty levels would quickly become truly catastrophic, and that even with attacks limited to "military" targets, the number of deaths in a substantial exchange would be almost indistinguishable from what might occur if civilian centers had been deliberately and directly struck. These possibilities pose a different moral question and are to be judged by a different moral criterion: the principle of proportionality.

181. While any judgment of proportionality is always open to differing evaluations, there are actions which can be decisively judged to be disproportionate. A narrow adherence exclusively to the principle of non-combatant immunity as a criterion for policy is an inadequate moral posture, for it ignores some evil and unacceptable consequences. Hence, we cannot be satisfied that the assertion of an intention not to strike civilians directly, or even the most honest effort to implement that intention, by itself constitutes a "moral policy" for the use of nuclear weapons.

182. The location of industrial or militarily significant economic targets within heavily populated areas or in those areas affected by radioactive fallout could well involve such massive civilian casualties that, in our judgment, such a strike would be deemed morally disproportionate, even though not intentionally indiscriminate.

183. The problem is not simply one of producing highly accurate weapons that might minimize civilian casualties in any single explosion, but one of increasing the likelihood of escalation at a level where many, even "discriminating," weapons would cumulatively kill very large numbers of civilians. Those civilian deaths would occur both immediately and from the long-term effects of social and economic devastation.

184. A second issue of concern to us is the relationship of deterrence doctrine to war-fighting strategies. We are aware of the argument that war-fighting capabilities enhance the credibility of the deterrent, particularly the strategy of extended deterrence. But the development of such capabilities raises other strategic and moral questions. The relationship of war-fighting capabilities and targeting doctrine exemplifies the difficult choices in this area of policy. Targeting civilian populations would violate the principle of discrimina-

tion—one of the central moral principles of a Christian ethic of war. But "counterforce targeting," while preferable from the perspective of protecting civilians, is often joined with a declaratory policy which conveys the notion that nuclear war is subject to precise rational and moral limits. We have already expressed our severe doubts about such a concept. Furthermore, a purely counterforce strategy may seem to threaten the viability of other nations' retaliatory forces, making deterrence unstable in a crisis and war more likely.

185. While we welcome any effort to protect civilian populations, we do not want to legitimize or encourage moves which extend deterrence beyond the specific objective of preventing the use of nuclear weapons or other actions which could lead directly to a nuclear exchange.

186. These considerations of concrete elements of nuclear deterrence policy . . . lead us to a strictly conditioned moral acceptance of nuclear deterrence. We cannot consider it adequate as a long-term basis for peace.

187. This strictly conditioned judgment yields *criteria* for morally assessing the elements of deterrence strategy. Clearly, these criteria demonstrate that we cannot approve of every weapons system, strategic doctrine, or policy initiative advanced in the name of strengthening deterrence. On the contrary, these criteria require continual public scrutiny of what our government proposes to do with the deterrent.

188. *On the basis of these criteria we wish now to make some specific evaluations:*

1) If nuclear deterrence exists only to prevent the *use* of nuclear weapons by others, then proposals to go beyond this to planning for prolonged periods of repeated nuclear strikes and counterstrikes, or "prevailing" in nuclear war, are not acceptable. They encourage notions that nuclear war can be engaged in with tolerable human and moral consequences. Rather, we must continually say "no" to the idea of nuclear war.

2) If nuclear deterrence is our goal, "sufficiency" to deter is an adequate strategy; the quest for nuclear superiority must be rejected.

3) Nuclear deterrence should be used as a step on the way toward progressive disarmament. Each proposed addition to our strategic system or change in strategic doctrine must be

assessed precisely in light of whether it will render steps toward "progressive disarmament" more or less likely.

189. Moreover, these criteria provide us with the means to make some judgments and recommendations about the present direction of U.S. strategic policy. Progress toward a world freed of dependence on nuclear deterrence must be carefully carried out. But it must not be delayed. There is an urgent moral and political responsibility to use the "peace of a sort" we have as a framework to move toward authentic peace through nuclear arms control, reductions, and disarmament. Of primary importance in this process is the need to prevent the development and deployment of destabilizing weapons systems on either side; a second requirement is to insure that the more sophisticated command and control systems do not become mere hair triggers for automatic launch on warning; a third is the need to prevent the proliferation of nuclear weapons in the international system.

190. In light of these general judgments *we oppose* some specific proposals in respect to our present deterrence posture:

1) The addition of weapons which are likely to be vulnerable to attack, yet also possess a "prompt hard-target kill" capability that threatens to make the other side's retaliatory forces vulnerable. Such weapons may seem to be useful primarily in a first strike;[29] we resist such weapons for this reason and we oppose Soviet deployment of such weapons which generate fear of a first strike against U.S. forces.

2) The willingness to foster strategic planning which seeks a nuclear war-fighting capability that goes beyond the limited function of deterrence outlined in this letter.

3) Proposals which have the effect of lowering the nuclear threshold and blurring the difference between nuclear and conventional weapons.

191. In support of the concept of "sufficiency" as an adequate deterrent, and in light of the present size and composition of both the U.S. and Soviet strategic arsenals, *we recommend:*

1) Support for immediate, bilateral, verifiable agreements to halt the testing, production, and deployment of new nuclear weapons systems.[30]

2) Support for negotiated bilateral deep cuts in the arsenals of both superpowers, particularly those weapons systems which have destabilizing characteristics; U.S. proposals like those for

START (Strategic Arms Reduction Talks) and INF (Intermediate-range Nuclear Forces) negotiations in Geneva are said to be designed to achieve deep cuts;[31] our hope is that they will be pursued in a manner which will realize these goals.

3) Support for early and successful conclusion of negotiations of a comprehensive test ban treaty.

4) Removal by all parties of short-range nuclear weapons which multiply dangers disproportionate to their deterrent value.

5) Removal by all parties of nuclear weapons from areas where they are likely to be overrun in the early stages of war, thus forcing rapid and uncontrollable decisions on their use.

6) Strengthening of command and control over nuclear weapons to prevent inadvertent and unauthorized use.

192. These judgments are meant to exemplify how a lack of unequivocal condemnation of deterrence is meant only to be an attempt to acknowledge the role attributed to deterrence, but not to support its extension beyond the limited purpose discussed above. Some have urged us to condemn all aspects of nuclear deterrence. This urging has been based on a variety of reasons, but has emphasized particularly the high and terrible risks that either deliberate use or accidental detonation of nuclear weapons could quickly escalate to something utterly disproportionate to any acceptable moral purpose. That determination requires highly technical judgments about hypothetical events. Although reasons exist which move some to condemn reliance on nuclear weapons for deterrence, we have not reached this conclusion for the reasons outlined in this letter.

193. Nevertheless, there must be no misunderstanding of our profound skepticism about the moral acceptability of any use of nuclear weapons. It is obvious that the use of any weapons which violate the principle of discrimination merits unequivocal condemnation. We are told that some weapons are designed for purely "counterforce" use against military forces and targets. The moral issue, however, is not resolved by the design of weapons or the planned intention for use; there are also consequences which must be assessed. It would be a perverted political policy or moral casuistry which tried to justify using a weapon which "indirectly" or "unintentionally" killed a million innocent people because they happened to live near a "militarily significant target."

194. Even the "indirect effects" of initiating nuclear war are sufficient to make it an unjustifiable moral risk in any form. It is not sufficient, for example, to contend that "our" side has plans for "limited" or "discriminate" use. Modern warfare is not readily contained by good intentions or technological designs. The psychological climate of the world is such that mention of the term "nuclear" generates uneasiness. Many contend that the use of one tactical nuclear weapon could produce panic, with completely unpredictable consequences. It is precisely this mix of political, psychological, and technological uncertainty which has moved us in this letter to reinforce with moral prohibitions and prescriptions the prevailing political barrier against resort to nuclear weapons. Our support for enhanced command and control facilities, for major reductions in strategic and tactical nuclear forces, and for a "no first use" policy (as set forth in this letter) is meant to be seen as a complement to our desire to draw a moral line against nuclear war.

195. Any claim by any government that it is pursuing a morally acceptable policy of deterrence must be scrutinized with the greatest care. We are prepared and eager to participate in our country in the ongoing public debate on moral grounds.

196. The need to rethink the deterrence policy of our nation, to make the revisions necessary to reduce the possibility of nuclear war, and to move toward a more stable system of national and international security will demand a substantial intellectual, political, and moral effort. It also will require, we believe, the willingness to open ourselves to the providential care, power and Word of God, which call us to recognize our common humanity and the bonds of mutual responsibility which exist in the international community in spite of political differences and nuclear arsenals.

197. Indeed, we do acknowledge that there are many strong voices within our own episcopal ranks and within the wider Catholic community in the United States which challenge the strategy of deterrence as an adequate response to the arms race today. They highlight the historical evidence that deterrence has not, in fact, set in motion substantial processes of disarmament.

198. Moreover, these voices rightly raise the concern that even the conditional acceptance of nuclear deterrence as laid

out in a letter such as this might be inappropriately used by some to reinforce the policy of arms buildup. In its stead, they call us to raise a prophetic challenge to the community of faith—a challenge which goes beyond nuclear deterrence, toward more resolute steps to actual bilateral disarmament and peacemaking. We recognize the intellectual ground on which the argument is built and the religious sensibility which gives it its strong force.

NOTES

1. *Pastoral Constitution of the Church in the Modern World,* par. 79.
2. Ibid., par. 82.
3. Ibid., par. 79.
4. Ibid., par. 80.
5. Ibid.
6. Augustine called it a Manichaean heresy to assert that war is intrinsically evil and contrary to Christian charity, and stated: "War and conquest are a sad necessity in the eyes of men of principle, yet it would be still more unfortunate if wrongdoers should dominate just men." (*The City of God,* Book 4, chap. 15).

Representative surveys of the history and theology of the just-war tradition include: F. H. Russell, *The Just War in the Middle Ages* (New York: 1975); P. Ramsey, *War and the Christian Conscience* (Durham, N.C.: 1961); P. Ramsey, *The Just War: Force and Political Responsibility* (New York: 1968); James T. Johnson, *Ideology, Reason and the Limitation of War* (Princeton: 1975); *Just War Tradition and the Restraint of War: A Moral and Historical Inquiry* (Princeton: 1981); L. B. Walters, "Five Classic Just-War Theories" (Ph.D. Dissertation, Yale University, 1971); W. O'Brien, *War and/or Survival* (New York: 1969); *The Conduct of Just and Limited War* (New York: 1981); J. C. Murray, "Remarks on the Moral Problem of War," *Theological Studies* 20 (1959): 40–61.

7. Aquinas treats the question of war in the *Summa Theologiae,* II–IIae, q. 40; also cf. II–IIae, q. 64.
8. *Pastoral Constitution,* par. 79.
9. For an analysis of the content and relationship of these principles cf.: R. Potter, "The Moral Logic of War," *McCormick Quarterly* 23 (1970): 203–33; J. Childress, "Just-War Criteria," in T. Shannon, ed., *War or Peace: The Search for New Answers* (New York: 1980).
10. Representative authors in the tradition of Christian pacifism and non-violence include: R. Bainton, *Christian Attitudes Toward War and Peace* (Abingdon: 1960), chaps. 4, 5, 10; J. Yoder, *The Politics of*

Jesus (Grand Rapids: 1972), *Nevertheless: Varieties of Religious Pacifism* (Scottsdale: 1971); T. Merton, *Faith and Violence: Christian Teaching and Christian Practice* (Notre Dame: 1968); G. Zahn, *War, Conscience and Dissent* (New York: 1967); E. Egan, "The Beatitudes: Works of Mercy and Pacifism," in T. Shannon, ed., *War or Peace: The Search for New Answers* (New York: 1980), pp. 169–187; J. Fahey, "The Catholic Church and the Arms Race," *Worldview* 22 (1979): 38–41; J. Douglass, *The Nonviolent Cross: A Theology of Revolution and Peace* (New York: 1966).

11. Justin, *Dialogue with Trypho,* chap. 110; cf. also *The First Apology,* chaps. 14, 39.

12. Cyprian, *Collected Letters;* Letters to Cornelius.

13. Sulpicius Severus, *The Life of Martin,* 4.3.

14. *Pastoral Constitution,* par. 79.

15. Ibid., par. 78.

16. United States Catholic Conference, *Human Life in Our Day* (Washington, D.C.: 1968), p. 44.

17. *Pastoral Constitution,* par. 80.

18. Ibid.

19. Pius XII, "Address to the VIII Congress of the World Medical Association," in *Peace and Disarmament: Documents of the World Council of Churches and the Roman Catholic Church* (Geneva and Rome, 1982), p. 131.

20. *Pastoral Constitution,* par. 80.

21. Ibid.

22. M. Bundy, G. F. Kennan, R. S. McNamara, and G. Smith, "Nuclear Weapons and the Atlantic Alliance," *Foreign Affairs* 60 (1982); K. Kaiser, G. Leber, A. Mertes, F. J. Schulze, "Nuclear Weapons and the Preservation of Peace," *Foreign Affairs* 60 (1982): 1157–70; cf. other responses to Bundy article in the same issue of *Foreign Affairs.*

23. Testimony given to the National Conference of Catholic Bishops' Committee during preparation of this pastoral letter.

24. Our conclusions and judgments in this area, although based on careful study and reflection of the application of moral principles do not have, of course, the same force as the principles themselves and therefore allow for different opinions, as the Summary makes clear. (See this volume, pp. 373–74. —Ed.)

25. Undoubtedly aware of the long and detailed technical debate on limited war, Pope John Paul II highlighted the unacceptable moral risk of crossing the threshold to nuclear war in his "Angelus Message" of December 13, 1981: "I have, in fact, the deep conviction that, in the light of a nuclear war's effects, which can be scientifically foreseen as certain, the only choice that is morally and humanly valid is represented by the reduction of nuclear arma-

ments, while waiting for their future complete elimination, carried out simultaneously by all the parties, by means of explicit agreements and with the commitment of accepting effective controls." See *Documents,* p. 240, cited in n. 19 above.

26. Particularly helpful was the letter of January 15, 1983, of Mr. William Clark, national security adviser, to Cardinal Bernardin. Mr. Clark stated: "For moral, political and military reasons, the United States does not target the Soviet civilian population as such. There is no deliberately opaque meaning conveyed in the last two words. We do not threaten the existence of Soviet civilization by threatening Soviet cities. Rather, we hold at risk the war-making capability of the Soviet Union—its armed forces, and the industrial capacity to sustain war. It would be irresponsible for us to issue policy statements which might suggest to the Soviets that it would be to their advantage to establish privileged sanctuaries within heavily populated areas, thus inducing them to locate much of their war-fighting capability within those urban sanctuaries." A reaffirmation of the administration's policy is also found in Secretary Weinberger's *Annual Report to the Congress* (Caspar Weinberger, *Annual Report to the Congress,* February 1, 1983, p. 55): "The Reagan Administration's policy is that under no circumstances may such weapons be used deliberately for the purpose of destroying populations." Also the letter of Mr. Weinberger to Bishop O'Connor of February 9, 1983, was a similar statement.

27. S. Zuckerman, *Nuclear Illusion and Reality* (New York: 1982); D. Ball, "U.S. Strategic Forces: How Would They Be Used?" *International Security* 7 (1982/83): 36; T. Powers, "Choosing a Strategy for World War III," *The Atlantic Monthly,* November 1982, pp. 82–110.

28. Cf. the comments in Pontifical Academy of Sciences "Statement on the Consequences of the Use of Nuclear Weapons," in *Documents* (see n. 19).

29. Several experts in strategic theory would place both the MX missile and Pershing II missiles in this category.

30. In each of the successive drafts of this letter we have tried to state a central moral imperative: that the arms race should be stopped and disarmament begun. The implementation of this imperative is open to a wide variety of approaches. Hence we have chosen our own language in this paragraph, not wanting either to be identified with one specific political initiative or to have our words used against specific political measures.

31. Cf. President Reagan's "Speech to the National Press Club" (November 18, 1981) and "Address at Eureka College" (May 9, 1982), Department of State, *Current Policy* #346 and #387.

21

Reflections on War and Political Discourse: Realism, Just War, and Feminism in a Nuclear Age

Jean Bethke Elshtain

How did we get from Machiavelli to MAD, to Mutual Assured Destruction? The tradition of realism that dominates our thinking about international relations not only presumes but requires a move "from . . . to" in ways I shall take up in the first part of this article as I examine realism's givens in light of feminist questions. In part two, I assay the most important historic contender against realism's discursive hegemony, just-war theory, with similar questions in mind. Because the central markers of realist and just-war thinking are well known, . . . I shall concentrate on rethinking the too-thinkable—exposing the presumptions that get wheeled into place when the matter at hand is collective violence. As the argument in parts one and two unfolds, feminism as a critical lever gives way to contemporary feminisms as articulated positions. I note the ways in which feminist thinking on war and politics may get stuck within received discursive forms, reproducing presumptions that deepen rather than challenge the present order.[1] I conclude with an interpretation of Hannah Arendt's *On Violence*, a text with animating symbols and images that suggest an alternative discourse.

WHAT MAKES REALISM RUN

Realism's bracing promise is to spring politics free from the constraints of moral judgment and limitation, thereby assuring its autonomy as historic force and discursive subject-matter, and to offer a picture of the world of people and states as they really are rather than as we might yearn for them to be. . . . The genealogy of realism as international relations, although acknowledging antecedents, gets down to serious business with Machiavelli, moving on to theorists of sovereignty and apologists for *raison d'état,* and culminating, in its early modern forms, with Hobbes's *Leviathan* before continuing the trek into the present. The contemporary realist locates himself inside a potent, well-honed tradition. Realist thinkers exude the confidence of those whose narrative long ago "won the war." Realism's hegemony means that alternatives to realism are evaluated from the standpoint of realism, cast into a bin labeled idealism that, for the realist, is more or less synonymous with dangerous if well-intentioned naiveté.[2]

But is the realist throne that secure? We are familiar with what modern realism presumes: a world of sovereign states as preposited ontological entities, each seeking either to enhance or to secure its own power. State sovereignty is the motor that moves the realist system as well as its (nearly) immutable object. Struggle is endemic to the system and force is the court of last resort. It cannot be otherwise, for states exist in a condition of anarchy in relation to one another. Wars will and must occur because there is nothing to prevent them. On one level, then, realism is a theory pitched to structural imperatives that are said to bear on all actors in the international arena. No state, argues the realist, can reasonably or responsibly entertain the hope that through actions it takes, or refrains from taking, it may transform the wider context. Given that context, conflict is inevitable. There is nothing to prevent wars. The only logical solution to this unhappy state of affairs is a unitary international order to remedy international chaos. . . .[3]

Historical realism involves a way of thinking—a set of presumptions about the human condition that secretes images of men and women and the parts they play in the human drama; and, as well, a potent rhetoric. Whether in its uncompromising Hobbesian version or the less remorseless Machiavellian narrative, realism exaggerates certain features of the human condition and downgrades or ignores others.[4] Interpreting foundational realist texts from a vantage point informed by feminist concerns, one is struck by the suppression and denial of female images and female-linked imperatives, hence alert to the restricted and oversimplifying terms through which realism constitutes symbolism and narrative roles more generally.

For example, Hobbes describes a world of hostile monads whose relations are dominated by fear, force, and instrumental calculation. Yet (and almost simple-mindedly) we know this to be anthropologically false. From the simplest tribal beginnings to the most complex social forms, women have had to tend to infants—no matter what the men were up to—if life was to go on in any sustained manner. That important features of the human condition are expunged from Hobbes's universe suggests that his realism is a dramatic distortion rather than a scientific depiction of the human condition at rock bottom. To acknowledge this by insisting that the state of nature is an analytic fiction fails to address the concerns I raise here. Fictions are also truths and what gets left out is often as important as what is put in and assumed.

To be sure, the contemporary realist is unlikely to endorse a full constellation of Hobbesian presumptions. He might reject Hobbes's vision of the state of nature, and his depiction of social relations, as dire and excessive. It is likely, however, that he would continue to affirm the wider conclusions Hobbes drew by analogy from the miserable condition of human beings in the state of nature to the unrelenting fears and suspicions of states in their relations to one another. Yet it seems plausible that if Hobbes omitted central features of human existence internal to civil societies and families, perhaps he is guilty of similar one-sidedness in his characterization of the world of states. To take up this latter possibility is to treat Hobbes's realism as problematic, not paradigmatic.

Machiavelli goes down more smoothly in large part because we have internalized so much of his legacy already. We all know the story. Human beings are inconstant and trustworthy only in their untrustworthiness. Political action cannot be judged by the standards of Christian morality. Civic virtue requires troops "well disciplined and trained" in times of peace in order to prepare for war: This is a "necessity," a law of history.[5] *Si vis pacem, para bellum,* a lesson successive generations (or so the story goes) must learn, though some tragically learn it too late, others in the nick of time.

Machiavelli's narrative revolves around a public-private split in and through which women are constituted, variously, as mirrors to male war-making (a kind of civic cheerleader) or as a collective "other," embodying the softer values and virtues out of place within, and subversive of, *Realpolitik.*[6] Immunized from political action, the realist female may honor the Penates but she cannot embark on a project to bring her values to bear on the civic life of her society. J. G. A. Pocock calls Machiavelli's "militarization of citizenship" a potent legacy that subverts (even for some feminists, as I argue below) consideration of alternatives that do not bind civic and martial virtue together. Military preparedness, in this narrative, becomes the sine qua non of a viable polity. Although women cannot embody armed civic virtue, a task for the man, they are sometimes drawn into the realist picture more sharply as occasions for war (we must fight to protect her), as goads to action, as designated weepers over the tragedies war trails in its wake, or, in our own time, as male prototypes mobilized to meet dwindling "manpower" needs for the armed forces.[7]

Rethinking realism using feminist questions defamiliarizes its central categories: the male *homme de guerre* retains his preeminent role, to be sure, but we recognize explicitly the ways in which his soldierly virilization is linked to the realist woman's privatization, and so on. But matters are never quite so simple. There are variants of modern feminist argumentation indebted to realist discourse in its Hobbesian and Machiavellian modes respectively.[8]

Hardline feminist realists, for example, endorse a Hobbesian social ontology and construe politics as a battleground, the continuation of war by war-like means. They advise women to learn to "fight dirty." Making generous use of military metaphors (Who is the Enemy? Where is he located?), Hobbesian feminists declare politics and political theory inevitably a "paradigm case of the Oppressor and the

Oppressed."[9] There is tough talk about sex-war, shock troops, and the need for women to be integrated into the extant power structure construed as the aggregate of all those who defend law and order, wear uniforms, or carry guns for a living—"the national guard . . . state troopers . . . sheriffs." Women are enjoined to prepare for combat as the only way to end their "colonization."[10]

Such feminist realists share with their Hobbesian forefather a self-reproducing discourse of fear, suspicion, anticipated violence, and force to check-mate force. Their discussions are peppered with worst-case scenarios and proclamations of supreme emergency that reaffirm the bleakest images of "the enemy" and pump up the will to power of combatants. Possibilities for reciprocity between men and women, or for a politics not reducible to who controls or coerces whom, are denied in much the same way Hobbes eliminates space for any noninstrumental human relations.

This hardline position is less important, however, than the modified realism, more Machiavellian in its claims and categories, expressed in a 1981 legal brief filed by the National Organization for Women as part of a challenge to all-male military registration.[11] Beginning with the claim that compulsory, universal military service is central to the concept of citizenship in a democracy, NOW buttresses an ideal of armed civic virtue. If women are to gain "first-class citizenship" they, too, must have the right to fight. Laws excluding women from draft registration and combat duty perpetuate "archaic notions" of women's capabilities; moreover, "devastating long-term psychological and political repercussions" are visited upon women given their exclusion from the military of their country.[12]

NOW's brand of equal opportunity or integrationist feminism here loses a critical edge, functioning instead to reinforce "the military as an institution and militarism as an ideology" by perpetuating "the notion that the military is so central to the entire social order that it is only when women gain access to its core that they can hope to fulfill their hopes and aspirations."[13] In its deep structure, NOW's legal narrative is a leap out of the female/private side of the public/private divide basic to Machiavellian realism and straight into the arms of the hegemonic male whose sex-linked activities are valorized thereby. Paradoxically, NOW's repudiation of "archaic notions of women's role" becomes a tribute to "archaic notions of men's role." Because of the indebtedness of their discourse to presumptions geared historically against women and the values to which they are symbolically if problematically linked, feminist realism, whether in its Hobbesian or less extreme "armed civic virtue" forms, fails to provide a sustained challenge to the Western narrative of war and politics. Ironically, female-linked symbolism is once again suppressed or depreciated this time under a feminist imprimatur as a male-dominant ideal—the "dirty fighter" or the "citizen-warrior" is urged on everyone.

JUST WARS AS MODIFIED REALISM

In a world organized along the lines of the realist narrative, there are no easy ways out. There is, however, an alternative tradition to which we in the West have sometimes repaired either to challenge or to chasten the imperatives realism claims merely to describe and denies having in any sense wrought.

Just-war theory grows out of a complex genealogy, beginning with the pacifism and withdrawal from the world of early Christian communities through later compromises with the world as Christianity took institutional form. The Christian saviour was a "prince of peace" and the New Testament Jesus deconstructs the powerful metaphor of the warrior central to Old Testament narrative. He enjoins Peter to sheath his sword; he devirilizes the image of manhood; he tells his followers to go as sheep among wolves and to offer their lives, if need be, but never to take the life of another in violence. From the beginning, Christian narrative presents a pacific ontology, finding in the "paths of peace" the most natural as well as the most desirable way of being. Violence must justify itself before the court of nonviolence.

Classic just-war doctrine, however, is by no means a pacifist discourse.[14] St. Augustine's *City of God,* for example, distinguishes between legitimate and illegitimate use of collective violence. Augustine denounces the *Pax Romana* as a false peace kept in place by evil means and indicts Roman imperialist wars as paradigmatic instances of unjust war. But he defends, with regret, the possibility that a war may be just if it is waged in defense of a common good and to protect the innocent from certain destruction. As elaborated over the centuries, noncombatant immunity gained a secure niche as the most important of *jus in bello* rules [;] responding to unjust aggression is central [to the] *jus ad bellum.* Just-war thinking requires that moral considerations enter into all determinations of collective violence, not as a post hoc gloss but as a serious ground for making political judgments.

In common with realism, just-war argument secretes a broader worldview, including a vision of domestic politics. Augustine, for example, sees human beings as innately social. It follows that all ways of life are laced through with moral rules and restrictions that provide a web of social order not wholly dependent on external force to keep itself intact. Augustine's household, unlike Machiavelli's private sphere, is "the beginning or element of the city" and domestic peace bears a relation to "civic peace."[15] The sexes are viewed as playing complementary roles rather than as segregated into two separate normative systems governed by wholly different standards of judgment depending upon whether one is a public man or a private woman.

Just-war discourse, like realism, has a long and continuing history; it is a gerrymandered edifice scarred by social transformation and moral crisis. A specific strength embedded in its ontology of peace is the vantage point it affords with reference to social arrangements, one from which its adherents frequently assess what the world calls peace and find it wanting. From Augustine's thunderings against the *Pax Romana* to John Paul II's characterization of our present armed-to-the-teeth peace as the continuation of war by other means—not war's opposite but one of the forms war takes in the modern world—just-war thinking has, from time to time, offered a critical discursive edge.[16]

My criticisms of just war are directed to two central concerns: One flows directly from just-war teaching; the other involves less explicit filiations. I begin with the latter, with cultural images of males and females rooted, at least in part, in just-war discourse. Over time, Augustine's moral householders (with husbands cast as just, meaning neither absolute nor arbitrary heads) gave way to a discourse that more sharply divided males and females, their honored activities, and their symbolic force. Men were constituted as just Christian warriors, fighters, and defenders of righteous causes. Women, unevenly and variously depending upon social location, got solidified into a culturally sanctioned vision of virtuous, nonviolent womanhood that I call the "beautiful soul," drawing upon Hegel's *Phenomenology*.

The tale is by no means simple but, by the late eighteenth century, "absolute distinctions between men and women in regard to violence" had come to prevail.[17] The female beautiful soul is pictured as frugal, self-sacrificing, and, at times, delicate. Although many women empowered themselves to think and to act on the basis of this ideal of female virtue, the symbol easily slides into sentimentalism. To "preserve the purity of its heart," writes Hegel, the beautiful soul must flee "from contact with the actual world."[18] In matters of war and peace, the female beautiful soul cannot put a stop to suffering, cannot effectively fight the mortal wounding of sons, brothers, husbands, fathers. She continues the long tradition of women as weepers, occasions for war, and keepers of the flame of nonwarlike values.

The just warrior is a complex construction, an amalgam of Old Testament, chivalric, and civic republican traditions. He is a character we recognize in all the statues on all those commons and greens of small New England towns: the citizen-warrior who died to preserve the union and to free the slaves. Natalie Zemon Davis shows that the image of warlike manliness in the later Middle Ages and through the seventeenth century was but one male ideal among many, having to compete, for example, with the priest and other religious who foreswore use of their "sexual instrument" and were forbidden to shed blood. However, "male physical force could sometimes be moralized" and "thus could provide the foundation for an ideal of warlike manliness."[19] This moralization of collective male violence held sway and continues to exert a powerful fascination and to inspire respect.

But the times have outstripped beautiful souls and just warriors alike; the beautiful soul can no longer be protected in her virtuous privacy. Her world, and her children, are vulnerable in the face of nuclear realities. Similarly, the just warrior, fighting fair and square by the rules of the game, is a vision enveloped in the heady mist of an earlier time. War is more and more a matter of remote control. The contemporary face of battle is anomic and impersonal, a technological nightmare, as weapons technology obliterates any distinction between night and day, between the "front" and the "rear." Decades before laser weapons, however, the reality of battle had undermined the ideal of the warrior. World War I constituted the foot-soldier as cannon-fodder. In the first day of the Battle of the Somme, July 1, 1916, 110,000 British men got out of the trenches and began to walk forward along a thirteen-mile front. They had no visible enemy to fight; they wore number tags hung around their necks; 60,000 were dead by the end of the day.

A just war requires agents to carry out its purposes. But if the warrior no longer serves as an avatar of justice, how is war itself to claim this imprimatur? If the present human condition can be described as the continuation of war by other means, a false peace, how can human agents legitimate their aims in the waging of a real war rather than the maintenance of a bogus peace? Does it make sense any longer to construe war as a coherent entity at all? These questions take me to my criticisms of just-war argument in our time.

Just-war discourse from its inception recognized the rights of political entities to self-defense. The moral requirements for waging war have also remained essentially unchanged from the fourth century to the present. Over time, of course, much has changed including the nature of political bodies, the context of international life, and the totalistic deadliness of weapons. Faced with historic transformations of such awesome magnitude, just-war thinkers seek valiantly to apply the appropriate rules to cover increasingly horrific situations. All agree that violence is regrettable, tragic, and to be avoided devoutly. But much slips through the cracks when one gets down to hard cases.

For example, in Michael Walzer's *Just and Unjust Wars,* the most lucid modern treatment of the topic by a nontheologian, queries concerning past practice (the British decision to engage in saturation bombing of German cities during World War II) and present policy (nuclear deterrence theory) are assessed on consequentialist criteria that frequently override the deontological formulae of classic just-war teaching (though it, too, required projections of consequence in certain situations). For example, Walzer justifies, with regret, British saturation bombing of German cities in light of the

Nazi threat and given the predictable outcome should Britain fall to Germany. Present threat and future danger override *jus in bello* rules.[20] By declaring Nazism an "immeasurable evil," Walzer foreordains his judgment: "Immeasurable" is an absolute and the "determinate crime" of terror bombing is clearly a lesser evil—it must be the way the issues get framed.

By continually adjusting to the realities of total war, just-war discourse is hard to distinguish from modified realism. I noted the example from World War II above in part because Walzer proclaims the present moment one of continuing "supreme emergency," analogous to the Nazi peril. If what we've got is supreme emergency, what we need—nuclear deterrence—is inexorable. Once again, Walzer regrets his own conclusion. Deterrence is a "bad way" of "coping" with supreme emergency but "there may well be no other that is practical in a world of sovereign and suspicious states. We threaten evil in order not to do it."[21]

Despite the impressive and determined efforts of Walzer, the U.S. Catholic Bishops, and others, the just-war frame is stretched to the breaking point as it can no longer provide a coherent picture of its discursive object—war in any conventional sense. Take, for example, Walzer's discussion of American use of the atomic bombs on Hiroshima and Nagasaki, unjustifiable, he argues, within a just-war frame. He goes on to ask: "How did the people of Hiroshima forfeit their rights?"[22] The language of rights and their forfeiture is impoverished in this context, inadequate to describe what happened on those dreadful days. The shakiness of just-war discourse, then, is forced upon us by "the nature of the modern state combined with the nature of modern total war."[23] In a twilight zone of false peace, with war deeply rooted inside the infrastructure of the modern state, the discourses of just war and realism link up to confront jointly the seemingly intractable present. . . .

Few feminist writers on war and peace take up just-war discourse explicitly. There is, however, feminist theorizing that may aptly be situated inside the broader frames of beautiful souls and just warriors as features of inherited discourse. This strongest contemporary feminist statement of a beautiful soul position involves celebrations of a "female principle" as ontologically given and superior to its dark opposite, masculinism. (The male "other" in this vision is not a just warrior but a dangerous beast.) The evils of the social world are traced in a free-flowing conduit from masculinism to environmental destruction, nuclear energy, wars, militarism, and states. In utopian evocations of "cultural feminism," women are enjoined to create separate communities to free themselves from the male surround and to create a "space" based on the values they embrace. An essentially Manichean vision, the discourse of feminism's beautiful souls contrasts images of "caring" and "connected" females in opposition to "callous" and "disconnected" males. Deepening sex segregation, the separatist branch of cultural feminism draws upon, yet much exaggerates received understandings of the beautiful soul.[24]

A second feminist vision indebted implicitly to the wider discursive universe of which just-war thinking is a part features a down-to-earth female subject, a soul less beautiful than virtuous in ways that locate her as a social actor. She shares just war's insistence that politics must come under moral scrutiny. Rejecting the hard-line gendered epistemology and metaphysic of an absolute beautiful soul, she nonetheless insists that ways of knowing flow from ways of being in the world and that hers have vitality and validity in ways private and public. The professed ends of feminists in this loosely fitting frame locate the woman as a moral educator and a political actor. She is concerned with "mothering," whether or not she is a biological mother, in the sense of protecting society's most vulnerable members without patronizing them. She thinks in terms of human dignity as well as social justice and fairness. She also forges links between "maternal thinking" and pacifist or nonviolent theories of conflict without presuming that it is possible to translate easily particular maternal imperatives into a public good.[25]

The pitfalls of this feminism are linked to its intrinsic strengths. By insisting that women are in and of the social world, its framers draw explicit attention to the context within which their constituted subjects act. But this wider surround not only derogates maternal women, it bombards them with simplistic formulae that equate "being nice" with "doing good." Even as stereotypic maternalisms exert pressure to sentimentalize, competing feminisms are often sharply repudiating, finding in any evocation of "maternal thinking" a trap and a delusion. A more robust concept of the just (female) as citizen is needed to shore up this disclosure, a matter I take up below.

RESCUING POLITICS FROM WAR: HANNAH ARENDT'S HOPE

Hannah Arendt's attempt to rescue politics from war deepens an important insight of just-war theory—underdeveloped in the theory itself—by insisting that the problem lies not only in the compulsions of international relations but in that ordering of modern, technological, society just-war thinkers call a "false" or "armed" peace. Dulled by the accretion of tropes, truths, necessities, and concepts that help us talk ourselves into war, situated inside a world of armed peace, Norman Mailer's claim in 1948 that "the ultimate purpose" of modern society is continuation of the army by other means seems exaggerated but not altogether far-fetched.[26] Michel Foucault, too, argues that 'politics' (the single quotes are his) "has been conceived as a continuation, if not exactly and directly of war, at least of the military model as a fundamental means of preventing civil disorder. Politics . . . sought to implement the mechanism of the perfect army, of the disciplined mass of the docile, useful troop," and so on.[27]

In an over-coordinated social world, violence may promise a release from inner emptiness or a temporary escape from overplanned pointlessness. Paradoxically, on this view, the routinization of everyday life, much at odds with a heroic or warrior society, nevertheless feeds rather than sates a deeper will to warfare as the prospect of escape from "impersonality, monotony, standardization," the chance to take and to share risks, to act rather than to persist in predetermined behavior.[28] That promise, however, is itself a victim of our armed peace. War technology devirilizes war fighting. The fighter exists for, and is eclipsed by, his weapons and an awesome nuclear arsenal.

More problematic than the inadequacies of just-war doctrine in light of social mimesis of military order, however, is the discourse of "disassociation" evident in contemporary rationalist, scientized realism. Such realists portray themselves as clear-sighted, unsentimental analysts describing the world as it is. At present, hundreds of think tanks, universities, and government bureaucracies support the efforts of "scientifically minded brain trusters" who should be criticized, argues Arendt, not because they are thinking the unthinkable, but rather because "they do not *think* at all."[29] The danger is this: a world of self-confirming theorems invites fantasies of control over events that we do not have. The scientization of rationalist realism eclipses the strengths classical realists could claim, including awareness of the intractability of events and a recognition that relations between and among states are necessarily alienated. Through abstracted models and logic, hyper-rationalism reduces states and their relations to games that can be simulated. Consider the following depiction of Western Europe by a strategic analyst: "Western Europe amounts geographically to a peninsula projecting out from the Eurasian land mass from which large continents of military force can emerge on relatively short notice to invade the peninsula."[30] Western Europe, reduced to an undifferentiated, manageable piece of territory, becomes (theoretically) expendable or indiscriminately usable for our strategic planning.

Modern thinkers of the abstracted unthinkable are not alone in doing violence to complex realities. "If truth is the main casualty in war, ambiguity is another," notes Paul Fussell, and one of the legacies of war is a "habit of simple distinction, simplification, and opposition."[31] Mobilized language, wartime's rhetoric of "binary deadlock," may persist and do much of our thinking for us. The absorption of politics by the language and imperatives of war becomes a permanent rhetorical condition.[32] J. Glenn Gray reminds us that one basic task of a state of war is to portray the enemy in terms as absolute and abstract as possible in order to distinguish as sharply as possible the act of killing from the act of murder. It is always *"the enemy,"* a "pseudo-concrete universal." This moral absolutism is constituted through language: there is no other way to do it. We are invited to hate without limit and told we are good citizens for doing so.

At one time war fighting often served, paradoxically, to deconstruct war rhetoric as soldiers rediscovered concreteness and particularity in tragic and terrifying ways. For example, Erich Maria Remarque's protagonist in *All Quiet on the Western Front* bayonets a frightened French soldier who, seeking refuge, has leapt into the trench beside him. Four agonizing hours later the Frenchman dies and when he has died Remarque's hero, his capacity to perceive and to judge concretely restored, speaks to the man he has killed: "Comrade, I did not want to kill you. . . . But you were only an idea to me before, an abstraction that lived in my mind and called forth its appropriate response. It was the abstraction I stabbed."[33] Gray, similarly, observes that the abstract bloodthirstiness expressed by civilians furthest removed from war fighting was often in contrast to the thinking of front-line soldiers whose moral absolutism dissolved once they met "the enemy" face to face.[34] Because it is now possible for us to destroy the enemy without ever seeing him or her, abstract hatreds are less likely to rub against concrete friction.

If realism's modern offspring invites dangerous disassociations, alternative discourse should be one less available for such purposes even as it offers a compelling orientation to the systemic imperatives at work in a world of "sovereign and suspicious states." Too often alternatives to "thinking war" reproduce problematic features of the discourse they oppose, for example, by insisting that we love (rather than hate) abstract collectives. But "the human race" is a pseudoconcrete universal much like "the enemy." Pitched at a level of abstract universals, the discourse of "the victims" falls apart if one moves to specify connections between its grand vision and political exigencies. Also, an alternative discourse must problematize war narratives with their teleological assurance of triumphant endings and their prototypical figurations of fighting men and weeping women, even as it acknowledges the attraction of the narrative.[35] Admitting rather than denying what Gray calls "the communal enthusiasm and ecstasies of war," we are invited to ask if we might not enlist our energies in some other way. Peace discourse that denies the violent undercurrents and possibilities in everyday life and in each one of us, perhaps by projecting that violence outward into others ("masculinism") is but the opposite side of the hard-line realist coin.

Hannah Arendt's *On Violence* responds to these concerns by exposing our acceptance of politics as war by other means. Arendt asks what historic transformations and discursive practices made possible a consensus "among political theorists from Left to Right . . . that violence is nothing more than the most flagrant manifestation of power?"[36] (The violence

Arendt has in mind is that of groups or collectives, not individual outrage culminating in a single violent act; Melville's *Billy Budd* is her example.) Her answer is multiple: teleological constructions of historic inevitability (known to us as Progress); theories of absolute power tied to the emergence of the nation-state; the Old Testament tradition of God's Commandments that fed command-obedience conceptions of law in Judaeo-Christian discourse; the infusion of biologism into political discourse, particularly the notion that destruction is a law of nature and violence a "life promoting force" through which men purge the old and rotten. All these "time-honored opinions have become dangerous." Locked into dangerously self-confirming ways of thinking, embracing "progress" as a standard of evaluation, we manage to convince ourselves that good will come out of horrendous things; that somehow, in history, the end does justify the means. Both classical liberals and their Marxist adversaries share this discursive terrain, Arendt argues, though she is especially critical of "great trust in the dialectical 'power of negation' " that soothes its adherents into believing that evil "is but a temporary manifestation of a still-hidden good."

By conflating the crude instrumentalism of violence with power, defined by Arendt as the human ability to act in concert and to begin anew, we guarantee further loss of space within which authentic empowerment is possible. In this way violence nullifies power and stymies political being. One important step away from the instrumentalism of violence and toward the possibility of politics is to resist the reduction of politics to domination. Arendt evokes no image of isolated heroism here; rather, she underscores the ways in which centralized orders dry up power and political possibility. If we recognize the terms through and means by which this happens, we are less susceptible to unreflective mobilization and more open to finding and creating public space in the current order. As citizens through their actions break repetitive cycles of behavior, power as the "true opposite" of violence reveals itself.

Arendt's discourse constitutes its subjects as citizens: neither victims nor warriors. She paints no rosy picture of her rescue effort. Just as Gray argues that the will to war is deepened by the emptiness of a false peace, Arendt believes that the greater a society's bureaucratization, the greater will be secret fantasies of destruction. She repudiates grandiose aims and claims, refusing to dictate what politics should do or accomplish instrumentally, for that would undermine her exposé of the future-oriented teleologies on which violence and progress feed. To the extent that we see what she is doing and let it work on us, her symbolic alternative for political being offers a plenary jolt to our reigning political metaphors and categories—state of nature, sovereignty, statism, bureaucratization, contractualism, nationalist triumphalism, and so on. If we remain entrapped in this cluster of potent typifications, each of them suffused with violent evocations or built on fears of violence, we will face only more, and deadlier, of what we've already got. Contrastingly, Arendt locates as central a powerful but pacific image that engenders hope, the human capacity that sustains political being.

Evidence of hopelessness is all around us. The majority of young people say they do not believe there will be a future of any sort. We shake our heads in dismay, failing to see that our social arrangements produce hopelessness and require it to hold themselves intact. But the ontological possibility for hope is always present, rooted, ultimately, in "the fact of natality." Arendt's metaphor, most fully elaborated in the following passage from *The Human Condition,* is worth quoting in full:

> The miracle that saves the world, the realm of human affairs, from its normal, "natural" ruin is ultimately the fact of natality, in which the faculty of action is ontologically rooted. It is, in other words, the birth of new human beings and the new beginning, the action they are capable of by being born. *Only the full experience of this capacity can bestow upon human affairs faith and hope, those two essential characteristics of human existence* . . . that found perhaps their most glorious and most succinct expression in the new words with which the Gospels accounted their "glad tiding": 'A Child has been born unto us.'[37]

The infant, like all beginnings, is vulnerable. We must nurture the beginning, not knowing and not being able to control the "end" of the story.

Arendt's evocation of natal imagery through its most dramatic *Ur*-narrative is not offered as an abstraction to be endorsed abstractly. Rather, she invites us to restore long atrophied dispositions of commemoration and awe; birth, she declares, is a "miracle," a beginning that renews and irreversibly alters the world. Hers is a fragile yet haunting figuration that stirs recognition of our own vulnerable beginnings and our necessary dependency on others. Placed alongside the reality of human beginnings, many accounts of political beginnings construed as the actions of male hordes or contracturalists seem parodic in part because of the massive denial (of "the female") on which they depend. A "full experience" of the "capacity" rooted in birth helps us to keep before our mind's eye the living reality of singularities, differences, and individualities rather than a human mass as objects of possible control or manipulation.[38]

By offering an alternative genealogy that problematizes collective violence and visions of triumph, Arendt devirilizes discourse, not in favor of feminization (for the feminized and masculinized emerged in tandem and both embody dangerous distortions), but politicalization, constituting her male and female objects as citizens who share alike the "faculty of action."[39] At this juncture, Arendt's discourse makes contact with that feminism I characterized as a modified vision of the beautiful soul. Her bracing ideal of the citizen adds political robustness to a feminist picture of women drawn to action from their sense of being and their epistemic and social location. Arendt's citizen, for example, may act from her maternal thinking but not as a mother—an important distinction that could help to chasten sentimentalism or claims of moral superiority.

But war is the central concern of this essay. Does Arendt's discourse offer a specifiable orientation toward international relations? Her discourse shifts the ground on which we stand when we think about states and their relations. We become skeptical about the forms and the claims of the sovereign state; we deflate fantasies of control inspired by the reigning teleology of progress; we recognize the (phony) parity painted by a picture of equally "sovereign states" and are thereby alert to the many forms hegemony can take. Additionally, Arendt grants "forgiveness" a central political role as the only way human beings have to break remorseless cycles of vengeance. She embraces an "ascesis," a refraining or withholding that allows refusal to bring one's force to bear to surface as a strength not a weakness.

Take the dilemma of the nuclear arms race that seems to have a life and a dynamic of its own. From an Arendtian perspective, we see current control efforts for what they are—the arms race under another name negotiated by a bevy of experts with a vested interest in keeping the race alive so they can "control" it. On the other hand, her recognition of the limiting conditions internal to the international political order precludes a leap into utopian fantasies of world order or total disarmament. For neither the arms control option (as currently defined) nor calls for immediate disarmament are bold—the first because it is a way of doing business as usual; the second because it covertly sustains business as usual by proclaiming "solutions" that lie outside the reach of possibility.

Instead, Arendt's perspective invites us—as a strong and dominant nation of awesome potential force—to take unilateral initiatives in order to break symbolically the cycle of vengeance and fear signified by our nuclear arsenals. Just as action from an individual or group may disrupt the automisms of everyday life, action from a single state may send shock waves that reverberate throughout the system. Arendt cannot be pegged as either a "systems dominance" nor "sub-systems dominance" thinker—a form of argumentation with which she has no patience in any case. She recognizes systemic imperatives yet sees space for potentially effective change from "individual (state) action." The war system is so deeply rooted that to begin to dismantle it in its current and highly dangerous form requires bold strokes.

At this juncture, intimations of an alternative genealogy emerge. Freeman Dyson suggests the *Odyssey* or the theme of homecoming rather than the *Iliad* or the theme of remorseless force as a dominant *Ur*-political myth if we break the deadlock of victims versus warriors. Socrates, Jesus of Nazareth, and Nietzsche, in some of his teachings, emerge as articulators of the prototypical virtues of restraint and refusal to bring all one's power to bear. For it was Nietzsche, from his disillusionment, who proclaimed the only way out of "armed peace" to be a people, distinguished by their wars and victories who, from strength, not weakness, "break the sword" thereby giving peace a chance. "Rather perish than hate and fear," he wrote, "and twice rather perish than make oneself hated and feared."[40] Historical feminist thinkers and movements who rejected politics as force take center stage rather than being relegated to the periphery in this alternative story.

To take up war-as-discourse compels us to recognize the powerful sway of received narratives and reminds us that the concepts through which we think about war, peace, and politics get repeated endlessly, shaping debates, constraining consideration of alternatives, often reassuring us that things cannot really be much different than they are. As we nod an automatic yes when we hear the truism (though we may despair of the truth it tells) that "there have always been wars," we acknowledge tacitly that "there have always been war stories," for wars are deeded to us as texts. We cannot identify "war itself" as an entity apart from a powerful literary tradition that includes poems, epics, myths, official histories, first-person accounts, as well as the articulated theories I have discussed. War and the discourse of war are imbricated, part and parcel of political reality. Contesting the discursive terrain that identifies and gives meaning to what we take these realities to be does not mean one grants a self-subsisting, unwarranted autonomy to discourse; rather, it implies a recognition of the ways in which received doctrines, "war stories," may lull our critical faculties to sleep, blinding us to possibilities that lie within our reach.

NOTES

1. A full elaboration of the major theoretical frames of contemporary feminism as political discourse appears in Jean Bethke Elshtain, *Public Man, Private Woman: Women in Social and Political Thought* (Princeton: Princeton University Press, 1981), Chap. 5.
2. This was one of the things I learned in graduate school.
3. Interestingly, Hannah Arendt, in *On Violence* (New York: Harcourt, Brace & World, 1969), seems to endorse this view. Yet she qualifies it and, as I argue in the final section of this article, finally undermines the ground on which such claims are based.
4. I am drawing on portions of *Public Man, Private Woman* for this discussion.
5. Niccolo Machiavelli, *The Prince and the Discourses* (New York: Modern Library, 1950), p. 61.
6. Ibid., p. 503. My views on Machiavelli are not widely shared, especially by those theorists who evoke his name as a father of civic republicanism. Nevertheless, I believe there is textual warrant for my claims. Women, or woman, also gets cast as a symbolic nemesis

in portions of Machiavelli's discourse, but I do not take up that theme here.

7. Nancy Huston, "Tales of War and Tears of Women," *Women's Studies International Forum* 5, no. 3/4 (1982), pp. 271–282, wonderfully evokes women's supporting roles in war narrative.

8. It should be noted that many realists of the "old school" express skepticism concerning the modern hyper-rationalized realism I discuss later on.

9. Ti-Grace Atkinson, "Theories of Radical Feminism," *Notes from the Second Year: Women's Liberation,* ed. Shulamith Firestone (n.p., 1970), p. 37.

10. Susan Brownmiller, *Against Our Will: Men, Women and Rape* (New York: Simon and Schuster, 1975), p. 388.

11. My point here is not to argue either the fairness or the constitutionality of the all-male draft but to examine the kinds of arguments NOW brought to bear in the case. It should also be noted that there was division inside NOW on this matter.

12. The brief is available from the NOW Legal Defense and Educational Fund, 132 West 42nd Street, New York, NY 10036.

13. Cynthia Enloe, *Does Khaki Become YOU? The Militarisation of Women's Lives* (London: Pluto Press, 1983), pp. 16–17.

14. The 1983 Pastoral Letter of the U.S. Bishops on War and Peace restored the pacifist tradition to a place of importance, however. The pastoral is printed in full in *Origins* (May 19, 1983), pp. 1–32.

15. Henry Paolucci, ed., *The Political Writings of St. Augustine* (Chicago: Henry Regnery, 1967), p. 151.

16. John Paul II, "On Pilgrimage: The UN Address," *Origins* 9, no. 42, pp. 675–680.

17. Natalie Zemon Davis, "Men, Women, and Violence: Some Reflections on Equality," *Smith Alumnae Quarterly* (April, 1972), p. 15.

18. G. W. F. Hegel, *The Phenomenology of Spirit,* trans. A. V. Miller (Oxford: Clarendon Press, 1977), pp. 399–400.

19. Davis, "Men, Women and Violence," p. 13.

20. Michael Walzer, *Just and Unjust Wars* (New York: Basic Books, 1977), pp. 251–263. A different view of the process is found in Freeman Dyson's *Disturbing the Universe* (New York: Harper Colophon, 1979). Dyson served in the "Operational Research Section" of British Bomber Command during the war, calculating probabilities for bombing raids without much of a "feeling of personal responsibility. None of us ever saw the people we killed. None of us particularly cared" (p. 30). But his reflections after the fact are mordant. He writes: "I began to look backward and to ask myself how it happened that I got involved in this crazy game of

murder. Since the beginning of the war I had been retreating step by step from one moral position to another, until at the end I had no moral position at all" (pp. 30–31).

21. Walzer, *Just and Unjust Wars,* p. 274.

22. Ibid., p. 264.

23. Gordon Zahn, *Another Part of the War: The Camp Simon Story* (Amherst, Mass.: University of Massachusetts Press, 1979), p. 251.

24. The separatist literature is vast but the strongest statement of its theory remains Mary Daly's works, including *Gyn/Ecology: The Metaethics of Radical Feminism* (Boston: Beacon Press, 1979). A softer version in which men may be redeemable is Helen Caldicott, *Missile Envy* (New York: William Morrow, 1984).

25. This perspective has past and present elaborations. See, for example, Jane Addams, *The Long Road of Women's Memory* (New York: Macmillan, 1916) and Sara Ruddick, "Maternal Thinking," which appears most recently in Joyce Trebilcot, ed., *Mothering: Essays in Feminist Theory* (Totowa, N.J.: Rowman and Allanheld, 1984), pp. 213–230. I have evoked Ruddick's formulation in several of my essays. The strengths and weaknesses of "maternal thinking" as a basis for political action are described in historic depth by Amy Swerdlow in her forthcoming work on the Mothers Strike for Peace.

26. Cited in Paul Fussell, *The Great War and Modern Memory* (Oxford: Oxford University Press, 1975), p. 320.

27. Michel Foucault, *Discipline and Punish* (New York: Vintage Books, 1979), pp. 168–69.

28. J. Glenn Gray, *The Warriors: Reflections on Men in Battle* (New York: Harper Colophon, 1970), p. 224.

29. Arendt, *On Violence,* p. 12.

30. Cited in E. P. Thompson, *Beyond the Cold War* (New York: Pantheon, 1982), p. 10.

31. Fussell, *Great War and Modern Memory,* p. 79.

32. See Fussell's discussion in *Great War and Modern Memory,* p. 108.

33. Erich Maria Remarque, *All Quiet on the Western Front* (New York: Fawcett, 1975), p. 195.

34. Gray, *The Warriors,* p. 135.

35. Huston's "Tales of War, Tears of Women" reminds us of the antiquity and pervasiveness of this narrative in Western history.

36. Arendt, *On Violence,* p. 35.

37. Hannah Arendt, *The Human Condition* (Chicago: University of Chicago Press, 1958), p. 247.

38. Arendt, *On Violence,* p. 81.

39. Arendt makes no gender-based distinction in this faculty though some commentators have argued—I am one of them—that the way she construes social arrangements contains its own built-in,

unacceptable restrictions on action for particular groups and classes. I am not as persuaded of the thorough soundness of this criticism as I once was. The most complete treatment of a strategic doctrine based on neither "warrior" nor "victim" thinking, but drawing from each, is Freeman Dyson's recent *Weapons and Hope* (New York: Basic Books, 1984).

40. Gray cites in full the paragraph from Nietzsche's *The Wanderer and His Shadow* in which he repudiates the corruptions that flow from being hated and feared, pp. 225–26. To be sure, one could count twenty declarations by Nietzsche in praise of war for every one condemning it but even in such passages an ironic ambivalence may be at work. A genealogy that locates Jesus and Nietzsche on the "same side" is provocative and I cannot make a full argument here. But see René Girard, "The Extinction of Social Order," *Salamagundi* (Spring–Summer, 1984), pp. 204–237 for a discussion of the Gospel deconstruction of mimetic (violent) rivalries and the mechanism of the scapegoat on which rests the "false transcendence" of violent systems.

22

In Defense of Creation: The Nuclear Crisis and a Just Peace

The United Methodist Council of Bishops (U.S.A.)

We write in defense of creation. We do so because the creation itself is under attack. Air and water, trees and fruits and flowers, birds and fish and cattle, all children and youth, women and men live under the darkening shadows of a threatening nuclear winter. We call The United Methodist Church to more faithful witness and action in the face of this worsening nuclear crisis. It is a crisis that threatens to assault not only the whole human family but planet earth itself, even while the arms race itself cruelly destroys millions of lives in conventional wars, repressive violence, and massive poverty. . . .

THE HERITAGE OF FAITH AND THE CALL TO PEACE

Biblical Foundations: *Shalom in Creation, Covenant, and Community*

. . . At the heart of the Old Testament is the testimony to *shalom*, that marvelous Hebrew word that means peace. But the peace that is *shalom* is not negative or one-dimensional. It is much more than the absence of war. *Shalom* is positive peace: harmony, wholeness, health, and well-being in all human relationships. It is the natural state of humanity as birthed by God. It is harmony between humanity and all of God's good creation. All of creation is interrelated. Every creature, every element, every force of nature participates in the whole of creation. If any person is denied *shalom,* all are thereby diminished.

To speak of the sovereignty of God over all nations and peoples is to testify to this ordering of the whole creation by the goodness and peaceable will of God. It is therefore to discern the inescapable reality of moral law in the universe. The creation is not a realm of chaos or meaninglessness, however much persons or nations may cause anarchy by their own behavior. This cosmic drama of moral struggle among the nations has been a persistent biblical theme in Methodist teaching about the fallenness of sinful human creatures. . . . Human sinfulness is, according to Scripture, a warrant for government, law enforcement, and defense against enemies—and also a warning against the iniquity of governors themselves.

Throughout both Testaments, there is a dual attitude toward political authority. The powers of government are legitimate expressions of the creation's natural order of political community among God's children, as well as constraints upon human sinfulness. Their authority is thus from God—at least provisionally. Rulers are ordinarily to be obeyed. Taxes are ordinarily to be paid. But the moral law implanted in creation transcends the laws of any state or empire. When governors themselves become oppressive and lawless, when they presume to usurp the sovereignty that belongs to God alone, they are rightly subject to criticism, to correction, and, ultimately, to resistance. . . .

The Old Testament speaks of God's sovereignty in terms of *covenant,* more particularly the "covenant of peace" with Israel, which binds that people to God's *shalom* (Isaiah 54:10; Ezekiel 37:26). In the covenant of *shalom,* there is no contradiction between justice and peace or between peace and security or between love and justice (Jeremiah 29:7). In Isaiah's prophecy, when "the Spirit is poured upon us from on high," we will know that these laws of God are one and indivisible:

> Then justice will dwell in the wilderness,
> and righteousness abide in the fruitful field.

And the effect of righteousness will be peace,
and the result of righteousness, quietness and trust for ever.
My people will abide in a peaceful habitation,
in secure dwellings, and in quiet resting places.
(Isaiah 32:16–18)

Shalom, then, is the sum total of moral and spiritual qualities in a community whose life is in harmony with God's good creation. It indicates an alternative community—alternative to the idolatries, oppressions, and violence that mark the ways of many nations. Israel's mission is to live out that alternative pattern of life in the world. . . .

The sovereignty of God means that vengeance in human hands is evil. When in the Song of Moses Yahweh proclaims "vengeance is mine," the message is not that God is violent but rather that the people of God have no right to usurp God's powers of ultimate judgment (Deuteronomy 32:35). We believe that particular biblical truth is directly relevant to ethical attitudes toward nuclear weapons.

To be sure, the Old Testament tells of much violence and warfare. In Israel's earliest traditions Yahweh is often portrayed as a warrior. God's victory over Pharaoh and the Egyptians to liberate Hebrew slaves discloses God's implacable opposition to oppression and injustice, which violate *shalom.* Exodus is liberation.

But liberation from oppression is hardly on the same moral plane as the building up of standing armies for nationalistic expansion and the oppression of weaker nations. It is when the elders of Israel forsake their moral covenant for warrior-kings that the nation begins its dismal descent into generations of exploitation, repression, and aggression—and then into chaos and captivity. Yahweh, the Creator, the Sovereign One, the transcendent God of the Covenant, becomes reduced to a domesticated and nationalistic idol. Ultimately, as Jeremiah has foreseen, destruction and exile come upon Jerusalem precisely as God's judgment upon nationalistic pride, religious arrogance, and excessive confidence in military power. Exile in Babylon is more than the loss of a war; it is the collapse of an illusion that military power, unrestrained by *shalom,* can offer security, peace, and prosperity.

We must look to the great prophets of that bitter period of Exile for the renewed vision of *shalom.* If Exodus is liberation, Exile is renewal. Ezekiel and Isaiah (40–66) reaffirm God's creation and redemption as universal in scope. Narrow nationalism is repudiated. Servanthood is exalted as the hopeful path to *shalom.*

Swords into plowshares, arms converted to food and death to life, no more wars or training for wars, peaceable kingdoms, joy and peace such that the trees clap their hands, new covenants written on the heart—these are the radiant images of *shalom* at the visionary heights of Old Testament prophecy. . . . The images forecast the coming of One who will be the Prince of Peace.

Jesus Christ is Our Peace

And so he comes. He comes heralded by angels who sing: "Glory to God in the highest, and on earth peace!" He invokes the most special blessings upon peacemakers. He exalts the humanity of aliens. He commands us to love our enemies; for he knows, even if we do not, that if we hate our enemies, we blind and destroy ourselves. *Shalom,* after all, is the heart of God and the law of creation. It cannot be broken with impunity.

There is a stark and sorrowful moment when Jesus, approaching Jerusalem from the neighboring heights, pauses to weep. And why does he weep? He foresees a terrible Day of Judgment when the Holy City itself will be totally leveled to rubble and dust without "one stone upon another." Why? Because the people there, even the most religious people in that supposedly sacred city, do not really know "the things that make for peace" (Luke 19:41–44). That moment is a powerful intimation of what false security policies based upon weapons of mass destruction can lead to. It is a poignant echo of Isaiah's lament from the Lord, the Redeemer, the Holy One of Israel:

> O that you had hearkened to my commandments!
> Then your peace would have been like a river,
> and your righteousness like the waves of the sea.
> (Isaiah 48:18)

New Testament faith presupposes a radical break between the follies, or much so-called conventional wisdom about power and security, on the one hand, and the transcendent wisdom of *shalom,* on the other. Ultimately, New Testament faith is a message of hope about God's plan and purpose for human destiny. It is a redemptive vision that refuses to wallow in doom. The author of the Epistle of James, which has been called "that secret little apocalypse," testifies to the power of this transcendent wisdom:

> The wisdom from above is first pure, then peaceable, gentle, open to reason, full of mercy and good fruits, without uncertainty or insincerity. And the harvest of righteousness is sown in peace by those who make peace.
> (James 3:17–18)

It is just after these verses that James asks: "What causes wars?" There follows a catalogue of human sins: excess passion, covetousness, pride, arrogance, evil judgments against brothers and neighbors.

Paul's letters announce that Jesus Christ is "our peace." It is Christ who has "broken down the dividing wall of hostility," creating one humanity, overcoming enmity, so making peace (Ephesians 2:14–19). It is Christ who ordains a ministry of reconciliation. Repentance prepares us for reconciliation. Then we shall open ourselves to the transforming power of God's grace in Christ. Then we shall know what it means to be "in Christ." Then we are to become ambassadors of a new creation, a new Kingdom, a new order of love and justice (2 Corinthians 5:17–20). It is Christ who has "disarmed the principalities and powers and made a public example of them, triumphing over them in him" (Colossians 2:15). To be citizens of this new Kingdom means that Christians are subject to conflicting loyalties—loyalty to one's nation and its government and a transcending loyalty to the "Governor of the whole universe" (John Wesley's term), whose laws may compel us to challenge our nation and its policies.

In Jesus Christ we know, when confronted with such conflicting loyalties, how costly the grace of God can be. This "only begotten Son" is sacrificed in a controversy with imperial and religious authorities so that we may know the full measure of God's love for us, even in our sinfulness, even when we crucify the Christ in our brothers and sisters. Yet we may still come to know that life never really ends but is transformed by eternal grace. Jesus never resorted to violence in his own defense. Somehow he had the power to forgive even his own killers. The Crucifixion is an eternal testimony to the transcendent power of forgiving love and nonviolence.

The Crucifixion was initially a political event—and a seeming defeat at that—but it quickly became transformed into a theological event, the ultimate act of our redemption. Christ is forever "making peace by the blood of his cross" (Colossians 1:19–20). Beyond all brutality, suffering, and death, God's costly gift of peace awaits us. Peace is the ultimate victory. . . .

THE ETHICAL SPECTRUM ON NUCLEAR WEAPONS

The sevenfold spectrum we offer here is largely concerned with what we . . . [call] the *primal issues:* the elemental questions as to whether any possession or use of nuclear weapons is morally permissible. . . .

Traditional Pacifism

Those who conscientiously repudiate all warfare and weapons of war have a clear answer to the question of nuclear weapons: No—no production, no possession, no deployment, no use. From this perspective, nuclear deterrence is illegitimate and immoral because it rationalizes the possession, if not the use, of the weapons themselves.

We believe the fidelity and endurance of this tradition among a sizable minority of Christians point to a fundamental question of the nuclear age: Can any major war remain non-nuclear? If not, hasn't rejection of war itself become an imperative for all our churches?

Our own United Methodist Church, while never claiming to be one of the historic peace churches or officially pacifist, has adopted by General Conference action a statement of Social Principles that declares:

> We believe war is incompatible with the teachings and example of Christ. We therefore reject war as an instrument of national foreign policy and insist that the first moral duty of all nations is to resolve by peaceful means every dispute that arises between or among them; that human values must outweigh military claims as governments determine their priorities; that the militarization of society must be challenged and stopped; that the manufacture, sale, and deployment of armaments must be reduced

and controlled; and that the production, possession, or use of nuclear weapons be condemned.

Nuclear Pacifism

Some Christians support conventional military forces and remain open to the possible justice or necessary evil of some wars or revolutions but say No to all nuclear wars and weapons. For them the "nuclear threshold" is an absolute moral boundary that must never be crossed. They may appeal to the historic prerequisites of a "just war" in Christian tradition, such as proportionality and civilian immunity, in judging that nuclear weapons are too destructive ever to serve the ends of justice. Or, oppositely, they may come to the conviction that the just-war tradition itself has been made obsolete by the enormity of any nuclear conflict. . . .

Yes/No Deterrence

While nuclear pacifists draw the moral line between conventional and nuclear weapons, others draw the line between *possession* of nuclear weapons and their actual *use.* They say Yes to having them but no to using them. They are prepared to maintain a nuclear arsenal for its presumed deterrent effect but they have absolute scruples against using the weapons.

Among Christian theologians confessing to such an ambiguous stance have been John C. Bennett, former president of New York's Union Theological Seminary, and David Hollenbach. . . . Father Hollenbach's recent book, *Nuclear Ethics,* pleads for a new synthesis of pacifist and just-war thinking. He candidly acknowledges the apparent inconsistency in his position:

> It would be easy to conclude that deterrence and the rejection of use are incompatible were it not for a single, massive historical fact: large numbers of nuclear weapons are already deployed and ready for use by both superpowers. Though incompatible on the level of ideas and logic, deterrence and non-use are concretely and existentially interlocked in our present world. This . . . is a prime example of what it means to live in a world which is not fully rational and which is broken by sinfulness.[1]

Critics of this position have dubbed it "bluff deterrence" . . . because its proponents are not really prepared to retaliate.

The credibility of yes/no deterrence is therefore a vexing question.

No First Use/Deterrence

Another moral boundary is drawn by those who approve of the possession and possible use of nuclear weapons, but absolutely oppose any use of them against a conventional attack. This restriction on nuclear retaliation to only a nuclear attack is termed a "no-first-use" policy.

Such a policy has yet to be adopted by the U.S. government. However, it was strongly recommended in 1982 by four eminent former officials: McGeorge Bundy (National Security Adviser), George F. Kennan (Ambassador to the Soviet Union), Robert S. McNamara (Secretary of Defense), and Gerard Smith (Director of the Arms Control and Disarmament Agency). Their advocacy of a "no-first-use" policy in a *Foreign Affairs* article raised the question as to whether NATO's conventional forces might need strengthening as a precondition of such a policy change. . . .[2]

First Use/Deterrence

A still lower nuclear threshold is advocated by those who want to preserve the option of nuclear retaliation against conventional attack. This has been a major element in U.S. and NATO policy since the early 1960s. That policy has tended to assume the possibility of a limited nuclear war—limited targeting, limited destruction, and the essential survival of belligerent nations.

The mainstream of official U.S. deterrence doctrine for many years has tended to assume not only the continued deployment of nuclear weapons into the far future but also the continuation of the arms race itself and the prospect of limited nuclear wars. Arms control, from this perspective, means "managing" the arms race so that a nuclear balance is maintained between the superpowers. Parity is the norm that matters. The title of a recent Harvard study, *Living With Nuclear Weapons,* suggests this position's skepticism about nuclear disarmament.[3]

This position also finds plausible support in the *jus in bello* norms of proportionality and discrimination as guides for the actual use of nuclear weapons. Thus a Christian case has been made for *counterforce* strategies—restricting the targeting of nuclear weapons to military forces and command centers while sparing civilian populations. Paul Ramsey has long been the most notable exponent of such a case, emphasizing that nuclear weapons cannot now be uninvented; that the moral boundary between nuclear and conventional weapons is not absolute; that "economy of force" should guide the design and possible use of nuclear weapons; and that Christians should be open to the support of new counterforce weapons like the single-warhead "Midgetman," which might be a move away from more-massive yet more-vulnerable strategic weapons such as a ten-warhead MX missile. . . .

[W]e are concerned that the doctrine of nuclear deterrence itself, which some churches justify by the just-war tradition, can be invoked for the most varied moral postures—from mere possession of nuclear weapons to their limited or even total use now, . . . to nuclear superiority and even the hope of victory in a nuclear war. We find no coherence in deterrence.

Counterforce Superiority

While counterforce principles may seek to restrain the destructiveness of nuclear weapons, they may also rationalize opposite tendencies: making the use of such weapons more "thinkable" and building up more-powerful and more-accurate weapons to achieve nuclear superiority. For some Americans, parity with the Soviet Union isn't good enough. Only when the United States can prove its capacity to outstrip the Soviet Union in the arms race will the Soviet Union begin seriously to negotiate arms control and accommodate to the demands of the United States on other issues—or so this position maintains.

In the early 1980s there was talk in high places in the U.S. of achieving a nuclear "war-winning capability." In the face of public criticism, Secretary of Defense Caspar Weinberger in 1983 denied that the U.S. really planned to "win" a nuclear war. The goal was rather to "prevail" in such a war. In 1984 President Reagan moderated his own language to declare that "a nuclear war cannot be won and must never be fought."

We have not been able to discern the difference between "winning" and "prevailing." On occasion, the same policies are propounded with the modest claim that the United States is only trying to restore a balance, which the Soviet Union is alleged to have upset by its own drive for superiority. At times official proponents of counterforce superiority characterize their position as one of "enhancing deterrence." The new counterforce threat, however, goes beyond retaliation against attack. Its very technologies are designed to destroy the adversary's own retaliatory forces—to have "hard-target kill capability," in official jargon. Such weapons tend to destroy confidence in whatever stability there may seem to be in mutual deterrence. Some official counterforce strategists, however, claim that deterrence itself is inadequate or immoral, or soon to be obsolete. Counterforce is thus justified as a critical alternative to deterrence. Once again we are concerned, and we ask all our members to be concerned, about the apparent lack of coherent and consistent guidance of U.S. nuclear weapons policy.

First-Strike Policies

Both the United States and Soviet Union now officially disavow any intention of preparing for a first strike—initiating an all-out nuclear attack that would destroy the other side's strategic nuclear forces and much else besides. In his *Annual Report to the Congress, Fiscal Year 1986*, Secretary of Defense Weinberger claimed: "We do not have, nor do we seek, a first-strike capability; we do not have a 'nuclear warfighting' posture; all of our exercises and doctrines are defensive in nature."[4]

But the Secretary of Defense went on to charge the U.S.S.R. with "development of a potential first-strike force of SS-18s and SS-19s" (heavy land-based missiles). Meanwhile, Soviet leaders regularly charge that the U.S. counterforce weapons (Minuteman III, Tridents, Pershing IIs, MX) amount to a growing first-strike threat against the U.S.S.R. They also remember the years of U.S. nuclear superiority in the 1950s when some American political and military leaders blatantly advocated a preemptive strike.

Whatever the intentions of government leaders, there is mounting evidence of genuine fear and suspicion in each country of first-strike plans on the other side. We believe that the technical characteristics of counterforce weapons—power, speed, unprecedented accuracy—understandably tend to escalate fear and suspicion. Such fear and suspicion are compounded by current efforts to develop space-based "defenses" that, if truly effective, could provide a cover for launching an offensive first strike. . . .

THE IDOLATRY OF DETERRENCE

For forty years the moral function of deterrence doctrine has been to justify the threatened use of nuclear weapons and an unending arms race. . . .

We do not doubt that the threat of nuclear retaliation can be, and has been, a factor inhibiting the resort to nuclear weapons. Fear is a powerful human motive—although its effects are notoriously unpredictable. . . . But we remain profoundly troubled by the military extremities which deterrence doctrines have legitimized if not motivated.

Deterrence has too long been reverenced as the unquestioned idol of national security. It has become an ideology of conformity too frequently invoked to disparage dissent and to dismiss any alternative foreign policy proposals. In its most idolatrous forms, it has blinded its proponents to the many-sided requirements of genuine security. There can be no unilateral security in the nuclear age. Security has become indivisible. Our vulnerability is mutual. Our security must be mutual. Security requires economic strength, environmental and public health, educational quality, social well-being, public confidence, global cooperation. In short, the indispensable moral qualities of security must not be forfeited to an uncontrolled arms race. . . .

Nuclear deterrence has become a dogmatic license for perpetual hostility between the superpowers and for their rigid resistance to significant measures of disarmament. Major General Kermit D. Johnson, former Chief of Chaplains of the U.S. Army, in written testimony submitted to our hearing panel, puts it this way:

> Before any nuclear weapons are ever launched, nuclear deterrence locks us into a permanent state of war, albeit a cold war, with the Soviet Union. They are regarded as an "enemy," imminently deserving of being threatened moment by moment with nuclear destruction. The overall political relationship between the U.S. and the Soviet Union is fixed by this military reality.

This primary reliance on unrelenting terror tends to perpetuate the most distorted and inhuman images of our "enemy." It forsakes the more prudent, positive strategies of offers, inducements, and incentives that might draw on the vast human, economic, and technological resources of the U.S. and its allies. . . .

It is the idolatrous connection between the ideology of deterrence and the existence of the weapons themselves that must be broken. Deterrence must no longer receive the churches' blessing, even as a temporary warrant for the maintenance of nuclear weapons. The interim possession of such weapons for a strictly limited time requires a different justification—*an ethic of reciprocity* as nuclear-weapon states act together in agreed stages to reduce and ultimately to eliminate their nuclear arms. Such an ethic is shaped by an acceptance of mutual vulnerability, a vision of common security, and the escalation of mutual trust rather than mutual terror. It insists that the positive work of peacemaking must overcome the fearful manipulation of hostility.

We believe that neither the U.S. nor any other nuclear power can extricate itself unilaterally from all nuclear perils. Indeed immediate and total nuclear disarmament by the U.S. might well tempt other countries to develop or expand their own nuclear arsenals, thereby increasing the risk of nuclear war. Whatever the objective truth about the effects of deterrence, faith in that doctrine will not die quickly. It will take prudent political leadership in partnership with all other nuclear-weapon states, including "enemies," to conceive and implement step-by-step approaches to disarmament. Prudence is always a moral obligation. . . .

THE ECONOMY

In the 1980s the U.S. federal budget has sharply focused the moral issues of national priorities. Military spending has doubled, amounting to $1.2 trillion in five years. That's about $5,200 for each citizen or more than $20,000 for a family of four. Between 1986 and 1990, $2 trillion more is projected, more than $34,000 for a family of four. In fiscal year 1986 military and related spending will amount to more than half of all discretionary spending by Congress, or more than half of all income tax revenue.[5]

The human costs of this buildup in the name of "defense" are borne most directly by those who are actually most defenseless: the poor, the elderly, and the very young, who are the main targets of severe cuts in social programs. U.S. "rearmament" is being purchased with food stamps, welfare checks, rent subsidies, Medicaid payments, school lunches, and nutrition supplements for poor mothers and their children. Half of the nation's Black children live in poverty, as do two-fifths of all Hispanic children. More than eight million adults are unemployed at a time of purported "recovery."

The productivity of the American economy has seriously slackened during these same years of high military spending. Not so long ago, the U.S. regularly enjoyed the world's highest productivity growth rates. In the past decade, the U.S. has slipped far behind many other industrial nations, failing to match the competition in more and more product lines, incurring enormous foreign trade deficits, and losing millions of industrial jobs.

We believe that industrial engineering in the civilian economy has failed to keep pace for at least three reasons: (1) the disproportionate allocation of scientific and technical personnel to military production; (2) the commitment of seventy percent of government research and development to weapons programs, and (3) the preference of basic U.S. industries for maximum short-term profits at the expense of long-term planning and modernization. Japan is only the most conspicuous example of a nation that, while holding its military spending to low levels, has invested its technological resources overwhelmingly in the civilian economy, thereby dramatically modernizing its industries, innovating products, playing an ascendant role in world trade, and accumulating enormous currency surpluses. Meanwhile, U.S. industries have suffered a loss of efficiency with the aging of machines and facilities and a corresponding loss of competitive prices and quality of goods. It is a sad measure of U.S. economic life at present that only foreign military sales provide a favorable trade category in durable-goods exports.

Even military production itself, however, is more and more revealed as plagued by wasteful management that often defrauds the government, operates without effective competition, and seldom avoids enormous cost overruns.

We believe there is no credible evidence that high levels of military spending contribute to high growth rates in the United States. In fact, the government's own research reports have repeatedly indicated that the civilian economy can generate enough aggregate demand to more than compensate for conversion from military to civilian production. One of the main tenets of communist ideology, especially in the works of Lenin, is that contradictions in capitalist economies drive them to militarism and imperialism. Some American corporation and labor leaders unwittingly take an almost-Leninist line in trying to prove how beneficial military industry is for the economy. We reject such claims. We believe that reduced military spending and conversion to civilian industry could prove extremely salutary to the American economy.

We are strongly committed to restoring the goal of full employment in the United States. We are convinced that, far from helping to solve the problem of unemployment, defense industry is a major part of the problem. Most Pentagon provider industries create fewer jobs per dollar than the median manufacturing industry. The basic reason is the increasingly capital- and technology-intensive nature of weapons production.[6] Switching military expenditures to the private sector could create hundreds of thousands of additional jobs if the nation made a political decision to do so. The safety of roads and bridges could be greatly improved; deteriorating urban infrastructures might be restored; affordable housing might be created; forests and lakes afflicted with acid rain might be saved; and nuclear and other industrial wastes might be more safely stored.

RACE AND THE ARMS RACE

The racial dimensions of this struggle over national priorities are increasingly acute. Approximately 40 percent of the U.S. black population are now concentrated in the deteriorating inner core of twenty cities plagued by severe unemployment, unsafe housing, and inadequate health services. Black unemployment in May 1985 was 15.6 percent compared to 6.2 percent for whites. Black teenage unemployment was 40.4 percent compared to 16.1 percent for white teenagers. Even more disturbing is the trend since 1965: a 22 percent increase in black teenage unemployment, with a scant 1.1 percent increase in white teenage unemployment. The continued movement of industrial jobs to the suburbs swells the ranks of hardcore unemployed among minority dwellers in the inner city.[7]

Without a sharp new governmental focus on inner-city peoples, their economy, and their environment, racial polarization is bound to intensify. In testimony to our hearing panel, Congressman Parren Mitchell of Baltimore spoke of the new "contempt for the poor" in the land, suggesting that "if the arms race were to stop tomorrow," there is no assurance that funds would be transferred to human needs. Minority group leaders report increasing awareness of inflammatory code words and diminished action by government agencies charged by law with enforcing civil rights, not to mention official efforts to reverse the civil rights gains of the past two decades. Clearly the demilitarization of America must be accompanied by a powerful new national commitment to equal opportunity and intergroup dependence for racially disadvantaged peoples.

PSYCHOLOGICAL AND SPIRITUAL DIMENSIONS

The consequent issues of the arms race ultimately have an impact on individual human beings. Systems decisively affect persons. Those charged with direct political and military responsibility for nuclear weapons are peculiarly subject to the strain of psychological contradictions—the rational management of weapons of suicidal terror. As citizens become conscious of the inability of their own powerful government to defend them and to curb the arms race, their personal insecurity and sense of powerlessness tends to increase. The technological complexity of military and arms control issues, the fear that only a few "experts" can cope with them, and the suspicion of being manipulated by propaganda aggravate the feelings of impotence. Economic maladjustments and racial polarization, made worse by the arms race, blight the hopes of many families and youth for a secure and prosperous future. Women are disproportionately victimized by the distortion of economic and social priorities of highly militarized states.

It is, however, the overhanging threat of nuclear annihilation with its impact on attitudes and behavior that has drawn the greatest attention among psychologists in recent years. The "nuclearism" that permeates a whole culture is reflected in what psychiatrist Robert Jay Lifton calls "psychic numbing": a simultaneous denial that the nuclear problem exists and a sense of helplessness to cope with it. "Nuclearism" seems to affect some policy makers rather oppositely. For three decades national security policy has become more and more obsessed with nuclear weapons to the neglect of political and economic factors. "Nuclearism" magnifies the tendency to escape into the wonderland of technology, to construct intellectual defenses behind jargon such as "nuclear exchange" and "strategic defense initiative," and to ignore the uniquely human and spiritual capacities of persons.

As bishops with pastoral responsibility for the whole church, we seek especially to underscore the consequences of "nuclearism" for families and for children. In testimony to our hearing panel, Washington psychiatrist Justin A. Frank pointed to a surprising contradiction. At the very time that anxiety about the arms race seems to have become a forbidden topic among many adults in a kind of "re-emerging Victorianism," field research indicates that the vast majority of children know about the consequences of nuclear war by the time they enter junior high school. A majority of teenagers rate the threat of nuclear war so highly that they do not expect to live out their normal life span. For parents and children to be unwilling or unable to communicate about such fears is a pastoral challenge of greatest importance. . . .

There is a deep-seated fear of "futurelessness" among many people. Some young parents agonize over the question of bringing children into such a world. Student vocational choices seem increasingly bounded by technical fixes and careerist anxieties, which are reinforced by educational pressures at all levels. Adolescent responses include "living in the fast lane" as if there is no tomorrow, cults, drug dependence, despair, and increasing suicide.

For young people and for all Americans, the legitimate need for self-respect as a nation must be lifted above the relentless barrage of aggressive, competitive, and chauvinistic sentiments that assault them not only in political rhetoric but also in commercial, recreational, and even educational institutions. The film and television industries' increasing resort to productions that promote suspicion, animosity, and contempt toward the Soviet Union must be challenged by our churches.

There is a powerful and more hopeful alternative theme in the struggle for nationhood: Working for peace and disarmament is working to strengthen the nation, its resources, its security, and its very soul. There is a heritage of humane values from earlier generations of Americans—values like fairness, pluralism, compassion, generosity, internationalism, rallying to the disadvantaged, a readiness to overcome past enmities, a respect for the rule of law and for peaceful change. Such values help nurture the spirit of reconciliation and the works of peacemaking. They could become once again the main marks of American nationhood. . . .

POLICIES FOR A JUST PEACE

Here we set forth . . . policy alternatives that may best express our own principles of peacemaking. We do so knowing that our knowledge is incomplete, that some Christians will conscientiously hold contrary positions, and that fuller understanding and changing historical circumstances may soon cause us to revise our own recommendations.

TOWARD A NUCLEAR-FREE WORLD

The necessity of reconstructing U.S.A.-U.S.S.R. relations is the crux of the nuclear crisis and an imperative of justice to all earth's peoples. That reconstruction involves developing a regular and systematic pattern of consultation, perhaps including an annual summit conference, between the highest political and military leaders of both countries. It requires a recommitment to substantial scientific, educational, and cultural exchanges.

The politics of reconstruction already have a sound if almost forgotten basis in a U.S.A.-U.S.S.R. agreement negotiated a quarter of a century ago. On September 20, 1961, these two governments signed the Joint Statement of Agreed Principles for Disarmament Negotiations, known as the McCloy-Zorin Agreement. That Agreement coincided with the creation of the U.S. government's Arms Control and Disarmament Agency and facilitated the Limited Nuclear Test Ban Treaty of 1963.

We urge the churches to rediscover the McCloy-Zorin Agreement and to press for government fidelity to it. It was endorsed unanimously by the United Nations General Assembly on December 20, 1961, and has guided UN deliberations on how best to achieve the Agreement's stated goal of general and complete disarmament. The Agreement is both visionary and prudent. It provides for a sequence of stages "within specified time limits," adequate verification and review, equitable balance, and eventual reductions to domestic police forces and an international peace-keeping force. Christians should not lose sight of the Agreement's practical wisdom about the requirements of transition to a peaceable world.

The particular measures we now commend are transitional policies in keeping with the principles of the McCloy-Zorin Agreement. The technical details of particular arms accords are less important than the political achievement of such accords and the direction in which they point. We believe the churches should be prepared to support any one or combination of the following four measures, whichever gives greatest promise of ending the new cold war and reversing the arms race:

1. Comprehensive Test Ban to Inaugurate a Nuclear Freeze. We support the completion at long last of a treaty banning all nuclear weapons testing. This action would redeem the solemn pledge of the 1963 Limited Test Ban Treaty and consummate two decades of nearly successful negotiations suspended in 1982. Such a treaty, perhaps more than any other step, would vindicate and strengthen the Non-Proliferation Treaty and thus help to curb the spread of nuclear weapons. It would do much to halt the development of new nuclear weapons. It is the most concrete step to implement a nuclear freeze, which The United Methodist General Conference supported in 1984—a mutual and verifiable freeze on the testing, production, and deployment of nuclear weapons and of missiles and new aircraft designed primarily to deliver nuclear weapons. We believe it is an evasive tactic to delay a comprehensive test ban over disputes concerning the verification of the 150-kiloton limit of the much less significant Threshold Test Ban Treaty of 1974. It is the occurrence of any major nuclear weapons test that must be verifiable, not the exact measurement of the explosive power of weapons, which should not be exploded at all. There is every reason to have high confidence in the verifiability of any major weapons test.[8]

2. *Consolidation of Existing Treaties and Phased Reductions.* We support an unequivocal reaffirmation of both the purposes and provisions of the ABM Treaty of 1972. Such action would help curb the costly, provocative, and illusory development of new "defensive" missile systems, whether ground-based or space-based. Such a reaffirmation would also help restore the vital role of the Standing Consultative Commission (established by the ABM Treaty) with its grievance procedures, thus defusing the incendiary propaganda on both sides concerning alleged treaty violations. Some updating of the unratified SALT II Treaty could reestablish the baseline principle of parity from which subsequent arms reductions can most readily be negotiated. We support the earliest possible negotiation of phased but rapid reduction of nuclear arsenals, while calling upon all other nuclear-weapon states to agree to parallel arms reductions, to the eventual goal of a mutual and verifiable dismantling of all nuclear armaments. All existing arms control treaties could be further strengthened by accords renouncing research and development of all weapons whose actual deployment is banned by those treaties.

3. *Bans on Space Weapons.* We support agreements banning both offensive and defensive weapons, which now threaten the increasing militarization of space. A ban on the further testing and development of antisatellite (ASAT) weapons would help to restore confidence in the satellite systems that monitor arms treaties and control the deployment of military forces. The U.S.S.R. stopped testing of a rudimentary ASAT system in 1982 and declared a unilateral moratorium as an incentive to negotiations. A ban on space-based "defenses" . . . would forestall their offensive and even first-strike implications, reinforce the ABM Treaty, facilitate negotiations on offensive force reductions, and avert what could become the most costly and most illusory weapons system ever produced.

4. *No-First-Use Agreement.* While we oppose any use of nuclear weapons, we support, as a transitional measure, a no-first-use policy by the United States and urge its reinforcement in an agreement with other nuclear-weapon states. The U.S.S.R. unilaterally announced its own no-first-use policy in

1982, having previously insisted on a bilateral agreement. Such an agreement should be accompanied by the withdrawal of all battlefield nuclear weapons from forward defense areas and also by assurances that no conventional force buildups are preconditions of such a policy. . . .

[Concerning the proliferation of nuclear weapons]: Joint U.S.A.-U.S.S.R. measures of significant nuclear arms control will do more than any other actions to restore the multilateral commitment required to curb the spread of nuclear weapons. But other actions are also needed, including: (1) firmer restrictions on nuclear trade with nations not party to the NPT; (2) effective incentives for persuading nonparties to become parties so that the treaty may approach the goal of universal adherence; and (3) more generous financial support of the International Atomic Energy Agency (IAEA) so that it may more confidently monitor compliance with the NPT. Curbing the perils of nuclear terrorism by revolutionary movements requires more than technical safeguards; it demands a prudent and humane strategy for removing the root causes of terrorism. . . .

While this study has not devoted major attention to the dismal subject of *chemical and biological weapons,* we are categorically opposed to their production, possession, or use. We therefore urge that treaties outlawing such weapons be reaffirmed and strengthened. . . .

EDUCATION FOR PEACEFUL ALTERNATIVES

We believe the prime alternative to hostility and violence is nurture in the ways of peacemaking itself. While peace research and peace studies have made some progress in the past two decades, we would urge a much stronger commitment to these fields on the part of educational institutions at all levels. . . .

We encourage the churches to mobilize support for specialized local, national, and international institutes for peace research and training along such lines. The U.S. Institute of Peace, recently established by Congress, can be a vital center for legitimizing and advancing peace research and training, providing that it (1) develops a broad and pluralistic approach and (2) preserves its academic freedom from domination or manipulation by official policy makers.

We encourage special study of nonviolent defense and peacemaking forces. In testimony to our hearing panel, Gene Sharp of Harvard University reported: "A vast—but neglected—history exists of people who have nonviolently defied foreign conquerors, domestic tyrants, oppressive systems, internal usurpers, and economic masters." Among notable modern examples are Gandhi's *satyagraha* (soul force) in India, Norway's resistance during Nazi occupation to keep schools free of fascist control, Martin Luther King, Jr.'s civil rights movement, and Solidarity in Poland. Every prospect that either military establishments or revolutionary movements might effectively replace armed force with nonviolent methods deserves Christian support. . . .

In this world of seemingly relentless violence, more and more of which might have nuclear implications, all Christians and their churches are clearly called to join in exploring every possibility of nonviolent means to a just peace. We recall once more that pacifists and just-war theorists share a moral presumption against violence; they have every reason to collaborate in peace research and education and to join in developing a more inclusive approach to peacemaking. . . .

NOTES

1. From *Nuclear Ethics: A Christian Moral Argument,* by David Hollenbach, S.J. (Paulist Press, 1983); p. 83.
2. See "Nuclear Weapons and the Atlantic Alliance," by McGeorge Bundy, George F. Kennan, Robert S. McNamara, and Gerard Smith, in *Foreign Affairs,* Spring 1982; pp. 753–68.
3. *Living with Nuclear Weapons,* by the Harvard Nuclear Study Group (Harvard University Press, 1983).
4. From *Annual Report to the Congress, Fiscal Year 1986,* by the United States Department of Defense, February 4, 1985; p. 45.
5. Congressman Parren J. Mitchell in testimony before our hearing panel, July 16, 1985. See also *The Fiscal Year 1986 Defense Budget* (Center on Budget and Policy Priorities, April 1985).
6. From "The Arms Race and American Society, Impact on the Economy," a statement prepared by Tex Sample for the Committee on Episcopal Initiatives, July 1982. See *Military Expansion, Economic Decline,* by Robert W. DeGrasse, Jr., Council on Economic Priorities (M. E. Sharpe, Inc., 1983); p. 29.

7. From "Impact on Health and Welfare," a statement prepared by Althea T. L. Simmons for the Committee on Episcopal Initiatives, July 1985.

8. See the section on verification in "Simultaneous Test Ban: A Primer on Nuclear Explosions," in *The Defense Monitor,* Vol. XIV, No. 5, 1985; pp. 10–12. See also "The Verification of a Comprehensive Nuclear Test Ban," by Lynn R. Sykes and Jack F. Evernden, in *Scientific American,* October 1982; pp. 47–55.

PART VI

The War Against Iraq

INTRODUCTION:
Applied Ethics and the Use of Force

On August 2, 1990, Iraqi forces invaded the sovereign nation of Kuwait, after which they set up a nine-man "Provisional Free Kuwait Government." A week later this government was dismissed and Iraq announced the annexation of Kuwait. On August 28, Kuwait was declared to be Iraq's nineteenth province, with Ali Hassan al-Majid, the cousin of Saddam Hussein, appointed as governor. Soon the international press and Amnesty International reported that occupying forces engaged in widespread destruction and looting of Kuwaiti property, including medical establishments and supplies. Reports also accused Iraqi forces of torturing and executing civilians, including children, detaining without trial hundreds of Kuwaiti citizens and deporting thousands more, and raping numerous Kuwaiti women before executing them.

Iraq's invasion of Kuwait was part of a historic territorial dispute, not without economic implications. Apart from seeking the systematic destruction of Kuwait's infrastructure, Iraqi forces endeavored to gain control of the oil-rich north-east strip of Kuwait and to acquire the strategic islands of Bubiyan and Warba. These claims accompanied a long-standing disagreement between Baghdad and Kuwait about the exact location of Kuwait's northern boundary.

Four days after the Iraqi invasion, the United Nations Security Council passed resolution 661, calling for economic sanctions against the Baghdad government and freezing its assets until Iraqi forces would withdraw from Kuwait. To enforce compliance with these sanctions, the Security Council soon passed resolution 665, authorizing member states to use their vessels to inspect all ships in the Persian Gulf to ensure strict enforcement of the U.N. embargo. Over the next three months, the council met numerous times to reiterate and develop its resolutions, culminating in November 1990, when the council authorized member states to use all necessary means after January 15, 1991, including military force, to uphold the U.N. resolutions should Hussein remain intransigent.

A coalition of Western and Middle Eastern forces, led largely by American troops, began the first phase of war—an air war—almost immediately after the deadline passed. Air raids sent Iraqis into bomb shelters and Israelis into sealed rooms as Baghdad responded by lobbing the first of what would be eighty-one Scud missiles into Israel. In addition, Iraqi troops embarked on a campaign of ecological terrorism in Kuwait's oil fields, creating an oil spill in the gulf between thirty and forty times in excess of the largest spill ever. The result was an oil slick that was reported to be one hundred miles long and from ten to twenty miles wide.

Soon the Allies were flying between two and three thousand sorties a day over Iraq. Within less than a month, the infrastructure of Baghdad was without water or electricity, and food was scarce for those who had failed to stockpile provisions. Reports indicate that sewage overflowed into the streets, raising the danger of widespread disease.

On February 23, Operation Desert Storm began its second phase—the ground war—by first invading from the south and then swinging east to envelop Iraqi forces. To the surprise of the Allies, forces on the ground were met with little resistance. Almost immediately, tens of thousands of Iraqi soldiers, many of them young boys, surrendered to Allied troops. Others made for a quick retreat, leaving Kuwait City in ruins and escaping with Kuwaiti prisoners. Seeking to complete their campaign of ecological terrorism, retreating Iraqi troops set hundreds of Kuwaiti oil wells ablaze, producing thick clouds of foul smoke that soon stretched from Turkey to Iran. Those fleeing along the road north to Basra were pummelled by Allied fighter-bombers, leaving a "wall of death" thirty-five miles long and four columns wide. One hundred hours after the ground war began, a cease-fire was declared, ending a seven-month-long occupation.

Within Iraq, however, a bloodbath ensued, as surviving Iraqi troops turned against Kurdish and Shiite minorities who aspired to overthrow the Ba'ath regime in the wake of a devastating defeat. Allied troops left those rebel forces to their own unhappy fate. Saddam Hussein, defeated and humiliated, remained in power.[1]

For those drawing on just-war criteria, the Allied war against Iraq provided a complex case for applied ethics, and attempts to apply just-war criteria to the war appeared in several public forums. Numerous academic conferences, newspapers, news weeklies, and magazines of public opinion in the secular and religious press all found a place to pose the question, Is some form of coercive response to Hussein's invasion justified? If so, what methods are appropriate? Several debates concerned (1) the relative merits of economic sanctions as an alternative to third-party military intervention, and (2) whether sanctions were given enough time to work before intervention occurred. For philosophers and theologians, the widespread currency of just-war tenets in these debates was more than a little impressive. But for those recalling the Manchurian crisis of the 1930s, the currency of just-war tenets in public discourse doubtless could not eliminate an acute sense of déjà vu.

NOTES

1. This information is compiled from data provided by Micah L. Sifry and Christopher Cerf, eds., *The Gulf War Reader: History, Documents, Opinions* (New York: Times Books, 1991); *New York Times* January 17, 1991, January 20, 1991, January 29, 1991, February 3, 1991, February 23, 1991, February 27, 1991, March 3, 1991, March 31, 1991; *Newsweek* August 13, 1990, March 4, 1991; Andrew Whitley, "Kuwait: The Last Forty-Eight Hours," *New York Review of Books,* May 30, 1991, pp. 17–18; Theodore Draper, "The Gulf War Reconsidered," *New York Review of Books,* January 16, 1992, pp. 38–45; "The True History of the Gulf War," *New York Review of Books,* January 23, 1992, pp. 46–53.

23

Letter to President Bush: The Persian Gulf Crisis

Daniel Pilarczyk, U.S. Catholic Bishops

I write as president of the National Conference of Catholic Bishops to offer our prayers for you, our president, at this time of difficult choices on how best to confront aggression and preserve human life and human rights in the Middle East. I also write to share our conference's deep concerns about the moral dangers and human costs which could be the result of war in the Persian Gulf.

The Catholic bishops of the United States met in our nation's capital this week and voted to affirm and make their own the enclosed letter of Archbishop Roger Mahony sent to Secretary Baker on November 7. The letter's central point was the urgent need to assess carefully and thoroughly the ethical and human consequences of war in the Persian Gulf. The letter strongly urges the moral imperative of persistent pursuit of non-violent international pressure to halt and reverse Iraq's aggression without resort to war.

As pastors we are deeply concerned about the human consequences of the crisis—the lives already lost or those that could be lost in war, the freedom denied to hostages, the suffering of victims of aggression and the many families separated by the demands of military service. As religious teachers, we are concerned about the moral dimensions of the crisis—the need to resist aggression, to protect the innocent, to pursue both justice and peace in a way that conforms with ethical criteria for the use of force. As U.S. citizens, we are concerned how our nation can best protect human life and human rights and secure a peaceful and just resolution to the crisis.

These are not new concerns for Catholic bishops. We are heirs of a long tradition of thought and moral reflection on issues of war and peace, including "The Challenge of Peace," our pastoral letter of 1983. Catholic teaching reflects our strong presumption against war while admitting the moral permissibility of the use of force under certain restrictive conditions. These traditional "just war" criteria limit strictly the circumstances under which war may be morally justifiable and also govern the means by which war may be carried out. Now our conference seeks to apply this tradition to the complex and changing situation in the Persian Gulf. While there may be diverse points of view on the specific application of these principles, our conference finds significant consensus on four key priorities:

1. Strong condemnation of Iraq's aggression, hostage taking and other violations of human rights and our strong support for worldwide peaceful pressure and action to deter Iraq's aggression and secure the peaceful liberation of Kuwait.

2. The urgent need for the careful consideration of the moral and human consequences of the use of force as well as the military and political implications.

3. Clear moral criteria must be met to justify the use of military force. As outlined in Archbishop Mahony's letter, these include questions of a clear and just cause for war, proper authority and sufficient probability of success to justify the human and other costs of military action. The criteria also ask whether war is genuinely a last resort; all reasonable peaceful alternatives must be fully pursued. Another criterion is proportionality: The human, economic and other costs of war must be proportionate to the objective to be achieved by the use of weapons of war. In this case, will war with Iraq leave the people of Kuwait, the Middle East and the world better or worse off? Our tradition also requires that the means and weapons used to pursue war must be proportionate as well and must discriminate between combatants and ordinary civilians. I fear that, in this situation, moving beyond the deployment of military forces in an effort to deter Iraqi aggression to the undertaking of offensive military action could well violate these criteria, especially the principles of proportionality and last resort.

4. Therefore, in our conference's view, our nation should continue strong, persistent and determined international and peaceful pressure against Iraq. Our conference understands that a strong military presence can give credibility to a vigorous pursuit of diplomatic and economic approaches to the crisis. Our concern is that the pressures to use military force could grow as the pursuit of non-violent options almost inevitably becomes difficult, complex and slow. We urge our government and our allies to continue to pursue the course of peaceful pressure and not resort to war. The use of weapons of war cannot be a substitute for the difficult, often time-consuming and frustrating work of searching for political solutions to the deep-seated problems in the Middle East which have contributed to this current crisis.

We are also concerned not only about the international consequences of possible war, but the domestic impact as well: the resources diverted, the human needs neglected, the political conflict and divisions within our society.

I believe, Mr. President, these are your concerns, even as they are ours.

I offer these reflections not to diminish in any way the necessary condemnation of Iraq's brutal actions. Rather, I speak with the firm conviction that our nation needs to continue to assess and discuss the ethical dimensions of this difficult situation. These discussions and this assessment must take place before, not after, offensive action is undertaken.

We stand with our government and the United Nations in the effort to halt and reverse Iraqi aggression, to condemn the taking of hostages and to secure their release. We strongly support and commend your efforts to build global solidarity and worldwide pressure against Iraq. Because of the serious moral and human factors involved, we ask you and the leaders of other governments to continue and intensify the determined and creative pursuit of a peaceful solution that seeks to bring justice to the region without resort to war.

Our prayers are with you as you face these awesome challenges and as you undertake a journey at this Thanksgiving season so important for our country and the world. We also pray that other world leaders meet their responsibilities to pursue both justice and peace. Our prayers also go out to all those directly touched by this crisis: the victims of aggression, the hostages, troops in the field and their families. We especially remember the members of our military forces, who face a difficult task in trying circumstances and who will bear the burden of the decisions made on how best to resolve this crisis. We hope and pray that these reflections from our conference's perspective as pastors and teachers will strengthen our nation's determination to pursue true justice through peaceful means.

24

Just-War Tradition and the War in the Gulf

James Turner Johnson

What moral judgment—as opposed to political, economic and other kinds of judgment—should be made on the use of force by the U.S. and the other members of the multilateral force to drive Iraq out of Kuwait? I want to address this question in terms of the just-war tradition of Western culture, or more specifically, by means of the seven criteria that must be satisfied to justify use of military force according to that tradition: just cause, right authority, right intention, overall proportionality of the good to be done over the evil, a reasonable hope of success, a situation of last resort, and the goal of restoring peace. These seven categories are deeply rooted in both Christian tradition and international law, and they are commonly used in contemporary moral debate, even by people who will not share the conclusions I am about to draw on the basis of these categories.

In my judgment these seven conditions were all met prior to the beginning of air attacks against Iraqi forces on January 16. Lacking Iraqi action to pull its forces out of occupied Kuwait and make amends for its invasion and systematic rape of that country, the United Nations–sanctioned coalition reached the position where the use of such force was the only remaining resort.

A *just cause* for use of force against Iraq has existed since last August, when Iraq militarily invaded Kuwait and then declared the area that was "formerly Kuwait" to be thereafter part of Iraq. Morally speaking, and in terms of international law, this was the crucial action: a flagrant case of aggression, violating the most fundamental norm of the international order. It was not the first time that Iraq under Saddam Hussein had been guilty of aggression against another country: we should not forget that Iraq, acting in the same way, started the lengthy and bloody war with Iran only recently settled. Iran then responded by using force in self-defense; what was different in August 1990 was that Kuwait was in no position to defend itself against Iraq and so it called for help from the international community. That help came in the form of the multinational coalition of forces placed in Saudi Arabia and the United Nations Security Council resolutions authorizing first the imposition of economic sanctions against Iraq and then the use of military force if Iraq still did not reverse its action of violence against international peace and order. These are responses in defense of both a tiny country and of the fundamental moral and legal norms that outlaw such aggression.

Historically, just-war tradition held that just cause for the use of force exists whenever it is necessary either to repel an unjust attack, to retake something wrongly taken, or to punish evil. International law has justified use of force only in response to aggressive attack. By either standard Iraq's attack against Kuwait was unjust and constitutes just cause for use of force to undo it.

The remaining six moral conditions have also been satisfied. In the international context, *right authority* was provided by the Security Council's resolution authorizing force. In the U.S., right authority consists in the powers granted to the president by the Constitution and by the War Powers Act and by the congressional resolutions decisively adopted on January 12 and 13 authorizing use of force against Iraq.

Right intention in this case consists in the aims of turning back and undoing aggression. There are no aggressive aims against the territory or people of Iraq. Right intention here also consists in deterring such aggression in the future, restoring the shattered peace of the Persian Gulf region, and attempting to set in place safeguards to protect that peace in the future. This right intention also satisfies the criterion of *the end of peace*.

As to the question of *proportionality* between the good such use of force would do and the evil that would result from allowing Iraq's violent aggression to stand, it must not be forgotten that Iraq has already brought great evil into being, and it is promising more. That country has already violated the rights of innocent people and caused great suffering and loss of life and resources by invading two of its neighbors, first Iran and then Kuwait. It has launched deliberate attacks on population centers in both Israel—which is not even a member of the coalition of nations seeking to enforce the U.N. resolutions against Iraq—and Saudi Arabia. It has developed chemical and biological weapons and is seeking to develop nuclear arms, and it has shown no hesitation in using its chemical weaponry both in war and in attacks against its own citizens.

By loosing crude oil into the Persian Gulf it has shown flagrant disregard for the fragile ecology of that region and the people who depend on the Gulf for food, water, and livelihood. Saddam Hussein has openly threatened to do more such damage, as well as to use weapons of mass destruction in the war. Coupled with all this, Iraq's militaristic aggressiveness, backed up by the most powerful military forces of any nation in the region, if left unchecked constitutes an unspoken but real threat to other neighboring countries. Allowing Iraq's aggression to stand is condoning an evil in itself and opening the door to yet further evil by a restless and aggressive Iraq. These are the issues in determining the existence of proportionality—not simply the costs expected from the use of U.N.-sanctioned forces against Iraq.

Is there *reasonable hope of success* in the use of force by the coalition allied against Iraq? The aim of satisfying this concern justifies the vigorous buildup of American and other military might in the region. While the presence of reasonable hope of success is always a matter for judgment, I note that responsible military and political parties possessing knowledge of the coalition's capabilities and intelligence information about those of Iraq conclude that use of force against Iraq will succeed.

Finally, was resort to military force a *last resort?* Iraq's intransigence and continued belligerence sadly left no other choice. Efforts to negotiate an Iraqi withdrawal failed. The sanctions imposed by the U.N., even if they had worked more effectively, in themselves were the source of moral harm.

Such sanctions, and not only military force, cause human suffering and loss of life. Moreover, the more effective sanctions are, the greater their inherent impact on those persons most remote from the wrongdoing of their nation's leaders and least able to bring about change: the poor, the aged, children, the infirm. These are exactly the people who, in war, are regarded most clearly as noncombatants. By contrast, the coalition's use of military force against Iraq aims at the military power behind Iraq's aggression: its combatant forces, its military resources and the leaders who have led it into aggressive wrongdoing. This is a more moral course than either condoning Iraq's aggression or continuing economic sanctions against the Iraqi people.

All the above considerations have to do with the decision to resort to use of military force and why I am convinced that, by the moral criteria of just-war tradition, that decision was justified. Just-war concerns require also that the means used in war be moral: specifically, that these means be *discriminate* and tactically *proportionate*.

Discrimination is the moral principle that seeks to protect noncombatants in war by prohibiting their being directly and intentionally targeted by military force. There is a vast difference, in terms of this moral principle, between the actions thus far of the coalition air forces and the actions of Iraq. The former have been directed at military targets and have employed weapons that by their nature are extremely accurate. By contrast, Iraq's Scud missile attacks have been direct, intentional attempts to harm the noncombatant inhabitants of Israeli and Saudi cities. Also by contrast, the flooding of oil into the Persian Gulf is an action inherently indiscriminate in its nature, with little direct military impact.

As for the principle of *proportionality,* when noncombatants are directly and intentionally targeted, any means at all are grossly disproportionate. Iraq's Scud attacks against population centers and its pouring of oil into the Persian Gulf thus fail the test of proportionality of means as well as that of discrimination. Only when the principle of discrimination is met does the question of proportionality of means come into play. In this regard it is important to note that the ability to make closely targeted strikes against military installations or associated support systems has produced a very different kind of war than was possible only a relatively short time ago, before contemporary guidance systems were available. A single "smart" bomb or cruise missile can do what, in Vietnam or Korea or World War II, it took an entire bombing raid to accomplish. Accordingly, the accuracy of contemporary weapons used by coalition forces means that the total damage done by an attack on a particular target can be much less than in earlier wars. The development of targeting technology shows that it is simply wrong to argue, as many people have argued in America in recent years, that contemporary war must of necessity be grossly and disproportionately destructive in its conduct. Rather, the means of war now available and in use by coalition forces against Iraq are inherently both more discriminate and more proportionate than means previously used. What remains is the need to continue to prosecute the war so as to make the fullest use of these abilities, despite the provocation inherent in nondiscriminate, disproportionate means of force by Iraq.

25

An Imperfectly Just War

John Langan, S.J.

The conflict in the Persian Gulf has been a war of mixed signals and contrary intentions; a war that many people feel need not have been fought; a war that is unlikely to resolve the problems of the Middle East. Both proponents and critics have attempted to evaluate it in moral terms. President George Bush assured the American people that this conflict was indeed a just war, a conflict between good and evil, right and wrong. The U.S. Congress debated the morality and the timeliness of the war and gave its less than resounding approval.

The critics of the war have had a hard time staking out a counterposition. It is not possible to offer a convincing apologia for Saddam Hussein, who has shown considerable ingenuity in finding ever novel ways to outrage world public opinion, from mistreating the citizens of Kuwait, to exhibiting prisoners of war on television, to polluting the waters of the Gulf, torching Kuwait's oil industry, and, most recently, crushing the Shiites and the Kurds. Saddam Hussein is a serial aggressor, a man ready to use lethal force against his opponents, a man who has invested large sums for a long time in building a war machine meant to bully and abuse his neighbors. In the face of the vast array of military personnel and technology that the coalition assembled, he refused to give up his hold on Kuwait. This combination—a bloodthirsty and tyrannical adversary and the mobilization of vast forces by a diverse coalition led and orchestrated by the United States—left much of the religious leadership of the United States in a quandary about whether to accept or to condemn our use of force against him. More broadly, an entire generation of Americans who acquired a deep distrust of government and the military from the sad experience of Vietnam was left searching for an appropriate framework for interpreting this very different situation.

The analogies that critics of the Gulf War tried to make to Vietnam and the war of attrition on the Western Front between 1914 and 1918 were rendered useless by the rapid pace and conclusion of the war. But so was Bush's comparison of Saddam Hussein to Hitler, which came to seem overdrawn as the weakness of the Iraqi forces became apparent. No doubt, such analogies provided orientation and legitimation for advocates of alternative policies as they confronted the uncertainties of the Gulf conflict, but finally they did not prove useful or convincing.

Just-war theory is the primary instrument that ethicists have for surmounting conflicting perceptions, analogies, and claims that naturally develop in any debate over a violent conflict. It commits us to a critical and questioning attitude to any war. Though the theory itself offers neither a blanket condemnation nor a blanket endorsement of this most dangerous and destructive human activity, it operates with a strong presumption against the use of violence. It includes elements that require the exercise of sophisticated and informed political judgment, and it recognizes the complexity of political disputes.

From August 2, 1990, when Hussein's troops seized Kuwait and converted it into the nineteenth province of Iraq, there was a strong basis for arguing that a war for the liberation of Kuwait was morally justified. A basic principle of international law requiring respect for the sovereignty of states was violated without warning. The brutal occupation of Kuwait, the seizure of its assets, the dispersal of large numbers of its citizens and residents compounded the original crime. Kuwait was entitled to wage a war of self-defense and to ask for help both from its allies and from states concerned over the threat to international order presented by Iraq. From the beginning the requirement that there be a just cause for hostilities was present.

But the course of events ensured that this factor counted for less than it would normally. First, whether as a result of the speedy response of the United States to the Saudi request for troops or because Hussein's original plans had not extended beyond Kuwait, it quickly became apparent that the Iraqis were not going to invade Saudi Arabia or to annex its oil-producing areas. Second, the Kuwaiti government was not able to mount a sustained resistance against the Iraqi invasions and occupation, which was carried out with overwhelming force. There is no evidence that any significant element of Kuwaiti society, with the exception of some Palestinians, preferred Iraqi occupation to the rule of the al-Sabah family. Third, once the occupation of Kuwait was complete and overt hostilities ceased, Iraq settled in to exploit its victim and to integrate Kuwait into its territory. The initiative—the decision to launch a war to undo the Iraqi aggression—passed to the United States and to those states that found Hussein's hold on Kuwait profoundly objectionable. All of these factors obscured reality: the fundamental act of war had been committed by Iraq with little provocation or warning. Then, it took several months for the coalition to assemble sufficient forces to make threats that would be plausible to Hussein, a guileful and unyielding leader. During that time, the allies and other concerned powers had time and opportunity to explore alternative ways of resolving the dispute without resorting to war. That interval was lengthy, but it makes more difference for political perception than for moral analysis.

It is true that the brutal character of Saddam Hussein's regime did not prevent various powers from collaborating with him before the invasion of Kuwait. France, Germany, the Soviet Union, and the United States had all in different ways provided support for what the world now agrees was a murderous, tyrannical, and aggressive regime. The history of Western dealing with Saddam Hussein's regime over the years before 1990 exhibits a mixture of wishful thinking and willful ignorance, of economic greed and legalistic formalism that Western governments often adopt when they find themselves facing a distasteful despotism with which, for various reasons (good and bad), they think they have to deal and which they think they are powerless to alter. It is true that large portions of the West, including governments and the media, have come relatively late to a clearheaded recognition of Saddam Hussein's threat to peace and order in the Middle East. But the failure to see this point early does not invalidate a policy that attempts to reverse a mistaken judgment before its consequences become catastrophic.

Another requirement that a just war must meet is that the war must be conducted by competent authority. In this regard, it is extremely important that the war on Iraq was authorized by the U.N. Security Council on behalf of the international community, by several states in the Middle East, and by the U.S. Congress. The Bush administration, which had unwisely attempted to operate on the principle that the war did not need congressional authorization, fortunately agreed to the congressional debate that took place before the January 15 deadline. Congress took its share of the responsibility for the decision, and the possibility that the war would lead sooner or later to a constitutional crisis was avoided. The debate reminded us both of the gravity and of the inescapably political character of the war.

Just-war theory also includes a requirement that the war being considered must have a reasonable prospect of success. From one angle, this was never a problem for the coalition in the Gulf. There was little doubt that the U.S. and its allies would prevail against the highly militarized but very vulnerable society of Iraq. The main uncertainty was not about ultimate victory but about the level of casualties that would be required to achieve this result and therefore about the willingness of the American public to sustain the war effort. The Iraqi army, while technologically inferior to the allies, was a large and experienced force. The key step for the allies was to convert their air superiority into a decisive edge in the ground war. This was done by hammering the ground forces from the air, by misleading the Iraqi command about our plan of battle, and by encouraging desertions from the relatively inexperienced troops near the frontier.

From another angle, the prospect of ultimate success was, and remains, uncertain. If we move beyond defining success only in terms of military victory and think of it as including significant progress toward making the Middle East a more secure and peaceful region, then we have to admit that our technological superiority and our ability to win battles in the air and on land can do little more than buy time for working out a settlement that the major players (including popular movements as well as governments) are prepared to live with for the short- and medium-term future. It may well be that "winning" in the present crisis does little more than preserve us and our allies from disasters that would have undermined our entire position in the Middle East if we had not successfully resisted Saddam Hussein.

Questions about success and objectives were given many different answers during the months from August to January. The lack of clear answers made it difficult to determine whether the military option met the just-war criterion of proportionality. Were the objectives sufficiently urgent and important to make war both necessary and plausible as a course that would prevent serious evils and were they likely to produce a better outcome than nonviolent alternatives? President Bush and the military leadership repeatedly spoke of our objectives as: (1) the eviction of Iraqi forces from Kuwait and (2) the enforcement of the relevant U.N. resolutions. This constituted what I would call the minimal objective for the coalition forces, and it enjoyed widespread support around the world. It was also an objective that was always obtainable by the free consent of the Iraqi government. But some government and military officials and many participants in the public debate spoke of more ambitious objectives. Occasionally, their language lacked conceptual precision and diplomatic finesse, for instance, when assault on various parts of Saddam Hussein's anatomy was presented as a desirable objective.

In the public discussion there was a certain inevitable escalation of objectives; these included the removal of Saddam Hussein and his regime as well as the removal of the weapons of mass destruction that the Iraqi military had been accumulating. The first of these more ambitious objectives would be attained, it was hoped, either as a consequence of defeat or as a result of an internal coup. It is a matter of regret to nearly everyone that this did not happen. The second objective is one that the coalition has chosen to pursue by limited means that fall between the complete occupation and demilitarization of the country, and a tortuous and lengthy process of arms control negotiation. Including the disarmament requirements within the cease-fire provisions was a positive move in that it combined two morally compelling objectives: the end of hostilities and restrictions on Iraq's ability to develop more weapons of mass destruction. Further objectives such as the territorial dismemberment of Iraq and the destruction of its people and culture were ruled out by President Bush. They were seen to be morally unacceptable and devastating for the long-term stability of the Middle East and for the future of American relations with the people of the region. At least this seemed to be the view that would have drawn general assent before the revolts in northern and southern Iraq. These revolts raised the troubling question of whether the unity of Iraq could be preserved without enormous human suffering or without reliance on dictatorial methods.

Clarifying the war's objectives came relatively late in the public debate, which made it difficult to determine whether the war could meet the just-war criterion of proportionality. My own judgment is that taken together the following factors justified the resort to war: (1) protecting the principle of the inviolability of sovereignty (especially in an area that contains a number of very vulnerable states); (2) preventing Iraq from achieving a weapons capability that would enable it to attack the major population centers of the region; (3) thwarting Saddam Hussein from achieving a predominant position in the world oil market; and (4) terminating the grave human rights abuses that his regime inflicted on the people of Kuwait and Iraq. I am not claiming that the United States and its allies have consistently defended these values in their foreign policy, only that these and related considerations about attainable objectives and values to be protected against an aggressor provide a reasonable basis for affirming that the test of proportionality between the means and the end was met in this decision to go to war.

Though the oil supply was a common theme of analysts and cartoonists, of commentators and protesters, no serious moralist regards the U.S. maintenance of gasoline at $1 per gallon as a justifying reason for any use of violence, much less for a fullscale war. Sustaining this folly is not worth the bones of a single American or allied soldier. Industrial economies have shown that they can make the adjustments required to pay for increased oil prices. Nonetheless, there was a morally serious reason for being concerned about higher oil prices: their negative effect on the nations of Eastern Europe and the third world. The history of OPEC shows that, even while the world depends heavily on a small number of producers in one highly volatile region, the direction of oil prices is not simply up and that the forging of a consistent policy within the oil cartel is extraordinarily difficult. What Saddam Hussein's seizure of Kuwait threatened to do was to start a chain of events that would give him both enormous wealth for carrying out further aggressions as well as a decisive voice in allocating one of the world's most essential commodities, particularly if he were to control, directly or indirectly, Saudi supplies.

The norm in just-war theory that has probably been most prominently invoked by critics of the Gulf War is that of last resort. This requires that alternatives to war be tried and found wanting and that the only way to maintain justice—and the values that are wrongfully threatened by the adversary—is to fight. Like the criterion of proportionality, it is applied through a judgment about a situation that is particular, complex, and changing. So we can expect significant and serious disagreements about whether this criterion is met or not. The major exception to this point is in cases of self-defense. Pearl Harbor and the subsequent German declaration of war abruptly terminated the internal American debate of 1940–41 about whether and to what extent the United States should intervene to stop Axis aggression in Asia and Europe.

There is no doubt that alternatives to fighting were offered to the Iraqi government and that the coalition would not have fought a war if Kuwait had been evacuated. But it also became clear that Saddam Hussein was not inclined to pull out of Kuwait even when the threat of war became credible and imminent. He resembled Don Giovanni in the last scene of the opera, who, with his hand firmly in the grasp of the Commendatore, persists in saying "no" to every urging that he change his mind. So far, Saddam Hussein seems to have fared rather better than the Don.

The key question about last resort is whether less coercive measures, particularly sanctions, would have been sufficient over time, and whether the diplomatic process was pursued with sufficient vigor and commitment from August through January.

We can see that the primary task of U.S. diplomacy was to build and maintain the coalition against Saddam Hussein. It was particularly important to cut the connections between Iraq and the Soviet Union, which had long been its primary source of weapons and military and technical expertise. On closer inspection, the worldwide coalition against Saddam Hussein is really divided into two coalitions. The first, a very broad coalition of states concerned about Iraq's violation of Kuwaiti sovereignty, was likely to be satisfied by achieving the minimal objective of evicting Iraq from Kuwait. The second, far narrower coalition demanded a decisive reorientation in Iraq's external policy, for which the defeat or removal of Saddam Hussein was an indispensable requirement. This coalition is unstable, since it agrees on the need to alter the direction of Iraq's foreign and military policies while its members disagree on how they understand this need and what they would put in place of Hussein's regime. Such disagreement is not surprising since this narrow coalition includes Kuwait, Saudi Arabia, Israel, Egypt, Syria, the United Arab Emirates, the United Kingdom, and the United States. It thus includes states that are not keen about being seen in public agreement with each other as well as states that have fought wars with each other in the recent past. The narrow coalition presents us with a situation in which nations are willing to take very strong measures against a common adversary but cannot be relied on to cooperate over an extended period of time. France, Germany, Japan, and the Soviet Union took positions that fall somewhere between the broad coalition and the narrow one.

The United States had to function as the leader of both. To maintain the broad coalition, Saddam Hussein was offered a no-frills deal: withdrawal from Kuwait without a retaliatory attack. But this left many observers unsatisfied, presumably not because they thought it unjust but because they thought it unlikely to be acceptable to a leader with his ambitions. At the same time, the United States had to avoid agreeing to concessions that would shatter the confidence of key members of the narrow coalition that the United States really was prepared to use force against Iraq. The Israelis, in particular, had strong and understandable objections to allowing linkage between the Gulf dispute and the claims of the Palestinians.

It is clear that no lasting peace in the Middle East is possible without a resolution of the Palestinian issue. Those who had been hoping for an international conference or some other process requiring the Israelis to deal with the Palestinians were too inclined to think that a complex negotiation aimed at a peaceful settlement of both Kuwait and Palestinian demands was an avenue worth exploring. This overlooked the possibility, indeed the likelihood, that the conference would fail on both counts with a consequent shattering of the coalition and with the Iraqis more deeply entrenched than ever in Kuwait. Of course, even an unsuccessful conference is less a disaster than war; but not if it ends in a way that makes a war on less favorable terms even more likely. It also overlooks the point that, precisely because there are important elements of justice in the Palestinian cause, it is important not to allow them to be captured and exploited by an unscrupulous demagogue like Saddam Hussein, whose interest in the Palestinians is secondary and manipulative. His invasion of Kuwait has cost the Palestinian community billions of dollars in aid from the Kuwaitis and Saudis, in remittances from Palestinians working in Kuwait, and in losses experienced by refugees and costs borne by those aiding them.

What about the sanctions? It seems to me that this was the hardest matter on which to come to a judgment. Clearly, it would have been a great gain for international order to have this kind of crisis solved with nonlethal measures. The best hope for sanctions did not turn on a general slowing down of the Iraqi economy or on the denial of essential food and medicine to the Iraqi people (which were not included in the embargo), but on the denial of spare parts and military supplies. But such a denial would only constitute serious pressure on Hussein if there were a powerful military force in the region capable of making the shortage of supplies a starkly urgent priority. Enforcing the embargo over a period of time, particularly since this would have meant maintaining the narrow coalition on a war-ready footing while preventing major evasions of the embargo, would have meant that U.S. allies in the region would have had to carry considerable stress in a situation of continuing tension. Given the requirement for a continuing deployment of substantial forces and the constraints that the climate and the religious calendar would have put on military operations and thus on the plausible threat to Iraq, a strong case can be made that the January 15 deadline was a reasonable decision.

I have grave reservations about the major increase in U.S.

forces after the November congressional elections. But this is primarily a problem about the administration's lack of candor in dealing with the American people. On the one hand, this deployment made our threats of military action against Iraq considerably more credible. Yet it inevitably created more pressure for a shorter timetable for the working of sanctions and other measures.

It will take independent scholars and observers a long time to determine what further steps the United States and its allies could or should have taken to achieve a diplomatic solution. But I believe that in the last analysis, the decisive judgment is one that was reached by most of the Middle East powers and that has been confirmed by Hussein's behavior during the last nine months. That judgment is that (1) Iraq under his rule was deeply committed to an aggressive and destructive policy; (2) Iraq posed a threat to almost all of its neighbors; (3) war with Iraq was inevitable at some point; and (4) such a war was best conducted before Iraq's arsenal was capable of dealing catastrophic blows to its neighbors. Those who hoped that this war could be averted or, at least, postponed did so in the honorable belief that better ways of resolving this dispute and others like it should be tried. This was not a false or foolish belief; the point is that the nature of this particular adversary and what we could reasonably expect from his regime made it inapplicable.

The course of the war made it clear that we had underestimated the tenacity and obduracy of the Iraqis and that we had overestimated their effective fighting power. This double error cuts two ways. In the first instance, it underlines the enormous difficulty that sanctions would have encountered in changing Iraq's policy. In the second, it undermines some of the more dramatic claims about what Iraq could have done to its neighbors and enemies. One important sign of progress is that a serious and conscientious effort was made to observe the principle of discrimination or noncombatant immunity. This was easy to do in the ground war which was waged in the desert; in the air war, new technology, and the nearly complete control the allies established over Iraqi air space made the observance of this principle much easier than it has been in previous wars. This did not eliminate the problem of civilian casualties, some of which are inevitable given the confusion and ignorance found in combat situations, and some of which are the result of inherently controversial judgments over how to proceed in attacking military targets embedded in an urban or civilian setting.

After the fact, more questions have been raised about whether the war was conducted in a proportionate way or, whether the allies inflicted excessive or unnecessary casualties and damage on Iraq. Granted that the electricity and communications systems are legitimate targets, was it possible to restrict the damage to Iraq's infrastructure so that the civilian population would be less at risk than it now seems to be? Answering such a question requires more knowledge than either proponents or opponents of U.S. policy possess. Looking to the future, I would argue that more care should be taken to protect civilians from the consequences of a catastrophic demolition of the infrastructure that modern societies rely on to sustain life. In this matter, however, the Iraqi people are as much the victims of their own government's intransigence (which makes humanitarian aid both hard to offer and hard to deliver) as they are victims of the coalition's bombs.

I have grave doubts about whether it was really necessary to bomb the Iraqi troops retreating from Kuwait as intensively as we did. Certainly, as the stories of their occupation of Kuwait made clear, many of them were no innocents. Later events also made it clear that Iraqi military power was far from totally destroyed. While retreating troops who have not indicated an intention to surrender are a legitimate military target, they did not constitute an immediate or serious threat to our own troops or military operations. Given the inevitable imprecision of warfare, it is reasonable to err on the side of mercy and life when one's forces are in an overwhelmingly dominant position, even if this means allowing some of the enemy to escape.

Whether the casualties inflicted by the air war on Iraqi ground troops meet the test of proportionality is a matter of some uncertainty. Part of this uncertainty is factual. It is very unlikely that anyone (Iraqi or American or other) knows with any accuracy the number of Iraqi soldiers killed by the air war. What can be given are reasonable estimates and neither side has been forthcoming about these. Another part of the uncertainty arises from the imprecision inherent in the notion of proportionality itself. For this reason, military officers and many moralists prefer to restrict their effective concern to the principle of discrimination. But this invites us to take the lives of soldiers too lightly; for surely it is possible to kill enemy soldiers without necessity or proportionate benefit, and this has to be wrong. But the criterion is extremely hard to apply in the course of war. Would it have been possible to stop the bombing and begin the ground war at a point where we would have lost a thousand troops and the Iraqis would have lost twenty thousand, rather than fifty thousand or more? Such an outcome seems preferable. But how is any commander in a position to make such calibrations with confidence that things will work out as anticipated? I leave aside the political difficulties involved in judgments that seem to trade American lives for enemy lives. The criterion of proportionality should direct military planners to prefer strategies that will minimize the loss of life on both sides; but once chosen, a strategy has to be pressed home vigorously. Whether there ever came a point at which reasonable commanders should have concluded that the Iraqi soldiers had taken enough punishment and that further hammering of their positions harmed them far more than it could possibly benefit us and our allies is something that I do not know.

Many of us, especially after the great changes in Europe in 1989, were hoping that prospects would brighten for more peaceful methods of settling disputes and that in the future, we would not have to confront the situations that have historically made just-war theory an essential part of social ethics and of Catholic moral theology. The fact that we have not reached such a point is a tragedy, especially for the people of Iraq. At the same time, it can be no surprise for those who have grasped the persistence of injustice in our world.

26

This War Cannot Be Justified

Jim Wallis

President Bush and his religious backers assert that the war in the Persian Gulf is a "just war." Indeed, every war in the history of this country has been called "just" by the president who waged it. It should come as no surprise that President Bush is now wrapping himself in the mantle of religion and morality as he pursues war in the Middle East.

But the war with Iraq cannot be justified on moral grounds. In resurrecting the language of moral discourse, the president and his theological advisers have failed to address the fundamental moral questions that have been at stake in this conflict since the beginning.

For more than five months before the war began, the American people wrestled with those questions in an unprecedented public debate, only to have them disappear in the illuminated skies over Baghdad. But the media's fascination with military technology, the collapse of congressional dissent, and the official pronouncement of this war's righteousness will not erase the basic moral contradictions of the Gulf crisis. The moral issues did not go away the day the fighting started. Indeed, they have become even more urgent and alarming.

To have put infinitely more energy and will into a military buildup than into political diplomacy in the Gulf crisis is a moral issue. This is not a war of "last resort," as the president has claimed. The many days and miles of shuttle diplomacy to which the president has referred were overwhelmingly directed toward building a military coalition against Saddam Hussein and authorizing its use rather than a serious attempt to deal with the underlying disputes and grievances at stake in the Gulf and, indeed, the whole region.

From the beginning, ultimatums substituted for negotiations and mutual threats pre-empted substantive dialogue. Without compromising on Iraq's withdrawal from Kuwait, there were and still are alternatives to war that address the underlying issues. The outbreak of war reveals a profound failure of political leadership on all sides. To now justify military conflict by claiming the failure of diplomacy is to compound the moral failure.

To unleash the demons of war in the Middle East is a moral issue. It risks engulfing the region in volatility, bitterness, ecological disaster, the possible use of chemical and nuclear weapons, and violence that will only multiply and reverberate around the Middle East and the world in the days ahead—and likely even for generations to come. George Bush has backed us into the corner of war with Saddam Hussein. And to back a dictator as dangerous and brutal as Saddam into such a corner, rather than to contain, undercut and defeat him in other ways, is a serious political and moral miscalculation.

In this crisis the United States is reaping what it has sown. For President Bush to justify the war as necessary to "protect our way of life"—a way of life in which six percent of the world's population consumes more than twenty-five percent of the world's oil—is a moral issue. The lack of an energy policy in the West that honors our responsibilities to both justice and the environment is a moral failure.

For the West to have so long controlled and manipulated the Arab world on the basis of an insatiable thirst for oil is a moral issue. Oil is still the real motivator in this crisis and has created a fundamental moral hypocrisy. If there were not oceans of oil beneath the Kuwaiti sands, would we be at war in the Gulf today? The United States has not acted out of President Bush's "conviction to oppose injustice" in myriad countries around the globe, from El Salvador to South Africa, from Haiti to Cambodia. In fact, in many cases, the United States has not only refused to oppose tyranny and aggression, but has been both a passive and an active supporter of repressive regimes—including Saddam Hussein's.

Should we declare war on China and begin bombing Beijing for its crushing of the democracy movement and its brutal invasion and occupation of neighboring Tibet? Should we bomb Moscow for the Soviet Union's violent repression of independence movements in the Baltics? The massive U.S. response to aggression and injustice in Kuwait, while virtually ignoring it or even supporting it in many other cases, is a moral double standard.

In particular, to have so long accepted and supported the injustice done to Palestinians through twenty-three years of brutal occupation underlies this conflict and is a moral issue. Just because Saddam Hussein has sought to use the Palestinian question for his own self-serving purposes does not diminish its importance on its own moral grounds. To delay further the legitimate grievances of Palestinians in order not to reward Saddam Hussein's aggression is morally unacceptable.

To undertake one of the greatest aerial bombardments in history is a moral issue of yet unknown proportions. We have confirmed reports of civilian casualties from refugees who have been eyewitnesses to the bombing and from church sources in the region. Destruction of homes, schools, hospitals, and churches are an ominous harbinger of human suffering yet to come.

To send hundreds of thousands of young Americans into battle is an issue of great moral consequence. We must all continue to support the American women and men in uniform. But as many of the families of soldiers in the Gulf have pleaded, the best way to support our troops is to bring them home physically safe and psychologically whole. It is crucial to begin to separate our support for the soldiers from support for the war and return to the fundamental moral questions that underlie this conflict.

That U.S. troops are disproportionately people of color reflects the moral injustice of this nation's continued racial polarization. It is a moral contradiction that young people, whose door to a better life is closed at home, have been promised an open door to the future through military careers and education only to see that open door now become a pathway to killing or being killed.

The cost of this war at home is a moral issue. Our cities suffer the ravages of poverty and neglect while the military consumes more than a billion dollars a day in the Middle East.

The bombs exploding in the Middle East also are exploding in many of our own neighborhoods, again deferring the hope of justice at home.

Bush claims that we are contributing to a new world order by intervening on Kuwait's behalf. But to turn away from the non-military instruments of sanctions, diplomacy, and multilateral political resolve in favor of the technology of war forestalls the hope of a genuinely new world order by again affirming the principles of the old world order—that "might makes right." And in Kuwait, as in Vietnam, it is possible that we may again be witnessing a U.S. campaign that destroys a country in order to save it.

Despite the claims of political leaders, our choices are not simply inaction or war, appeasement or conflagration. This war has been created by political leaders with limited vision and abundant technology. And a last-minute, just-war defense is merely a cynical replacement for persistent diplomacy and moral reflection.

In his address to the National Religious Broadcasters Convention, President Bush claimed that the forces of the world arrayed with us against Iraq are on God's side. But are we? When Gabriel Habib, general secretary of the Middle East Council of Churches, was recently asked by the BBC, "Whose side is God on in this war?" his response was, "God is on the side of the suffering."

God's blessing cannot be invoked either for George Bush's moral crusade or Saddam Hussein's holy war. The true face of God is always revealed in compassion for those who suffer in war the consequences of human failure.

The [illegible] experience in the Middle East also [illegible] [illegible] [illegible]

[illegible] [illegible] intervening [illegible] [illegible] [illegible] the [illegible] [illegible] [illegible] [illegible] [illegible] [illegible]

[illegible] the [illegible] [illegible] [illegible] [illegible] [illegible] [illegible] [illegible]

[illegible] [illegible] [illegible] [illegible] [illegible] [illegible] [illegible] [illegible]

[illegible] [illegible] [illegible] [illegible] [illegible] [illegible] [illegible] [illegible]